preserving
the japanese way

Traditions of Salting, Fermenting,
and Pickling for the Modern Kitchen

Nancy Singleton Hachisu

Foreword by David Tanis
Photographs by Kenji Miura

 Andrews McMeel
Publishing

Kansas City • Sydney • London

DEDICATED TO THE HOUSE
THAT HOLDS US SAFE IN HER HEART
AND THE LAND AND SEA THAT FEED US

CONTENTS

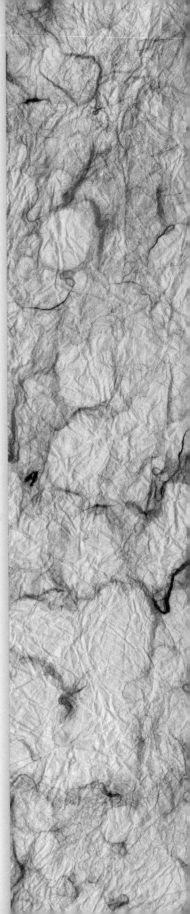

FOREWORD BY DAVID TANIS	IV
PRESERVING A WAY OF LIFE	V
CHAPTER ONE: SALT, WIND, AND SUN	1
CHAPTER TWO: MISO	45
CHAPTER THREE: SOY SAUCE	87
CHAPTER FOUR: FISH SAUCE	117
CHAPTER FIVE: RICE VINEGAR, SOUR PLUMS, AND PERSIMMONS	143
CHAPTER SIX: KOJI, SAKE LEES, AND RICE BRAN	185
CHAPTER SEVEN: TOFU, NATTO, AND KONNYAKU	227
CHAPTER EIGHT: KATSUOBUSHI, KONBU, AND NIBOSHI	247
CHAPTER NINE: CHILE PEPPERS AND KIMCHEE	277
CHAPTER TEN: SAKE, SHOCHU, AND TEA	295
AFTERWORD: THE SNOW OF 2014	334
ACKNOWLEDGMENTS	337
GLOSSARY OF JAPANESE PRODUCE	339
FRUITS AND VEGETABLES BY PICKLING METHOD	345
FISH AND SHELLFISH BY PICKLING METHOD	346
RESOURCES	348
BIBLIOGRAPHY	355
METRIC CONVERSIONS AND EQUIVALENTS	356
INDEX	357

FOREWORD BY DAVID TANIS

Nancy Hachisu's new cookbook, she says, is about preserving foods in the Japanese way. And it is, but it is so much more.

It is also about living and thinking in a Japanese way, as seen through the eyes of a plucky American expat who married a Japanese farmer, transplanted herself, and took on a thousand projects, each one a quest for flavor and spirit.

As a cook, her passion is learning to do things the old way—as things were done when families on working farms still produced all their own food and rarely bought anything from stores.

She lives, along with her husband and sons, in a century-old farmhouse. They grow their own rice, soybeans, mustard greens, and rows of the Japanese leek called negi. But if she hears of someone in another village who is producing something different, off she goes in search of it. She is especially eager to talk food and make food with the elders, the aunts and grandmothers. They have the knowledge of traditional ways to make the pickles and fermented products now produced mostly in factories.

Nancy's food is simple. Introductions to her recipes frequently begin with something along the lines of, "It may seem intimidating, but it is easier than you imagine." And it's true, even if, with some, you may need to wait a couple of years to sample it. Though nothing could be simpler than the salt massage she recommends for making quick pickled mizuna greens with kumquat. Or rolling up shiso leaves around a bit of miso for an easy snack.

Even before you arrive at Chapter One, Nancy sets the stage by familiarizing the reader with ingredients they will encounter throughout the book. Then she throws in a story or two about daily life, both modern and historical, and a glimpse of the community in which she is involved and a tour of the house she and her family inhabit and care for.

There's a discussion about knives, about tea, about seaweed.

You'll learn, among other tangential odysseys, at least five traditional ways to preserve fruits, vegetables, and fish: with salt, with miso, with fish sauce, by air-drying, and with sake lees. You'll also learn to make a fermented vinegar mash with persimmons.

Should you choose to follow Nancy's inspiring example, you'll want to put the following chores on your to-do list: Make your own miso from brown rice; make your own rice vinegar; make your own tofu; even your own sake. Not to worry, the recipes in the book don't require that you do. But isn't it wonderful that you could? And the information is right here.

Years ago, I visited friends in Japan in a small town during cherry blossom season, a rather magical time of year. I was able to observe firsthand how the locals would gather in the public spaces to picnic beneath the blooming trees for hours, often sharing little cups of sake or high-octane shochu. An appreciation bordering on love for the everyday Japanese ways with life and food was instilled in me during those few weeks, yet somehow I never returned.

I am grateful to have this book to spend time with, to rekindle those feelings. With Nancy's encouragement, I am anxious for spring to arrive, for now I know how to salt and pickle cherry blossom buds and sprinkle them over a bowl of steamed rice.

preserving a way of life

In the post-WWII exodus from the country to the city, many farms lay fallow, and it became difficult for urban Japanese to continue life as they had known it before the war. The traditions of preserving food largely passed from the country grandmothers into the hands of professionals, though, if one looks more closely, some grandmothers are still making pickles here and there. And some young fermenting and pickling aficionados are taking up the mantle as well. After the war, farming families who could make a living remained on their land and ate what they grew. But they raised their children with the goal of attending university and working in nonagrarian jobs. The countryside is wide open, so often a convenient place for large companies to build plants. And these plants provide jobs. Most sons (or daughters) of farming families did not follow in their parents' footsteps. My husband, however, did.

Like so many, I took my mother-in-law for granted, thinking she would always be there. But somewhere along the line I noticed that she was no longer making miso. I blinked twice and saw that she had given up on making *takuan* (page 217) and *hakusai* (page 11). They were easier to buy. I had my hands full with Western conserves such as marmalade, jams, pickles, sauerkraut, confit, and chorizo, so put the Japanese pickles on a back burner. "I'll learn how to make them later" was my excuse.

But after renovating and moving into the family farmhouse in 2000, my position in the family shifted. I could no longer shirk my responsibilities as the *oyome* (bride). I needed to steward the house along with Tadaaki. Tadaaki had thus far been the main Japanese cook of our household, while I cooked from the rest of the world. But being installed in the family home meant taking an active part in extended family dinners during Japanese holidays, not just as assistant, but as co-cook. And through this transition period, I found that many dishes fared well in my hands. My children were getting older, and I became more serious about my writing. People wanted me to write about the food we eat and the life we lead, so I did. In doing so, Tadaaki's food evolved into something more personal: It became mine. And I liked it better for the lightness and brightness that I brought to our Japanese farm food.

In writing *Japanese Farm Food*, I developed self-confidence in pickling, fermenting, and salting, which had always seemed mysteriously Tadaaki's purview, not mine. The second winter I made *takuan* and *hakusai*, Tadaaki pronounced them "just like my grandmother's." Thus began my odyssey of Japanese preserving.

The easiest preparations involve salt and air-drying. Half-day dried fish (page 35) has taut slightly salty flesh that firms up when broiled and is surprisingly delicious. Or even more basic: Cut up some eggplant or shiitake (page 18) and set them to dry in the sun until they are completely desiccated. I joined our friend's miso-making group (page 49) and wondered why I had not done so years earlier. Around the same time, a young couple living in a nearby mountain town started a soy sauce—making co-op that I was able to jump into. All of a sudden, I was making my own miso, soy sauce, and the most traditional Japanese pickle trilogy: *umbeboshi*, *takuan*, and *hakusai*. All of a sudden I was a real Japanese farmwife, and it felt good.

And as I took control of the family fermenting projects, my attention also focused on the ingredients we used in our kitchen. I knew our vinegar was excellent, but I wanted to know more. What was the difference between the clear organic rice vinegar that my husband bought and the organic brown rice vinegar that I bought? How were they made? What would be the difference in the food? This journey led me to Fujisu: an organic Japanese vinegar made from local Japanese rice by Iio Jozo (page 159) and Kakuida in Kagoshima (page 150). Our vinegars, albeit organic, had been made with American rice. I had heretofore been happy to have good-quality organic rice vinegars in the pantry, but once I knew which ones had been produced by Japanese rice, and once I met the vinegar makers themselves, I started using those vinegars (though I still use the more cost-effective American-grown rice vinegars for large-batch pickles).

Fuji TV filmed a 20-minute documentary sequence around vinegar, which included our trip to a vinegar maker. The director asked a sampling of people on the streets of Tokyo if they knew how rice vinegar was made, and none of them did (despite the fact that it is a centuries-old Japanese food tradition).

I also discovered that a large portion of Japanese did not know how soy sauce and miso were made, and I started a crusade to lay bare the methods for creating these elemental Japanese ingredients. Granted, not everyone can purchase local and artisanal 2-year-aged organic soy sauce and miso. We are eternally grateful to live in the same town as Yamaki Jozo (page 106). There are not enough soybeans in Japan to supply Kikkoman and Yamasa (the largest soy sauce companies), so the majority of soy sauce must be fermented from American-grown beans. Certainly not everyone is willing

to pay three times as much for artisanal soy sauce over the least expensive variety. Nonetheless, it is important to understand why artisanal is more expensive: It is fermented from whole soybeans, whereas the cheapest soy sauce is quick fermented from defatted soy grits (the by-product of making soybean oil). It became an obsession of mine to introduce these foods in their best forms to the world. The taste speaks for itself.

I had long been fascinated with katsuobushi (simmered, smoked skipjack tuna that is fermented and sun-dried) and wanted to visit the katsuobushi producer for this book. Fuji TV was interested in tagging along, because they wanted to place katsuobushi more in the public eye. At the katsuobushi producer, I learned that 90% of all packaged shaved katsuobushi has only been smoked and not fermented and sun-dried. Shocked, I vowed to go back to shaving as needed from a whole katsuobushi filet and have done so. The visit to Sakai Katsuobushi (page 255) in Kagoshima connected me with the producer, and I share that connection in this book. Not everyone can travel to where these products are made, but by introducing them here, I hope that readers can catch the enthusiasm and excitement. Now when I shave katsuobushi for lunch at my English immersion preschool, Sunny-Side Up!, the children gather round, fascinated, and stick out their hands eagerly when I ask, "Who wants katsuobushi?"

I never lack for things to do, so in the past I often put off preserving projects until too late. The best strategy with preserving is to balance out the quick souses and salting methods with a few of the long-term pickles. Pick ones that sound appealing, that you think you might be able to do. Remember that preserving and fermenting are processes. Don't be afraid of them, but do keep in mind that it is necessary to monitor your pots and barrels.

And when fruit is ready, it is ready. You cannot shilly-shally. As the resident wife in this ancestral Hachisu farmhouse, I knew that processing the fruit from the trees was another responsibility I bore. And truthfully,

I did not always fulfill my obligation. Sometimes I was overwhelmed by other projects, and sometimes I was out of town. Through the odyssey of writing this book I have realized that incorporating the seasons of preserving into my life makes me feel rooted, not always ricocheting from one project to the next. My life is ordered by the pull of the land and the need to be here when I should be.

I still cannot organize my life entirely around the land because there are times when I must be in the States, but I can be much more mindful of the seasons, taking advantage of what we have and not let our fruits and vegetables go to waste. I can try to be a good farmwife.

THE ROLES OF MEN AND WOMEN

One early morning weeding in the field before the sun became too unbearable, I started to think about how the lines had blurred and how much more difficult it is to live as a modern couple. There are so many choices: what career you will pursue, who you will marry, how you will set up your family life. And in these choices, there are inherent conflicts. Both members of the couple vie with each other to carve out their own time, as they divvy up the work that is needed for the home, the kids, and the land. Typically the woman's job, my

husband does the laundry, while I help in the fields. When asked, our sons pitch in here and there with farm work and cooking, but no cleaning.

The trade-off for gender equality and being able to choose one's own way is the fallout of more unclear duty lines and rivalry for free time.

I grew up in an equal household during the 1960s with two progressive, intellectual parents. There were three boys and three girls in our family, all two years apart, all born in a girl-boy pattern. We all did the dishes, we all cleaned, and we all helped with the laundry. And we were all told we could be doctors or lawyers—whatever we wanted. I believed anything was possible. That is perhaps why I'm fearless about diving into even the most foreign fermentation projects such as *narezushi* (page 207) or fish nukazuke (page 224). Nothing like a healthy dose of confidence to help you through tight spots. Tadaaki still shakes his head at some of my exploits, though in some way, I have stepped into his world and have usurped his place as the preserver in our family—only because I have made it a priority.

Tadaaki is wondering what his next steps are in the aftermath of the unprecedented snowfall that demolished his chicken coops (page 334). Fuji TV is talking about filming us together as we travel to locations about Japan. Now that the children are almost grown, maybe that is the next step: where we become partners once again, rather than competitors carving out separate directions.

TAKING RISKS

Sandor Katz wrote that you should not be afraid of mold. I agree. Also do not be afraid to try a preserving project that might take 3 months . . . or 3 years, especially if there is not much actual work involved, just waiting. The empowerment when you succeed is matchless. The raw materials will not set you back much, and the learning curve is exhilarating. But perhaps it makes sense to get your sea legs with some of the quicker pickling techniques. There is a myriad of simple methods to preserve, souse, and dry. Massage some salt into sliced vegetables, wrap tightly, and store in the fridge for a quick pickle (page 5). Throw a piece of squid in soy sauce and grill (page 77). Embed young green beans in miso (page 59) and leave overnight. Dunk young ginger or *myoga* buds in plum vinegar (page 175) for a few hours and you have an instant pickle. Drizzle with shio koji instead of a sprinkling of salt or shoyu koji in place of soy sauce, to transform even the simplest vegetable preparation such as grilled shiitake (page 198) or sliced tomato wedges (page 204).

But also start a few long-term pots that don't take much vigilance. I encourage you to put up a pot of chopped fish and salt to ferment for 2 to 3 years. And I am completely enthused about my pot of sake lees that sits alongside the fish sauce mash. It should be ready to press into red vinegar in 3 years (right about the time the fish sauce is ready). In the meantime, Persimmon Vinegar (page 177) only takes 3 months to ferment and produces a startlingly fragrant vinegar. Fermented Napa Cabbage (*hakusai*, page 11) would be the first of the "harder" fermented pickles to make, and I also recommend trying your hand at making miso. You will be very pleased with the result, as there is no substitute for homemade miso.

Each miso is different because each person is different and each locale has its own airborne spores that affect the miso (for the better). Neither quick pickles nor long ferments take much time to put up because farmers were busy people. And once the pickles are done, they are extremely useful to have in the larder to pull out for drinks before dinner, casual buffets, or as a palate cleanser for almost any meal. There are plenty of simple pickling methods in this book, but once you've gained assurance, you might want to try some of the more traditional methods, for through accomplishing those, you will have climbed an important personal mountain.

FORGIVING YOURSELF

There are the times when you don't succeed as well as you had hoped. It could mean that you did not watch the thing as closely as you should have. You were busy or out of town. This is not cause for alarm.

I ran into my friends Bill and Christine Campbell of Hotei Wines at a signing event I did at the Tokyo American Club. Bill is a fellow Stanford grad and also my wine supplier. We swapped stories about making *umeboshi*, and they told me their woes of the previous year. After their shipment of organic *ume* arrived, they salted them and immediately went out of town for several weeks. When they returned to Japan, 4 out of 5 of the crocks holding the salted *ume* were moldy. They rued the $64 paid for the 4 pounds of *ume* and promptly threw them out. My advice: Carefully pick off the mold and start drying the *ume* in the bright sun immediately (page 168).

While I don't have to buy my *ume*, I do have to gather them, and that takes several hours. So for me, when mold forms on my *ume*, it's less about the wasted money than the responsibility of having been less than vigilant. I should have checked the *ume*. Learn from your mistakes. Fix them. Each year you will get better. And realize that the window to perform many of these projects is short. Try approaching them without

ego. Rather than deciding when "you" want to do it, determine the best timing for your area and climate and give in to that.

Less decisions mean less anxiety. Let the seasons call the shots. The amount of choice that we have in this modern world, and particularly in the United States, is bewildering and frequently upsetting. Sometimes it's nice to do what is mandated by conditions rather than personal whim.

More and more I just try to be the best me I can, regardless of American or Japanese customs: The best Nancy Hachisu in the Hachisu house that I am able to be, and that means every day, or every month, or every year trying to become a more fully integrated person with the house and the lands and the country.

TRYING AGAIN

Do not be afraid to try again. The main difference I have found between America and Japan is the idea in America that we can always improve ourselves. We can go back to school or succeed in school later in life, we can change careers midstream without eyebrows raised, we can slough off bad habits and become better people. We can have second chances.

This concept is less a part of Japanese society, likely because of the deeply entrenched Japanese notion that there is one path set out and one must follow that path without deviation. Because the path is so firmly in place, it is terrifying, if not unimaginable, to deviate. How could one return?

The U-turn precept is where rural people such as Sakai-san from Sakai Katsuobushi (page 255) go to urban areas to attend college and work but eventually return to the rural area to raise their families and perhaps take over the family business. But we are also now seeing another phenomena called "I-turn," where urban people like Yuka and Kazushi Murakami of the soy sauce community (page 93) are leaving the city to start lives in rural areas. Perhaps they feel they can reinvent themselves out of their comfort zone. The reason why many Japanese are afraid to speak English is because they do not want to seem stupid or to make mistakes. This is crippling. And this fear is probably the reason why fewer and fewer young Japanese are cooking today. They are afraid of failure. If you use good ingredients and approach projects with conviction, the chance of failure is slim. It's important to try and to stay on top of the process: Check your fermenting pots regularly. And it's a way to monitor your own personal balance.

When my father-in-law to-be asked me if I thought I could be a bride in this farming family I immediately said, "Yes, of course!" not knowing what it really meant. That's a great thing about us Americans—our eternal optimism. But we are also naïve. There were plenty of customs I had a hard time following, and it took many years before I was firmly entrenched in this often maddening culture. When you marry into a farming family, the daughter-in-law is expected to jump into the mother-in-law's kitchen and take over the job of cooking for the family. In our case, however, we had built our own house separate from the parents. And although I have been cooking since elementary school, when we were first married, I let my husband cook the Japanese food. We occasionally went to Tadaaki's parents' house to eat, and at that time Tadaaki was the main cook, just as he had been for the seven years living in his parents' home following university. I thought it made complete sense for Tadaaki to do the cooking, since he knew what he was doing. My father-in-law did not agree.

There were four mysterious elements of Japanese country cooking that held me back from diving wildly in: the very fine cutting techniques with the scary-sharp Japanese knife; the roasting, then grinding of sesame seeds in the *suribachi* grinding bowl; the making of the ubiquitous dashi stock; and the rolling of udon noodles with the Japanese noodle rolling machine. In our area of Saitama prefecture, farm families grew rice and wheat on a rotating basis in the same field and ate udon noodles for dinner. My mother-in-law made udon noodles for her husband every night for about 50 years despite the fact that she hated udon. Clearly she was a better wife than I.

One day, when I was pregnant with my first son, I decided to make lasagna. Lasagna takes several hours to put together, so I had to start while Tadaaki was still working. He gave me a quick lesson on the noodle-rolling machine, and I started out with determination. You feed the dough through the rollers to make thinner and thinner sheets of pasta. To do this you have to rotate the screws a tad to narrow the gap between the rollers. The problem is that I got off balance on my screw tightening, so the gap was not evenly spaced. The dough came out raggy, a bit zigzaggy. A mess. I gave up. I was completely intimidated by the noodle machine.

Eighteen years later, writing the Japanese farm food book, I knew I needed to climb that mountain again. We had a photo shoot scheduled for a magazine article, so I thought I'd better enlist the help of Christopher, my oldest son, who was home from college for winter vacation. I prepared the dough. Christopher kneaded the plastic bag of dough with his feet and rolled it with the machine. Miura-san captured a series of great shots, then Christopher said he was finished and took off. "Hey, what about the rest of the dough?" I asked. Christopher gave me a quick refresher on the machine and I gathered myself up, centered myself, and said, "You can do this." Quietly, patiently, I fed the dough through the machine, and the noodles came out perfectly. At that moment, I knew I could do anything.

It is not just the Japanese kitchen that calls for personal balance, but also the Japanese farmhouse. The 100-year-old sliding *shoji* doors (page XII) require a gentle touch as you open and close them. Old *tansu* (page XIII) drawers must be pulled out evenly, without tugging or forcing, otherwise they stick. The obstinate drawers drove my father crazy, but that is what I love about living in a Japanese farmhouse. Every day I can fix my balance.

May 2014

THE FIRE

"This is how I think about our house," my husband, Tadaaki, informed me as he handed me an oversized book, appropriately called *The House*. Implicit in the gift was that somehow I did not feel the same, and that somehow he desperately needed me to understand his deep love for the house itself and his deep responsibility toward its stewardship. Our house was built by my husband's grandfather almost 90 years ago. And in years when Tadaaki's grandparents were alive, all surfaces in the house were rubbed lovingly every day, because the idea of caring for the house as if it were a living, breathing entity was part of that generation's psyche. But in the intervening years, the children grew up and moved out, and the house began to accumulate more and more stacks of books, papers, and unneeded clutter. The back storage area was stacked high with futons from long-gone days when the aunts and cousins would come back to their family home during the holidays. Tadaaki's father effected some modernizations in the 1970s, but the piles increased.

When Tadaaki and I renovated the house prior to moving in with the parents-in-law in 2000, we sorted through the accumulation of the last fifty years before finally just moving the boxed-up books and clothes to a 150-year-old outbuilding that, along with the house and the barn, forms an enclosed compound on our property. The boxes of books and clothes gathered dust, and eventually dirt, spiders, and other creatures. I spent the following five months washing down the 100 sliding wooden and glass doors (*shoji*, page XII) that would be papered along with some heavy wooden doors

(*fusuma*, page XII) that would be used as is. And I wiped all surfaces of the house—every crack and crevice from floor to ceiling.

On May 11, 2014, at around 2 a.m., that storage house erupted in fire and a series of staccato explosions. The storehouse burned to a hollowed-out shell, and the firemen stayed until the sun came up.

As I stood in the street, hair awry, barefoot, clad in a T-shirt and flimsy jammies, clutching my laptop and one sandal (grabbed in my panic while searching for my cell phone), I ached for the house and wanted to hold her. It was a miracle that the fire did not spread to our house, only 6 feet away from the burning storehouse. Like my parents-in-law, we have let her become piled with papers and books and other miscellany over the years. The outside buildings are likewise stacked to the gills, almost overflowing. I dragged out the book that Tadaaki gave me that past Christmas and remembered a favorite book from my childhood: *The Little Stone House*. He and I were not so different in how we carried the concept of house in our hearts. I had just grown up with a more cavalier attitude than he. Immediately, and viscerally, I understood his pain at how we had let things go and vowed to spend the following months culling the accumulation, polishing the house, and once again letting her shine.

DAILY LIFE AND TRADITION

Every home has its own personality and life and idiosyncrasies. And a Japanese farmhouse also carries a weight of traditions, practical customs, and some superstitions. The traditional materials of a farmhouse are relatively fragile—wood, earth, paper, tatami flooring. Wooden surfaces, floors as well as chests, need to be wiped with a damp cloth. Papered *shoji* screens are particularly vulnerable to careless punctures; repapering them is a big chore. Sweaty and oily palms are the cause of unwashable dirt on white-plastered walls; similarly, when passing through the split curtain (noren) in entryways and between rooms, you push it aside with the back of your hand. These little things might seem excessive to urban apartment dwellers, but they are simply part of life in our house and are as natural as breathing.

Each part of the house has its traditions, ambience, and character, and I have included a brief glossary of terms and customs. Of course, the kitchen is where to start. Most of the tools on the list have admirable substitutes in the Western kitchen, though I do strongly recommend a sharp, all-purpose Japanese knife such as a *bunka bocho* (page XXII). No need for fancy handles or signed blades; get an unpretentious one with a sharp edge. It is also worth searching out the largest grinding bowl (*suribachi*, page XVII) that you can find, along with the wooden pestle (*surikogi*). Not only for Japanese food, the *suribachi* is extremely useful in the Western kitchen. (I use mine for pounding salt cod for brandade, and pork for chilorio and rillettes.) And although a decent-sized *shichirin* (page XVI) can be a major purchase, it could be the most useful barbecue implement you will ever use.

There is a plethora of folk arts and objects still being made in Japan. Handcrafted objects are understandably expensive and, as they approach fine art, are almost out of reach for most of us. However, folk objects are still quite findable at flea markets and antique junk stores. I collect these items because I see their numbers dwindling over the years and so cannot pass them by.

THE HOUSE

DOMA: Our kitchen is located in what used to be the *doma* (literally "earthen room"). Originally, the floor surface of the *doma* was sweepable packed earth. My father-in-law covered the earth floor with linoleum in the 1970s, and we installed a floor heating system and Mexican tile in 2000. The *doma* was the work area of the farmhouse and thus a place under the roof where footwear was worn. Our current kitchen is a no-shoes area, though because of the in-and-out dogs, I'm not sure it should be.

SHOJI: Wooden framed sliding screens or doors, often made with sections of glass. The wooden lattice portions of *shoji* are mounted with thin Japanese paper (*washi*, page XIII). My favorite *shoji* in our house are a pair of fancy ones from an upscale antique market that stand majestically behind our dining room table, and the mouse-eaten closet doors in our bedroom, which had been covered with newspaper by Tadaaki's grandmother for insulation to keep the silkworms they raised warm. The burnished gnawed doors framed against the white paper are arresting when the closet is lit. They have atmosphere; they are cool. And I am also partial to the *senbongoshi* "thousand-slatted" partitions that Tadaaki bought for $30 each but would cost at least $1,000 each IF someone could make them today.

FUSUMA: Solid sliding doors made with a lacquered frame and constructed with complex layering of paper; paper on both surfaces. Wooden sliding doors, colloquially called *fusuma*, are actually *itado* and may have papered surfaces to resemble a *fusuma*. The paper surfaces may have striking texture, color, and even paintings such as intricate landscapes. The oblong metal door pulls often have an interesting relief pattern and are worth noticing.

BYOBU: Literally "to make the wind lie down"; hinged lacquer-framed standing screens constructed with layered paper similar to *fusuma*. *Byobu* are highly decorative and used as room dividers in distinguished houses or temples. Some of Japan's greatest paintings are found on *byobu*.

TANSU: Japanese traditional chests. There are many styles, ranging from the oversized kitchen chests (*mizuya dansu*) to the elegant (and expensive) stair chest (*kaidan dansu*) to the most common two-tiered clothes chest (*yofuku dansu*) to the more elegant "tea" chest (*cha dansu*) to small, multidrawered merchant chests. In our house we have several *mizuya dansu* for large storage items, many *yofuku dansu*, sometimes with single tiers used as coffee tables, a few *cha dansu,* and some small *tansu* scattered throughout the house.

HAICHO: A screened cupboard ranging from mini to slim refrigerator sized, used to store food. The screening allows air circulation and keeps the flies out. I use our *haicho* for wineglasses and overflow pottery.

KOTATSU: A square, low table frame over which a padded cloth is draped and covered with a square tabletop. People sit around the table on the tatami matting with the cloth draped over their knees. This was the family center and where people ate meals or watched TV. A heating element is attached to the underside of the frame, which emits a gentle warmth welcome in the frigid Japanese farmhouses. As Japanese moved to urban areas, they took with them the custom of eating and living around the *kotatsu*, despite the introduction of wall-based heating elements and electric carpets. Even today, central heating is not common in modern Japanese houses; however, tables and chairs are, so life around the *kotatsu* may eventually become obsolete.

HORIGOTATSU: A wood-framed square hole in the floor just deep enough to dangle legs over which a *kotatsu* is set. The heat source at the bottom was at one time charcoal-fueled but is now electric. Our house had a *horigotatsu*, but we floored it over for the living room area in our house renovation. In modern Japan, *horigotatsu* are more often found in restaurants than homes.

CLOTH AND PAPER

NOREN: The hemp or cotton split curtain that hangs in the inside and outside entryways of houses and restaurants. Noren act to provide privacy as clever dividers of space and can be gorgeous to boot.

TENUGUI: A long rectangular cotton cloth with countless uses (sometimes called a "hand dryer"), used in the kitchen for steaming, straining, wiping, or drying. A *tenugui* can also be fashioned into a head cloth or twisted into a band to tie around the head (such as some sushi chefs do). Many shops and restaurants make *tenugui* each New Year to hand out to their customers as a thank-you gift. *Tenugui*, once a ubiquitous part of the Japanese country kitchen, has now become a collectable item.

SARASHI: A 13-inch (34-cm) wide bolt of cotton or linen cloth traditionally used as a loincloth, bandaging, to wrap a woman's tummy during pregnancy, or to fashion diapers. These applications were still current when I came to Japan over two decades ago but are almost nonexistent today. *Sarashi* is also useful to line the steamer for cooking big batches of rice or soybeans or to cover preserving projects. In recent years, pieces of *sarashi* are sold cut and hemmed.

FUROSHIKI: A large square piece of cotton, linen, silk, or synthetic fiber used as a carrying cloth and to wrap gifts. *Furoshiki* may be plain or strikingly patterned. *Furoshiki* are now again in vogue as a multiuse wrapper/carrier (kind of a reaction against plastic bags).

WASHI: Often called "rice paper" for some inexplicable reason. *Washi* literally means "Japanese paper" and is handmade from paper mulberry (*kozo*), *mitsumata*, or *gampi* fibers. *Washi* is also hand dyed and can be used decoratively in the house as a covering for *tansu* or on *shoji*. In the late 19th century there were thousands of types of *washi* being made throughout the archipelago. Japan was truly a paper country. Today the craft is maintained by only a scattering of dedicated people. Due to increased paper imports from China and Thailand, this millennium-old cottage industry is

PRESCHOOLERS AND PAPER

Going anywhere with a motley crew of preschoolers is always a challenge, guaranteed to tax anyone's patience. But try packing a gaggle of exuberant little English-speaking Japanese kids onto an excursion bus for a craft museum visit. Even a 5-minute walk to the field leaves us harried and exasperated. But that doesn't mean we don't do it. Because we do.

I'm constantly scrounging around for a new venue for field trips with my Sunny-Side Up! preschool students. One little impediment is that most places only conduct classes or demonstrations in Japanese. Since we're an English immersion preschool, that doesn't work. Several years ago, we were visted by Sam Seager, a photographer from England. He was in Japan shooting mountain towns to document their unfortunate demise. I took him to Ogawa-machi, a culturally and agriculturally thriving little town about 40 minutes away by car. I hadn't been there since my first year in Japan, so didn't know what to expect. We had no joy at the craft beer place, since Monday is the day they are closed. We also never found Frostpia, a well-known organic farm owned by Yoshinori Kaneko, where I have been taking visitors recently. On one last whim, we followed the signs to a place optimistically named Saitama Traditional Craft Hall. They, too, were shuttered up. I suppose nothing much happens on Mondays in Ogawa-machi. But peering through the windows, the craft hall looked promising, and so the next day I had my assistant make the call.

For about $2 per person, the kids could each make a sheet of paper. Since it sounded like a good deal, we reserved for an upcoming field trip. The issue of explanations in Japanese would be dealt with when we got there. My plan: The paper-making ladies could tell the teachers the instructions in Japanese, and we would explain to the kids in English. That was the theory.

The Japanese part was a disaster, but the kids had fun, and the paper turned out beautifully. Why obsess about the language? Unless we strictly enforce the "no Japanese" rule, the children will speak to the teachers in English but will naturally speak to their friends in Japanese. And once they create these relationships in Japanese, it will be almost impossible to bend them into English. We learned this through experience. In the early days of SSU!, not wanting to introduce "language negativity," we never told them "no Japanese." I assumed the kids would organically begin switching over to English as they got better in the language. That did not happen.

Early in the second year, we initiated the "no Japanese" rule, which has been in place ever since. It took me the following two years to wrest the group into an English-only environment using various methods, which involved private sessions at "Nancy's House" (everyone is desperate to come) and well-placed money rewards. No shame here—it worked.

I take seriously the responsibility of growing little human beings and believe deeply that we are planting seeds in these children that will flourish for many years to come. It is heart-breaking when children leave the fold, but

I know we've touched their lives, so derive comfort from that. Even now I get visits from ex-English conversation students from the early years when "the school," called "Nancy's English Club," was merely a classroom in our home. They often report that they've continued with English, or perhaps have spent time living abroad, and it is warming to know that I made a lasting impression in their lives.

As I write about my life here in Japan I think a lot about how the house is the center of our life. I also think about the Japanese-influenced oiled redwood house, in which I grew up, with the rice paper plants that germinated a seed in me that grew and eventually brought me to Japan.

As I child, I thought our rice paper plant with its wide canopied leaves was used for making what we Americans call rice paper. In fact, handmade paper is most appropriately called *washi* (literally "Japanese paper"). Some *washi* is air thin, while other types have a gorgeous tactile texture that absorbs dyes well. The folksy style of *washi* is my new favorite present to bring to the U.S., if I can just figure out a way not to smash it in transit.

Here's how we made *washi* with the kids: The teacher sets a screen (*su*) made of fine bamboo splints on top of a wooden frame. With her help,

the child dips the frame into the pulpy water. With back-and-forth motions, the child swishes the frame to catch the pulp. It's harder than it looks (we adults did not fare so well). Once the screen has accumulated enough paper pulp, the teacher releases it from the frame. She gently lifts the pulp-coated screen from the frame and carries it gingerly to the pile of still wet papers the kids have made (each with a piece of *washi* marked with their name). The teacher expertly positions the screen precisely on the pile (pulp side down) and lifts the screen away from the pulp, leaving the wet sheet behind on the pile of other just-made paper. The stack of freshly made paper is pressed to expel water and then dried on a rack. The sheets magically separate when fully dried, thanks to the mucilage added to the pulp solution.

After the field trip, I returned to Ogawa-machi many times to visit a paper-making family down the street from the craft center where we made paper with the SSU! kids. The shelves are stacked with vibrant colored *washi* of different textures and varying thicknesses, and I wander about the shop, leafing through the piles. But the pieces that invariably draw me are the crumpled pieces (*momigami*) marbled with multicolored filaments. That powerful, striking paper appears in this book, separating the chapters.

threatened. In November 2014 Hosokawa *washi* (from Ogawa-machi and Higashi-Chichibu) was added to UNESCO's Intangible Cultural Heritage List. The *washi* used in this book was all produced by Kubo Shotaro Washi, my favorite paper makers in the nearby town of Ogawa. Kubo-san generously (and enthusiastically) gave me permission to use his original works in the hopes of increasing awareness and spreading appreciation of this important craft to the world at large.

CALLIGRAPHY PAPER: Thin rectangular paper (larger than legal sized) sold in packs of 100 or so. Calligraphy paper is a delicate paper that is very handy to have around for lining plates of tempura. The paper is folded on the bias to form an asymmetrical shape. Available at many Japanese grocery stores and online at Japan Bargain (see Resources).

FIRE VESSELS AND TOOLS

SHICHIRIN: A round or rectangular tabletop barbecue used for grilling meat or air-dried fish. *Shichirin* are fired from carved diatomaceous earth (page 41), and the name comes from the seven copper rings that are hammered around the circumference of the barbecues. Available online through Korin (see Resources).

KONRO: Any tabletop cooking stove, which includes *shichirin*, gas-fired large cooktops, or portable butane-fueled burners. The butane-fueled burners are useful for tabletop cooking such as one-pot dishes (*nabe*). Available through kitchenware stores or Amazon.

KAMADO: A brick or earthenware stove with one or more large circular openings to hold pots for cooking. Underneath the opening is the fire chamber. *Kamado* are fueled by wood rather than charcoal and are typically used to cook rice or noodles in a flanged iron pot. The intense heat of the wood-burning fire causes the grains to swell and cook evenly. A *kamado* is often an inside fixture in the *doma* (page XII); we used to have one in the kitchen until our house renovation in 2000. Sadly, there was no room to keep it, so it now sits outside our kitchen door.

IRORI: A sunken hearth with smoldering coals around which the family gathered for warmth and to cook food. Tubers such as potatoes, sweet potatoes, and taro (page 339) can be buried directly in the embers, fish skewered on sticks and stuck in the ash to grill slowly, or a pot of water or soup is hung from the giant hook (*jizaikagi*) suspended from the ceiling. While some mountain homes still have *irori*, you will find them more likely as a novelty in specialty restaurants.

HIBACHI: Hibachi are porcelain pots or portable wooden boxes with copper linings that are filled halfway with ash to hold charcoal embers, which provide heat. In English they are sometimes called hand-warmers. While some friends still use hibachi, they are more a collectible than a part of current Japanese life.

HIOKOSHI: A small, wood-handled, cast iron charcoal starter. Put a heaping pile of charcoal in the *hiokoshi*, set it over a gas flame, and wait until the charcoal has gone from black to red to a little white on the edges. Available online at Korin (see Resources).

PICKLING CONTAINERS AND ACCOUTREMENTS

TARU: Wooden barrels (page 54) fashioned from cedar or cypress slats that are held together with rings of braided bamboo strips. These are the traditional containers for pickling and fermenting but are not used much today. *Taru* need to be used, or at least filled with water periodically, otherwise they will fall apart since they maintain their shape by the snugness of the slats and the integrity of the encircling bamboo bands. If not stored upside down, the wood can shrink, causing the bamboo rings to slip down and the bucket to fall apart. Leaky *taru* are fixable by filling with water to swell the wood and close up the cracks. If there is still an issue with seepage, rub salt inside a dampened barrel and turn upside down overnight before filling again with water. The benefit of using *taru* is that they breathe—air can enter all of the seams, thus allowing for a quicker and more even fermentation. The downside is a possibility of mold, though the mold can be scraped off and the sides sterilized with shochu (page XXXII) or vodka.

KAME: A lidded (usually brown) ceramic pot that ranges from small to quite large to huge. *Kame* are not only tastefully made, but also very useful for many preserving and fermenting projects such as *umeboshi* (page 167), miso (page 51), and *doburoku* (page 311). Easily available at hardware stores in Japan and perhaps at selected Japanese kitchenware sections abroad. Substitute any crockery pickling pot available through The Brooklyn Kitchen, Quitokeeto, Gardener's Supply Company, or Cultures for Health (see Resources).

POLY TARU: Ubiquitous yellow food-grade plastic tubs for pickling. These tubs are sold with a drop lid and top. Substitute Western-style tubs sold on Amazon or Lexington Container Company (see Resources).

POLY BUKURO: A food-grade plastic bag used for pickling. Sold all over Japan at vegetable stands, grocery stores, and hardware stores. Most likely available during pickling season at large Japanese grocery stores abroad or on Amazon.

TSUKEMONOKI: A modern plastic container (of various sizes) with a spring-action screw mechanism that substitutes for the barrel and rock weights. One benefit of these contraptions is that they fit in the fridge. We use zippered bags instead of a *tsukemonoki* for quick pickling jobs.

OTOSHI BUTA: In cooking, a drop lid. In pickling, a wooden or plastic drop lid used to distribute the weight of the stones placed on top of it to press miso or vegetables evenly during fermentation.

OMOISHI: Literally "heavy rocks": any heavy objects used as weights for fermenting and preserving. Typically garden rocks or river stones were used in Japan, though nowadays ceramic or plastic-covered iron weights can be purchased at home centers. I prefer rocks because there is an art to piling them on and this is one more instance where experience brings improvement.

FOR VEGETABLES, SEEDS, BEANS, AND DOUGH

TAWASHI: A hemp palm–bristled brush for scrubbing vegetables (and anything else). Rather than peel root vegetables such as daikon, carrots, gobo, and turnips, we usually scrub them. Substitute a Western vegetable brush if you cannot find the "Turtle" *tawashi* made in Japan. *Tawashi* are also useful for cleaning the grooves of a *suribachi* (grinding bowl) or scrubbing iron pots (*tetsunabe*, page XIX). Check Japanese grocery stores or the Natural Import Company (see Resources).

TOFU TSUKURUKI: A plastic, metal, or wood form for tofu-making. Japanese ones have joined corners, are fashioned from Japanese cypress, and are available from Soy Milk Maker and Cultures for Health (see Resources). Amazon is selling a larger American-made one of less aromatic wood, with small nail pins holding it together (this style used to be sold at Soy Milk Maker).

SURIBACHI: A grooved ceramic bowl used for grinding seeds, nuts, or tofu. You can substitute a coffee or nut grinder for the seeds, a miniprep for the nuts, and a food processor for the tofu; however, the *suribachi* is the most satisfying way to grind these and any foods. But do not bother with a small *suribachi* since the seeds will jump out and make a mess. If you decide to take the plunge, get the biggest one you can find. Sold at Japanese grocery stores, Korin (see Resources), or Amazon.

SURIKOGI: The grinding pestle that is used with the *suribachi*. Again, look for the largest pestle that fits reasonably with the size of your bowl. A wider bottom on the pestle will mean quicker dispatching of the grinding process. The best *surikogi* are made from the thick branch of a *sansho* (prickly ash) bush, a relative of Sichuan pepper. The knobby surface makes getting a purchase on the pestle easier than slick wood.

TAKE BURASHI: A small, rectangular bamboo "brush," sometimes sold with *suribachi* sets, which is handy to have for removing foods that cling stubbornly to the grooves of the *suribachi*. Also good for scraping the last grated ginger or wasabi off the *oroshigane* grating plate.

OROSHIGANE: A handled, rectangular metal sharp-toothed plate for fine-grating ginger, daikon, and wasabi. A wide-bladed Microplane™ is a fine substitute.

OROSHIKI: Technically any grating tool. We use a circular ceramic grating plate with a trough surrounding the round raised, textured grating area; the finely grated daikon slides down and is held in the trough as you grate.

WASABI OROSHI: Wasabi is conventionally grated on a handled wooden board covered in sharkskin. Unless the grater is fairly large, it takes a bit of time to grate the wasabi. Also you will need to replace the grater periodically since the sharkskin dulls over time and tends to warp. I prefer using a wide antique copper-toothed grater (*oroshigane*). You grind wasabi in a circular motion.

MUSHIKI: A tiered bamboo steaming basket. Easily available in Chinese or Japanese cookware stores or online at Korin (see Resources).

SEIRO: A square (or round) wooden or metal stackable steamer. Can be found online at Korin (see Resources) and possibly at Asian kitchenware stores.

KONEBACHI: Large "kneading bowls," usually made of thick wood or stoneware, the latter probably dating back to the late 19th century. No longer common in the modern Japanese kitchen, these heavy bowls have been replaced by lighter, more easily storable ones made of tin or stainless steel. I have an ever-growing collection of various antique bowls (*hachi*) stacked inside my kitchen cabinets, on the kitchen floor, and in several outbuildings of our house. My bowls range from quite small to very large, and some of the smaller-sized bowls have spouts for pouring (*kataguchi*). The larger bowls can be taxing to heft when full, but the pleasure they give far exceeds the effort (and the room they take up in the kitchen).

RICE- AND SOUP-RELATED

SUIHANKI: Japanese-style electric rice cooker easily found at most kitchenware stores. However, I would advise buying this appliance at a large Japanese grocery store. A good rice cooker is not cheap. The Japanese-made Zojirushi will run about $300 and the Chinese-made Zojirushi around $200. I bought the Chinese-made Zojirushi for events in the U.S. and found I needed to recalibrate my rice cooking method: The amount of water had to be decreased a bit.

DONABE: A lidded ceramic casserole-style vessel used for cooking one-pot dishes (*nabe*) or rice over an open flame. Rice cooked in a *donabe* (or cast iron pot) is more toothsome than that steamed in the rice cooker and thus superior, to my mind. Those who are used to having warm rice on the ready from a rice cooker may not like the fact that the rice does not stay warm in a *donabe*. Black-glazed Iga ware *donabe* from Nagatani-en are available in the U.S. from Toiro Kitchen (see Resources). *Donabe* are expensive but a useful and beautiful multipurpose addition to your kitchen. Buy the one that can cook rice and use it for simmering a Japanese

one-pot dish (*nabe*) at the table or a Western stew. A Western ceramic casserole will not substitute because it cannot be used on a direct flame.

SHAMOJI: Thick, flat bamboo, plastic, wooden, or ceramic paddles for serving rice. Twenty years ago, bamboo paddles were the norm; now textured plastic paddles are favored. I have a ceramic paddle from the Blue & White in Tokyo (see Resources) that I love, while my husband and sons use the paddle that came with the rice cooker. It sits in a stand on the counter—not too aesthetically pleasing but certainly convenient.

HANDAI: A round, low-sided, wide wooden tub used for cooling and aerating rice as you add in the sweetened vinegar for making sushi rice. The back of a large wooden cutting board or an ultra-clean butcher-block table can provide the same function of sucking the excess moisture out of the rice.

TETSUNABE: Prior to WWII, iron pots were cast from unique handcrafted molds and copper pots were hand-hammered. However, the war effort appropriated metals, and handwork all but ceased. Rebuilding infrastructure took precedence in postwar Japan over reviving local crafts; and most artisanal production of cookware died. At the end of the WWII, the Oigen factory in Iwate prefecture restarted their production of *tetsunabe*, though converted over to machine-made molds. In the interest of regrowth, and due to the lack of artisanal workers, they gave up making cast iron kettles, however took the local Nambu Tekki (see *tetsubin*) cast iron tradition and developed high-quality cookware. Cast iron ware acts as a partner in the cooking process, and iron is exceptionally eco-friendly since less energy calories are needed to cook the food. (Also a cast iron lidded pan acts like a stovetop oven.) Oigen ironware is available through Korin in New York City and Chef's Armoury in Australia. Personal factory direct import is also possible via email (since1852@oigen.jp).

TEA-RELATED

TETSUBIN: Cast iron kettles used to heat water for brewing tea—the Nambu Tekki cast iron tradition of Iwate prefecture has an international reputation. Nanbu Tekki kettles are not only beautiful, but also functional. They are cast in molds of sand and clay, in which designs/patterns are drawn by hand into the mold wall. It takes two weeks to create one mold. And although a skilled artisan can reuse his mold as many as ten times, more often, each mold can only be used three times before it is destroyed in the process of freeing up the cast kettle. This 400-year-old ironware technique was designated an official Traditional Craft Industry in 1975.

Artisanally made *tetsubin* are dear, though in light of the workmanship, a bargain. Especially considering that, with care, the kettle will last for generations. We finally had to retire our kettle inherited from Tadaaki's grandmother after more than 100 years of daily use but have replaced it with a couple of other kettles bought at the local flea market. (Be warned, antique kettles are known collectibles, so no cheaper than the new ones.) *Tetsubin* typically hold about 1 liter of water.

KYUSU: Small teapots used for brewing tea. Japanese *kyusu* are made of ceramic or iron and usually hold from .3 to .6 liter. Nambu Tekki *kyusu* are popular in Europe and available at specialty tea shops abroad.

KNIVES

Tadaaki and I each have our own personal *bunka bocho*, and our sons use them indiscriminately. A *bunka bocho* is literally an "everyday knife" that can be used on meat and vegetables or even fish. However, if you are attempting to cut sashimi, it is best to invest in a slim *sashimi bocho*, since the knife will cut through the fish like butter (provided you keep it sharp). We have several *sashimi bocho* in our house; I bought my own a few years ago at the advice of the fishmonger. He told me that it is better to use the same knife while gaining skill in cutting

sashimi. Thick and heavy fish knives (*deba bocho*) are also useful in any kitchen, since they can be used for cutting up poultry and large pieces of meat. Japanese knives are the right tools for the job—well made and reasonably priced (except for the fancy ones marketed in fashionable kitchenware emporia). Hida Tool in Berkeley, California, or online (see Resources) is an excellent source for authentic Japanese knives and tools and will not break the bank. The only caveat is that the blades are carbon steel, so you must rinse without soap after use and immediately dry—and keep the blade sharp.

BUNKA BOCHO: There are several types of these everyday knives: *banno bocho*, *santoku bocho*, and *funayaku bocho*. We use a relatively inexpensive ($35) *banno bocho* made by our local knife maker (page XXV), Hitoshi Matsunaga. Although 12 inches (30.5 cm) long, our *banno bocho* is light as a feather at 4.4 ounces (125 g), so your arm does not get tired holding it for long periods of time while you slice and dice. The blade is also razor-thin, thus excellent for cutting fruit, vegetables, meat, and fish, but nothing crusty or hard, such as levain bread or kabocha. Check the weight and blade thinness before you buy. The back edge of our *banno bocho* tapers from ⅛ inch at the base to very thin at the tip, though for the most part is about 1/32 inch. The back is curved, but the blade is straight, so you do not make rolling cuts. You slice down emphatically and quickly, using your curled fingers as a guide. If you buy one Japanese knife, choose a *bunka bocho*.

DEBA BOCHO: Also called a *sakana bocho* (fish knife). *Deba bocho* are wide-bladed knifes of varying sizes that are typically used for butchering fish, so the base of the knife is thick enough to cut through fish or poultry bones. A smallish 9¼-inch (23.5-cm) *deba bocho* would be the second Japanese knife to add to your collection; it is especially useful in Western cooking since it can cut through small bones. A 12¼-inch (31-cm) *deba bocho* is handy for cutting up large pieces of fish or meat and can whack through soft bones.

SASHIMI BOCHO: If you plan on doing any sashimi slicing, this knife is indispensable. There are two basic styles of *sashimi bocho*: *takobiki* and *yanagiba*. The *takobiki* has a squared-off rectangular blade, while the *yanagiba* blade tapers to a pointed tip. Tadaaki generally uses a *takobiki*, while I use a *yanagiba*. It's purely a matter of personal choice.

HASAMI: These butterfly-shaped iron scissors are exquisitely crafted and a joy to hold in the hand. (This basic design is seen in the Roman Empire.) Every time I touch these scissors I want to stroke the smooth curves. *Hasami* are useful for harvesting vegetables in the field or snipping flowers and herbs in the garden. The blades are carbon steel, so be sure to wipe dry after use or they will rust.

BENRINER: A Japanese mandoline useful for large-job cutting projects such as Thinly Sliced Ginger Pickles (page 156) or Dried Daikon Threads (page 16). Available at Japanese cookware suppliers or on Amazon.

TOISHI (WHETSTONE): There are plenty of YouTube videos out there if you want to learn how to sharpen a knife, but there is no substitute for practice and a bit of self-confidence. Rather than relying on an outside knife-sharpening service, it makes much more sense to hone the blade on your knife regularly. Even if you are not extremely skillful at first, eventually you will be. A diamond-surfaced hand sharpener is also useful to have around for a quick touch-up.

PANTRY

There are not a lot of special ingredients that you will need for Japanese preserving and fermenting, though the main one is salt. Since preserving projects could require fairly large volumes of salt, you must weigh the costs. I don't use my most expensive salt for salting, but do use responsibly produced Japanese sea salt. I have found that Italian Trapani salt is the closest to Japanese sea salt and like Japanese sea salt, it comes in varying grades. I prefer a salt with slightly flaky crystals for most of my cooking, while a finer-textured, less expensive sea salt is fine for pickling or fermenting. Likewise, when selecting miso or soy sauce as a pickling medium, rather than a flavor for a certain dish, cost comes into play.

Many of these pickling or sousing methods that use copious quantities of one ingredient are generated from a time or place where those ingredients were plentiful. Fish sauce quantities are small for the most part, so if you cannot find Japanese fish sauce, I would recommend using Red Boat for methods that call for larger amounts and Nettuno Colatura for dribbling or for adding that indescribable hidden taste. Beyond that, finding the best possible katsuobushi, konbu, and niboshi is certainly a quest worth investing some time in, since those are the subtle seasoning components of dashi (page 253).

As for koji, sake lees, and rice bran, try to get these from as close to the source as possible (i.e., koji from the miso maker, sake kasu from the sake brewery, and rice bran from the miller or grower). Mirin and sake can be purchased at Japanese grocery stores. Take care to only purchase hon mirin, which is naturally sweet through fermentation rather than from added sugar. Find a medium-priced bottle of sake and stick it in the fridge for sousing or cooking. For sautéing and salads, use a clear, preferably organic oil, such as Spectrum Organic Canola Oil. I also recommend a small bottle of organic sesame oil, either Eden Foods or Ohsawa (see Resources). The best-quality Japanese grocery stores are often local ones like Tokyo Fish Market in Berkeley, California, or Anzen Hiroshi in Portland, Oregon. Nijiya is a small California chain that is dedicated to putting artisanal, organic, and other high-quality products on the shelves. On the other hand, I have found large-scale Japanese supermarkets abroad to be bewildering and difficult to navigate.

Internet-based Japanese food suppliers are increasing in number, so it is worth doing a Google search periodically for a hard-to-find product. Every year there are more available than the year before and Amazon has also increased its Japanese food supplies exponentially. All that said, I remain steadfast in recommending the top online macrobiotic Japanese food sources: Gold Mine Natural Food Co., Natural Import Company, as well as Eden Foods (see Resources).

SHOKUNIN

Jiro Ono of Sukiyabashi Jiro is the ultimate *shokunin* (craftsman). I have had the honor of being a guest at Jiro-san's sushi restaurant four times over the last several years, thanks to my friendship with Jiro-san's editor, Yasushi Ozaki. Each time, the sushi experience is a like a nuanced symphony, and I feel the power of being in the presence of a great man. I wish I could absorb some of his strength, like osmosis, though no such luck. Jiro-san's 80+ years of work shows in the upright way he holds himself and the relaxed stance of his body. Jiro-san's sushi is well worth the tariff, though I go for the chance to sit under his watchful eye (wondering whether I measure up) and for the chance of a lively repartee now that he has warmed up to this irreverent Californian.

Even before being an audience to Jiro-san's impressive sushi-making artistry, I thought of *shokunin* as the treasures of Japan. After watching David Gelb's portrait of Jiro-san, *Jiro Dreams of Sushi*, I became more enthralled with Jiro-san because the thoughts he expressed about *shokunin* were exactly mine. I felt he was a kindred spirit, and this made his sushi and being in his presence that much more meaningful. In some strange way, he became a mentor I looked up to and appreciated as embodying the heart of Japan. Every day Jiro-san comes to work to treat the fish and create sushi that is better than the day before. Every day.

Japanese have great reverence for the artisanal restauranteur, and it is commonly understood that it takes seven years apprenticing a specialized Japanese culinary art before one can be called "master." Our friend Kanji Nakatani owns two soba restaurants in our area and his customers come from as far away as Tokyo as well as from the neighboring towns. "Kanchan," as he is affectionately known, periodically stages soba dinners at Chez Panisse in Berkeley, California, and is the mentor of our three sons. Kanchan says that he operates his restaurants like a hobby: He does it because he loves it. He knows fish intimately, so fish figures strongly on his menu along with the soba. He is enthralled with architecture, interesting (old and new) plates, bowls, glassware, art, and interior aesthetics. His restaurants both reflect this appreciation for crafts and art . . . along with eclectic music. Kanchan says that if you follow what you love, money will follow.

Shokunin (職人) literally means "working person"; *shokunin* are craftsman. The term gained true meaning during the Edo period when the concept of making things for the sake of the thing and not for money gained ground. And through the making of quality crafts, artisans developed pride in their work. Fine Edo period workmanship is renowned in Japan for its quality and it is heartbreaking that our Edo period storage building recently burned to a charred shell (page XI). Fortunately we have a close Canadian friend who graduated from a Japanese trade college and is a certificated Japanese carpenter, now building traditional Japanese houses. And the carpenter who worked on our farmhouse renovation was so remarkably skilled that he crafted a seamless extension of the antique copper roof we added to the front door area of the house. Perhaps one of those carpenters, skilled in traditional Japanese building practices, will rebuild our Edo period storage building.

We also value the tools of the past. Apart from the pottery made by my husband and sons, we mostly use 50 to 100-year-old baskets, bowls, buckets, and pots. I do not know the people who made these implements, but I can feel the weight of the ages, and I derive strength from the farmwives who used them in their own preserving and cooking endeavors. And that makes me feel connected, like I belong in the compendium of this local life.

Also at the flea market is the knife maker from whom we buy our knives and farm tools, Hitoshi Matsunaga. Over the years, young Matsunaga-san has become skilled at his craft under the tutelage of his father. And what was once a monthly presence in the flea market has become weekly, a testament to hard times. People are buying at generic home centers. Knowing the person who crafted the knife that you use is part and parcel with knowing who grows your food. Even when I am not in the market for a knife, I always stop by Matsunaga-san's stand when taking a turn through the flea market. His wide, smiling face never fails to lift my spirits, and I almost wish I were buying a knife, though make up for it by buying a dozen or so as presents before trips abroad.

On the opposite end of the spectrum of artisanal craftsmanship is Gyokusendo, a 200-year-old tin and coppersmith in Niigata prefecture. What struck me first when we strolled up to Gyokusendo was that the lovingly cared for traditional building hailed back to another era and was an anomaly on the modern street where it stands. The entryway skirted a spare garden that gave a sense of peace to the

room where we drank tea from Gyokusendo copper and tin hand-hammered cups. What also struck me about this coppersmith was that the artisans worked side by side: seasoned craftsmen and budding apprentices. The rhythmic *ton-ton* of the hammers was soothing and somehow comforting, never irritating. I asked why they did the work, and their answer was that each piece may appear the same, but ultimately was subtly different, and this kept the work interesting and fulfilling. Most of the intricate inlaid pieces fashioned by Gyokusendo were priced out of sight, though I did splurge on two beer cups for Tadaaki's Christmas present. Beautifully made things, whether they are expensive hand-hammered cups or reasonably priced well-made knives, are a pleasure to hold and will last forever, so ultimately worth the investment.

Up until WWII, Japan was 90 percent agricultural, and each farmer had his own plot of land to grow food for his family. The national character of Japan is deeply embedded in this agrarian society's set of values, which puts the cooperative community above all. Inherent in all of this is pride, commitment, value, respect, connection, and belonging. And it is those farm boys who rose up after WWII to build Japan into the modern powerhouse that it is today. Japan is well known for its dichotomy: the modern juxtaposed with the traditional. And while quite a bit of attention is focused on the car and electronic industry or manga, we should not overlook the craftsmen, farmers, fishermen, and local artisanal producers of traditional Japanese foods who all contribute to the crucial fabric of Japan. They represent the heart of Japan and the deep pride that Japanese have in a job well done.

Even if you cannot follow an agrarian or artisanal life or work style, you can value it, and knowing it is there keeps Japanese people feeling connected. We who live in Japan belong to this culture, which values ALL workers. Having a job is the value. In the end, the reason why Japanese work so hard is that there is this underlying and pervasive culture of valuing a job. A commitment to each other and respect for society is passed on from generation to generation. And it exists because of the deep connection to the land and sea that still gives Japan a feeling of historical grounding.

I asked my farmer husband why he believes Japanese work so hard. His answer: "Japanese believe there is a soul in every object, every part of life. They don't even think about it. It is in their DNA, so it is impossible not to do a good job. It would be disrespectful to the soul of Japan."

In the Edo period (1603–1867), sugar was refined in a unique method from "bamboo" sugarcanes to create *wasanbon* (page XXXIII), a melt-in-your-mouth tan powder with a subtle fragrance valued for confectionary even today. While difficult to find, it is obtainable online through Ueno Gourmet (see Resources). Adding sugar to savory foods is a custom that came about post–WWII to compensate for the lack of intrinsic flavor in foodstuffs. Overuse of sugar is rampant in modern Japan; better to use moderately and to use a good organic sugar or *wasanbon*.

Because of arsenic scares in rice, organic rice in the bulk section would be a safe choice. Alternatively, order online from Lundberg Family Farms or Koda Farms, a Japanese family that has been growing rice in California since 1928 (see Resources). For fresh seasonal foods that will have good intrinsic flavor, hold up well in storage, and be safe for consumption, please visit the farmers' market, fish market, and butcher. Buying from the source is cost-effective in the end, if you factor in the added benefits of flavor, safety, and freshness.

SALT-RELATED

SHIO (SEA SALT): The Meadow, a salt and chocolate shop in Portland, Oregon, and New York City, is run by the very passionate and very knowledgeable Mark Bitterman. According to Mark, Japanese artisanal salts are the best in the world. While I agree, their prices abroad are completely out of sight for preserving projects. Find a bright sea salt such as the Sicilian Trapani salt or bulk sea salt in the organic section. Flaky *fleur de sel*, *fiori di sale*, Maldon, or some of the local Maine or Northwest salts are also good choices for finer uses such as sprinkling on fish or vegetables. If possible, avoid mass-produced salts and choose the best sea salt in your price range for the job.

MISO: Miso is widely available in mainstream supermarkets abroad as well as specialized Internet sites (see Resources). There is not a large variation in miso prices, though if you are planning on doing miso preserving, it might be wise to buy bulk miso from Gold Mine Natural Food Co. It probably makes sense to choose two types of miso at first: a mild one and a darker one, until you are ready to branch out. Best to read Choosing, Storing, and Using Miso (page 70) before venturing out to the market.

SHOYU (SOY SAUCE): In Japan, the supermarket shelves are filled with a variety of soy sauces, mainly produced by the two largest brands: Kikkoman and Yamasa. Since offering multiple choices is not really a Japanese custom, I would guess these products were originally developed for the large U.S. market. You don't need more than one soy sauce, and for Japanese food, select a Japanese one. We use Yamaki Jozo (page 106) organic soy sauce and my homemade soy sauce. Our locally made Yamaki soy sauce is repackaged by Ohsawa as Nama Shoyu (written in script on a yellow ochre label) and is easily found in natural food stores as well as online at Gold Mine Natural Food Co. Eden Foods is bottling artisanal Japanese soy sauce as well, and I also like the Blue Grass Soy Sauce made in Kentucky, especially for salads (see Resources). If these artisanal soy sauces are out of your price range, choose an organic or at least a whole bean soy sauce made by Yamasa or Kikkoman; otherwise you will be getting a soy sauce made from defatted soy grits rather than real soybeans (page 90).

GYOSHO (FISH SAUCE): The generic term for fermented fish sauce, known in Akita prefecture as *shottsuru* and on the Noto Peninsula as *ishiru* or *ishiri*. *Shottsuru* is typically fermented from sandfish (*hata hata*), but can also be made from anchovies or sardines (*iwashi*). A barrel of *ishiru/ishiri* used to be a fixture in most Noto Peninsula fisherman households until about twenty years ago. The waters off of the Noto Peninsula contain a wealth of fish and sea creatures, all of which can be fermented into fish sauce. Use as a substitute for, or in addition to, salt or soy sauce. A few drops in a salad dressing or in a soup provide a hidden pop to the dish. A thorough treatment of fish sauce can be found in Chapter Four (page 117). Nettuno Colatura is the closest substitute for mild Japanese fish sauce, though Red Boat is also a good choice.

SHIO KOJI: Rice koji and salt water that have fermented for 7 to 10 days at room temperature. Used for quick pickles or marinating poultry, meat, and fish before grilling. Keeps for one year, refrigerated. Easy to make at home (page 192), but also available at some Japanese grocery stores and on Amazon.

SHOYU KOJI: Rice koji and soy sauce fermented for 7 to 10 days at room temperature. Drizzle on vegetables or marinate meats in place of soy sauce. Keeps for one year, stored chilled. Homemade from good-quality soy sauce is best (page 202), but also available at selected Japanese grocery stores and on Amazon.

NIGARI (BITTERN; MAGNESIUM CHLORIDE): The coagulant used for making tofu: Nigari is the liquid left over after all salt solids have been extracted from seawater. Sold in liquid or crystal form. Available from Gold Mine Natural Food Co., Cultures for Health, and Natural Import Company (see Resources).

VINEGARS

RICE VINEGAR: The least expensive rice vinegars are quite harsh due to accelerated production methods and the low percentage of rice per liter. I almost only use brown rice vinegar because it has a rounder, more well-balanced flavor than clear ones made from white rice. Natural Import Company sells a sushi rice vinegar that is probably the best-quality clear rice vinegar available in the United States (and, despite the name, is unseasoned). Avoid seasoned rice vinegars like the ones prepared for making sushi rice, since they usually contain MSG. Sushi rice vinegar is simple to make. For 6 cups cooked Japanese rice: 6 tablespoons rice vinegar, 3 tablespoons organic granulated sugar, and 2 teaspoons fine sea salt.

BROWN RICE VINEGAR: As far as I can tell, all of the brown rice vinegars being sold by Eden Foods, Natural Import Company, and Gold Mine Natural Food Co. in

the U.S. and Clearspring Ltd. in the U.K. are all technically black vinegar (page 152) fermented in stoneware pots in Kyushu. These are your best bet for a soft, full-flavored rice vinegar. Highly recommended (see Resources). In Japan, brown rice vinegar is fermented from brown rice sake and some seed mother from previous batches.

BLACK VINEGAR: Although a bit of a misnomer, black vinegar is actually brown rice vinegar that has been fermented outside in stoneware pots from cooked brown rice, brown rice koji, and spring water.

RED VINEGAR: Red vinegar (page 165) is pressed from 3- to 5-year aged sake lees thinned with water. Very difficult to purchase, even in Japan, though available through professional channels (see Resources). Technically, red vinegar is required to make true Edomae sushi (sushi as we know it today).

OTHER PICKLING MEDIUMS

SAKE KASU (SAKE LEES): Used to pickle fish or vegetables and flavor soup (page 210), but also lovely in ice cream (page 215). Available in Japanese grocery stores or from sake breweries such as Artisan SakeMaker (see Resources).

KOJI (ASPEGILLUS ORYZAE): Spores used to ferment miso, soy sauce, sake, shochu, mirin, and rice vinegar. Koji spores are produced by a small number of labs in Japan and are generally purchased by professional makers rather than home fermenters. Already inoculated grains such as brown rice koji and barley koji are available online through the Natural Import Company or Cultures for Health. Rice koji can be purchased through miso makers such as South River or Cold Mountain (see Resources) and is sold as loose grains. Compressed "cakes" of rice koji are available at Japanese grocery stores, though must be broken into individual grains before using.

SOYBEANS

TOFU: There are several artisanal tofu makers in the U.S. making a decent product (page 230). The one that tastes the closest to Japanese-made tofu is Meiji Tofu in Gardena, California, but many other companies are doing an admirable job of producing fresh tofu. For Japanese dishes, avoid the spongy long-shelf-life blocks of bean curd often found in U.S. supermarkets. Also if tofu is not locally available, it is not difficult to make your own (page 236), though it does require a bit of patience to produce homemade soy milk.

USUAGE: Tofu blocks, sliced horizontally into thin (about ¼-inch/6-mm) slabs, weighted to press out liquid, deep-fried once at a lower temperature to cook and again at a high temperature to puff up. To date, I have not been impressed with the *usuage* (also known as *abura age*) sold abroad. Look for bright-colored pieces that seem appealing and not saturated with oil. Degrease by pouring hot water over before using. Often added to stir-fries and soups, or simmered in dashi and stuffed with sushi rice. Sold frozen outside of Japan.

NATTO: Fermented soybeans inoculated with *Bacillus natto* (page 230). Natto is sold in small foam packs with tiny packages of hot mustard and dashi-soy sauce. Most natto abroad is sold frozen. However, local, organic natto is being produced by MegumiNATTO in Sebastopol, California, and Natto du Dragon in France (see Resources) and is available via the Internet. Before eating, natto is usually whipped up with chopsticks to create a creamy mass of beans suspended in sticky threads. Keeps for several weeks in the fridge.

OKARA: Soybean pulp: A by-product of making soy milk that is usually given away free by tofu shops. Often stir-fried with vegetables (*unohana*) or used as a degreasing and softening agent for Pork Belly Simmered with Daikon and Leeks (page 161).

YUBA: Soy milk skin skimmed off the surface of scalding soymilk during the tofu-making process (page 233) and rolled into delicate, flat cylinders (or dried). Highly perishable, so must be eaten within a day or so of making. Drizzle with soy sauce or sprinkle with sea salt and eat with a dab of freshly grated wasabi, if you have it.

DRIED FISH

KATSUOBUSHI: Dried, smoked skipjack tuna (often called bonito) that is shaved on a razor-sharp planing blade set into a wooden shaving box (*katsuobushi kezuriki*). The curled flakes are used to make stock or to flavor vegetables. *Arai kezuri*: Thickly shaved (slightly leathery), rust-colored pieces good for making stock. *Hanakatsuo*: Pinky-tan, fine flat shavings for topping cooked vegetables. Once opened, store in the fridge.

NIBOSHI: Juvenile sardines that are salt-simmered before air-drying until completely dessicated (page 252). Used for making Niboshi Dashi (page 274) or Soy Sauce–Simmered Niboshi (page 275). Also eaten as a healthy snack (or manna for cats).

AGO: Juvenile flying fish, salt-simmered or charcoal-grilled before sun-drying. Used to make ago dashi.

SAKURA EBI: Tiny shrimp from the deep-sea waters of Suruga Bay in Shizuoka, Japan, during two seasons annually: April through June and October through December. Sold in dried form. Used in stir-fries such as Fish Sauce Fried Rice (page 140) and kimchee (page 280).

CHIRIMIN JAKO: Larval-stage teeny fishes of the sardine family (whitebait) that are salt-simmered and semidried in the open air. Eaten on top of rice or mixed with seaweed, sesame seeds, katsuobushi, and *shichimi togarashi* (page XXXI) to form a condiment called *furikake*.

SURUME IKA (AIR-DRIED SQUID): Used to make *matsumae zuke* pickles (*Japanese Farm Food*, page 71). Also eaten torn into strips as an accompaniment to sake after being wafted over low-ember coals (a technique known as *aburi*). *Surume ika* is whole, flat sun-dried squid that is usually sold unpackaged. Look for it in authentic Asian markets, such as those in Chinatown. Avoid packaged shredded *surume* as it contains MSG and sugar. (Or make your own by drying whole squid stretched flat in the sun until completely dehydrated.)

SEAWEED

KONBU (KELP): Giant wild or farmed kelp harvested in the northernmost island prefecture, Hokkaido. Sold folded in long packages and most likely will be ma konbu or possibly Hidaka konbu. Break into manageable pieces and store in the cupboard in a well-sealed plastic bag. Wild Japanese ma konbu is available from Eden Foods in small packages (see Resources). Use for dashi, in simmered foods, for pickling, and on its own in Soy Sauce–Simmered Konbu (page 273).

TORORO KONBU: Ma konbu or Rishiri konbu that has been pickled in vinegar and then scraped, dried, and pressed into thin sheets. Used primarily in the Hokuriku area of central Japan that includes Ishikawa, Fukui, Niigata, and Toyama prefectures. Eaten in udon noodles, in place of nori as a wrapper for rice balls, and as the base for a simple soup with hot water, yuzu peel, chopped scallions, and soy sauce (similar in theory to Chabushi, page 261).

WAKAME: Fresh wakame may be found in fish markets or Japanese grocery stores. Use as is in miso soup or vegetable salads. Dried wakame is available through Gold Mine Natural Food Co. and Eden Foods (see Resources) and sometimes can be found salted in the refrigerator section. Either way, you will need to soak the wakame for at least half an hour in cold water to desalinate or reconstitute before using. An extremely invasive seaweed, wakame has been eaten in Japan since prehistoric times. Currently also being cultivated in Brittany and gathered wild in Maine (see Resources).

HIJIKI: Black needle-like tips of a seaweed variety that grows wild in vast underwater forests off the coast of Ise, Japan. Soak for 15 minutes before using. Simmer for 15 minutes before chopping and adding to stir-fries, soups, or salads. Sold dried and available through Eden Foods as hiziki (the Latin name) and Gold Mine Natural Food Co. (see Resources).

ARAME: Gathered off the coast of Ise, arame can be used in place of hijiki, but only soak for 5 minutes before using. Wild dried Japanese arame is available through Gold Mine Natural Food Co. and Eden Foods (see Resources). Arame is milder than hijiki, so it's an excellent seaweed for novices.

MOZUKU: Slippery, threadlike brown algae that flourishes in shallow temperate waters (such as Okinawa) from winter to spring, but dies back in the summer. Although mozuku can be found fresh, it is usually preserved in brine. My husband makes a saladlike concoction with mozuku called dashi that is one of our son Christopher's favorite summer dishes. Soak mozuku in cold water for 20 minutes, drain, and cut into easy-to-eat segments. Toss with thinly sliced okra rounds, julienned Japanese cucumber, finely slivered ginger, and shiso leaves cut into chiffonade. Season lightly with soy sauce and a mild rice vinegar.

AONORI: Aonori also grows in the coastal waters of Ise. After harvesting, this green laver is washed and sun-dried. Delicious as tempura, though more commonly used in the powdered form sprinkled on soups, rice dishes, and in shichimi togarashi (page XXXI). Raw aonori is a delightfully briny delicacy in the early spring. Powdered aonori is available at Japanese grocery stores.

NORI (LAVER): While the most famous nori is produced in the Ariake Sea in Kyushu, several other prefectures around Japan are making nori. The current processing methods were developed during the Edo period and resemble paper making, where raw filaments of red algae are spread on wide screens to air-dry. Although sometimes called "laver" in English, nori is now a household word, thanks to the worldwide craze for sushi. Nori is typically sold toasted, ready to use in zippered packages. It is wise to double-bag nori in one more heavy resealable plastic bag to keep it from losing its snap. Nori can be recrisped by holding both sides over a stove burner flame, though a low-ember charcoal stove works better. Seasoned or flavored sheets of nori and packs of small rectangular pieces all contain MSG.

CHILES AND MUSTARD

TOGARASHI (CHILE PEPPER): Chile japones, a small, hot chile used fresh (red or green) during the summer. The plants are yanked out of the ground before the first frost, hung to dry, and the dried red chile japones is used throughout the year. Available through Purcell Mountain Farms (see Resources) and Japanese grocery stores. Substitute chile de árbol, but use less.

SHICHIMI TOGARASHI (7-SPICE POWDER): Contains red pepper, *sansho*, tangerine peel, white and black sesame seeds, hemp seeds, dried ginger, and *aonori*. Used for sprinkling on *nabe* (one-pot dishes) or hearty soups, and soupy noodles (udon, etc.). Readily available at Asian markets. Buy one that is roughly ground and has visible colors (not pulverized into a homogeneous powder). Store in the fridge and replace every few months. Also sold as *nanami togarashi*.

ICHIMI TOGARASHI (GROUND RED CHILE POWDER): Powdered chile japones. Available at Japanese grocery stores.

GOCHUTGARU (KOREAN GROUND RED CHILE POWDER): Powdered Korean hot chile. Available at Korean and Japanese grocery stores.

RAYU (HOT CHILE OIL): Chile-infused sesame oil used when eating *gyoza* and ramen. Also good on soy sauce–dressed salads.

YUZU KOSHO (FRESH CHILE AND YUZU PEEL PASTE): A spicy condiment developed about 50 years ago in Kyushu and recently popularized. Made from pounded yuzu peel, fresh chiles, and salt (page 281). *Yuzu kosho* can be red or green: Green chiles are pounded with green unripe yuzu peel, whereas fresh red chiles are pounded with ripe yellow yuzu peel. Good dabbed on sandwiches, noodle soups, and with rice. Available at selected Japanese grocery stores and online at Amazon.

KARASHI (ORIENTAL MUSTARD POWDER): Powdered mustard used to flavor soy mustard pickles (page 103) or

to make a paste to eat with Chinese-style dishes such as Pork Belly Simmered with Daikon and Leeks (page 161). Available in Japanese grocery stores, though I would recommend buying from Penzeys (see Resources).

FERMENTED AND DISTILLED LIQUIDS

MIRIN: We don't use much mirin, but when we do, we use only hon mirin ("true" mirin). Mirin is fermented from glutinous rice and koji in a series of steps similar to making sake. Unlike sake, mirin is allowed to develop a much more pronounced sweet flavor profile, but like sake, it should have depth and character, not just sweetness. Inexpensive or generic mirin relies on added sugar or corn syrup to make it sweet and lacks the complexity of hon mirin, so probably should be avoided.

SAKE: We use a middle-grade sake for cooking. Store in the refrigerator after opening and use within a few months, though you might want to start with a small bottle. Following the same principle as cooking with wine, you don't want to use the rotgut stuff but also probably don't want to spring for the *daiginjo* (page 301) either.

SHOCHU: Depending on the grade, shochu is used in Japanese cocktails or as the base for fruit-flavored cordials (in this case sold as "white liquor"). Aged shochu is like top-shelf tequila and is drunk neat or on the rocks. Shochu is commonly distilled from sweet potatoes, barley, or rice, but can be made from other substances as well.

AMAZAKE: A nonalcoholic cultured rice product sold as amazake concentrate through Natural Import Company (see Resources) or easily made at home with a yogurt maker or rice cooker (page XVIII). Amazake is naturally sweet, so an excellent sugar substitute. Also good served cold or warm diluted with equal parts water for an afternoon pick-me-up.

TEAS AND INFUSIONS

RYOKUCHA (GREEN TEA): Most commonly known as *ocha*. A subtle green tea (page 325) that brews a beautiful pale green. Green tea has many healthy components and has been proven to be anticarcinogenic. Widely available abroad at tea shops and online tea suppliers (see Resources).

HOJICHA (ROASTED GREEN TEA): A toasty charcoal-roasted green tea (page 306) that is experiencing great popularity abroad. Available through tea suppliers (see Resources).

MATCHA (POWDERED GREEN TEA): Stone-ground, high-quality, powdered green tea (page 331) used most commonly in the tea ceremony but also in desserts and other culinary applications (e.g., mixed with salt for dipping tempura). Available through Breakaway Matcha in the U.S. (see Resources) and many tea sources worldwide.

KOCHA ("BLACK" TEA): *Kocha* (page 326) is fermented from green tea leaves and is a dark reddish color (the Japanese name *kocha* means "red tea"). When brewed, *kocha* is a pale brown and has a gorgeous floral aroma. In Japan, all brown-colored teas are indiscriminately referred to as *kocha*, though true *kocha* is truly exceptional and nothing like black teas. Available though tea suppliers (see Resources).

MUGICHA (BARLEY TEA): Powdered crushed barley tea is sold in sachets at Japanese grocery stores. However, whole-grain roasted barley is worth seeking out (page 332).

SOBACHA (BUCKWHEAT TEA): Roasted buckwheat, sold in 1-kilo bags in Japanese grocery stores (page 333).

KONBUCHA (KONBU TEA): An infusion made from powdered konbu or konbu strips (page 307), not to be confused with kombucha, a fermented drink recently popular abroad. Often *umeboshi* is added to *konbucha*, and thus called *ume konbucha*. Widely available in Japanese markets. The powdered variety is usually sold in little red tins with a small measuring spoon inside.

SEEDS AND NUTS

KIN GOMA (GOLD SESAME): Hard to find abroad, golden brown *kin goma* is sold unroasted and unhulled at vegetable stands in Japan. After roasting, *kin goma* develops a robust, toasty sesame profile and thus elevates sesame treatments such as *goma-ae* or *shira-ae* (page 182). Preroasted sesame seeds (*iri goma*) are sold in Japanese grocery stores, but should be avoided since they will not be fresh. Use sesame seeds found in the bulk section of natural food stores.

KURO GOMA (BLACK SESAME): Good for adding color to dishes such as rice balls (page 172). Roast lightly to bring out the seeds' subtle aroma.

SHIRO GOMA (WHITE SESAME): Used as a mild alternative to *kin goma*. Also pretty sprinkled into green vegetable treatments.

ONIGURUMI (BLACK WALNUTS): A rich, intensely flavored Japanese native black walnut whose name means "devil walnuts." Very difficult to crack without a hammer or a special nutcracker, though absolutely worth the effort. These walnuts grow in the hills above us, and I stock up when they hit the tables at the local farm stands in early winter. Most urban-dwelling Japanese have never seen or tasted *onigurumi*. Use black walnuts or local conventional walnuts in place of *onigurumi* for Wild Arugula with Walnut Miso (page 75).

RICE

KOME (RICE): Japanese short-grain rice (Japonica), which belongs to the same family as Arborio (used to make risotto). Sometimes labeled abroad as "sticky rice" or "sushi rice" (also sold in the U.K. as pudding rice). Japanese rice should be scrubbed, rinsed repeatedly until the water runs clear, and cooked with equal parts water in a rice cooker, cast iron kettle (*tetsunabe*, page XIX), or refractory clay pot (*donabe*, page XVIII).

GENMAI (BROWN RICE): Brown rice is hulled, unpolished rice, though some brown rice might have a small amount of the outside bran polished off for making sake or vinegar. Brown rice is cooked with one and a half times the amount of water as white rice. Massa Organics in California sells excellent organic brown rice grown on a family farm along the Sacramento River (see Resources) and can be found at many Bay Area farmers' markets.

MOCHIGOME (GLUTINOUS RICE): Glutinous rice is often packaged abroad as "sweet rice" and can contain cornstarch, iron, niacin, thiamine, and folic acid. Best to check the label before buying. Glutinous rice contains no gluten; however, the grains exude a glutinous texture that results in a pleasantly sticky rice good for Japanese sweets. Mirin is fermented from glutinous rice.

OILS

CANOLA: Originally known as rapeseed oil, the oil is extracted from the rape plant (similar to rapini) and is the oil used by generations of Japanese farm families. Unclarified rapeseed oil is almost orange in tint—similar to mustard oil, but not as pungent. I use a clarified rapeseed that is reminiscent of the organic canola oil sold by Spectrum in the United States. The oil should be pleasant and fresh tasting, not flat, heavy, or flavorless.

RICE BRAN: Another light oil used in Japan. My favorite potato chips are fried in rice bran oil.

COLD-PRESSED SESAME: A mild oil that generally lacks character and has no intrinsic sesame taste. Better to use canola or rice bran.

DARK SESAME: I changed my mind about using sesame oil after I found good-quality organic ones. Use sparingly along with a lighter oil in stir-fries and salad dressings. Natural Import Company (see Resources) sells an organic Japanese sesame oil packaged by Mitoku. Eden Foods's organic sesame oil is Japanese as well and available at natural food stores. A little goes a long way, so don't gasp at the price.

SUGARS

ORGANIC GRANULATED SUGAR: Unlike white sugar, organic granulated sugar adds complex, flowery notes along with sweetness to a dish. A kitchen staple, though mainly for desserts.

KUROZATO (OKINAWAN BROWN SUGAR): This dark, molasses-rich native sugar is available at Japanese grocery stores. Good for adding a darker note to deeply flavored dishes such as Soy Sauce–Simmered Konbu (page 273) or Soy Sauce–Simmered Niboshi (page 275).

WASANBON (JAPANESE SUGAR): This dense, fine-grained sugar is produced in the southern islands of Japan. Traditionally, crystalized sugarcane juice diluted with water was pressed through linen bags (*shibori bukkuro*) and stacked in a weighted pressing "boat" (*shibori fune*) in the same manner as sake, mirin, vinegar, and soy sauce (page 99). After the molasses is squeezed out, the solids are dried on trays in the sun. *Wasanbon* is the very top pale tan powder that accumulates on the raw sugar. *Wasanbon* is highly prized for Japanese sweets due to its distinctive yet subtle overnotes of molasses and its powdery, melt-in-your-mouth texture. Processing sugarcane into *wasanbon* only produces one-fourth the yield as conventional sugar. Add in the weather-reliant nature of its production, *wasonbon* is understandably dear. Many confectionaries use substitutes such as *sanonto* (light brown sugar) and *kurozato* (dark brown sugar). *Kurozato* is similar to *wasanbon* in process, but has a much more pronounced molasses flavor.

塩風と太陽

1

salt, wind, and sun

SALT RECIPES

BABY TURNIPS WITH SALT-WILTED GREENS	5
SALTED YOUNG SHALLOTS	8
FERMENTED NAPA CABBAGE	11
SALT-FERMENTED MUSTARD	14
DRIED DAIKON THREADS	16
BAACHAN'S DRIED EGGPLANT	18
SALTED RED SHISO LEAVES	19
SALT-MASSAGED SHISO BUDS	20
SALTED CHERRY BLOSSOMS	23
SALT-DISTRESSED MIZUNA WITH KUMQUAT	24
SALTED EGGPLANT WITH MYOGA AND SHISO	27
SALT-DRIED GREY MULLET EGGS	29
SLIGHTLY DRIED SQUID	30
SALT-DRIED SALMON	33
HALF-DRIED BARRACUDA	37
AIR-DRIED SARDINES	38
SEMIDRIED HERRING	43

Salt is ground zero for preserving. It is present in almost all forms of natural preservation, so embracing salt as your friend and understanding the interplay between salt and what you are preserving is crucial. Salt is the underlying element in miso, soy sauce, and fish sauce—all of which are used in many Japanese pickling operations. Salt is added even when pickling in vinegar (although vinegar pickles are not the most common form of preserving in Japan and are more often called *sunomono*, "vinegared things"). But the easiest (and perhaps most common) use of salt is for air-drying, a deceptively simple operation whose nuances ultimately rely on experience. Many pickling or preserving methods begin with a short air-dry or presalt because salt helps the vegetable or fish expel some of its inner moisture and thus aids in preventing mold and spoilage. The trick here, though, is that too much salt will hinder the growth of healthy bacteria and thus impede fermentation, leaving you with a salty but not pleasantly sour end product. It's all about balance and a sense of feel. That is what makes salt preservation so fascinating: finding the balance. Salt preservation is almost like a mini lesson in life. When I am on my game, I am confident of success; when I am harried or out of sorts, who knows what the results will be. . . .

Salt and pepper have interested me for many decades. As a little girl, I shook salt with abandon on my boiled spinach (with a memorably disastrous result). As a young adult, I sprinkled sea salt on my food and carried my own pocket pepper grinder. But now I carry my sea salt in a baggy, since restaurant food is often flat or devoid of character and good salt can mitigate what's lacking. My salt epiphany came after reading Susan Herrmann Loomis's *French Farmhouse Cookbook*, where she introduced me to *sel gris* from Guérande. I became an aficionado of this coarse, mineral-packed yet soft-flavored grey salt. And I yearned to go to Bretagne, where I could see the salt rakers at work.

As the years went by, more often than not I reached for the elegant, bright *fleur de sel* over the more homely *sel gris*. But it was in Italy that I found my next perfect everyday salt: *sale marino di Trapani*—sea salt from Sicily. I loved the sparkling white brightness of the salt and that the crystals were a mix of semifine to coarse—perfect for the cook and eater in me. (I pinched up coarse crystals when flavoring in cooking, medium for salting salads and vegetables, and fine when at the table.) But it niggled at the back of my mind that I was using Italian salt when I lived in Japan—an island nation.

I began using Japanese salts more and more but never found "the one" until I attended a meeting at Shogakukan—the large Japanese publisher. At that meeting I was introduced to a woman who represented a salt maker in Wajima on the Noto Peninsula. She passed around some samples and, not wanting to wait until I got home to taste, asked if I could open mine. I shook out some crystals on the palm of my hand and immediately was excited by the look and feel of them. I licked up a smidge and then a bit more. It was explosive, yet gentle and not hit-you-over-the-head salty, lovely. Wajima Kaien is the name of the salt and is the salt I now use daily, sometimes even for pickling when I am feeling especially extravagant. I recommend Sicilian Trapani salt as a close substitute for Japanese salt, as it is equally bright and also comes in different grades: from inexpensive coarse crystals to flaky fine. The Meadow and Amazon are good sources for a range of sea salts (see Resources).

While salt is the vehicle to hasten the drying process, without sun and wind you would be hard-pressed to dry your fruits, vegetables, and fish. But do not despair if your living quarters or local weather render drying outside a challenge. It is possible to jerry-rig up a drying chamber inside that simulates warm balmy seaside air. This will involve a fan or two, so be prepared to give over some space to your project. While I love the romantic idea of fish flapping in the seaside wind, the reality is that many drying operations have moved inside to covered areas coveniently located to allow a year-round work area protected from the elements. When a hot summer sun is required for drying vegetables such as Baachan's Dried Eggplant (page 18) or Dried Daikon Threads (page 16), you will need a bit more creativity to accomplish this inside. Sissi from *With a Glass* blog recommends 4 to 5 hours on a parchment-lined cookie sheet in a 122°F (50°C) low oven. I found this an admirable compromise solution.

Many of the recipes or methods in this chapter will seem mindlessly simple. As they should. Salt, sun, and wind are age-old drying methods and cannot be improved upon by technology or newfangled improvisations. Also keeping patience and trust is the most arduous element in the process for us modern beings zinging from here to there. For nature cannot be hurried and the weather cannot be manipulated. Perhaps that is what draws me to salting as the most primal preservation method.

I was in the San Francisco Bay Area to help with soba chef pal Kanji Nakatani's third soba event at Chez Panisse, so Sylvan Mishima Brackett of Peko Peko Japanese Catering organized a pop-up as a collaboration of friends. Normally we would slice the turnips and cut the leaf and stem ends into segments before massaging in the salt and other aromatics, but I had found baby turnips at the farmers' market. It seemed wasteful to lose the gorgeous natural shape of the baby turnips, so I quartered them instead. After massaging some salt, red pepper, and yuzu into the greens, I showed them to Kanchan (as we call Kanji Nakatani). His response: "More." I showed him the greens a few additional times and each time his gravelly voice dictated, "More, more!" so I massaged them until the greens were completely broken down. And I served them on the side next to the turnips. The plates were ravaged quickly as soon as the servers dropped them on the communal food table. These pickles are bright with the hot pepper and lemony peel and go well with cocktails.

baby turnips with salt-wilted greens SERVES 6

KABU NO SHIOZUKE

2 small bunches baby turnips, with tender greens attached (about 1¾ pounds/800 g)

2 tablespoons fine sea salt

Zest of 2 yuzu or 1 Meyer lemon

2 small dried red chile peppers (japonesa or árbol)

Whack off the greens, leaving 1 inch (2.5 cm) of the stem. Set the stems aside, keeping the stem ends aligned.

Soak and scrub the turnips in a large bowl of cold water. Pull one turnip out at a time, lop off the tail end, and shave off any brown spots around the top with a sharp knife. Drop as you go into a metal strainer. When all of the turnips are cleaned, give them one last rinse and set the strainer over a medium-sized bowl. Dump the cold water in the bowl down the sink and refill with more cold water.

Pick through the turnip greens and toss any of the leathery or brown ones into your compost pile. Keeping the greens aligned at the stem end, swish them in the cold water, then lay them on a clean kitchen towel and roll up to pat dry.

Pat the turnips down with a clean kitchen towel and cut them into quarters or halves depending on their size (you want a mini bite of about ½-inch (1.25-cm) wide wedges. Massage with 1 tablespoon sea salt until some of the liquid is released. Sprinkle in half of the aromatics, massage those in as well, and slide the seasoned turnips into a gallon-sized resealable freezer bag. Refrigerate for an hour or so before eating (if you are able) but no longer than a couple of days, as the turnips will become progressively saltier. Grab a handful of turnips at a time and squeeze out the salty liquid before serving.

baby turnips with salt-wilted greens

Slice the stem ends into ½-inch (1.25-cm) segments and the leaves into 1-inch (2.5-cm) pieces. Massage in the remaining tablespoon of salt, zest, and chile pepper until the leaves have completely broken down as if they were cooked. Refrigerate in a quart-sized resealable freezer bag for at least 30 minutes if possible. Squeeze before serving a small mound alongside the salt-pickled turnips.

VARIATIONS: Eliminate the citrus and use some finely slivered ginger in its place. Fresh red or green chile pepper instead of dried also works.

Rakkyo (Japanese shallots) are multiplying onions that will take over your garden if you are not careful, or if you are lucky, depending on how you look at it. True *rakkyo* are probably hard to come by commercially outside Japan, though West Coast U.S. farmers could well be growing them. On the other hand, *rakkyo* bulbs are available for purchase through HeirloomOnions.com and I recommend reserving a corner for them in your garden. One recent summer, Suka-san's wife dropped by our house with a large bag of *rakkyo*—a gift from her mother-in-law (page 242), my mentor in preserving methods and old Japanese ways. My son Christopher was working at my English immersion preschool, Sunny-Side Up!, that summer, so I asked him to take on the tedious task of peeling off the dried outer skins under running water. It took him all afternoon. I stopped by the school to pick up the *rakkyo* and discovered that Christopher had left the teeny root end intact rather than snapping it off with his thumb. Obviously my instructions had been lacking. No matter—the root ends did not bother me a whit. I left them on and proceeded with my salting operation. We ate the salted *rakkyo* for tea breaks along the side of the rice fields the day we planted rice and washed them down with organic ginger ale. I munched the shallots, roots and all, though some people spit the roots out.

salted young shallots MAKES ABOUT 2 POUNDS (1 KG)
RAKKYO NO SHIOZUKE

2 pounds (1 kg) Japanese
   shallots (*rakkyo*)

3 tablespoons (50 g) sea salt
   (5% of the cleaned shallot weight)

Collect a metal strainer with feet and a medium-sized bowl from your kitchen. Head outside and grab a bucket. Fill the bucket with cold water from the garden faucet and dump in the *rakkyo*. Pull up a stool and scoop out a clump of *rakkyo* from the water. Separate each *rakkyo* from the root end and peel off the darkened outer skin. Drop the peels in the bowl and the cleaned *rakkyo* into the strainer. You can cut off the small root filaments, but do not cut off so much that the bulb separates; leave at least 1 inch (2.5 cm) of the top tendril. This will take a while, so you might want to put in some earbuds and crank up the tunes.

Once all the *rakkyo* are cleaned, give them a last rinse under cold running water; dump the bucket of water and toss the skins in the compost. Head back to your kitchen and lay out a large kitchen towel on the counter. Strew the *rakkyo* on the towel and pat dry with another clean kitchen towel. Put the *rakkyo* in a gallon-sized resealable freezer bag and toss with the salt. Press all the air from the bag, roll, and refrigerate for 1 week. Serve without rinsing, as a snack to accompany cocktails or a full-bodied beer. Stays fine for a few weeks in the fridge; if any longer, I would pickle in a sweetened vinegar solution (Pickled Young Shallots, page 155).

VARIATIONS: Any fresh, sweet allium such as ramps or fat chives will substitute nicely here. Tender young gingerroots also are delicious salt-pickled in this method, though take care to obtain thin roots and separate them into individual stalks that can be eaten as is.

THE SALT RAKER

Since I had never given up my dream of viewing the salt fields in Bretagne, I arranged a visit to the salt maker in Wajima. The promotional materials for Wajima Kaien salt showed the salt maker with his beaming face turned toward the sun, the dark blue sea in the background—taken while he was out on a boat pumping up deep-sea water. My romantic fantasy of watching the salt raker at work was not to happen the day of our visit. The salt maker met us at the door of a small building. His browned face was again tilted toward the sun and he had a wide welcoming grin as he beamed at us through thick glasses.

Hajime Nakamichi only started making salt in 2000. Having grown up on Hegura-jima, an island off Wajima in Ishikawa prefecture, he was a master fisherman by trade before working in the fish processing industry producing partially dried fish. In Japan, 98% of the fish destined to be partially dried (such as *himono* and *mirinboshi*) is caught in far foreign waters, and the resulting fish product is sold for less than Japan-caught fresh fish. This somehow seemed wrong, so Nakamichi-san began producing partially dried fish from the Sea of Japan with salt he had extracted from the Sea of Japan as well. Ultimately, however, he decided that making salt was more deeply interesting than producing partially dried fish. Providentially these enterprises roughly coincided with the abolition in 1997 of the 90-year-old government salt monopoly. Another element that drew Nakamichi-san to producing local, artisanal salt was that he would be creating a product that was in the hands of the gods: Each batch of salt he makes varies, naturally, in taste and texture. Ultimately, he decided that making salt would

be more interesting than fishing. We are all glad that he thought so, because Nakamichi-san's salt has soul. I got that flash of excitement when first tasting it several years ago and now buy it by 2-kilo bags.

Nakamichi-san takes his boat out from Hegura island and pumps up pristine deep-sea water. The saltwater first goes through a cleaning process where he removes the scum (calcium). This purification step is skipped in cheaply produced salts. The purified saltwater is pumped into a drying table over which hang drying lamps to simulate the sun. An oscillating fan buffets the drying brine with a tepid breeze. While his drying operation is not conducted out in the salt flats, the resulting salt is exquisite and the process is all very low-tech.

As the warm air wafts over the table, salt crystals begin to form after about 18 hours. The crystals are mesmerizing in the glow of the table lights. I wanted to scoop my hand into the brine and run my fingers through the mica-like formations. Five thousand liters (5 tons) of deep sea water yields 600 liters of concentrated saltwater, from which 250 kg of salt can be harvested. Nakamichi-san rakes out the salt each day over the course of about one week. As the salt crystals are removed from the brine, what Nakamichi-san calls "pancake salt" solids form in the water, signaling that no more salt can be harvested. What was

once 3% saltwater has become *nigari* (bittern), the coagulant used for making tofu, with a salt content of 23 to 32%. The final step involves a small centrifuge resembling a washing machine. Each day Nakamichi-san packs the harvested salt in net bags and sets them on the spin cycle to remove excess moisture.

"Although the salt tasts the same throughout the seasons, when you sample the salt in the winter months it feels saltier on your tongue than during the summer," Nakamichi-san revealed. While perhaps not intuitive, this made perfect sense to me. The sharp taste of salt in some way combats the cold of winter, while in the sultry Japanese summers our bodies lose salt through sweat and thus absorb salt with pleasure. I cannot say that I am able to pick up the nuanced differences of how salt reacts in my mouth in summer and winter, but I am able to identify Wajima Kaien every time. Because it is my salt and I bring it with me wherever I go.

But preserving can put a serious dent in the salt barrel, so you have to weigh cost against the importance of the salt in any project. I use Wajima Kaien when salt is the main component and the amount is relatively small. Otherwise I use Japanese sea salt sold in 2-pound (1-kg) bags through a natural food supplier. As always, the choice is purely personal and comes down to priorities (money vs. taste). So far I am fine using the salt packaged by the natural food supplier, though I'm ready to ask Nakamichi-san if he will part with some of the B-grade salt he sells to local producers. I've been hesitating because I did not want to be pushy. Now I am ready to be bold for the sake of the pickling.

I cut my fermentation eyeteeth on fermenting napa cabbage, so am particularly proud of producing these pickles each winter. Initially I used a food-grade plastic pickling barrel, but after switching over to a wooden barrel have never looked back. There is something incredibly empowering about slapping the cabbage wedges back into the barrel if you decide to rotate the bottom cabbage to the top. I follow Katchan's method on this with a little advice from other sources as well. (Katchan is Tadaaki's aunt and is often at our house.) This is the first Japanese preserved vegetable that I would suggest tackling because even if the souring does not happen, the salty cabbage will be delicious. And you will learn an invaluable lesson in the process. These pickles should be made in the winter when napa cabbage is in season and the days are cool.

fermented
napa cabbage MAKES ABOUT 5 POUNDS (2.5 KG)
HAKUSAI NO TSUKEMONO

8 small heads Chinese cabbage, quartered vertically (about 1⅓ pounds/600 g each)

135 g sea salt (3% of cabbage weight)

8 small garlic cloves, thinly sliced

8 small dried Japanese (or 6 árbol) chile peppers

Peeled strips from 4 small yuzu or Meyer lemons (avoid the white bitter pith)

Remove any outside wilted leaves and dry the cabbage quarters for 1 day under the cold winter sun on sheets of newspaper set directly on the ground.

Line a plastic or wooden pickling tub with a large pickling-grade plastic bag (see Note). Pack one layer of the slightly dried Chinese cabbage, cut side down, on the bottom of the pickling container, rubbing each one with salt before you set it in the tub. Sprinkle the layer of cabbage with some of the sliced garlic, chile peppers, and yuzu zest. Continue until all the cabbage quarters have been rubbed with salt and packed in the pickling tub. Don't forget to throw in some garlic, chile peppers, and yuzu peel before you start each new layer. Make sure the cabbage is snugly packed and flatten the excess portion of the plastic bag across the surface of the cabbage, pressing out the air to create a seal. Set the pickle tub's drop lid on top (or find a suitable substitute), weight with a rock or other heavy object (about the equivalent weight of the cabbage), and cover. Let sit outside in a cold shady spot, out of direct sunlight, for a couple of weeks. (Check after a few days to make sure enough brine has been exuded to cover the cabbage. If not, sprinkle in a little more salt.) If mold forms, lift it off the pickles gently and wipe any mold spots on the plastic bag or wooden tub with a neutral alcohol such as shochu or vodka.

The pickles can be eaten any time, but perhaps better to wait at least 2 weeks. They reach optimum flavor after 1 or 2 months, and stay good while the cold weather holds (store in the refrigerator if the days turn warm).

fermented napa cabbage

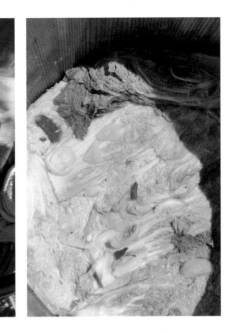

VARIATIONS: You can easily substitute savoy cabbage or another Asian-style green such as bok choy.

NOTE: If you are feeling particularly adventurous, you could forgo the plastic bag. I do. In this case, make sure your drop lid and weights are well washed before placing the drop lid directly on the surface of the cabbage. If using rocks, place them thoughtfully, keeping in mind that you want the pressure on the cabbage to be even. Set the top on the barrel and cover with a large muslin cloth secured by tying a piece of twine around the circumference of the barrel to keep out flying dust and debris.

I am part of a team of long-residence foreigners who consult on projects promoting food and other local cultures around Japan. This team is called the Japan Local Innovator's Committee. One of the projects on which I consult is for a travel restaurant created by the visionary owner of Roppongi Nouen restaurant, Hima Furuta. The first time I tasted these wild pickles was on a trip to Niigata prefecture with the travel restaurant. Several weeks later my good friend Matsuda-san (page 78) served the very same pickled greens at lunch after our yearly miso-making session (page 49). Traditionally made from a type of mustard called *takana*, these salt-fermented greens can be made from any variety of bitter green from the mustard family. Although autumn is the true season to start these fermented greens, fate told me that I must put up a batch even though we were almost into spring, so I did. Their salty bitterness is captivating and good as a palate cleanser alongside almost any full-flavored savory dish. Rinse or not before eating; it's up to you. (Best made in the late autumn or late winter, when the weather is neither too cold nor too warm.)

salt-fermented mustard MAKES ABOUT 4 POUNDS (2 KG)
KOMATSUNA NO TSUKEMONO

6 bunches (about 8 pounds/ 4 kg) *komatsuna* (page 341), bok choy, turnip greens, or mustard

1 pound/432 g fine white sea salt (12% of vegetable weight)

Trim off any brown leaves from the mustard green bunches and cut off the very bottom end of the stems (but leave the greens connected). If your greens are gritty, fill a large bowl or basin with cold water and swish 2 bunches of greens at a time around in the water before shaking off well and laying on a clean kitchen towel. Roll in the towel to pat dry. If the greens feel clean and perky, proceed with the salting without the water swish.

Working over a small wooden or food-grade plastic barrel (or large ceramic pickling pot), rub the stems and leaves generously with salt. Make sure you work the greens well enough so they exude a bit of water. Allign a layer of greens side by side across the bottom of the barrel with the stems flush against the side of the barrel. Curl the tops to fit, if need be. Smash each layer down with your flat hands before starting to lay the next layer crosswise over the previous layer. Cover the greens with a piece of food-grade plastic sheeting, if you like, and set a drop lid approximately the same size as the surface of the greens on top of the cloth, and place enough weights to equal double the weight of the greens. Store outside in the cool autumn weather a few weeks before the cold winter days begin to approach. Check after a couple of days to make sure that the liquid has risen and the greens are submerged. Press down with your clean hands to check if the water is accumulating below. If the greens do not have a lot of give, sprinkle a cup or two (250 cc to 500 cc) of 6% salt water over the greens, re-cover with the cloth or plastic, and replace the weights. Depending on the weather, the greens

will take about a month to ferment properly. Remove one strand from the barrel, squeeze, and check for doneness. They should be a pleasantly soft dusky dark green, with a bitter-salty profile. If they retain any feeling of rawness, put them back in the barrel and give them more time to ferment. When sufficiently fermented, squeeze down the length of each strand of greens and store in resealable gallon-sized freezer bags, rolled up with the air squeezed out. If you find the greens too salty, you can rinse (or soak) in cold water to desalinate before squeezing again for serving. Cut into 1-inch (2.5-cm) lengths and arrange alone on a plate or as part of an assorted pickle platter.

VARIATIONS: These leafy pickles make a striking contrast to bland rice as a wrapping for rice balls (page 172). Check the salinity, as you may need to rinse and squeeze before using. Rapini-like flowering brassicas would benefit from this fermenting method. Be sure the rapini stems are not too thick or woody, however.

Kiriboshi daikon was one of those mysterious foods I would see around at the farm shops but that barely registered since my husband Tadaaki did not use them much. A while back, my farmwife friend, Junko Suka, gave me a bag of *kiriboshi daikon* that she had dried from daikon they had grown. Anything that comes from the Suka household is worthy of great respect, so I credit this gift as the impetus that galvanized me into putting *kiriboshi daikon* on my cooking radar. I asked Junko how she prepared *kiriboshi daikon* for her family, and that was all I needed to jump in feet first. And I'm glad I did. These dried daikon threads keep forever, so handy to have around in a pinch to add to stir-fries or soups.

dried daikon threads MAKES ABOUT 3 OUNCES (85 G)
KIRIBOSHI DAIKON

1 large daikon (about
 1¾ pounds/800 g)

Scrub the daikon with a rough hemp-bristled vegetable brush (*tawashi*, page XVII). Dry. Lop off the top light green or spongy portion of the daikon. (After the frost, the top exposed portion of the daikon freezes in the night, so it cannot be used.) Using the julienne blade of a mandoline or a Japanese tooth grater (like a Benriner), grate the daikon into thin strips: Grasping the bottom end portion of the daikon in your dominant hand, stroke the daikon across the blade at a slight diagonal until you can no longer take a pass without drawing blood.

Line two (or more) wide-open baskets with butcher paper and dry the threads in the hot sun for as long as it takes (about 1 week, depending on the weather). Store inside the house or garage at night. Junko dries hers initially in a dehydrator until almost dried (for the most part dried, but thicker sections are not quite). She then spreads them under the winter sun for 2 or 3 days (bringing in at night) to infuse the daikon with natural energy from the sun. Bear in mind that unless you use a dehydrator like Junko does, your dried daikon threads will not be quite as stiff as the ones pictured on the opposite page.

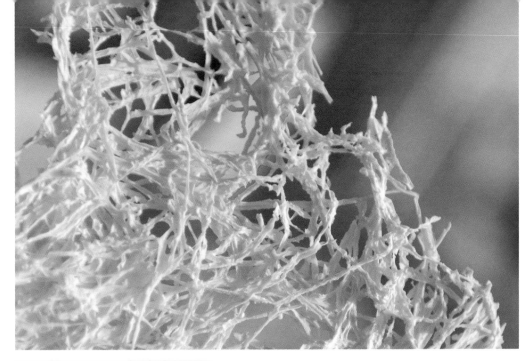

Soak dried daikon threads in cold water for about an hour, or warm water for 15 minutes, to reconstitute before using. (Beware: After soaking, the dried daikon will have grown fourfold!) Use in stir-fries such as *kimpira*: Sauté with julienned carrots in a little oil and dried red chile pepper. Throw in some julienned thin-fried tofu (*usuage*, page XXIX) if you can find it, and season with soy sauce before serving. Or skip the dried chile pepper but follow the rest of the previous method, and drizzle in some of the soaking liquid or dashi along with a few tablespoons soy sauce. Sprinkle with shaved katsuobushi before serving.

VARIATION: For *wariboshi daikon* cut the daikon into 3-inch (8 cm) lengths and shave off ⅕-inch (5-mm) thick slices of daikon with a mandoline or flat cutting blade. Stack about 4 slices at a time and cut those into ⅕-inch (5-mm) wide strips. Dry in the same way as for *kiriboshi daikon*. The strips should be desiccated, but they will still have a little bend to them. Soak in dashi or with konbu in water for 1 hour before squeezing and pickling in Soy Vinegar (page 150) with a little sugar and torn dried red chile.

Although I wrote a story in my first book about my mother-in-law drying eggplant, I did not include a recipe. Really there is not much of a recipe, which I find oddly comforting. When I dry these eggplants I always think of Baachan (as we affectionately call grandmothers). I miss her pestering me and wish I had mined more of her pickling expertise before she left this earth. Also now that Baachan is no longer at the family dinner table, somehow I have become the one who gets corrected or commented upon by the know-it-all teenaged boys in our house. I miss my female ally! Dried eggplant paired with dried shiitake and a piece of konbu will make a spectacularly nuanced vegetarian dashi. Please try it.

baachan's
dried eggplant MAKES ABOUT 2 POUNDS (1 KG)
BAACHAN NO HOSHINASU

4 pounds (2 kg) eggplant,
   preferably Japanese or another
   thin, long Asian variety

Wipe the eggplant of any dust or dirt, but try to avoid washing. Slice off the top calyx and cut the eggplant into 1-inch (2.5-cm) thick rounds. Lay the pieces out flat on bamboo baskets for several days or until completely desiccated and hard to the touch. You will need to turn the pieces occasionally to ensure even drying. Also the eggplant should be collected before nightfall into a straw basket and covered with a clean cloth. Put the eggplant back out in the sun the following morning, but not if the day is cloudy or rainy. Dry on sunny days. Store the balsa wood–like light pieces in a cool, dark place in a glass jar. Soak for an hour before using with the soaking liquid as the base for a vegetarian Japanese-style soup.

VARIATIONS: Shiitake are dried in the exact same way, though they may take longer to dry, depending on the weather. Some thrifty housewives or shopkeepers use the fresh shiitake tops for grilling or in one-pot dishes (*nabe*) and then chop up the stems to dry for making dashi. Our friend Suka-san's mother also dries the bottom root tendrils of the Japanese leeks (negi) she grows and uses this for making dashi as well. Dried shiitake, eggplant, and negi bottoms sound to me like the perfectly balanced vegetarian stock, especially if you pop in a square of konbu.

Though in our house we do not add salted red shiso leaves to our salted sour plums (*umeboshi*), many people do. (Mysteriously, my *umeboshi* end up a dusky pink despite the lack of red shiso. Perhaps the variety?) I can barely remember to take the salted plums (*ume*) out of the brine at the correct time, let alone plan to pickle the red shiso leaves midway through the *ume* salting operation. (*Ume* are harvested before the red shiso is ready, so the salted red shiso is introduced after the *ume* have been salting for a week or two.) But I was grateful for putting up a batch of salted red shiso one recent summer because it was the perfect foil for my Sour Plum Cordial Cocktail (page 318).

salted red shiso leaves MAKES ABOUT ½ POUND (225 G)
AKAJISO NO SHIOMOMI

6 tablespoons fine white sea salt

½ pound (225 g) red shiso leaves

Spread a layer of salt in the bottom of a small crockery pot. Stack the red shiso leaves by 10s and lay the first stack of 10 leaves on top of the salt in the crock. Sprinkle more salt on top of the leaves (not a thick layer, but enough so that the leaves have a light salt coverage), then lay in another stack of leaves. Alternate leaves and salt until you have placed all of the leaves in the crock. Finish with a last layer of salt to cover the top leaves so none are exposed. Cover with a piece of muslin cloth and weight. Store in a cool, dark place for a couple of weeks to a month. Squeeze before using. Add to *umeboshi* (page 167) during the salting and drying process or preserve in *umesu* (page 147) to keep longer. Great chopped up and stirred into a cocktail of *umeshu* over ice, topped with sparkling water.

Toward the end of my first book tour for *Japanese Farm Food*, we held a book party at Pizzaiolo in Oakland. Owner Charlie Hallowell has a sprawling back area behind Pizzaiolo, which includes a beehive and plenty of herb beds. His shiso had already gone to seed, so, though no leaves were to be found, there were massive amounts of shiso buds. Siew-Chinn (The Ramen Shop) offered to harvest the stalks and scrape off the seed clusters. Charlie was making Japanese-style pizzas that night, so the idea of salt-massaging the buds to take off some of their menthol-like tannins jumped to mind. A few strewn over pizza hot from the oven gave the perfect pop.

salt-massaged shiso buds SERVES 6
HOJISO NO SHIOMOMI

8 stalks of budding shiso
(*hojiso*, page 343)

Flaky sea salt

Give the stalks a quick rinse under cold running water if they are dusty or weather worn. Shake off the excess water and scrape the buds into a medium-sized bowl: Hold the stalk in your nondominant hand by the cut end, then run the thumb and index finger of your dominant hand down the length of the stalk to remove the bud clusters. Sprinkle a fine coating of sea salt over the surface of the shiso buds and massage the salt in well until their natural liquids are exuded.

Taste. If overly salty, squeeze by handfuls before storing in a rolled-up resealable plastic bag. Alternatively, pack in a crock, but press a piece of muslin or plastic directly on the surface of the salted buds before covering to avoid oxidation. Use fairly soon as a garnish for simple Japanese-style dishes such as Shio Koji–Grilled Pork (page 201), tofu marinated in shio koji (page 65), or as part of an assorted pickle plate. Squeeze before serving.

VARIATION: If you have access to fresh sansho (page 343) seeds, they can be preserved using this method.

Tadaaki served these to me on our first Valentine's Day after being married. I came home from teaching that day to a cherry blossom–themed dinner. While I don't remember what else he served that night, I do remember the salted cherry blossoms, which he sprinkled over the rice. My pal, Sylvan Mishima Bracket, has a complicated method of drying the blossoms, then salting them and drying again before storing in vinegar. In Akita prefecture as well, the blossoms are salted before preserving in vinegar. Naturally salty plum "vinegar" (*umesu*, page 147) would be my vinegar choice. Since these blossoms are not commercially available, look for a Japanese cherry or plum tree in your neighborhood and ask if you can use some of the buds.

salted cherry blossoms MAKES ABOUT 1 CUP (250 CC)
SAKURA NO SHIOZUKE

1 cup (250 cc) cherry blossom buds before flowering

Best-quality fine white sea salt

Snip off the cherry blossom buds from a nonfruiting Japanese cherry tree. Do not wash. Clip off any stem ends and drop the blossoms into a bowl or basket. Sprinkle a layer of salt in the bottom of a small crockery container and strew a thin layer of blossoms on top of the salt. Sprinkle more salt on top of the blossoms (like a frosting, but not a thick layer) and continue alternating blossoms with salt until you have used all of the blossoms. End with a thick layer of salt and set aside for a month or so in a dark, cool closet. Alternatively, you could press a small piece of muslin cloth on top of the salt surface and set a clean weight on top of the cloth until the brine rises. Sprinkle on top of hot rice as a salty condiment. Use within a couple months since the buds will eventually discolor.

For longer storage, squeeze well and soak in rice vinegar or plum vinegar before eating as a mouth-puckering pickle.

VARIATIONS: Plum or peach buds could be substituted for the *sakura*.

Ever since my mother-in-law died in 2011, I have been missing an older person in my life. Luckily, my farming friend Toshiharu Suka's parents (page 242) are often to be found packing vegetables with their son and daughter-in-law. Suka-san's mother has her own personal field, separate from the income-generating fields, where she grows vegetables for the family. She and her husband have been growing without pesticides, chemical fertilizers, or animal by-products for over sixty years. Occasionally Suka-san's mother gives me some vegetables from her private stash, and the mizuna she grows is incredible, actually unforgettable. Suka-san's mother is quite proud of her field, and rightfully so. If given the chance, she will talk your ear off about the soil. I willingly and happily listen. I plucked a couple of kumquats off our tree to massage in with the mizuna, as they give a nice sweet citrus note that results in a striking color palette.

salt-distressed mizuna with kumquat SERVES 4

MIZUNA NO SHIOMOMI

1 large bunch (about
  1 pound/450 g) mizuna

1 ounce (14 g) best-quality
  flaky sea salt

3 kumquats

Pick through the mizuna, carefully removing any tough or browned leaves. Set a large mixing bowl in the kitchen sink and fill with cold water. Douse the mizuna in the water, swishing it around for a minute or two. Lift the greens out of the bowl, shake off the water, and drop into a colander to drain further. Discard the water in the bowl, pick up the draining mizuna with both hands, and set in the empty bowl. Massage in the salt until you can feel it weep a tad, cover the surface with a drop lid or plate, and weight with whatever you have handy in the kitchen. Let sit for an hour or so, or until the naturally exuding water rises to the surface.

Squeeze down the length of each mizuna bunch to press out the excess water. Cut each kumquat in half through the midsection and remove the seeds and most of the pith. Slice the kumquats into fine threads and toss in with the squeezed mizuna to distribute. Cut the greens into 1½-inch (38-mm) lengths, mound attractively on a contrasting but complementary colored plate, and serve as an appetizer or to accompany any meal (Japanese or Western). Keeps for a few days in the fridge, stored in a rolled-up, resealable freezer bag.

VARIATIONS: This is fantastic made from edible chrysanthemum or dandelion greens, though in this case omit the kumquat. Instead, toss in some thin rounds of dried red chile. For longer-term pickles, increase the salt to 5% of the vegetable weight (¾ ounce/22 g).

On my first book tour for *Japanese Farm Food*, Andrew Knowlton invited me to prepare a few raw dishes in the *Bon Appétit* test kitchen. It was all in a bit of rush, as we only had the kitchen for a short window. In my flurry, I cut the eggplant too thick—more like for sautéing than eating raw, but I liked it that way. I also like the idea of a thicker than normal cut of *myoga* buds so you can really taste their earthy freshness, and as a result, the thick cut of eggplant cries out for a slightly wider than normal chiffonade on the shiso.

salted eggplant with myoga and shiso SERVES 4
NASU NO SHIOMOMI

3 (4½-ounce/125-g) Japanese eggplants

2½ tablespoons sea salt

4 small *myoga* buds (page 343)

½ tablespoon shiso leaves, cut into a thick chiffonade

Slice the eggplants down the middle lengthwise with a sharp knife, then diagonally crosswise into slightly less than ½-inch (1-cm) pieces. Drop in a medium-sized bowl with the salt and a handful of ice cubes. Cut the *myoga* buds into ¼-inch (12-mm) thick slices lengthwise and stir in with the salted eggplant. Let sit for 10 minutes more. Squeeze out the water, dump the salty water down the drain, and return the squeezed eggplant to the bowl. Drop in the thick shiso chiffonade and toss gently with chopsticks. Mound in a small bowl and serve immediately, as the eggplant will begin to discolor over time.

VARIATIONS: Throw a handful of pepper cress sprigs in with the eggplant instead of the *myoga*, and omit the shiso. Use only 1½ tablespoons salt, and toss with a few drops of mild Japanese fish sauce before serving (substitute Italian Colatura, page XXVII).

THE ROOTS OF KAISEKI

I got the email the day before Christmas: Would I like to go to Nara with Fuji TV to find out about *So*, an ancient native Japanese cheese? Hell, yes. Too busy to focus on anything beyond Christmas Day preparations, I did not have time for much more than a cursory glance at the itinerary that involved a five-hour train transit from my town to Nara. While the travel details were exacting, the subject of the shoot was not: cooking. Already on my way, I regretted not grabbing my apron.

Luckily, it was not me who would be doing the cooking. I was along to taste and comment on a meal prepared by the head chef at the Park Hotel in Nara. While the Park Hotel has various menus, they specialize in reproducing food (and atmosphere) from the Tenpyo era—roughly around the year 1300. As I parted the noren (page XIII), a server in period dress encouraged me to don a Tenpyo-style vest. From the vestibule, I was ushered into a dark, spare room adorned simply by a large, low table capable of seating twenty in a pinch. It was a *horigotatsu* (page XIII): a table set over an open cavity into which you can comfortably dangle your feet.

The silent yet smiling server reappeared and whisked a tray in front of me, while the chef knelt by my side to describe what I was eating: various dried fish that had been reconstituted in sake; dried, then pickled vegetables . . . and a splash of period-style pink *nigorizake* (page 301). One element that attracted me to this style of food was the purity of the ingredients. In the Tenpyo period they salted with a light hand, thus the Park Hotel served the seasonings separately for the diner to use sparingly as he or she wished.

This Kyutei Ryori (Imperial Cuisine) meal inspired by Tenpyo era preservation methods is where the roots of Kaiseki cuisine lie. Before refrigeration, seasonal lines were slightly blurred due to the practice of air-drying most fruits, vegetables, and fish. This plethora of dried foods resulted in a great variety on the table at any given time. Most of the fish was salted and air-dried before soaking in sake to reconstitute. If not used right away after soaking, the fish was kept in a cool place buried in rice koji (page XXVIII).

I was particularly taken by the *hoya* (sea squirt) dried for two weeks and the squid preserved in rice koji, as well as by the octopus legs dried for one week before grilling lightly. Seeded summer cucumbers had been dried for three days and pickled in a gentle brown rice vinegar solution for two weeks. The daikon was cubed, lightly salted for one day, rinsed, then dried for one week in the winter sun. The daikon was then preserved in a bed made from smashed rice koji, simmering water from cooked soybeans, and soy sauce mash (*moromi*, page 114). It was stunningly delicious. Actually each bite of that meal was better than the last, with the exception of a darkly flavored rice dish that was not to my palate. My director admonished me not to eat too much, as we had dinner reservations, but to this day I regret following his advice. Our late-night pizza could not erase the yearning for the food on the tray I had been foolish enough to leave.

I fell in love with *bottarga* in Italy when attending Slow Food's mega food conference, the Salone del Gusto in Turin, Italy. Yet it had not registered that we have a very similar preparation in Japan—probably because *karasumi* does not cross the Japanese farm table very often. Our friend Kanchan of Soba Ro and Soba Ra restaurants makes a version that rivals the Italian *bottarga* in taste and texture. Kanchan shared his method with me, though since I can't readily put my hands on grey mullet roe I usually substitute cod roe. If the sacs become overdried, you can soak them in sake for a day or two to soften them.

salt-dried grey mullet eggs MAKES 6
KARASUMI

Fine sea salt

6 grey mullet roe sacs

Shochu, for brushing

Line a rack with absorbent spongy-style paper towels. Salt the paper, lay the roe sacs on top of the salt, and sprinkle enough salt around the tops and sides of the sacs that all of the surfaces are covered but you can still see the eggs under the salt layer. Set the rack of roe on a drip pan, drape with plastic wrap, and refrigerate for 3 days.

After 3 days, soak the salted roe sacs in a solution of 2% brine to desalinate for 12 hours. Pinch a little of the roe from the center opening to check the salt. If too salty, soak for another 12 hours in 2% brine. If not salty enough, best salt lightly for a day. Drain, pat dry, and brush with shochu (or vodka) to guard against mold developing in the drying process.

Hang the sacs in a net basket for 1 to 2 weeks in a cool, shady spot that gets good air currents. Brush each day with shochu. The roe is properly dried when there is no longer any give in the center, but the tips of the lobes are not hard.

Slice and serve as an accompaniment to sake. Also sensational paired with small slices of chayote (*hayato uri*).

VARIATION: Can be made quite successfully with small cod roe sacs, though watch the drying time since they are smaller than grey mullet sacs and so will dry more quickly. Large cod roe sacs can also be used though the color will not be as nice since they are more tan than orange.

On one of our winter photo shoots, I made *Ika no Shiokara* (Raw Squid in Coral, page 287) with my photographer Kenji Miura giving advice. Miura-san is from Hokkaido, the land of salmon, squid, sea urchin (*uni*), and konbu. When preparing *ika no shiokara* you invariably end up with more raw squid than can really be included with the squeezed stomach contents without throwing off the balance of the dish. Miura-san recommended drying the excess squid bodies and legs, so I did. I loved the simplicity and flexibility of this method. If it is evening by the time you are done cleaning your squid, no matter; leave it in a cool place to begin the air-drying process, then stick it out in the morning sun when you wake up the next day. As an American, it has taken me a while to get used to the trust that Japanese have in this system that eschews refrigeration, but then Japanese houses are naturally cool by design.

slightly dried squid SERVES 6
IKA NO ICHIYABOSHI

2 very fresh squid

Sea salt

Soy sauce, for serving (optional)

Wedges of yuzu or Meyer lemon, for serving (optional)

Clean your squid following the method described in Raw Squid in Coral (page 287). Sprinkle both sides of the fileted squid bodies and tentacles (still attached at the top) lightly with salt. Drape across a bamboo basket and dry in the direct sunlight for 2 to 4 hours until the skin has tightened and developed a slightly leathery texture. Turn once. If you have crows in your area, a nylon fish-drying basket comes in handy. If you clean the squid in the late afternoon or evening, leave it on the basket at cellar temperature and dry outside the next morning. Grill lightly over low-ember coals or on a rack set in the second slot from the top of an oven broiler for about 2 or 3 minutes on each side. Julienne, and eat dipped in soy sauce or salt for a before-dinner snack or light lunch. Also nice with a squeeze of yuzu or Meyer lemon. Uncooked dried squid keeps wrapped in the fridge for about a week.

THE SALMON WHISPERER

Before even crossing the threshold, I knew that Kikkawa (home of Murakamisake dried salmon) was a place worth visiting. Besides the well-kept throwback architecture, the polished vintage automobile and bicycle parked next to the building showed where the owners' value set lay. People after my own heart.

Stepping into the cavernous room opening up behind the shop (half house, half barn), I felt like I had entered another era. The salmon hanging from the rafters were slightly surreal, with faces resembling prehistoric fish. I wandered around, awestruck by the nobility of the ancient building. My eyes were drawn to a large cedar water tank, fashioned decades ago by a local cooper. I also was grateful to see a collection of smaller-sized wooden buckets still in daily use. I turned to meet Akira Yoshikawa, the gregarious 70-something owner, decked out in indigo workers' clothes and wearing a skullcap. He enthusiastically (without taking a single breath!) regaled us with the several-hundred-year-old history of his family's salmon salting operation, doing business since the Edo period (1603–1868). Yoshikawa-san is the 14th generation of this venerable house.

Yoshikawa-san walked us through the salting process, starting with how he chooses the fish. The fishermen lay out 500 fish, and from those 500, Yoshikawa-san only selects 5 or 6. How does he make his selection?, I ask. The fish call to him, is his response. How much salt do you use?, I ask. The fish tell me, he says with a small knowing smile. Can I make this is in my area?, I wonder. Emphatically no, Murakamisake can only be made in Murakami according to

Yoshikawa-san. I understand that it will not be the same, or anywhere close to being as good as what you make, but it is possible to make in my area, right? No. Akira Yoshikawa, 14th-generation salmon whisperer, will not budge on this. But I am not to be deterred and will try my hand at salting my own fish.

There were more than one hundred different ways to treat salmon in Murakami, but over the course of the last 50 or 60 years those local methods have lost favor. New preparation methods, vaunted under the guise of being "efficient and modern," use chemical processing rather than local, time-worn methods. The Yoshikawa family continued to produce this very local dried fish under their Kikkawa label even during the toughest times, when it was difficult to sell their product. But luckily food climates

change, and in recent years there is a renewed interest in local products. And thanks to media attention and the ease of Internet ordering, this artisanal product can be savored by all of us who do not live in Murakami.

I recently tried the *shiobiki* salmon that I had ordered from Murakamisake. It was out-of-this-world incredible. Before grilling over low coals, the flesh was a soft pinky color and delectably salty, yet not oily. After a quick grill on both sides the salmon became a translucent orange pink. I served it as handheld sushi rolls made from Iio Jozo Akasumeshi Su—an unusual vinegar made from aged sake lees (Red Vinegar, page 165) and Iio Jozo's premium vinegar. Unforgettable all the way around. I could barely keep up with the SSU! kids asking for "more please!"

I've been fascinated with air-dried salmon since I took a trip to Niigata a couple of winters ago, so decided to take a stab at salting a whole fish myself. At first I had to confirm that my area was cold enough, since you need the temperature to remain around 50°F (10°C) during the salting period. As I was still in the mulling process, I noticed some small, whole salted salmon hanging at our local fish market. My fishmonger explained their process. Basically they salted the fish and left it in the naturally cool fish market air until it was dried. As simple as that. Their wild makeshift preserving method emboldened me to salt my own fish roughly following the method kindly described on the Iwafune Web site (another salmon salter in Murakami). As I am not a salmon whisperer (page 31), the fish did not call to me, nor tell me how much salt to use, but I used good salt and the result was not half bad. Actually the fish was delicious.

salt-dried salmon MAKES 1 LARGE DRIED FISH
SHIOBIKI SHAKE

1 very fresh small whole salmon
    (about 3½ pounds/
    1.6 kg), guts intact

Good-quality fine white sea salt

Remove the skin slime from the salmon with a bamboo scraper or a nontreated wire scrubby. Rinse thoroughly with plenty of cold running water and cut out the gills by inserting a thin blade and scraping up to the back of the eye (this is important for ensuring that the salt absorbs properly). Pull the gills out by hand. Grab the tail and make a deep incision about a quarter of the way up from the tail end of the ventral side. Hold your flat hand on top of the fish and make a running slit up the tummy to the midsection fin. Optional: Leave an uncut portion of about ¾ inch (2 cm) at the midsection fin (a custom that stems from the dislike of *seppuku* (hari-kari [*sic*] in the era of the samurai). Make another incision above the ¾-inch (2-cm) uncut portion and continue slitting up to the fins underneath the jaw.

Remove the guts and discard. Scrape out the insides very well with a blunt knife or your fingernails, taking care to remove any remaining gills and blood vessels, as well as the kidney-like organ adhering to the middle bone. Starting from the inside working out, flush the salmon well with cold running water to rinse off any lingering guts or blood.

Using a circular motion, massage salt onto both surfaces of the fish, starting from the tail section, moving up toward the head. Don't neglect the backbone and back of the head. Massage more salt generously into the open midsection as well, leaving some loose salt inside. Be sure to work the salt in well around the eye area and any crevices such as the cleaned gill area and the jaw. Massage salt into all surfaces one more time for good measure.

salt-dried salmon

Place the salted fish in a wooden or Styrofoam box (anything OK!) and leave uncovered in a cool spot (important: not warmer than 50°F/10°C) for 3 days. Flop the salmon over and leave for 3 more days to ensure even distribution of the salt.

After a total of 6 days, rinse off any visible salt crystals and soak the salmon in plenty of cold water for 10 to 15 hours. This step is the most important (besides choosing the fish!) and also the trickiest to get right. The soak time will determine the end flavor of the fish: whether it will be *karashi shio* (salty) or *amajio* (sweet). Like most things, it takes practice to figure out which taste you prefer. I took the middle ground and went with a 12-hour soak.

Remove the fish from the water bath and scrub one last time with a bamboo scraper or wire scrubby to remove any residual skin slime or lingering gut particles. Rinse thoroughly in cold running water and pat dry with a clean kitchen towel.

Hang the fish from the tail (head down) in a well-ventilated cool place (at least 50°F/10°C or colder) for 7 to 10 days. If the air temperature rises or is humid due to precipitation, there is danger of the fish turning, so take care to monitor the weather. In Murakami, most families hang their fish under the eaves of the house, but the drying operation can also be done successfully in an open garage or other sheltered area. It is possible to semidry the fish in the fridge, though in this case eliminate the cold water soak and leave the first salt.

Butterfly the fish by slicing from head to tail through the stomach area with a thick fish knife. Finish cutting the fish in half by cutting through the backbone, or just remove the bones altogether. Keeps well in the refrigerator for a couple of weeks or in the freezer for several months. Grill for 10 minutes on each side over low-ember coals or on a rack set over a foil-lined cookie sheet in the third slot from the top of a broiler until the flesh has turned from creamy pink to translucent coral. Eat as is or wrapped in a piece of nori with vinegared sushi rice (page XXVIII).

VARIATIONS: Although I have not tried it, I suppose it is possible to substitute another similar-sized ocean fish or a large salmon trout.

WAJIMA AIR-DRIED FISH

Before visiting the Noto Peninsula I asked around about any producers hanging fish right by the water to air-dry naturally in the salty sea air. Here again, I had a romantic picture in my mind of the small fish twisting gently in wafts of wind coming off of the water. Instead we were introduced to a fisherman's house, where a team of three family members cleaned and salted the daily catch in the space normally designated as a garage. The team consisted of a middle-aged couple and the sister-in-law.

Squatting on turned-over plastic milk boxes, the women swapped stories and cackled as they worked. The man hid behind dark sunglasses and kept his laconic self steady to the task. I immediately squatted on my own crate and took copious notes as the women explained what they were doing. It took a bit of prying and cajoling to jolly the man to give up some of his fish-preserving secrets, but in the end he did. Being able to sit and watch professional hands cut, scrape, clean, and salt is mesmerizing—and ultimately illuminating. I had salted and dried fish on my own, but essentially I was working in a sort of vacuum. Going to the source gives you context and a fuller understanding of the process. I was lucky to be there and hung on every word.

The catch comes in in the morning. The three spend all morning cleaning and salting the fish and shellfish before threading with glutinous rice straw. After about a half hour of salting, they rinse the fish and hang them on poles above where they work until the next morning when the fish are ready to be sold. In Wajima, people eat this semi-air-dried fish and seafood (*himono*) for lunch and there are hand-pulled

carts or mini pickups that troll the city in the mornings selling *himono* and the fresh catch of the day.

I also learned that any fish or shellfish can be salted and air-dried for *himono*. *Any.* I'm not sure why this had such a huge impact on me other than the fact that this concept made so much sense. Of course! When the catch comes in you need to decide how to preserve it. Certainly eating the fish or shellfish raw as sashimi is one option, but ultimately there must be preserving methods in place for dealing with larger catches. *Asazuke* means "morning pickles" and refers to any quick souse. Douse some squid in soy sauce for 30 minutes and voilà, an instant "pickled" fish ready for grilling. In Wajima, salt and fish are plentiful so the quick air-dried process of making *himono* is completely intuitive, as is fermenting all of the by-product fish guts from the *himono*-making process with salt to make local fish sauce (*ishiru*). The Noto Peninsula also grows rice, so the rice bran that comes from polishing rice is mixed together with *ishiru* to make a Noto-style *nukadoko* pickling bed for a longer-fermented fish (page 224). What comes clear from seeing the methods in situ is that they developed from what was naturally available, and while fewer and fewer people are making their own *ishiru* or *himono* (or fish *nukazuke*, for that matter), I get a sense of warm comfort in seeing these methods continue today, deeply entrenched in the local food culture.

Like most preparations, there is no one way to make air-dried fish (*himono*). My fishmonger recommends using a brine bath at the same salinity as saltwater (3%), while the artisans we visited in Wajima salted by feel. Either way the general salting time is 30 minutes. Both methods produce delicious results, so in the end (like most things) it comes down to personal preference.

half-dried barracuda SERVES 6
KAMASU NO HIMONO

3 small barracuda or other medium-sized whole fish (about 8 ounces/225 g each), gutted and butterflied without the head

Fine white sea salt

Lightly squeezed grated daikon (optional)

Soy sauce (optional)

Rub the butterflied barracuda (*kamasu*) generously with salt. The salt should be visible on the surface but not a heavy blanket. Leave the fish to absorb the salt for 30 minutes, then soak in several changes of cold water for 30 minutes to remove some of the salt's intensity.

Poke a bamboo skewer through the top portion of one side and pass it across the surface of the fish through to the top portion of the other side. Thread a piece of kitchen twine around each end of the skewer and tie around a horizontally hung pole or thin tree branch. Make sure the fish is tied evenly on each side, not lopsided. Hang in a well-ventilated spot (in the indirect late afternoon sun) until the following morning. Refrigerate until ready to cook. Grill lightly for 10 minutes on the stomach side and 5 minutes on the skin side over low coals or on a rack set over a foil-lined cookie sheet in the third slot from the top of the oven broiler. Serve communally or ½ fish per person on individual plates. Dollop some squeezed grated daikon alongside and serve with soy sauce, if using.

VARIATIONS: Instead of rubbing with salt, soak for 30 minutes in a 3% brine. Hang directly after soaking without rinsing. Dry outside for 1 to 2 days in the bright winter sun. Bring in at night. Instead of the daikon and soy sauce, also excellent with squeezed yuzu or Meyer lemon juice and a little salt.

Sardines are tricky. They are almost too big to eat as tempura and can quickly overcook when grilled. I've always been partial to sardine sushi: two delicate pillows of sushi rice with glistening ultrafresh seasonal sardines draped across, brushed with soy sauce and dabbed with grated ginger. Heaven. Also marinated sardines are a huge favorite. What is appealing about air-drying the sardines before grilling is that because the fish are half-dried, they don't seem to get that chalky dried-out texture that can destroy grilled sardines. I also like that you can store these in the fridge for a few days before you are ready to cook them, as it is always a great boon to have ready-to-make food in the house.

air-dried sardines SERVES 6
IWASHI NO HIMONO

½ tablespoon fine white sea salt

6 very fresh sardines
    (5 ounces/150 g each), gutted,
    deheaded, and butterflied

3 small yuzu, halved (or 1 Meyer
    lemon, cut into sixths), for serving

Flaky white sea salt, for serving

Stir the salt into 1 cup (250 cc) of cold water to dissolve. Rinse the sardines and submerge in the water to soak for 30 minutes. Remove the fish from the water and pat dry. Poke a bamboo skewer through the skin side right above the gill area of one side of the fish, passing the skewer across the top front of the butterflied sardines, and poke the skewer in above the gill area on the opposite side. Set the open-threaded sardines onto a grate and place it in the direct winter sun, cut side out, for 3 or 4 hours, depending on the time of day and intensity of the light. Flip the fish halfway through drying to expose the skin side.

Grill for about 3 minutes per side over low glowing coals or on a wire rack set over a foil-lined cookie sheet in the third slot from the top of an oven broiler. Serve each fish on a small individual plate with half a yuzu or wedge of Meyer lemon. Mound a tiny pile of best sea salt next to the citrus for dipping. If the bones and heads are soft enough, they can be eaten. Your choice.

VARIATION: Instead of deheaded, butterflied sardines, you could use gutted whole ones. Use glutinous rice straw or some other equally stiff twine or fine wire to thread 2 fish together through their mouth areas as if they were kissing. Tie the straw or wire to form a bowed-out shape for hanging. Hang outside to air-dry without salt for 1 to 3 days, depending on the weather (but bring in at night). When the fish no longer retain any natural moisture, they are ready to be grilled.

FUNABA SHICHIRIN

I had tagged along to the Noto Peninsula with veteran editor (and expert in things Japanese) Kim Schuefftan and my photographer, Kenji Miura. They were on a magazine shoot, while I was fulfilling the long-held desire to visit Sakamoto, an inn (ryokan, page 126) well known for its understated and very personal local food. It is owned by old friends of Kim, so going as friends would enhance what already promised to be a once-in-a-lifetime experience.

We followed Sakamoto-san as he buzzed around the sweeping curve that leads up to Funaba Shichirin, makers of tabletop barbecue sets (shichirin, erroneously called hibachi in the U.S.). Surrounded by rice fields, one got the sense that this was God's country. This part of Noto has huge deposists of diatomaceous earth, and the Funaba company carves grilling sets of various sizes and shapes from blocks of this fossilized plankton. We donned rubber boots and tromped across the road to the hillside mine. Claustrophobic, I could not be persuaded to follow photographer Miura-san into the bowels of the hill. While Kim remained behind to get his story from the owner, I strolled back to the office with the owner's wife, Yoneko, to share a cup of tea. The first thing she asked me as we headed across the road was, "Have you gone through menopause?" If you have heard stories about the reticent Japanese, they were certainly not talking about countrymen or women. No holds barred there. With that opening, we were fast friends and spent the next three quarters of an hour exchanging stories of being mothers and wives. Our different nationalities had no play in the bond that we formed that afternoon.

When I was heading back to Noto to capture stories for this book, I was intent on revisiting Funaba Shichirin. By Googling shichirin in Japanese, I found one company nearby the Sakamoto ryokan. The fortunate part about being a foreigner who happens to also be a farmwife is that people tend not to forget you. I called the shichirin place but my description did not ring a bell. I asked if another place had a very friendly, talkative wife. The wife of this particular shichirin company laughed and immediately replied, "Ah, yes, you must mean Funaba-san—the wife is very chatty!" Success. I immediately called the number given me and reconnected with my pal, Yoneko Funaba. Thirty minutes later, we had hashed over our lives from the last year and a visit was on the calendar.

The second time I visited Funaba Shichirin their son was our guide. Newly back from spending ten years attending university and working in Tokyo, Shinichi Funaba is aiming to transition the family business into a more modern profile through the World Wide Web. As his father reflected, Shinichi may not have the wherewithal to cut clay from the mountain, but he brings other expertise like familiarity with computers to the family enterprise. We splashed our way through the water puddled up on the packed clay surface of the new mine the family had recently taken over. Thankfully this mine had been tunneled out taking a wide swath, so my borderline claustrophobia was not an issue. We paused to watch the skilled worker cut out massive blocks of packed, moist diatomaceous clay using a wooden wedge and mallet to cut each side and a long metal tool to tip it free from the mountain. I asked what

drew him to this solitary, physically demanding work, but he could not answer, perhaps because his boss was standing right there or perhaps because he had not thought much about it. I learned later that in the past there had been workers in their seventies still cutting the blocks—as this is a job that requires adept leverage more than brute force.

We emerged from the mine and strolled over toward the 100-year-old processing barn. Stopping at the handcrafted firing kiln, I could hear the pride in Shinichi's voice as he showed us his family operation. Each block is hand shaved by two artisanal workers or Kazuo Funaba, the father. While a machine drills out the centers of the round *shichirin* to create a chamber for the charcoal, the rectangular ones are carved out by hand, thus more dear. The *shichirin* are fired, then painted by hand by workers before brass fittings are hammered in place. Funaba Shichirin is the oldest of three makers left in Noto who are fashioning their *shichirin* completely by hand. I thought they would be (should be?) more expensive, but was agreeably surprised that these hand-cut and individually crafted *shichirin* were incredibly reasonably priced at about $90 for a large rectangle barbecue and $30 for the medium-sized round ones we usually use on top of the table, though I imagine I got the friends and family discount.

But no amount of money can match the absolute and deep pleasure derived from grilling Air-Dried Sardines (page 38) over artisanal Ohno charcoal (page 329) in a Funaba *shichirin*. All from the Noto Peninsula. I know I left a part of myself there and am always wondering when I can go back.

Round-headed fish such as horse mackerel or butterfish are often butterflied with the head intact to make a beautiful circular shape that is dried. Long fish such as saury or flying fish can also be butterflied to a dramatic effect. Although herring and barracuda are commonly butterflied without the head, herring can also be left whole. Rather than hanging, it is fine to set the fish on a rack tilted toward the sun after threading with a bamboo skewer through the gills to keep flat. In this case, be sure no dogs are in the area because if you turn your back, your wily hound may gobble them up. (I speak from experience!)

semidried herring SERVES 6

NISHIN NO HIMONO

4 very fresh herring (about 8 ounces/225 g each), gutted and butterflied

Fine white sea salt

Freshly grated daikon, squeezed lightly

Soy sauce (optional)

Put some fine white sea salt in a small bowl next to your work space and rub salt generously all over each fish, taking care to really get into the gill area and all crevices. Let the fish macerate in the salt for 30 minutes, then rinse in a basin with cold running water. Hang outside (or in an open garage) in a well-ventilated spot with indirect sunlight from midafternoon to the following morning.

Poke a bamboo skewer through the skin side right above the gill area of one side of the fish, passing the skewer across the top front of the butterflied herring, and poke the skewer in above the gill area on the opposite side. Set the open-threaded herring onto a grate and place it in the direct winter sun, cut side out, for 3 or 4 hours, depending on the time of day and intensity of the light. Flip the fish halfway through drying to expose the skin side. The flesh should be moisture-free, and the skin should not have any lingering shininess.

Grill over smoldering coals or on a rack set over a foil-lined sheet in the third slot from the top of a broiler for 5 minutes on each side, or until the skin oil is crackling and the flesh is cooked. Serve communally with the grated daikon and pass the soy sauce, if using.

VARIATION: Also nice with squeezed citrus juice such as yuzu or Meyer lemon; in this case, I would use salt instead of soy sauce if the fish needs it.

みそ

2

miso

MISO RECIPES

HOMEMADE BROWN RICE MISO	51
SHISO ROLLS	57
KABOCHA IN MISO WITH RED PEPPER	58
GREEN BEANS CLOAKED IN MISO	59
APPLE PEARS IN MISO	60
GARLIC EMBEDDED IN MISO	61
TOFU MARINATED IN MISO	65
MISO-CURED EGGS	66
YUZU MISO	69
MISO-MUSTARD RAPINI	74
WILD ARUGULA WITH WALNUT MISO	75
MISO SQUID	77
COUNTRY MISO AND VEGETABLE SOUP	80
COLD MISO SOUP WITH CUCUMBER AND MYOGA	82
CARROT SALAD WITH MISO VINAIGRETTE	83
SHISHITO PEPPERS SAUTÉED WITH MISO AND GINGER	85

I first arrived in Japan in the summer of 1988. I had eaten miso soup, but otherwise really had no idea of how to use miso or what exactly miso was. Each trip to the supermarket was like a bewildering excursion through unknown territory. What were all those strange packaged foods? In the United States we have whole walls of shelves dedicated to breakfast cereal or soft drinks. In 1988 Japan, rice held a prominent wall, as did miso. I remember shelves of plastic containers and bags of miso. I was convinced that those containers held peanut butter, not miso. That shows you how insular I was despite my so-called worldly outlook. Over the years, ironically I lost the taste for peanut butter but developed one for miso with a vengeance—the strange has become commonplace and vice versa.

Miso has been so intertwined with our culinary life that I never gave it much thought. In the early years, my mother-in-law was still making her own miso, so we always had some of her homemade miso in the fridge. But our stock miso was Yamaki Jozo's inaka miso (literally "country miso"). Inaka miso is made from white rice koji, so it is light in color but has the full flavor of a two-year fermentation that Kyoto-style white miso does not.

In our house, miso was just miso; we never talked varieties and never used the term "red" miso. In fact, it was not until I started thinking about and writing about Japanese farm food that I began to delve beneath the surface of the hows and whys of traditional Japanese foods. I used to take things at face value: Knowing something was well made was enough; I didn't need to obsess about exactly how it was made. That point of view has changed, though. Many Japanese have lost touch with how traditional foods are made. Consequently, my current mission is to visit the producers of artisanal Japanese foods and share their stories with the Japanese public through my periodic Fuji TV segments.

I also realized that it was simply not enough to gather information. I had to participate in the making of as many of these traditional foods as possible—for the sake of passing on the preservation practices to my sons and future daughters-in-law, and to develop a deeper understanding of the processes. Making miso as a community effort gave me self-confidence and a feeling of personal power. "You can do it!" is a litany I often say to my preschool kids (and to myself). And it is what I want to say to all of you reading this book: You can do it!

You can make miso.

MAKING MISO

I had heard about Matsuda-san's miso-making confabs for years but was never able to participate. February was the time we left for a month for our annual SSU! school trip, piggybacked on to a long family trip with my sons, as well as periodic soba dinners at Chez Panisse with chef friend Kanji Nakatani. Early winter was always occupied with trip preparations, marmalade making, and graduation plans at Sunny-Side Up! No room for miso making on the schedule.

But in writing my last book I became completely immersed in all things Japanese and thus was ready to jump into the miso-making group as well. I did a dry run by attending a class at Yamaki where you sit at a table and make the miso without getting your hands mussed. When you climb the stairs adjacent to their shop, you come upon a room of glossy wood tables with indigo-cushioned stools. In front of each place is set a 2-kilo bag of cooked soybeans, a 1-kilo bag of rice koji, a 400-gram bag of sea salt, a large food-grade plastic bag, and a rubber band. The idea is to dump all of the ingredients into the plastic bag along with a small ladle of "seed miso" water (water into which miso has been whisked to the consistency of a very weak miso soup). The participants then seal up the bag with the rubber band and proceed to shake and mash the beans through the plastic. Always the renegade, I just plunge my whole arm in and squeeze the beans through my fingers to get the chunky texture I like for miso. The miso is so good (dark, naturally sweet, beguiling!) I make four batches worth each year. Although I get a discount for the multiple batches, it still comes out to be much more expensive than making

miso with Matsuda-san. No matter—I can enjoy the miso all year long. I like having both types on hand: the rich brown rice koji miso I make at Yamaki as well as the light, bright miso I make under Matsuda-san's tutelage.

When we arrive around 9 a.m. at Matsuda-san's mayonnaise company compound in the hills, Matsuda-san is already steaming the beans in steamer boxes about nine tiers high set over an iron cauldron of boiling water fueled by a raging wood fire. A tall pot of warm water in which Matsuda-san has dissolved some of his previous year's miso as a starter for the new miso is cooling on the gas burner in the makeshift kitchen underneath the mayonnaise company. Plank tables have been rigged up to create elevated work spaces so we don't all have to work Japanese-style, crouched over bowls placed on the floor. There is a grinding machine affixed to one table for those who care to make swift work of mashing the steamed soybeans. I have brought my largest *suribachi* and *surikogi* (Japanese grinding bowl and pestle) and set about smashing my allotment of beans in batches. My old friend/ex-student Yoshie Takahashi starts squeezing her steamed soybeans between her thumb and index finger while waiting to use my *suribachi*. As it turns out, I take so long with my two batches that she is finished by the time I can pass her the grinding bowl. Not a problem: Mashing by hand is a tactile and perfectly doable alternative to the machine grind or mortar smash.

We take turns mixing in the smashed soybeans with the salt, koji, and seed miso (last year's miso diluted in water) in an oversized soba-kneading

bowl (*konebachi*, page XVIII). The orange lacquer bowl is a remnant of the days when Matsuda-san also ran a soba shop in one of our neighboring towns (a short-lived operation when he was feeling particularly enterprising). My friend Adam Zgola offers to knead my first batch while I am still occupied smashing the second. I decline and, as an artisanal Japanese carpenter (page XXIV), he instinctively understands why. I want to put my soul into the miso, to be the one to lay my hands on it and knead in my own personal energy.

Matsuda-san rolls up balls of freshly made miso mash and thwacks the balls into his yellow plastic barrel from the year before (the previous year's miso clinging to the sides of the container will act as a starter for the new batch). I just smash my two batches into plastic bags to take home and pack later into my wooden barrel after removing last year's miso to the fridge.

We eat together in the former café, a traditional storage building that was transported from elsewhere in Japan and rebuilt by Matsuda-san and his friends. The wood fire spreads a welcome warmth in the room as we gather for a simple lunch of rice balls (just pressed triangular shapes, no nori wrapping), assorted pickles made by Matsuda-san, and a light miso soup with root vegetables—the quintessential Japanese farm meal. It is days like this that make me feel part of a whole, and I appreciate the people who make that possible—people like Matsuda-san, Yoshie, and Adam.

Although tackling making miso may seem intimidating, it is really much simpler than you may imagine. I encourage you to take the plunge because when you end up with a vat of bright homemade miso that has your own taste, the sense of accomplishment is unrivaled.

Mitoku organic brown rice koji and barley koji can be ordered through Cultures for Health or the Natural Import Company, an excellent source for top-quality Japanese ingredients, and white rice koji is available online at South River in Massachusetts or Cold Mountain Miso (see Resources). This method follows the one used at the Yamaki Jozo miso-making workshop. The large percentage of koji results in a full-flavored, almost sweet miso. Good-quality dried soybeans are readily found in the bulk organic section of your best organic shop. Though I use Japanese sea salt, just use a good-quality local or even Italian white sea salt, preferably naturally dried. Make miso in the cool months from late November through early March to give it time to rest before the fermentation arc starts to climb as the weather warms in the spring and summer

homemade
brown rice miso MAKES 6 POUNDS (3.5 KG)
TEZUKURI GENMAI MISO

2 pounds (1 kg) best-quality non-GMO dried soybeans

2 teaspoons best-quality organic miso (or previous year's homemade) to use as seed miso for the new batch

2 pounds (1 kg) brown rice koji (page XXVIII)

14 ounces (400 g) fine white sea salt

Soak the soybeans for 18 hours in a large pot of cold filtered water. Drain the beans, return them to the pot, and refill the pot to about 5 inches (10 cm) above the beans. Bring to a boil over high heat, lower to a simmer, and cook for about 1½ to 2 hours, uncovered, until the beans are soft. The idea here is to simmer the beans in just enough liquid so they cook well but eventually most of the liquid is boiled away by the time the beans are cooked. Traditionally, the beans are steamed for 1½ hours in wooden steaming boxes stacked over a large cauldron set over a very hot wood fire. The beans can also be cooked in batches in a pressure cooker for about 20 minutes over high heat. (N.B.: If you steam the beans you will need to double the amount of seed miso and water that you add to the mash with the koji and salt.) While the beans are cooking, slowly whisk ½ cup (125 cc) of hot water into the 2 teaspoons seed miso and cool to room temperature (the solution should be like a very thin miso soup in consistency).

Drain the cooked beans and start mashing them to a coarse consistency. I like to grind them roughly in batches in the Japanese grinding bowl (*suribachi*). Alternatively, you could run the cooked soybeans through a sterilized meat grinder. Or you can opt for the low-tech squeeze between your thumb and index finger method. When the beans are smashed to your satisfaction (chunky or smooth), they will also be cooled enough to measure in the koji— they should be just off warm at the most (too hot and it kills the spores). Sprinkle in about 80% of the salt along with the seed miso (miso thinned with water). Knead well to distribute the koji and salt with the mashed beans.

homemade brown rice miso

Form tennis ball–sized spheres of bean mash and *throw* them into a large crockery pot, small wooden barrel, or food-grade plastic vat *with all of your might. Whack! Splot!* The container should be set on the floor, and it probably makes sense to have a piece of plastic sheeting underneath the container to catch any misthrows. You are looking for a satisfying splat that sounds like *thunk* rather than a weak *glurp*. Or (if you are lazy like me, with stunningly bad aim), you might mash the balls in with your fist and the heel of your hand to ensure that all air pockets have been filled. The bean mash should only fill the container about half full. Pat down the surface of the mash with the flat of your palm and sprinkle with the remaining 20% portion of salt.

Smooth a clean muslin cloth across the surface of the mash and let it drape down over the sides of the container to keep out flying leaves or other debris. Place a wooden or plastic drop lid on top of the cloth-covered mash surface and weight evenly with rocks or heavy objects that equal at least the weight of the mash. Cover with one more large muslin cloth and wind some twine a couple of times around the circumference of the barrel to tie the cloth in place. The cloth will act as a mold barrier and will become scarily dusted with green mold spores, so don't skip or replace with plastic. Carefully remove to wash when you stir the miso.

Let the young miso sit undisturbed in a shaded area outside until the weather warms. From May, start stirring the miso about once a month to avoid mold as the fermentation arc starts to ramp up. During the hottest period, you should probably stir the miso (from the bottom up) every 2 weeks to avoid mold forming. Ideally the weather should become muggy, and the temperatures should rise to about 100°F (38°C) at the height of the summer. But avoid direct sunlight. If you see any mold on the surface, carefully scrape it off. Clean the inside surface walls of the container with a vodka- or shochu-soaked cloth to deter mold. If you are feeling particularly adventurous, you could smooth a 1-inch (2.5-cm) layer of sake lees across the surface of the miso in June or July to seal and inhibit mold produced by oxidization. In this case, you really want to completely cover the surface to make a homogeneous layer (you still need to use the cloth, drop lid, weights, and outside cloth cover). Peel off the sake lees when the weather turns cool in the late fall, and recycle the lees as an instant pickling bed.

If you have not sealed the miso with sake lees, check the miso after the summer to see if it has mellowed to your liking. At this point, you can refrigerate it or just leave the miso in its fermenting container until you start your next batch in the coming winter. No need for weights once the miso is done—you can leave it outside if the weather is cool; otherwise store it in the fridge.

VARIATIONS: I have heard of people using different beans such as chickpeas or azuki; I would not. In Japan miso is always made from soybeans. Also it is fine to use white rice koji or barley koji instead of the brown rice koji.

THE BARREL MAKER

One day when I was rummaging around in our neighborhood hardware store (not the chain home center), I notice a medium-sized pickling barrel perched on the highest shelf. I could tell by the color of the barrel that it had been there for a while and asked the storekeeper to lift it down to check the price. It was marked $100; though she knocked off 20% it was still expensive, but I bought it. I had become obsessed with switching over from plastic to wood and was excited at the prospect of making my Fermented Napa Cabbage (page 11) in the new barrel. The newness of the cedar leached out a bit and a small amount of mold developed, but I was thrilled that I did not need to use a plastic bag like when I made sauerkraut. I'm not into the whole sterilization process (too much trouble), so I like to find alternative methods that actually work.

Thus began my quest for used barrels, which proved very hard to find. Over the years I have collected plenty of wooden buckets, but they require care. One day they are standing tall, the next they have collapsed because the bamboo rings that keep the slats in place have loosened and slipped down. You need to store them upside down, and you need to use them. My flea market vendors told me that used pickling barrels were virtually nonexistent (considered dirty?), so I explored other options on the Internet. I Googled *barrel* in Japanese (樽, *taru*) and came up with taruya.com. I liked the feel of the site with its rustic drawings and general sense of style, but could not figure out the size or type of barrel needed so gave up for the time being.

It was the spring of 2013, and I was about to leave the country for another six-week *Japanese Farm Food* book tour in the States. I sent the barrel maker an email asking him to send me the barrels, but he never did. He sometimes ignores English emails (which turned out to be providential). After I returned to Japan, Fuji TV approched me to do some filming, and we were able to capture on film the dramatic unpacking of the barrels, finding the sake lees that the barrel maker had included as a present, and filling the 4-*to* barrel with water from the garden hose to soak for 24 hours. All with the SSU! kids in tow. The director was so enthused about my soy sauce— and miso-making activities that she proposed a visit to the barrel maker. I asked Miura-san to tag along and off we went to Kobe.

Earlier, when I joined a soy sauce–making community, the juxtaposition between the handcrafted soy sauce pressing apparatus and the yellow plastic barrels struck me as odd, and that feeling stuck with me. At the second annual soy sauce pressing event, I had a conversation with the master presser, Iwasaki-san. Having already decided to ferment my own barrel of soy sauce at home rather than leave my share to ferment in the plastic tubs with the other members of our cooperative, I questioned him about the size of barrel I would need. Barrels are sized by a unit called *to*. I needed a 4-*to* barrel for my soy sauce. Armed with this information, I called the barrel maker and a 45-minute conversation ensued. For fermenting soy sauce, the barrel maker advised me to use a recycled 4-*to* barrel in which ceremonial sake had been stored and a new 2-*to* barrel for miso.

Yashima Nishikita stepped out of his workshop sporting a white T-shirt with a bat stamped across a yellow circle (which he later, inexplicably, changed into a bright yellow one with the words *Fiat 500* blazed across the chest in red). His stiff black hair was shot with grey and held back in a thick ponytail. He had an unusually wide smile and bright round eyes gleamed from deep sockets. It was a striking picture—Nishikita-san standing in front of his ancient workshop with a graveyard of used sake barrels stacked up outside. The sake barrels were waiting to be refurbished and sold to fermenting maniacs (like me). Nishikita-san even sends his barrels to a pickling aficionado in Washington, D.C.

We followed Nishikita-san into his workshop to watch him and his master craftsman put together a barrel or two. The workshop was stacked high

on one side with barrels, and the only place to walk was on the bamboo strips, which would be woven together to form the rings that keep the wooden barrel slats in place. I gingerly balanced my way across the bamboo strips, akin to walking a tightrope, and found a small out-of-the-way corner to rest my notebook. Fascinated, I watched the craftsman knock the slats in place using a couple of metal hoops as a guide.

"Chotto majiku mitai," Nishikita mused with a knowing smile . . . "It's a little like magic."

The whole process took about thirty minutes before he carried the barrel over to the tightening machine. Not satisfied with the job he had done (the slats were marginally off balance), he removed the barrel from the machine, slipped off the bamboo rings, and started again. It's easy to understand why the new barrels go for about $160, which is cheap when you consider the time, workmanship, and materials. Nishikita-san is an 8th-generation barrel maker who has been doing it for over thirty years. He went off to the city to sow his wild oats but returned to take over the family business in his early thirties. Kobe is an international seaport, and he was proud to report that he still had many foreign friends (including an American ex-girlfriend in his past). Nishikita-san has his one master craftsman to assist in the barrel-making operation but now is teaching two more young men to learn the craft. Barrel making is a dying art in Japan, but hopefully it will survive for a couple of more generations.

On a visit to the Oigen ironworks in Iwate prefecture, I was fortunate enough to spend the morning with Tami-san, the ninety-nine-year-old mother of Oigen's owner, Kuniko Oikawa. Tami-san was slightly hard of hearing in one ear, so most questions I asked had to be repeated by one of her daughters. We had a grand old time swapping pickling methods, and I wished the morning would last forever. Right before we were wrapping up the session, Tami-san suddenly began to tell me about these shiso maki. Despite already having more than enough recipes for this book, I knew these rolls had to make it into the mix. The beauty of shiso maki (besides being completely addicting) is that the compacted rolls keep for many months in the fridge and make a quick savory-sweet bite with afternoon tea or a bowl of rice when there is not much else in the fridge.

shiso rolls MAKES 50
SHISO MAKI

5 tablespoons organic granulated sugar

30 tablespoons (600 g) brown rice miso

2 or 3 small dried red chiles, cut into fine rings

10 tablespoons finely chopped walnuts

5 tablespoons black sesame seeds, warmed

Pinch of salt

50 large green shiso leaves (page 343)

Canola oil, for frying

Mix the sugar into the miso with the chile and heat in a small frying pan over low heat to melt the sugar crystals. Fold in the chopped walnuts, black sesame seeds, and pinch of salt. Let cool.

Do not wash the shiso leaves. If you want to remove dust or dirt, wipe with a slightly damp kitchen towel (introducing water in oil-frying is not good). Working at a large table or counter area, lay the shiso leaves out, bright green side down. Spoon a heaping ½ tablespoon of the miso mixture onto the base of each leaf. Make sure you have enough filling before rolling. Roll the leaves up and stack onto a dinner plate.

Film a small amount of oil into a large, heavy frying pan and warm over low heat. Fry the rolls lightly on sides until bright green, but not brown or blistered.

Eat hot when freshly fried or cold directly from the refrigerator. The leaves will darken slightly, but the rolls keep for several months, stored in a plastic container in the fridge.

These pickles take a few weeks to mature but are well worth the wait. The earthy, rustic salt of the miso complements the naturally sweet pumpkin. This pickle was culled from William Shurtleff and Akiko Aoyagi's excellent tome, *The Book of Miso*. Despite the unusual name, I had never put together the fact that William Shurtleff is a relative of my sister's mother-in-law, Willi Hilliard (the woman I admire most in this world). Willi and Bill Shurtleff's father, Lawton (also a gifted author), are cousins. The connection did not click until just recently when I was seated across the table from Lawton's widow, Anneke, one night at Willi's up on Chalk Hill Road in Healdsburg, California. I had been wanting to be in touch with Bill and Akiko for years so the circle became complete—funny how the link came from such an unexpected non-food-related source—and from someone who is almost family.

kabocha in miso
with red pepper SERVES 6 OR MORE
KABOCHA NO MISOZUKE

1 tablespoon sea salt

½ medium-sized kabocha (about 1⅓ pounds/600 g)

About ½ pound (250 g) brown rice or barley miso

7-spice powder (*shichimi togarashi*, page XXXI)

Fill a medium-sized, heavy pot three-quarters full of water, throw in the salt, and bring to a boil over high heat.

Scoop out the seeds and pulp from the kabocha, peel, and slice into ½-inch (12-mm) thick wedges (measured from the back edge) with a sturdy kitchen knife. Blanch for 1 minute in the boiling water, remove with a fine-mesh strainer, cool under cold running water, and let air-dry for an hour or so on a clean, dry dish towel.

Spread the miso around the pieces of kabocha, sprinkling in *shichimi togarashi* to taste, and pack in a resealable plastic bag. Store in the fridge for a few weeks, but start tasting after 1 week. When the kobocha has sufficiently softened, it is ready to eat. Carefully remove a slice or so from the miso and wipe before eating. If the miso starts to overwhelm the kabocha flavor, scrape off all of the miso and store in a clean bag. Reuse the miso pickling bed for making miso soups.

VARIATIONS: Any dense, flavorful winter squash could be substituted successfully here. Some slivered yuzu or Meyer lemon peel adds a bright note to the miso bed or, instead, can be sprinkled on the kabocha when serving.

In my mind, beans or peas and miso are a logical combination—perhaps because miso is made from mature soybeans. I like miso dressing on blanched spring snap peas and sautéed green beans flavored with sake-thinned miso. As an extension of that philosophy, I felt these green beans in miso made perfect sense.

green beans cloaked in miso SERVES 6

INGENMAME NO MISOZUKE

½ pound (225 g) thin green beans

1 tablespoon coarse white sea salt

4 tablespoons sake

1 cup (250 cc) brown rice miso

1 tablespoon slivered ginger

7-spice powder (*shichimi togarashi*, page XXXI)

Do not top or tip the green beans, but pick through them and discard any floppy or brown beans. Trim off any long stems to leave just a pretty little stem portion of about ⅛ to ¼ inch (3 to 6 mm). Rub the salt into the beans and let sit for 10 minutes in a fine-mesh strainer.

In the meantime, mash the sake into the miso and warm the mixture in a frying pan, stirring over low heat for 1 or 2 minutes, until fragrant and the miso smells a bit like beer. Cool.

Rinse the beans, align them on a clean kitchen towel, and roll up to dry. Smooth a thin layer of cooled miso in the bottom of a small enamel or plastic rectangular container. Arrange several green beans on top of the miso, smoothing more miso over the beans (you will still be able to see the beans poking through the miso). Continue making layers of green beans and miso until all the beans have been placed in the container. Finish with one last layer of miso. Store in the refrigerator overnight (or at least half a day) to mellow. Scrape off most of the miso before serving as a side dish to any Japanese or simple Western meal. Garnish with the slivered ginger and sprinkle with 7-spice powder before serving. Reuse the pickling miso for flavoring sautéed vegetables such as shishito peppers (page 85) or a rustic miso soup (page 80).

VARIATIONS: Wedges of green peppers, baby turnips with a half-inch of greens attached, thick slices of peeled lotus root, and Japanese cucumbers are also fantastic in this miso treatment.

I came up with this idea because apple pears seem to want something. Our town, Kamikawa-machi, is known for its apple pears, and we have our share during the summer season. The fruit is less about flavor as it is about the crisp, wet crunch that is so welcome in the height of our muggy summer. A half day in miso gives the apple pear slices a nice salty tang.

apple pears in miso SERVES 6
NASHI NO MISOZUKE

2 apple pears, about ¾
   pound (350 g) each

1 cup (250 cc) barley miso (page 72)

Ichimi togarashi (page XXXI)

Peel the apple pears, cut in half through the stem end, and quarter. Cut out the cores and slice into 1-inch (2.5-cm) wedges (measured at the thick end).

Spread the wedges with the miso, sprinkle on a little *ichimi togarashi*, and store in the fridge for 1 hour. Scrape off the miso, drop the apple pear in a clean container, and store in the refrigerator until serving time. Reserve the miso for cold summer soups (page 82), if you don't mind the chile pepper. Serve the apple pear slices with tea in the afternoon or before dinner with a cold beer.

VARIATION: It is possible to substitute a very sweet pale apple such as Golden Delicious for the apple pears.

Immediately after turning in my first book manuscript I emailed my editor to announce my next book plan: a preserving book. Her return mail: "Let's get this one done first!" (Wise words that I did not heed.) Before the editing process of my first book plunged me into a monumentally busy five months, I had Miura-san come out for some photo shoots. At one of the shoots I poked garlic in miso and subsequently forgot about it. For about one year. When I dug the garlic out, it was sublime. You don't have to wait one year, though I would suggest trying these every few months. You can keep them in a ginger jar on the counter or in the fridge, whichever works for you. I love miso as a pickling medium because you don't need to add anything to it and there are enough different types of miso to give you a variety in the pickling process. This miso pickling bed should not be reused for miso soup, but a dab of it in a Western stew could be all the salt you need—just a hint for that hidden taste. This garlic-infused miso is also fantastic dolloped on a hot bowl of rice or smeared on grilled eggplant.

garlic embedded in miso SERVES 6
NINNIKU NO MISOZUKE

4 heads of garlic

1 cup (250 cc) barley miso

Peel the garlic and separate into cloves. Pare off the root ends of the cloves. Smooth the miso into a ceramic, glass, or plastic container. Poke the cloves into the miso and leave for a month or so. Taste periodically. Store in the fridge or at room temperature. Scrape off the miso or wash the cloves before serving. Good as part of a pickling plate or with drinks before dinner.

VARIATION: Parboil the unpeeled garlic for 5 minutes before peeling and embedding in the miso. This will cut the pickling time down to about a week.

NEW GARLIC AND MISO

When I mentioned seasonal garlic in one of my recipes, a friend asked, "Garlic has a season?"

Oh, yes, everything has a season. We just may not see it, especially for those ubiquitous everyday ingredients like potatoes, onions, and garlic. But seasons they do have and their seasons should dictate how you use them.

As with many people who do not grow vegetables professionally, there are times when our fields are lean and we must buy from other farmers or make do eating negi every day (negi are Japanese leeks and are an almost year-round crop on our field). Family members tend to rebel, so we are lucky to have other organic grower friends in our area to turn to when we are between seasons. Late May is the most barren season of all and is called *hazakaiki* (literally "on the edge of the season"). Late winter and early spring vegetables have come and gone, while the early summer shoots are still struggling their way to maturity. Farmers who started their seeds in greenhouses are beginning to crop their vegetables, so I break some of my unwritten rules about waiting to buy edamame, tomatoes, or potatoes before ours are ready. I cook lunch for the kids at my immersion school Sunny-Side Up!, and the vegetables that Fukuda-san, Suka-san, and Iwata-san grow give me the essential inspiration and energy I need to create daily meals for those kids.

Garlic, though, is one of our crops that never manages to last a full year. So, no guilt there about buying locally. And by some lucky stroke of fate, a few farmers in the next town are growing rose garlic. I first read about rose garlic in the Seeds of Change catalog. I loved the sound of the small cloves with their purported delicate flavor. I'm more of a small-is-better kind of person, so don't buy into the gigantic fruit varieties that have been historically popular here in Japan. Tracking down Japanese heirloom seeds is getting easier, but twenty years ago it was nearly impossible. We ordered our seeds from Seeds of Change, and along with those seeds, a couple pounds of garlic. Too bad they didn't make it through the agriculture inspection.

As for our garlic "seeds," since I discovered those farmers growing rose garlic in a neighboring town, we have our own local source. Rose garlic appears in the beginning of June and is sold out by the end of the month, so every year I order about 10 kilos to get me through the year. The alternative is white elephant garlic from China, a bit pungent for my taste.

Over the years, I've tried various storage methods. Tadaaki always insisted on hanging the small crop of garlic that he grew under the eaves of the chicken coops. But the cloves turned to dust after several months and never made it to Christmas. Tadaaki completely ignored my logical advice, but not having grown the garlic, I had to shrug that off. I learned to use our homegrown garlic quickly, before it disintegrated. However, the local garlic I bought was mine to store as I liked. I tried refrigeration, but the air was too moist, and the garlic tended to sprout. Room temperature in the larder was not the answer either. Eventually, I found the garlic stayed best when packed loosely in thick American supermarket bags (rolled up, but not

sealed airtight) and left in the *kura*, a traditional storage house that stays at cellar temperature throughout most of the year. There are some mice that scamper about, and although they gnaw at the wine bottle foils, they don't get into the garlic. And these days, Tadaaki has given in about where I store his garlic as well: I keep it in a box in the garage.

Tadaaki grows garlic most years, though his crop is usually small and would be quickly depleted should I use it to feed the SSU! kids. I ration his garlic out bit by bit, usually only for salads constructed from our own baby lettuces. Also, the garlic bulbs we grow sometimes melt in the field, engulfed by monster weeds. In a fit of I-don't-know-what, Tadaaki decided to till the field where he had planted onions and garlic one year, so he cropped them early. Too early. To give Tadaaki his due, it was a miserable crop to begin with and probably not worth leaving in the field. Much nicer to gaze over the pristine, rich, brown dirt, nary a weed in sight, and begin one's summer planting with a clean canvas. Much more satisfying than a single scraggly line of alliums marring the vista.

I found Tadaaki's newly cropped garlic in a heap on the garage floor, mingled with some fresh-cropped onions. Moist earth still clinging to their bulbs, the garlic and onions were all in danger of going moldy. I separated the bulbs and dried the garlic a bit on the gravel in front of our house, heated by the late afternoon sun. I also brought a few teeny bulbs into the house and set to work peeling them to mash up with salt and put in my salad that evening.

But as I peeled, a thought came to me. Miso. These teeny little cloves, not much bigger than a one-year-old's pinky, must be sensational dipped in the organic brown rice miso I had in my fridge. I tried one. Juicy hot garlic against the earthy, rustic miso. I had to try another, and another, but finally forced myself to stop after about eight of those weency cloves. Before bed, I had to have just a few more though regretted it the next morning. I woke up to garlic on my brain. Over the course of the following two weeks, I was addicted to this little snack and had to keep myself in check. The only reason I stopped was because I ran out of that special miso and my everyday one was too light to be an effective foil to the garlic. I've been busy writing, so have not had time to make the trek up to Yamaki to buy more. The taste haunts me, and now I'm craving that miso with Tadaaki's new garlic. Perhaps I'll go today.

Whenever visitors come to town I always take them up to our local organic soy sauce, miso, and tofu place, Yamaki Jozo. If the shop is slow, the veteran staff members bring out some special tasters for our guests. I was astounded by how close to cheese tofu becomes when marinated in miso. This is a very old method that hearkens back to the days without refrigeration, when preservation was a necessary way of life.

tofu marinated in miso SERVES 6
TOFU NO MISOZUKE

1 (10.5-oz/300-g) block Japanese-
 style "cotton" tofu

1 tablespoon hon mirin (page XXXI)

2 tablespoons barley miso

½ tablespoon chiffonaded
 shiso leaves (optional)

Remove the tofu from the package, but do not throw away the tub in which it was sold. Set the tofu on a cutting board propped up at one end, angled into the kitchen sink for draining. Place another chopping board on top of the tofu and leave to press out the moisture for 1 hour. The board should not be so heavy that it smashes the tofu. Smooth the mirin into the miso and spread half of the mixture in the bottom of the saved tofu tub. Return the tofu to the miso-lined tofu tub. (Alternatively, you could use another plastic container with a lid if you prefer.) Spread the rest of the miso on top of the tofu and seal the whole package well with plastic wrap. Refrigerate for 3 days to fully cure. Remove the tofu from the tub and spoon onto small saucers for a salty snack with drinks before dinner. Garnish with the chiffonaded shiso leaves, if using.

VARIATIONS: Tofu also transforms brilliantly by marinating it in soy sauce, shoyu koji (page 202), or shio koji (page 192). Smear 1 teaspoon of the marinating medium in the bottom of the tofu container, replace the water-expressed tofu into the container, spread another teaspoon of the marinating medium on top of the tofu, and cover well. Refrigerate for 3 days and serve as you would the miso tofu. Garnish with complementary aromatics as you like.

At the advice of the barrel maker, I made the mistake of sprinkling a heavy layer of salt on my miso as a ploy to avoid mold. The extra salt layer was not a disaster, but the salt did leach down into the miso, leaving it a tad saltier than I would like. I scraped off the top few inches of the saltiest portion of the miso and stored it for future pickling projects. Perfectly boiled eggs with a slight orange center begged to be enveloped in miso. I had already been pickling my eggs in soy sauce, so knew the theory was sound. These eggs provide great balance to a pickle plate (Western or Japanese). Do not be put off by the large amount of miso required, as it can be reused for future egg-pickling projects.

miso-cured eggs SERVES 6
TAMAGO NO MISOZUKE

6 medium farm eggs, at
    room temperature

1 pound (450 g) miso

Set the eggs in a metal mesh strainer with a handle. Bring a medium-sized pot of hot water to a boil and lower the eggs gently into the boiling water. Cover and cook over high heat for 9 minutes. If the eggs are knocking about the sides of the pan, crack the lid and lower the heat a smidge. Place a medium-sized mixing bowl in the kitchen sink and fill with cold water. After the eggs have boiled for 9 minutes, scoop them out of the pan with the mesh strainer and plunge the eggs (still in the strainer) into the bowl of cold water in the sink. Immediately run a continuous stream of cold water until the eggs are cool. Or dump a tray of ice in the bowl to minimize water use. Once the eggs are well cooled, scoop them out of the water, shake off the excess drips, and tip onto a clean kitchen towel. Rap each egg smartly against the kitchen counter (go easy here, don't smash!) and peel carefully by slipping your thumb under the thin membrane between the egg white and shell. Fresh eggs will not peel easily. Some people age their eggs to ensure a smooth surface. I do not.

miso-cured eggs

Pat out about 2½ ounces (75 grams) of miso in your nondominant palm. Place 1 peeled egg on the miso and smooth the miso around to cover the whole surface of the egg. Nestle the eggs in a resealable plastic bag or storage container and refrigerate for 4 hours. After 4 hours, regardless if you are ready to serve or not, remove the miso from the eggs by scraping your thumb gently across the surface of the egg. Repack the miso into a resealable plastic bag and refrigerate for subsequent egg pickling. Store the eggs in the fridge until ready to serve. Cut in half lengthwise with a very sharp knife and wipe the knife each time between cuts to keep the inside free of miso.

VARIATIONS: For larger egg-pickling operations it is possible to spread a thin layer of miso in a plastic food storage container, arrange the cooked eggs side by side, then spread another layer of miso on top of the eggs. Depending on the amount of miso covering, it might be prudent to wait 6 hours before serving. Also, I would avoid stacking the eggs more than 2 high, as the bottom ones will crush under the weight of multiple layers. These 9-minute eggs are equally distinctive marinated in a scant ½ cup (100 cc) of soy sauce, shoyu koji, or shio koji (and certainly less time-consuming—though rotating the pickling bag is highly recommended to ensure even distribution of the pickling liquid). The shio koji version was told to me by Max Bernstein, a Japanophile Berkeleyite who has visited our farm a few times on his travels.

Right about now, you might be thinking it is time to get a yuzu tree. We use yuzu a lot. And why not in miso as well because yuzu goes with just about everything.

While the classic aromatic miso is made with *fuki no to* (page 342), a hauntingly bitter mountain vegetable bud, here yuzu makes an admirable alternative. Morita-san from Yamaki recommends adding koji to the miso. If possible, try to add the same kind of koji as the miso you use. I also prefer mirin over sake here. Any way you make it, this yuzu miso goes well spooned onto your bowl of rice or as a dipper for fresh vegetables.

yuzu miso MAKES 2 CUPS (500 CC)

4 medium-sized yuzu or
  3 Meyer lemons

4 tablespoons hon mirin (page XXXI)

1 cup (250 cc) flavorful miso
  (brown rice or barley)

¼ cup (125 cc) brown rice or
  barley koji, optional

Shave the peel off of the citrus with a very sharp knife. Stack into small piles and slice into thin slivers. Stir the mirin into the miso to make a smooth paste and cook in a frying pan over low heat to dissipate a bit of the alcohol. Stir in the citrus peel and koji, if using, while the miso is still warm. Use right away or store in the refrigerator indefinitely. However, the citrus will lose spark over time. Serve spooned on top of a bowl of steaming rice or as a dipper for crudités such as cucumber, celery, or green pepper.

VARIATIONS: Instead of yuzu, fold chopped, parboiled, and refreshed *fuki no to*, watercress, or wasabi stems into the sake-seasoned miso. Omit the koji.

CHOOSING, STORING, AND USING MISO

Pre-WWII most agrarian families made their own miso from the rice and soybeans they grew. The koji was obtained from the local koji maker and the salt from the vendor who sold staples that were not produced at home, such as konbu, katsuobushi, vinegar, and salt. The Kansai area (Kyoto/Osaka) prides itself on a lighter, more delicate cuisine; mountainous and northern areas such as Gifu and Tohoku favor dark misos and deeply flavored foods; whereas Greater Kanto (Tokyo) tends toward a midrange salty palate. In Kyushu, the southern island of Japan, the cuisine is characterized by very fresh fish and, inexplicably, sweetened soy sauce (not to my taste). Seaside areas use less miso than mountainous areas; instead, several abundant varieties of fish are fermented to make fish sauce (*shottsuru*, *ishiri*, *ishiru*, page 119) as the condiment of choice (besides soy sauce).

Misos are named for the area they come from (i.e., Saikyo or Hatcho) or the grain used to incubate the koji (brown rice, barley, or soybean). All miso is made from soybeans, koji-inoculated grain, salt, and bit of seed miso (the previous year's miso diluted in hot water). Inaka miso (country miso) is made from white rice koji and is perhaps named as such because it is the most-used miso in farm cooking. Town people and restaurants tend to use white miso. We have never bought white miso because our local miso company makes 2-year fermented organic misos, and white miso only requires a 30-day to maximum 3-month ferment. My new pal, Myoho Asari (The Kojiya Woman, page 194), "made" white miso in the studio during the course of a 1½-hour Fuji TV program in which we both appeared. She used a pressure cooker

to speed the cooking, and the miso contained a high percentage of white rice koji and salt. It was salty but good, though perhaps not quite "miso" in my mind.

As for selecting miso outside of Japan, there is good news and bad. The good news is that miso is widely available at all supermarkets, not just organic shops or Japanese markets. The bad news is that most of the miso I have come across is oxidized, or in any case darker than its Japanese equivalent. For instance, inaka miso is as dark as the brown rice miso sold in Japan, and the brown rice miso can be as dark as the dark chocolate brown soybean miso (*mame miso*). For a long time I puzzled at why cooks I respected hugely, like David Tanis (formerly co-chef of Chez Panisse, now of the *New York Times*) used white miso for my recipes they reviewed. It seemed so odd, since the country kitchen does not normally stock white miso. Finally I understood after buying and testing numerous American-made and Japanese-made misos sold in the U.S. The solution: Use white miso to lighten brown rice or barley miso. Inaka miso is only available as an imported product, though some companies such as Aedan in San Francisco are making a modified version. I keep a 1-kg bag of Yamaki inaka miso in the fridge and a 500-g bag of Yamaki brown rice miso; I also make both of those kinds of miso. My homemade brown rice miso is naturally sweeter than the commercially produced Yamaki counterpart; and my inaka miso is more compacted than the Yamaki one because I don't grind the beans by machine and I probably add less seed miso. I sometimes buy barley miso for variety, but seldom buy soybean miso because I am less

enamored of dark tastes (though am currently reconsidering this bias).

There is much talk about red miso in the States. I had never heard that term, so asked my husband what he considered to be red miso (*aka miso*). He tilted his head and told me he did not think of miso in those terms. The family always made just one kind of miso (country-style with white rice koji), and after his mother gave up producing miso for the family, he replaced it with Yamaki's inaka miso. Simple as that.

SHIRO MISO (WHITE MISO): is made with 1.5 to 2 times as much white rice koji as cooked soybeans and 4 to 5 percent salt, and is fermented for 1 to 3 months, depending on the salt content. White miso will commonly range from a light tan to yellow ochre. It is sometimes known colloquially as Saikyo miso from the well-known Kyoto miso style and is often thinned with sake and spread on gauze-wrapped fish to marinate before grilling (*saikyo yaki*).

INAKA MISO (COUNTRY MISO): The inaka miso we make under Matsuda-san's tutelage is made from 10 kg of cooked soybeans, 2 kg of rice koji, 1 kg of sea salt, and seed miso (about 75 cc of miso diluted in 600 cc hot water). Inaka miso is the most versatile miso and most commonly used in farm kitchens. Good in light salad dressings, as a flavoring for sautéed vegetables, and as a gentle pickling bed, inaka miso should be the color of coffee with milk.

GENMAI MISO (BROWN RICE MISO): is perhaps my favorite miso to eat raw with vegetables. Along with barley miso, it also makes a flavorful pickling bed. Genmai miso (page 51) is made in a similar way as inaka miso, but with brown rice instead of white and perhaps a higher percentage of rice koji. I recommended using brown rice miso in most of the recipes containing miso in my first book. However, I was subsequently dismayed to find out how dark the brown rice miso was in the States, even the one made at Yamaki and repackaged by Gold Mine Natural Food Co. I hope this oxidation issue in misos will resolve itself in the coming years. It won't be from lack of my trying! Genmai miso is generally the color of burnished milk chocolate and should not be dark, dark brown.

MUGI MISO (BARLEY MISO): resembles genmai miso in appearance and flavor profile, though has pleasant wheat overtones. Good raw or as a pickling bed; also excellent used to flavor hearty soups or stir-fries. Mugi miso is made in a similar method to inaka miso and genmai miso, with barley instead of rice and is about the same color as genmai miso, but just a hair darker.

MAME MISO (SOYBEAN MISO): is produced in the same way as the other standard misos (inaka, genmai, and mugi), but partially cooked soybeans (instead of rice or barley) are inoculated with koji and added to the cooked, smashed soybeans along with the salt and seed miso. Mame miso is a dark chocolate brown, almost black.

HATCHO MISO: is a miso made in Aichi prefecture by a specialized process dating back several centuries. The steamed beans are left to steep overnight and thus darken before being ground. After smashing, the beans are formed into large crosslike shapes to increase surface area, dusted with crushed barley, and inoculated with koji spores. The koji spores are allowed to propogate around the smashed beans and barley for three days before being mixed with salt and a small amount of water. The miso mash is packed in huge cedar vats, then the surface is covered with cloth and a wooden drop lid before being weighted with 3 tons (almost 3,000 kg) of stones piled on so carefully that the resulting pyramid is stable even during an earthquake. Hatcho miso is left undisturbed for two to three years to ferment and mellow. Because of its dark-nuanced profile, Hatcho miso lends itself to deep stews. Eden Organic sells true Hatcho miso repackaged as Hacho Miso [sic].

CHOOSING MISO: Top-quality Japanese misos are available through online macrobiotic sites such as Gold Mine Natural Food Co. or organic sites such as Mitoku Company, Ltd. Eden Foods, found at Whole Foods or small organic shops in the U.S., is also a good source for organic Japanese products. Clearspring in the UK is the main supplier of most of the best Japanese and organic foods in Europe. South River Miso Company sells their misos in Whole Foods and many organic shops across the United States—and is perhaps the best miso available at this time. Jorinji in Portland, Oregon, is (was?) also top-notch, but at the time of this printing, they may not still be in production due to variables outside of their control. Cold Mountain Miso in Southern California also looks promising, though I have not tasted their products. I liked the flavor of Miso Master (Blue Ridge Mountains, North Carolina) when I used it for some cooking classes in Texas, but found the consistency and color to be a bit dense for my purposes. Also pockets of artisanal miso makers, such as Aedan Foods (San Francisco), are popping up here and there at farmers' markets, so the miso scene outside of Japan is showing great promise (see Resources). Nonetheless, I encourage you to make your own!

STORAGE: Miso (and soy sauce, for that matter) keeps forever. Truly. But it does darken in both flavor and color. Press some cooking paper or plastic film on top of the surface of the miso to slow oxidation. If your miso is sold in a plastic bag, store in a clean resealable bag after opening. Change the outside bag periodically, as the inside bag does get to be a bit of a mess. Avoid repacking, however, because that will encourage oxidation.

In the springtime the fields are filled with flowering reseeded greens and I am deeply appreciative that the field is giving us back something so delicious yet so happenstance. Rapini seems to have a long growing season in the States from what I have observed in jaunts to farmers' markets in California and New York. I look for rapini or any flowering brassica that is perky and not too thick stemmed.

miso-mustard rapini SERVES 6
NANOHANA NO KARASHIMISO

1½ teaspoons Oriental mustard powder

1 bunch (about ¾ pound/ 350 g) fine-stemmed rapini

2 tablespoons sake

1 tablespoon brown rice vinegar

7½ tablespoons (150 cc) inaka miso (page 72)

1 tablespoon freshly shaved katsuobushi or 2 tablespoons *hanakatsuo* (page XXIX), for garnish

Muddle ¼ teaspoon water into the mustard powder and invert the bowl on the counter.

Pick over the rapini and pull off any brown or wilted strands. Slice off the very tips of the stem ends to refresh. Bring a large pot of hot water to a boil and place a large mixing bowl of ice water in the kitchen sink. Hold the rapini by the tops and lower the stems into the boiling water. Count to 5 or 10 (depending on the thickness of the stems), then drop the rapini into the pot and cook for 1 to 3 more minutes. Scoop out the greens with a fine-mesh strainer and drop them immediately into the cold water. If the hot rapini causes the temperature of the water to warm, add cold running tap water to compensate. Pull out a few connected strands at a time and squeeze down the length of the greens to press out excess water. Lay all of the squeezed rapini on a cutting board and slice into 2-inch (5-cm) lengths. Dump the rapini into a large bowl and scissor lightly with your fingers to separate the squeezed pieces.

Smash the mustard, sake, and brown rice vinegar into the miso. Scrape the miso-mustard over the rapini and gently toss to distribute. Cover the surface with plastic wrap and leave to mellow for about 1 hour. Alternatively, pack in a container and refrigerate overnight. Sprinkle with the shaved katsuobushi right before serving.

VARIATION: Also pretty (and delicious) garnished with some slivered yuzu or Meyer lemon peel instead of the katsuobushi.

In the spring of 2013 I made this from beautiful California walnuts and wild arugula I found at the Marin Civic Center Farmers' Market. I met Anthony Starelli at the market, and we wove our way through the vendors, searching out the day's most vibrant vegetables for a dinner at Saltwater Oyster Depot in Inverness. I had received an email from Nancy Beck, the owner of Osprey Peak B&B in Inverness: "Would you be interested in coming to Point Reyes, California, for a book signing?" Absolutely. Point Reyes has oysters and great cheese (home of Cowgirl Creamery): God's country in my book. Nancy offered a room in her Japanese-influenced B&B and also organized a dinner at Saltwater under the helm of the ever irrepressible and creatively forward-thinking Luc Chamberland. I used a five-year aged brown rice vinegar known as "black vinegar" (*kurosu*) made by Kakuida in Kagoshima. If your vinegar is too puckery, I would suggest sprinkling in a small amount of organic sugar to fix the balance.

wild arugula with walnut miso SERVES 6
RUKKOLA NO KURUMI-AE

1½ pounds (675 g) wild arugula

10 heaping tablespoons whole walnuts (about ¼ pound/100 g)

4 tablespoons brown rice miso

1½ to 2 tablespoons brown rice vinegar, depending on its intensity

Bring a large pot of hot water to a boil and place a large bowl of cold water in the kitchen sink. Throw the wild arugula into the pot of boiling water, push down under the surface of the water, and immediately scoop out with a wire-mesh strainer. Shake off the hot water and plunge the strainer into the cold water. Turn on the tap to introduce a steady stream of cold running water for a couple of minutes to cool the steaming greens. Once cooled, scoop the arugula out of the water and shake off. Squeeze the arugula by handfuls, but reserve the squeezed juices to lighten the walnut mixture. Lay the squeezed handfuls of arugula on a cutting board as you go, then chop roughly.

Drop the walnuts into a *suribachi* (Japanese grinding bowl) or mortar and smash well until the oil has exuded from the walnuts and a rough paste has formed. (Alternatively, the food processor can preform this task.) Add the miso and rice vinegar to the mortar and blend until creamy. Mash in a little of the squeezed juices to lighten the mixture, if needed. The walnut-miso mixture should be creamy white, not oily light brown. But go easy here—the beauty of this dish is in the interplay of the walnut-miso-vinegar. Adding too much liquid will dilute the trilogy. Dribble in just enough liquid so that the creaminess starts to come out.

Fold the roughly chopped arugula gently into the dressing by scooping from the bottom of the *suribachi* to dislodge the dressing and scissoring the greens with your fingers to distribute the dressing evenly. Serve in the *suribachi* or an attractive pottery bowl.

We are fortunate to have a constant supply of very fresh squid in Japan. If you have any doubts about the freshness of your squid, you might want to perform a boiling water–ice bath operation a couple of times by pouring a stream of boiling water over the squid for 10 seconds, then plunging in a bowl of ice water to refresh (*yudoshi*). Also squid is one sea creature that does not suffer much from freezing, so frozen squid is an alternative to fresh. Miso tends to burn, thus low-ember coals or far away from the broiler is best. Squid stands up to the miso and the long, slow cook more than fish, as its surface is naturally taut and becomes slightly caramelized. Utterly delectable as a before-dinner snack or appetizer. Also excellent cold the following day.

miso squid SERVES 6
IKA NO MISOZUKE

5 small fresh squid (about ⅓ pound/150 g each)

½ teaspoon fine sea salt

1 tablespoon sake

4 tablespoons brown rice or barley miso

1 to 2 small dried red chiles, sliced into fine rings

Clean your squid following the method described in Raw Squid in Coral (page 287). Blot well, drape across a dinner plate, and sprinkle all sides with the salt. Stash in the fridge for 1 to 2 hours uncovered.

Muddle the sake into the miso and spread over both surfaces of the squid bodies with a small rubber scraper; smooth around the tentacles (still attached at the top) with your fingers. Return the squid to the refrigerator for 2 or 3 hours more for a deep, dark taste. Grill slowly over low-ember coals or on a rack set in the third slot from the top of an oven broiler for about 5 minutes on each side. Julienne and eat as is for a before-dinner snack.

VARIATION: The laconic gentleman who hid behind dark glasses at the Wajima air-dried fish place (page 35) parted with his favorite way to make squid: Marinate in soy sauce for 30 minutes and grill. Simple. I like to serve it with a squeeze of yuzu or Meyer lemon.

MATSUDA-SAN: MENTOR, MOTIVATOR, FRIEND

Twenty years ago when Masashi Matsuda dropped into our midst, I resented him for eclipsing my husband. Matsuda-san was like a whirling dervish, kicking up a huge dust storm of group projects. He had come from Tokyo to build a small organic mayonnaise factory, and bringing all of that dammed-up creative energy from years of city living, he dove into country life with a vengeance.

Matsuda-san appears in *Japanese Farm Food* in the photo montage from our annual Edamame Cropping Slow Food event at his place in the hills above us. He was the guy sporting traditional indigo garb tending the iron cauldron of boiling edamame. He has a shock of white-grey hair and a well-trimmed beard to match. But mostly you remember his welcoming smile.

In his heyday, besides the very successful mayonnaise company, Matsuda-san was running an organic café and a soba restaurant. The soba restaurant was top-notch; nonetheless it tipped the scales on his busy barometer and he let that go first. The café morphed from an organic lunch spot to a brick oven pizzeria, but eventually it too went the way of the soba restaurant. The hand-constructed brick oven remains, and Matsuda-san organizes pizza-making parties there when he's in the mood. In one of the first years after he arrived, Matsuda-san bought a traditional storage building (*kura*) from Kirin beer in some northern area, relocated it, and rebuilt it with friends

following the traditional building practice of walls made from a bamboo frame, filled with straw and surfaced with earth. The *kura* housed the café and now serves as a clubhouse for our various soy sauce– and miso-making events.

These days Matsuda-san looks less to building businesses than to increasing his quality of life and the quality of life of others. He has a great interest in horses, so in 2004 built stables for native Japanese horses (*dosanko* from Hokkaido and a Kishu horse from central Honshu) in the hills nearby his mayonnaise company and started a horse co-op for members to share exercising and care of the horses. It is always on my list to join. I suppose I need to take a lesson or two from Matsuda-san about setting priorities and making time for leisure.

Although Matsuda-san's tornado-like energy eventually calmed to an even breeze, he continues to make his own levain, natto, pickles, koji, miso, soy sauce, *doburoku* (homemade sake, strictly illegal), and beer. He grows the soybeans and wheat for our soy sauce–making group; and also organizes the miso-making cooperative by providing the space, the beans, the homemade koji, and the sea salt. He continues to be an essential source of inspiration and know-how for all of us in this locale. Without Matsuda-san I would be rudderless in this country life. He generously offers the knowledge of a country grandma without the added family baggage. He is a kind and supportive friend.

I love the idea of flavoring this soup with a veil of miso—its very lightness compelling you to pick up the bowl and slurp the broth in between bites of softened vegetables. Inaka miso (literally "country miso") is made from white rice, so paler in color and slightly milder than brown rice miso. It is the Japanese farm kitchen's daily miso in our area. If you have access to sake lees (page 188), then by all means measure a tablespoon or so of them into a bowl and whisk in some of the broth to soften before adding the sake lees to the soup.

country miso and vegetable soup SERVES 4 TO 6

INAKA NO MISO SHIRU

1 medium carrot, about
    ¼ pound (115 g)

¼ medium daikon, about
    ¼ pound (115 g)

1 medium negi (or fat spring onion)

2½ cups (600 cc) Katsuobushi
    Dashi (page 253)

1½ tablespoons organic inaka miso

1 finely chopped thin
    scallion, for garnish

Finely slivered peel from 2 small
    yuzu or 1 Meyer lemon

Cooked Japanese rice, for serving

Scrub the carrot and daikon but do not peel unless the skins look tough or blemished. Halve the carrot lengthwise, cut into ⅛-inch (4-mm) half-moons, and dump into a small bowl. Slice the daikon lengthwise into quarters, cut into ⅛-inch (4-mm) thin wedges, and put into a medium-sized bowl. Peel off any discolored outside layers from the negi and slice off the bottom root and dark green tops (reserve in the fridge for another dish such as Western stocks). Cut the white or pale green portion into 1½-inch (3-cm) pieces. Toss the negi pieces into the bowl with the daikon.

Heat the dashi in a largish saucepan until it comes to a gentle simmer. Slide the carrot pieces into the simmering dashi and cook for 3 minutes over medium heat. Drop in the negi and daikon as well and cook for another 3 minutes.

Measure the miso into a medium-sized soup bowl and scoop in a dollop of broth. Whisk to blend, then dip the bowl back into the soup, swishing around a little to capture all of the miso adhering to the side of the bowl. Ladle into generous-sized soup bowls, sprinkle with the scallion and yuzu peel, and serve immediately with a bowl of rice and one or two other vegetable dishes for a light supper. (N.B.: Once the miso is added, the soup should be removed from the heat source.)

VARIATIONS: Substitute a large handful of napa cabbage cut from a quartered head, sliced crosswise into 1½-inch (3-cm) pieces, for the negi (or just add it into the mix). Add after the daikon has simmered for 3 minutes, cook for 2 minutes more, then serve. Also lovely with a poached egg: Bring 2 cups (500 cc) water with 1 tablespoon brown rice vinegar to a bare simmer in an 8-inch (20-cm) frying pan. Crack 6 room temperature eggs, each into its own small bowl. Slip the eggs one by one into the barely simmering water and cook for about 10 minutes, or until the whites are just set. Lift the eggs out with a slotted spoon onto a dinner plate. Slide a poached egg into each bowl of soup before garnishing with the scallion and yuzu.

One day I was chatting before lunch with the very kind president of Yamaki Jozo, Tomio Kitani (page 106). We were talking miso when all of a sudden Kitani-san began to describe his grandmother's cold miso soup. I could not wait for the weather to turn warm to try it. Kitani-san told me his grandmother's soup was only adorned with sliced cucumbers and maybe a little chopped negi. I thought a bit of *myoga* might be nice as well and maybe some ground roasted sesame to give it a speck of richness. Serve this when you are looking for a cold bite to cool the sweat dripping from your brow. This soup can be as simple as just cucumbers or as "complex" as the addition of *myoga* and sesame.

cold miso soup
with cucumber and myoga SERVES 6
KYURI TO MYOGA NO HIYASHI MISO SHIRU

1 small Japanese cucumber,
  about ¼ pound (100 g)

2 *myoga* buds (page 343, optional)

4 tablespoons brown rice miso

2½ cups (600 cc) Katsuobushi
  Dashi (page 253), chilled

1 tablespoon finely chopped scallion,
  green and white parts included

Slice the cucumber into thin matchsticks and divide among 6 miso soup bowls. Cut the *myoga* buds in half lengthwise, if using. Lay the cut side down on the chopping board and slice the *myoga* thinly. Distribute among the miso soup bowls.

Measure the miso into a small bowl and whisk in a splash of the chilled dashi to thin the miso to a loose paste. Scrape the miso into the chilled dashi and whisk to incorporate. Ladle the cold miso soup into the bowls with the cucumbers and *myoga*, if using. Garnish with the chopped scallion and serve immediately.

VARIATION: Adding ground toasted sesame seeds will bring a richer, deeper note to the soup. In this case, set a small frying pan over high heat and toss in 1 tablespoon sesame seeds when you can feel the warmth rise from the surface of the pan. Toast the sesame seeds until they start to pop and are fragrant. Be careful not to burn, though. You may have to lift the pan off the heat and also shake the pan as you are toasting. Pour into a *suribachi* (Japanese grinding bowl) and grind to a flaky consistency with a *surikogi* (Japanese pestle). Alternatively, pulse in a clean coffee or nut grinder.

The key here is to slice the carrots with a razor sharp knife to obtain the very thin julienne. I tend to dress carrot salads a bit more heavily than other salads because they can stand up to the vinaigrette, whereas leafy greens get soggy. I am particularly fond of this combination and make it a lot for the kids at my immersion school, Sunny-Side Up!, because carrots have several growing seasons and our friends produce extremely flavorful carrots that are never woody.

carrot salad with miso vinaigrette SERVES 6

NINJIN SARADA MISO VINEGURETTO

3 cups (750 cc) finely julienned carrots, about ⅔ pound/300g

2 tablespoons julienned scallions or spring onions (white and light green parts)

1½ tablespoons inaka miso (page 72)

1½ tablespoons brown rice vinegar

3 tablespoons best-quality canola oil

Throw the carrots and scallions into a large bowl. Muddle the miso with the vinegar and whisk in the oil. Scrape the miso vinaigrette over the carrots and scallions and toss until well distributed. Serve with a simple preparation such as sake-steamed fish or Shio Koji–Grilled Pork (page 201). Always serve salads from the bottom, since the dressing tends to pool in the bottom of the bowl. This is still delicious the next day for lunch.

VARIATIONS: Substitute julienned daikon or turnip with a small handful of chiffonaded bitter green tops instead of the carrots and scallions. Finely shredded cabbage also goes well with the miso vinaigrette—in this case perhaps some slivered citrus peel would make a nice aromatic instead of the scallion. You could also toss in or garnish with a handful of *mitsuba* (page 343) leaves.

Shishito peppers are all the rage in Northern California and easily obtainable. I love them charred in oil, served with a sprinkling of salt, but the salty, earthy miso treatment here complements the bitterness of the peppers. A bit of heat from the chile and pop from the ginger make this a can't-get-enough dish. Padrón peppers can be substituted, but omit the chile, as Padróns are plenty hot on their own.

shishito peppers sautéed with miso and ginger SERVES 6

SHISHITO NO ABURA MISO

4 or more teaspoons sake

4 teaspoons brown rice miso

¾ pound (350 g) shishito peppers

1 tablespoon organic canola oil

1 small dried japones or ½ arból chile pepper, torn in thirds

2 teaspoons slivered ginger

In a small bowl, mash the sake into the miso. The resulting paste should be loose enough to slurp around the peppers, so if your miso is unusually stiff, splash in a bit more sake.

Leave the stems intact on the shishito peppers, but snip off the discolored tips of the stems to refresh. Heat the oil with the dried red chile pepper in a large wok over medium heat until the pepper turns bright red. Throw in the shishito peppers and toss to coat with oil. Scatter in the ginger and toss gently for several minutes, until the peppers start to jump and pop and small blisters appear here and there on their skins. Remove the pan from the heat, scrape in the miso-sake mixture, and stir quickly with a flat wooden spoon so the peppers are coated evenly but the miso does not burn from the heat of the pan. Slide into a serving bowl as soon as the miso is incorporated, since the peppers will deflate and lose some vibrancy if left in the hot pan. Serve with drinks before dinner or alongside Soy Sauce–Soused Steak (page 111).

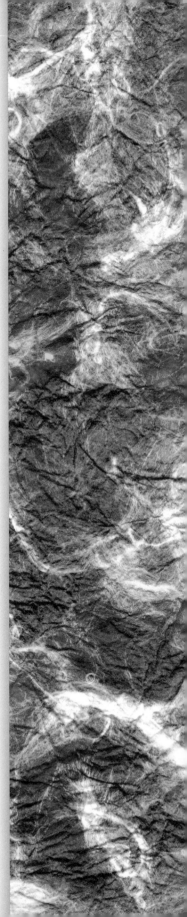

3

soy sauce

SOY SAUCE RECIPES

BROCCOLI IN SOY SAUCE WITH RED PEPPER | 92

WASABI LEAVES IN SAKE AND SOY | 98

CUCUMBERS SOUSED IN SOY | 101

MOUNTAIN YAM IN SPICY SOY | 102

EGGPLANT PICKLED IN SOY MUSTARD | 103

SOY SAUCE–CURED SALMON ROE | 104

GINGER-SOY PORK SANDWICHES | 109

SOY SAUCE–SOUSED STEAK | 111

TOMATO, ONION, AND PEPPER SALAD | 113

While I thought I knew how soy sauce was made, I actually only had a vague glimmering until I began writing about Japanese food and the artisanal producers around Japan. The cheapest soy sauces are made by mixing hydrolyzed vegetable protein with caramel color, corn syrup, and salt; but all brewed or so-called natural soy sauce contains salt, water, and koji. No mistake there. However, large companies use a base of processed defatted soybeans (脱脂加工大豆, *dasshi kako daizu*) instead of whole soybeans and sometimes wheat bran instead of whole wheat berries to create their soy sauce. In Japan, the labeling is strict about whether or not the soybeans are whole, though less so about wheat (no differentiation between wheat bran or wheat berry, just unhelpfully listed as "wheat"). More discouraging is that Kikkoman and Yamasa, the two largest Japanese soy sauce brands, do not disclose the use of processed defatted soybeans on their U.S. Web sites or labels (although Yamasa kindly gave me the information when I sent a query). Both companies purport to still be producing soy sauce in the timeheld traditions of their over 400-year history, in actuality the truth is a bit more blurred. Romantic photos on their Web sites of wooden tanks holding soy sauce mash (*moromi*, page 114) only lull the customer into believing a half-truth: Yes, the soy sauce is made with a soybean product and wheat product, but most of these companies' soy sauces are no longer made in the traditional method. For one thing, there are no more cedar barrels to be had (so virtually impossible for U.S.-based soy sauce companies to be using them). The shape-shifting bothers me in this world, where we need to trust our food producers.

CHOOSING JAPANESE-STYLE SOY SAUCE: The good news is that the majority of major-brand Japanese soy sauces are naturally brewed (as opposed to HPV/chemically produced products). However, there is a world of difference between the 18- to 24-month fermentation process, which involves two summers (the main fermentation period) at ambient temperature and a 3- or 6-month soy sauce (to which stronger spore strains have been added) that has been manipulated by temperature controls used to force the soy sauce into a longer false summer of fermentation. But of course the greatest difference between artisanal soy sauce (*shoyu*) and most large-producer soy sauce is that *shoyu* is made from 100% soybeans (with the best makers using 100% organic Japanese soybeans; one rank down, using nonorganic Japanese soybeans; next rank down, organic U.S. soybeans; the lowest in the artisanal category, nonorganic U.S. soybeans). The soy sauce I recommend without reservation is made by our local organic soy sauce company, Yamaki Jozo (page 106), and is repackaged by Ohsawa Japan as Nama Shoyu. This soy sauce is readily available in the U.S. at Japanese grocery stores, organic shops, and Amazon.com. However, Nama Shoyu is three times as expensive as Kikkoman or Yamasa Marudaizu Soy Sauce (*marudaizu* = "whole bean"), and twice as expensive as Organic Kikkoman Soy Sauce, Kikkoman Tamari, and Organic Yamasa Tamari (all whole bean). N.B.: Tamari, which traditionally was the puddled syrupy liquid that pooled up naturally on the surface of the miso, is now man-made by fermenting soybeans with a small amount of or no wheat. I do not fuss around with low-sodium or so-called light soy sauce (*usukuchi shoyu*), which is actually higher in salt content than conventional soy sauce. Considering the small amount of soy sauce you might be using at any one time, weighed against the pivotal importance of that base seasoning, it makes sense to spend more on a better product (1 tablespoon of the least expensive Kikkoman or Yamasa soy sauce made from defatted soy grits will cost you 14¢; whole bean accelerated fermentation types, 22¢; and artisanal Nama Shoyu, 44¢ per tablespoon). Naturally, some of the soy sauce sousing/dousing/pickling projects will require more than a tablespoon, so do the math and make your decision. Even in Japan, many people have no idea that their favorite brands of soy sauce are made from defatted soy grits instead of whole soybeans.

OHSAWA NAMA SHOYU: This is our local organic soy sauce that is fermented in cedar barrels then blended to produce a beautiful, well-balanced, deeply nuanced soy sauce. It does not get any better. Made responsibly by the Kitani family from organic soybeans grown by some of our closest farmer friends. Strongly recommended.

EDEN SOY SAUCE: Eden is perhaps the last single-owner natural food company in the U.S. and Eden sources many of their traditional organic Japanese ingredients directly from Japan, including this 2-year soy sauce fermented in cedar casks. Also highly recommended.

BLUEGRASS SOY SAUCE: This bourbon barrel–aged Kentucky soy sauce is absolutely delicious and perfect on salads. Tasted side by side with the Ohsawa Nama Shoyu, I found some herbaceous notes that I could do without. But this is being very picky. I use this soy sauce for my events in the U.S. when I cannot find Nama Shoyu, and I am delighted to do so, since it is American made.

SAN-J SOY SAUCE: I have used this soy sauce in a pinch when cooking in the States. For me, it lacks flavor and character. Japanese participants in my classes agreed, but you decide.

KIKKOMAN ORGANIC SOY SAUCE: Not a bad choice for people on a budget.

YAMASA ORGANIC TAMARI: Responsibly made and a good alternative for a gluten-free soy sauce.

OHSAWA ORGANIC TAMARI: Twice as expensive as the Yamasa, but worth the extra money if you can spare it. Gluten free.

Once I started making my own soy sauce I had a revelation about its use. Artisanally made, 2-year fermented soy sauce is dark, rich, and deep with flavor. Homemade, while quite delicious, is typically thinner, since we add hot water to the mash in order to adjust the salt and to aid the soy sauce pressing process. In the farm kitchen, we often omit dashi in many preparations and just use soy sauce alone for dipping or drizzling. Here, I decided to cut the powerful soy sauce with a bit of dashi to soften the pickle. It is not strictly orthodox, but one thing I have learned in my travels around the outlying areas of Japan: Every area has its own approach to the most simple dishes and there are even variations between each cook within that locale. The hot pepper is a key ingredient, so do not omit. The addition of katsuobushi is purely mine.

broccoli in soy sauce with red pepper SERVES 6
BUROKKORI NO SHOYUZUKE

3 small heads of broccoli
(about 2 pounds/900 g)

6 tablespoons Katsuobushi
Dashi (page 253)

8 tablespoons soy sauce

3 small dried red chile peppers,
coarsely crumbled

2 tablespoons freshly
shaved katsuobushi or 3
tablespoons *hanakatsuo*
(page XXIX), for serving

Bring a medium-sized pot of hot water to a boil and place a bowl of cold water in the kitchen sink. Trim the fibrous bottom portion off the stems and discard. Lop the stem off of the top flower cluster and free up bite-sized broccoli florets by slicing off the remaining top stem. Depending on the toughness of your broccoli, peel the skin off the tender stem portion you did not discard. Cut the stems into pieces roughly the same size as the florets or a bit smaller.

Drop the broccoli into the pot of boiling water and cook for 3 minutes. Scoop the pieces out with a strainer and dump them immediately into the cold water. Turn on the tap and run cold water into the bowl to cool the broccoli stems and florets. Once cooled, drain in the strainer, then pat dry with a clean kitchen towel.

Toss the broccoli with the dashi, soy sauce, and red chile peppers in a medium-sized bowl. Press a drop lid or piece of plastic wrap on top of the surface and let sit macerating at room temperature for 30 minutes. Best freshly made, though still good if stored in the refrigerator for a few days. Drain the marinade before storing since the broccoli will discolor. This fiery bite is a welcome addition to a bento or the perfect complement to a heady glass of local beer. Spoon into a small bowl and sprinkle with katsuobushi before serving.

VARIATION: For a livelier version, use 1 tablespoon of slivered citrus peel (such as yuzu or Meyer lemon) instead of katsuobushi.

MAKING SOY SAUCE

I jumped into a soy sauce–making community the day they were pressing their first batch. After the fall soybean and wheat harvest, the beans and grains are stored for making the year's miso, soy sauce, noodles, and breads. In the early spring, soybeans are steamed, cooled, mixed with roasted wheat, and inoculated with koji to carefully culture over the course of three days in a controlled environment. After three days, the temperature of the cultured soybeans and wheat has risen, so they must be shocked with salt (*shiokiri*) to slow fermentation. We sing songs to the beans as we dig our hands into the warm pile of soybeans covered with a dusky coating of cultured koji. The final step is dumping the cultured soybeans into barrels (food-grade plastic or wood) and adding spring water. When this is left in the hot Japanese summer sun, fermentation happens quickly. Nine months later we press the soy sauce.

When I finished my manuscript of *Japanese Farm Food* in early September 2011, I felt a bit discouraged about the future of Japan. The weight of caring too much pressed down on me: I saw old houses being destroyed, trees being cut down to make way for ugly buildings or more grave plots, old farm implements being jettisoned because they were not valued, and food traditions being passed over for lack of appreciation or understanding. Even my husband was sometimes buying meat and vegetables at the supermarket when it was expedient. In a desire to leave an optimistic note in the book, I wrote about community. That sense of community has brought me great comfort and hope for the future of this local area and for the future of Japan at large. So in

a way, the glimmering of hope I dug out of the rubble became a reality.

One huge turning point came in the form of the soy sauce–making community I joined in February 2012. After all the years of organizing Slow Food events for members that spread out from our local area to Tokyo, I had grown weary of being the main impetus for these community gatherings. Becoming a passive member was gloriously freeing. I loved being told when to show up and what to bring. I loved not being in charge. And I deeply appreciate the time and energy that Yuka and Kazushi Murakami, the young couple who manage the soy sauce–making community, put into the group. But perhaps more than that, I gain energy from their youthful excitement to learn more and more about all portions of the miso- and soy sauce–making process. They have been fixated on how to grow koji for making miso or soy sauce, and, in turn, I am galvanized to do the same. It is through Yuka's encouragement that I am fermenting my own soy sauce in a wooden barrel. The rings of my community have circled out like Venn diagrams, and that extended community has made this next phase in my life and this current book possible.

A central figure in our life remains Masashi Matsuda (page 78). Matsuda-san continues to be one of Tadaaki and my closest friends and colleagues, but he has also extended his mentorship from miso-making weekends (page 49) to growing soybeans and wheat for the soy sauce community. While group members do support the growing process—planting, weeding, cropping, and sorting—nonetheless, the lion's

share falls on Matsuda-san and some of his close acolytes. Still, it is encouraging to see the effects of his mentorship through the young men and women he has encouraged and taught farming practices to as they return to assist in the times when group labor is needed. I go when I can, though the summers prove difficult, so I never have gotten to any of the weeding "parties." I hate not pulling my weight, but our summer fields, summer pickling, and summer programs at Sunny-Side Up! leave me with little room to do much else.

We ship "our" soybeans and wheat to a small soy sauce producer in Nagano prefecture who cultures the grains for us. I tagged along on a trek up to Nagano one year to fetch the bags of newly cultured soybean and wheat from the soy sauce producer. It was a 4-hour drive. We pulled into a minuscule parking lot next to a coffee shop and unfolded ourselves from the car. The shop was located directly across the street and the façade told the story of its long history. Seeing these 80-year-old buildings still in use is reassuring, yet there is always that uncomfortable feeling in the pit of my stomach: Will it still be there next year, or will they tear down and modernize? As we filed into the shop, the ancient soy sauce barrels, burnished from decades of use, caught my eye. The twelve of us could barely fit in the shop, so I wormed my way forward to hear what was being said. I wish I had not.

The forty-something soy sauce maker was berating us in a low voice for the difficulty it took to deal with our soybeans and wheat. He did not like that the wheat had some chaff or debris. Perhaps he was more used to large-scale harvested wheat berries rather than ones from a small farm that used imperfect machines for separating wheat from chaff. Heads bowed, we took the lecture onto our shoulders, apologized profusely, and silently hefted the bags across the street. Despite the irritation he put into the soybeans, we were able to press some of the best soy sauce to date from the mash that year. I suppose the "laying on of hands" by the members when they came to perform their regular stirring duties helped put the love back into the soybean mash (*moromi*, page 114). I dipped my whole arm into my own *moromi*, so was able to replace the negative with positive energy too. Unfortunately, Matsuda-san is still not set up to culture more than enough soybeans and wheat for his private stash of soy sauce, so we will continue to use the Nagano maker for now.

Back on the road, we caravaned through the Nagano countryside before turning off onto a dirt road that led to a B&B operated by a macrobiotic cooking teacher. She had generously offered her garden as a place for us to mix salt into the koji-cultured soybeans and wheat to stop the mixture from generating heat that could damage the koji. The culturing of koji is quite specific: Once the spores have grown in a warm, moist environment for three days, the koji-inoculated grain must be cooled down immediately lest it lose its crucial flavor-inducing properties. We spread blue plastic sheets brought for the task and dumped out one bag at a time of the inoculated beans. That day we would only mix in half of the required salt, since the other members who could not

come with us would want to dip their hands into the beans as well. The beans were slightly furry, almost frosted with the koji, and gave off a heady kind of musty aroma that made me want to keep tasting them. So I did. While the others tore open bags of Vietnamese salt that year, I had brought Japanese sea salt sourced through my farmer friend, Junko Suka. It did not seem to make sense to go to the trouble of making our own soy sauce from locally grown soybeans and wheat only to douse it with Vietnamese salt. But that's where my mind goes. With the bags all repacked into the cars, we perched on the wooden porch and overturned tree stumps to eat bentos we had brought with us before hitting the road for the drive home.

The following day I packed the SSU! kids in station wagons and drove up to Matsuda-san's house to finish the "salt cutting" (shiokiri) before sharing a communal lunch. We were told to wear masks, but I ignored that helpful piece of advice. For one thing, I relish breathing in the koji-inoculated dust that flies up while we mix in the salt, and for another thing, masks make me claustrophobic. I encouraged the kids to taste the beans—which they all pronounced "yummy!"—and was particularly proud that those little Japanese kids could experience such a quintessentially traditional food culture while attending English immersion school. The lovely juxtoposition of it all tickled me. We dumped the soybean mixture back into the paper feed bags and carted them back to my house along with a plastic tub full of spring water that Matsuda-san's strapping acolytes had fetched from the mountains. My wooden barrels had not yet arrived, so we sloshed the soybeans and

spring water into the plastic tub for a few days. Perhaps not the typical field trip, but it was nonetheless fun and educational to boot.

I had entered the soy sauce group at the tail end of the first year during the pressing event. The second year I went along for the ride with everyone else, sharing in the tasks of mixing the soy sauce mash (moromi) throughout the year (more frequently in summer) by dumping each full barrel, one at a time, into an empty barrel, thus ensuring a true mix from bottom to top. I use the term "barrel" loosely, as in fact they were yellow food-grade plastic tubs. By the third year I had developed the self-confidence to strike out on my own. My wood barrel stood in front of my house all year long, a proud testament to my accomplishment. Actually, I did not do much to care for it. I stirred the moromi mash when I thought about it and added water a few times as well when I felt it was evaporating too much. Although not spring water, it did come from our family well. The mash became completely mine in its imperfection—an accurate reflection of who I am. I heard from my friend Yoshie that the group's 2013 soy sauce is the best yet. I have yet to compare mine with theirs, but shall. In any case, it gave me deep pleasure to share the evolution of the moromi mash with the SSU! kids and to be able to give foreign or city-dwelling guests a taste of the fermenting mash. I wondered and fretted a bit at why my beans were not disintegrating like they do at Yamaki, and consequently decided to only press half of the moromi in the winter of 2013 and leave the rest to ferment for two years. I also mashed the beans a bit to hasten the softening. Even bottle aging changes the flavor of the soy sauce, since it is alive, so I eagerly anticipate a whole barrel two-year fermentation, starting with my 2014 soy sauce, which will be pressed in 2016. Luckily the barrel maker (page 54) sent me an extra barrel or two in thanks, for which I will keep him supplied with soy sauce and miso.

The soy sauce presser (page 99) called me one night in the early winter of 2013 to apologize for not being able to come as scheduled and that he had rescheduled when I would be out of the country. He had double booked. Touched, I felt some responsibiity to live up to the task. That year, Matsuda-san had commissioned a local furniture maker to build him a wooden soy sauce pressing apparatus (*shibori fune*). I attended the pressing event at Matsuda-san's place and felt I could do it on my own with some help from my Sunny-Side Up! teachers, Alyssia and Alice. I invited the SSU! kids and Fuji TV. We felt the lack of adults, especially since the pressing mechanism was missing from the apparatus (due to a design flaw that was being repaired by the builder). However, Tadaaki rigged up a method to press using gravity and the slow weight of a grinding stone that he hung from the end of a wooden pole, which acted as a lever. The weight frightened me, as the children, focused on the soy sauce dribbling out, did not seem to heed the possible danger of the several-hundred-pound weight. We could barely keep them away from the steady stream of light brown, salty, delightfully funky elixir. Actually, we encouraged them to stick their fingers in to grab as many tastes as they liked. It was highly addicting!

When Tadaaki and I were first married, we still went foraging in the woods for wild berries, mushrooms, and wasabi. Tadaaki had a special spot off of a road in the hills above us where he had found wasabi growing by a mountain stream. It takes wasabi rhizomes many years to develop in the wild, so the rhizomes we were able to gather were never much fatter than my pinky. But we could find a copious amount of leaves and stems, which we brought home and pickled. (I first fell in love with this pickle at Kozushi in Kumagaya, my favorite sushi shop, whose master is an inspired pickle maker.) Our foraging days have, for the most part, come and gone, but occasionally we get the urge for wasabi leaf and stem pickles, so return to our secret spot. In the States, wasabi stems and leaves are available through Frog Eyes in Oregon (see Resources).

wasabi leaves
in sake and soy MAKES 1 POUND (500 G)
HA-WASABI NO TSUKEMONO

1 pound (500 g) wasabi
  leaves and stems

½ cup (125 cc) best soy sauce

½ cup (125 cc) sake

Freshly shaved katsuobushi,
  for serving (optional)

Position a large bowl of ice water in the half of the kitchen sink that is away from the drain and bring a teapot of water to a boil over high heat. Pick through the wasabi stems and leaves: Pare off and discard any brown or black portions, including any discolored stem ends. Place a wire-mesh strainer in the other half of the sink that contains the drain and nestle the cleaned leaves into the strainer. Pour the boiling water over the stems and leaves in a continuous stream for about 10 seconds. Set the teapot back on the stove to get it out of the way. Immediately pick up the strainer, shake off the excess hot water, and plunge it into the ice water bath. (This process is called *yudoshi*.) When the wasabi stems and leaves are cool to the touch, scoop a handful out and squeeze gently. Drop onto a clean kitchen towel as you go. After all of the stems and leaves have been removed from the water and squeezed, roll them up in the towel for one last chance to remove water. Lay the stems and leaves on a cutting board, cut off the end tips, and slice into 1-inch (2.5-cm) lengths.

Drop the cut stems and leaves into a resealable gallon-sized freezer bag and pour in the soy sauce and sake. Slosh around to distribute and store in the refrigerator for 24 hours to absorb the pickling solution. Scoop out some leaves and stems with a slotted spoon and serve in a small, pretty bowl to add a welcome spicy note to any kind of cold collation, either Western or Japanese. Sprinkle with shaved katsuobushi, if using, right before serving.

THE SOY SAUCE PRESSER

We wound our way up the steep mountain road that etches a path through the hills above our house. The email had said: "Wear boots and an apron; bring a scarf and a lunch." I had thrown together sandwiches for photographer Miura-san and me, not thinking about the soy sauce we would be pressing. Japanese-style bentos would have made more sense. The steeper the climb, the cooler the air felt. I had heard about this soy sauce–pressing event from my ex-student, now close friend, Yoshie Takahashi. Yoshie is part of the younger set of semihippie types that live up in the mountain towns close to us. She has spent quite a bit of time working in Africa and appreciates a simpler way of life in a setting even more rural than our township, Kamikawa-machi.

The pressing site was an abandoned mountain school that had been taken over by Yuka and Kazushi Murakami. They board a small group of Tokyo kids who attend the local elementary and junior high school. Yuka and Kazushi also manage the soy sauce–making cooperative to which I belong and they had organized this pressing event.

As we were milling about, a minipickup pulled up to the old school. Out jumped Yozo Iwasaki, the soy sauce presser, clad in purple rain gear and a wool cap. He set about removing the blue tarp that battened down the equipment he had brought for our event. Iwasaki-san seemed diverted by my efforts to assist in the unloading of his truck, as some of the various bits and pieces needed for setting up the soy sauce–pressing apparatus were heavy—very. He had also schlepped from Nagano the hollowed-out drum can and iron cauldron we would need to

first heat the water we add to the soy sauce mash (*moromi*, page 114) and to later pasteurize the pressed soy sauce. As the day meandered along, it became patently clear that Iwasaki-san was completely comfortable chatting with a foreigner (in fact, it turned out we had friends in common). I stuck close by his side most of the day because I wanted to learn as much as I could from a true countryman. Also, we cared about the same traditional Japanese cultural practices, and he too lamented their loss. Or maybe I just found his twinkling-eyed amusement at all of our clumsy efforts to be refreshing.

SOY SAUCE PRESSING

- Stir hot water into the *moromi* (fermented soybean mash) to bring the heat up a bit and to thin to the desired consistency and 18% salinity.

- Scoop the diluted *moromi* into hemp or thick cotton bags (*shibori bukuro*).

- Fold the edges of the bag under itself and lay flat in the wooden trough of the soy sauce–pressing apparatus.

- Stack additional *moromi*-filled bags on top of the first bag.

- Screw down the wooden press to slo-o-o-owly express the raw soy sauce.

- Pasteurize over a wooden fire.

The following year, I got a late start, so missed half of the pressing operation. But I made up for my lapse by bringing a couple of freshly dead chickens (they had been stepped on by their brethren, so had died naturally the day before). I am always amazed that even mountain folk have never plucked a chicken. That day there was a

group of about ten adults and kids observing and marveling at my (not so finely honed) skill at breaking down the chickens. I did not bother with plucking them, as I intended to steam the meat in sake with grated ginger. Always happy to provide a teaching moment, I was ultimately glad to have taken the time to round up the chickens and all of the ingredients needed to cook them for our communal meal. I had also brought pickles.

That year I did not get as much time as I would have liked chatting with Iwasaki-san. Nonetheless we were able to catch up before lunch as he manned the pressing apparatus. Each year friendships deepen, so I was thankful I had gone. Of course, there had never been a question of not going because, even more than the soy sauce community, I did not want to let down Iwasaki-san. And we were able to discuss barrels. Iwasaki-san advised me on the size of barrel I would need to ferment my soy sauce that year while I madly pecked notes on my iPhone. When we sat down for a potluck lunch, all of the food was made from home with love—nothing store bought in sight. My favorite (besides the steamed chicken) were raw mountain yam slices that we dipped in the scum skimmed off of the pasteurizing soy sauce. Who would have thought that scum could be so intoxicating and not "scum-like." Which begged the question: Why remove it? Probably for aesthetic purposes. In any case, I could not stop reaching over for another slice.

The beauty of soy sauce (and miso) is that it is already a fermented product and contains enough salt to pickle on its own. I adapted this method from a recipe in *The Well-Flavored Vegetable*, ghostwritten by veteran Kodansha International editor Kim Schuefftan with Eri Yamaguchi, a *tsukemono* maven. The recipes are from before Japanese cuisine got intense attention and are a tad dated, but I love hearing Kim's voice in the headnotes he wrote twenty-five years ago. The salt roll is used to break down the skin a bit so the cucumbers can absorb the soy sauce. Fear not: The salt is washed off quickly. If you are worried about wasting good soy sauce on these pickles, you could get away with less, but you will need to rotate the bag every 15 minutes instead of 30 to ensure even absorption. You could save the soy sauce marinade for adding to soups such as Country Soup Flavored Four Ways (page 138).

cucumbers soused in soy SERVES 6
KYURI NO SHOYUZUKE

1 tablespoon fine sea salt

1¾ pounds (800 g) Japanese cucumbers (5 or 6 medium)

2 dried Japanese red chiles or árbols, broken in small pieces

2 tablespoons finely slivered ginger

½ cup (125 cc) best-quality soy sauce

8 shiso leaves (optional)

Sprinkle the salt on a cutting board and roll the cucumbers in the salt using fairly strong pressure (lean your body into it!). Rinse the cucumbers in hot tap water and pat dry. Lop off the bitter ends and slice into ¼-inch (6-mm) rounds. Drop the cucumbers, torn chiles, and ginger slivers into a resealable gallon-sized freezer bag and pour in the soy sauce. Stack the shiso leaves, if using, roll into a cigar shape, slice into fine tendrils, and toss into the bag with the cucumbers. Roll the bag up, squeezing out the air as you go, and refrigerate for 1 hour. Flip the bag once after 30 minutes so the soy sauce is evenly distributed.

Remove from the refrigerator when ready to eat and drain the cucumbers in a wire-mesh strainer set over a bowl. Discard the soy sauce souse, mound in a small pretty bowl, and serve before dinner with drinks or as a side dish to Semidried Herring (page 43) or Slightly Dried Squid (page 30). Keeps for several days stored in the fridge, though the cucumbers will weep a little.

VARIATIONS: Omit the ginger and shiso from the marinade, and serve the drained cucumbers sprinkled with 2 tablespoons freshly shaved katsuobushi or 3 tablespoons *hanakatsuo* (page XXIX). Substitute Western cucumbers, but peel and seed first.

You may want to wear plastic gloves or cover your hands with a plastic bag when you peel and cut these itchy-fleshed tubers. The mountain yams you find perhaps will not have been grown locally, but once in a while it's OK to cheat. These quick pickles are worth breaking the rules, since the tubers travel well and the texture is deliciously unusual. Mountain yams are either long cylinders like daikon or almost clubfoot-shaped; either one will work fine here, though the clubfoot shape will require creativity in cutting. Ruth Reichl told an audience at the CIA Worlds of Flavor Japan conference that learning to love slimy Japanese foods such as these mountain yams is the new threshold that sets real Japanese food lovers apart from others (in the past raw fish was the wall). Personally, I am in love with the crispy crunch of the tuber. (They also say slimy foods are good for male potency.)

mountain yam in spicy soy SERVES 6
YAMAIMO NO SHOYUZUKE

1 mountain yam (14 ounces/400 g)

⅓ cup (80 cc) good-quality soy sauce

2 tablespoons sake

1 or 2 dried red chiles, torn into small pieces

2 tablespoons thinly snipped nori slivers

Don a pair of plastic gloves to protect your hands from the itchy white flesh if you like and peel off the chalky brown, eye-speckled skin of the mountain yam. Slice the yam into ⅓-inch (8-mm) thick half-rounds or rounds, depending on the size of the yam. Drop the yam pieces into a reseable gallon-sized freezer bag and pour in the soy sauce and sake along with the red chile. Shake to distribute and roll up the bag, squeezing out the air as you go. Refrigerate for several hours or overnight (depending on how much soy sauce you want the yams to absorb), flipping the bag occasionally to counteract the bottom-pooling souse. Scoop the yam pieces out of the souse and sprinkle with the nori threads right before serving. Drain the yams once they have absorbed enough soy sauce and store in the fridge without liquid. Goes well with a traditional Japanese breakfast or as a snack before dinner with beer or Homemade Ginger Ale (page 324).

VARIATIONS: Substitute a small handful of *hanakatsuo* katsuobushi flakes (page XXIX) or a few tablespoons of freshly grated katusobushi instead of the nori threads.

Eggplant can be pickled successful in any medium: salt, miso, soy sauce, fish sauce, vinegar, koji, sake lees. But there is something about the combination of mustard and soy sauce that mitigates eggplant's natural bitterness and brings out its creaminess.

eggplant pickled in soy mustard SERVES 6

NASU NO KARASHI-ZUKE

1¾ pounds (800 g) Japanese eggplants (7 or 8 small)

1½ tablespoons salt

2 teaspoons Oriental mustard powder (page XXXI)

2 tablespoons sake

2 tablespoons soy sauce

8 shiso leaves, cut into a chiffonade

Slice the eggplants down the middle lengthwise, then diagonally crosswise into slightly less than ½-inch (1-cm) slices. Discard the calyx portion. Drop the eggplant slices into a gallon-sized freezer bag and massage in the salt with your hands. Roll the bag into a tight cylinder, squeezing out the air as you go. Let the eggplant macerate in the refrigerator for 1 hour. About 30 minutes before the eggplant is done macerating, measure the mustard powder into a small bowl and muddle in ½ teaspoon water to form a stiff paste. Turn the bowl upside down on the counter to develop the flavor. When the appropriate time has elapsed, remove the eggplant from the fridge and drain. Dump the salty liquid that has accumulated and wipe the inside of the bag clean. Squeeze the salted eggplant by handfuls to express any excess water and drop into a small pretty bowl. Whisk the sake slowly into the mustard to make a smooth paste. Whisk in the soy sauce slowly as well. Pour the soy mustard mixture over the eggplant, toss with the shiso leaves, and serve immediately. Good as a side dish with any simple fish or grilled meats. Best the first day since eggplant tends to discolor. If you do have leftovers, store without the soy mustard.

While I was writing this book, I collaborated on a *Japanese Farm Food* dinner with Sylvan Mishima Brackett of Peko Peko Japanese Catering in Oakland, California. Sylvan usually washes his salmon eggs in sake, then seasons them with soy sauce, and I was game to follow his method. It was the beginning of October, so early in the season. Unfortunately the salmon roe we got from Monterey Fish, though ultrafresh and totally delicious, were just too small to successfully break them away from the sac filaments without smashing the eggs completely. I decided to marinate them in Shio Koji (page 192) instead, then scoop them out into small dishes for service. I thought the eggs were phenomenal. When I returned to Japan, I began adopting Sylvan's sake-wash, soy sauce–flavoring method and never really went back to the salt and sake method I had previously used—though eventually I suppose I will. Or maybe I'll adopt the shio koji marinade instead. . . .

soy sauce–cured salmon roe SERVES 6
IKURA NO SHOYUZUKE

1 very fresh sac of salmon or salmon trout roe (about 7 ounces/200 g)

½ cup (125 cc) sake

2 tablespoons best-quality soy sauce

Slivered yuzu or Meyer lemon peel (optional)

Set a medium-sized bowl in the kitchen sink and fill with tepid water. Submerge the egg sac in the water and gently pry the roe from the outer membrane by scraping your fingertip along the membrane. Remove the membrane tendrils from among the eggs. If this task takes an inordinate amount of time and produces sticky white filaments that adhere to your hands, you are in for a rough ride. Some seasons are easier than others— it's a potluck kind of thing. Drain the eggs as you go in a wire-mesh strainer set over a bowl.

Dump the milky water used to soak the sacs down the drain; rinse, wipe, then slide the separated salmon eggs back into the wiped bowl. Pour in the sake and let soak for about 30 minutes. Drain, measure in the soy sauce, and taste. Add a dash or more soy sauce, if necessary. The eggs should be balanced between their natural sweetness and the deeply flavored soy sauce but should not be too salty. (N.B.: Because the roe is only lightly cured, it will be fairly perishable.) Serve as an appetizer in a small, colorful bowl with soy sauce saucers and chopsticks alongside. Garnish with a little slivered yuzu or Meyer lemon peel, if you like.

VARIATION: You could just as easily season with salt, though be sure to use a mild white sea salt and start with about 2 teaspoons.

YAMAKI JOZO

Although rice is certainly the king of Japanese food, soybeans are the queen. Small miso, soy sauce, and tofu makers dot the landscape of Japan, but blink once and you will notice that the local shops are closing up as the supermarket culture takes over daily life.

Up in the hills above our town lies Yamaki Jozo, an organic miso/soy sauce/tofu/natto/pickle company surrounded by organic vegetable fields and thoughtfully designed Japanese gardens. The ultimate wabi-sabi experience. But it is not just for the elegance of this so-called soy sauce plant that I bring all visitors there (foreign and Japanese alike). What Yamaki offers is myriad and only depends on time and the emptiness of your stomach.

When we have advance notice, I book seats at their weekend tofu restaurant, Shisuian, a steal at less than $30. Otherwise we just hop in the car willy-nilly and cruise up the winding road to the Kamikawa-machi hills, about 15 minutes from our farmhouse. After sampling the various tofus (silk, cotton, yuzu, sesame, yuba), misos (inaka, brown rice, barley, soybean), and pickles (too many to list!), we climb the stairs from the retail shop and peer through the glass at the gigantic cedar barrels of soy sauce fermenting over the course of two years. Upstairs is where Yamaki holds miso-making workshops, soy sauce–pressing or tofu-making demonstrations, and tastings. (I occasionally bring my little English immersion preschool students there for a tour, conveniently conducted in English.)

Yamaki Jozo is all about transparency, and the current plant was built with the visitors who would cross through their halls, all wanting to see exactly how the soy sauce, miso, and tofu are produced, firmly in mind. But more than that, Yamaki built the plant thinking of the restful feeling we would get as we wind our way along the path leading toward the whitewashed buildings, or when we turn a corner and come across ikebana moments upstairs. Here is Japan at its best: delicious-tasting wares, responsibly grown organic ingredients, and a pristine setting.

I sometimes sneak away for a little curry lunch or udon set prepared by the excellent cooks who "man" the Yamaki retail shop. There are three veteran ladies who are in charge of the retail shop, and I often ask for their sage advice in pickling or using koji. They are the smiling (and knowledgable) faces of the shop. And I never leave empty-handed. Yamaki products are my favorite present to take when I go overseas. The packaging has that elegant aesthetic sense one often associates with Japan (but is sometimes hard to find), and what is inside the packaging is absolutely top quality.

Although Yamaki is several generations old, it was the current president, Tomio Kitani, who, inspired by veteran natural farmer Kazuo Suka (page 242), committed to using 100% organic soybeans about 40 years ago. Historically the

miso and soy sauce fermenting was done in Honjo, a neighboring city; and the tofu-making operation was located in Kamiizumi-mura, the neighboring mountain village that was recently merged with our town, Kamikawa-machi. Tofu (and soy sauce) rely on the best water available, so being near the mountains from which the clear spring water is trucked was essential. Yamaki built the current plant on the site of the tofu operation in 2002 and moved all of the soybean-related activities up to the Kamiizumi-mura hills.

Kitani-san views organic farming as normal—the natural way to grow food. Consequently, he feels an innate responsibility to make traditional Japanese products in the way they have been made for generations and not to use modern shortcuts. That sense of history is exactly why Kitani-san is aligned with the venerable House of Shijo in support of the ancient food traditions of Japan. Tsukasake Shijo, the 41st-generation Shijo family head of this very old Kyoto family, comes out to Yamaki Jozo twice a year for the ceremonial rice planting and rice harvesting, and invites Kitani-san each year for an audience with the emperor to present Yamaki *shoyu*.

Kitani-san puts the current food culture into perspective by these apt words: "It has taken only 70 years to destroy a 1000-year-old food tradition." Framed like that, people might want to think twice before reaching for mass-produced soy sauce over artisanal, family-made soy sauce—especially now that Washoku has been designated as an Intangible Cultural Heritage by Unesco. Perhaps we should actually live up to the honor.

When I serve these juicy sandwiches to guests, foreigners and Japanese alike swoon. Somehow I overlooked putting *shoga yaki* (ginger-soy marinated pork) in the last book, even though it is one of our family's standard dishes. Tunnel vision, I suppose. In Japanese, *tsukemono* (pickles) means things that have something done to them or put on them. Since the pork slices are marinated in soy sauce and grated ginger, that worked for me in this chapter. The idea came to me as a riff off the strange *tonkatsu sando* (breaded pork cutlet on bread—how does breading + bread work?) you see in Japan. I reinvented that breaded pork sandwich with a much more sensible meat choice and of course the best ingredients.

ginger-soy pork sandwiches SERVES 6
SHOGA YAKI SANDO

2 tablespoons grated ginger

14 ounces (400 g) thinly sliced
   pork butt with some fat

½ cup (125 cc) soy sauce

Mayonnaise, preferably
   homemade (see Note)

2 small onions

1 small head of red leaf
   or butter lettuce

12 slices pain de mie or another
   soft bakery bread

Dijon mustard

About ½ tablespoon sesame
   oil, for cooking

Scrape the peel off of the ginger with the back of a spoon and grate. Place the pork slices in a medium-sized bowl, pour the soy sauce over them, and drop the grated ginger into the bowl as well. Pick up the pork slices one by one to smoosh in some soy sauce and grated ginger until all of the slices are coated with soy sauce and no longer pink. Slide the pork slices and marinade into a resealable gallon-sized freezer bag. Roll the bag up, squeezing out all of the air as you go, and refrigerate for at least 1 hour but preferably overnight.

Assemble the sandwich components when you are about 45 minutes or so from eating.

Make the mayonnaise, if using homemade (see Note); otherwise use jarred French mayonnaise. Avoid Japanese Kewpie mayo because it contains MSG. Cut the ends off of the onions, peel, and slice crosswise into ¼-inch (6-mm) half-rounds. Wipe the lettuce and make a stack of around 18 leaves (about 3 per sandwich) depending on the size of each leaf. (I prefer a thick layer of lettuce to one scraggly leaf.) Set up a bread station by laying the slices side by side on the counter or cutting board. Arrange them in a row of top pieces and a row of bottom pieces. Slather on the mayonnaise, dollop ½ teaspoon mustard onto the bottom slices, and spread. Lay 2 pieces of lettuce on each of the bottom slices of bread and strew some onion half-rings on the lettuce. Lay another piece of lettuce on each of the top slices of bread.

ginger-soy pork sandwiches

Set a large frying pan over high heat and film with a small amount of sesame oil when the pan is hot (hold your palm over the surface of the pan and you will feel the heat start to rise). Lift the pork pieces out of the soy-ginger marinade, shake off the excess liquid, and throw the pork pieces into the hot pan. Cook by tossing and separating the pieces that are clinging together with tongs until the pieces caramelize a bit over high heat.

Lay 2 to 4 slices of pork on top of the piece of bread with the sliced onions and cover with the top slice of bread. Cut in half and serve immediately. Be warned—you may want more than one!

VARIATION: Throw on a couple of slices of ripe tomato in the summer.

NOTE: To make homemade mayonnaise, stir 1 teaspoon Dijon mustard (or ¼ teaspoon dried mustard) and ½ teaspoon brown rice vinegar into a farm-fresh egg yolk at room temperature. Whisk in about ¾ cup (180 to 200 cc) best-quality canola oil at room temperature very, very slowly. Once the mayonnaise looks like a creamy sauce (not oily looking), you can add the oil a bit faster. Season with a sprinkling of fine sea salt and dribble in a bit more brown rice vinegar to taste, if you like. Stir in ½ to 1 teaspoon sugar or honey if you prefer a more Japanese style of mayonnaise.

We had always eaten thick steaks grilled on the barbecue, Western style. But when I began writing my first book, I remembered the thin Japanese-style steaks that restaurants served and decided to break out of our Western mold. Middle son Andrew, ever the epicure, offered a variation to the version I made (and served) with salt: "Marinating the meat in soy sauce with a splash of sake would be good." And so it was. We served this steak at the book launch dinner at Chez Panisse in September 2012 and at many others. It never fails to receive compliments. The four-hour cure is perfect, but you can get by with three.

soy sauce–soused steak SERVES 6
STEIKI NO SHOYU MARINE

2 (¾-inch/2-cm) thick, well-marbled grass-fed sirloin steaks (about 1 pound/500 g)

½ cup (125 cc) top-quality soy sauce

1 tablespoon sake

A couple of pieces of best-quality beef suet

Slide the steaks into a resealable gallon-sized freezer bag and measure in the soy sauce and sake. Marinate in the fridge for 4 hours, but turn after 2 hours to distribute the sauce, as it tends to pool in the bottom of the bag. After 4 hours, remove the steaks from the soy sauce marinade and pat dry with thick paper towels. If you are not cooking the steaks right away, put them on a plate in the refrigerator until you are ready to cook.

Heat two heavy cast iron pans over high heat and rub each with a piece of suet until some of the fat has rendered and filmed the pan. Discard the suet.

Slap a steak in each of the pans and cook for 30 seconds on each side. Cover, and cook 1 minute more on each side for rare or 2 minutes for medium-rare. Add 1 more minute for each degree of doneness. Water will bead up on the inside of the lid, so be sure to wipe the condensation a few times during the cooking process. If you only have one pan, cook the steaks one by one. Be sure to wipe out the pan before repeating the process with the second steak.

Let the steaks rest 5 minutes before cutting crosswise into ¼-inch (6-mm) strips. If the strips are too long, cut in half, as the pieces should be able to be eaten with chopsticks in one bite but also should remain large enough to be attractive. Serve with a soy vinaigrette summer salad such as Tomato, Onion, and Pepper Salad (page 113). Also makes delicious leftovers for a cold supper or Japanese-style sandwiches similar to Ginger-Soy Pork Sandwiches (page 109). Substitute the cold soy sauce steak for the warm ginger-soy pork.

At the end of the summer, when we still have plenty of cherry tomatoes, peppers, and onions, I love to compose them in a salad dressed with soy sauce. Drizzling each component of the dressing separately makes for a brighter result, as each bite is subtly different.

tomato, onion, and pepper salad SERVES 6
TOMATO, TAMANEGI TO PIMAN SARADA

1 pound (450 g) large organic cherry tomatoes

4 small green peppers (about 3½ ounces/100 g)

1 small onion (about 1¾ ounces/50 g)

1½ tablespoons organic canola oil

½ tablespoon organic dark sesame oil

1 tablespoon organic soy sauce

1 tablespoon brown rice vinegar

4 shiso leaves, cut into threads (optional)

Right before serving your meal, cut the cherry tomatoes in half with a very sharp knife, and scatter on a pretty plate. Cut the tops off of the peppers, halve vertically, remove the seeds, and slice crosswise into ⅛-inch (3-mm) slivers. Distribute the slivers evenly across the surface of the tomatoes. Slice off the root and top portion of the onion, cut in half lengthwise, and peel. Slice crosswise into ⅛-inch (3-mm) half-moons. Rub the half-moon shapes between your fingers to dislodge into slivers and scatter on top of the tomatoes and peppers. Drizzle the salad with the oils, followed by soy sauce, and finish with the vinegar. Strew with the shiso threads, if using, and serve immediately.

VARIATION: Substitute 5 smallish, firm tomatoes cut into ¼-inch (6-mm) slices. Arrange the slices attractively in a slightly overlapping circular fashion on a pretty plate before strewing with the pepper and onion. (N.B.: Shake the oils, soy sauce, and vinegar in a jar and you will have soy sauce vinaigrette.)

MOROMI

I am enamored with everything that our local soy sauce and miso producer makes, but most of all I am drawn irresistably to a mysterious dark, heady substance kept in a metal tin with a white plastic cover upstairs at Yamaki Jozo (page 106). It's called *moromi*.

I am not sure why it took me so long to understand what *moromi* actually is. Gaps in my Japanese vocabulary? Whatever the reason, until I began making my own miso and soy sauce, I was unclear on how the processes differed and what exactly *moromi* was. Our pal Masashi Matsuda (page 78) smears a thin film of his *moromi* on pizza dough, sprinkles it with slivered onions and a flavorful cheese such as fontina, then bakes it in his burning-hot pizza oven before serving with some fresh carrot fronds (heaven!). When we staged a Japanese Farm Food event at Pizzaiolo in Oakland, I concocted a mixture of Ohsawa Tamari and Ohsawa Brown Rice Miso to roughly replicate *moromi*. Owner Charlie Hallowell valiantly

used the mixture on some of the pizzas he was throwing out that night. I thought the substitution worked, though I should have told Charlie a little goes a long way. Think thin—a barely perceptible smear, where you see the mostly white dough steaked with brown.

Each time I ran into Kazuhiko Morita at Yamaki, I would beg him for a little taste of the *moromi*, since it reaches deep into my whole being as a primal flavor. One time I asked Morita-san if I could buy the Yamaki *moromi*. "It would be like selling our soul," was his reply. Put simply, *moromi* is the soy sauce mash from which soy sauce is pressed. And in the case of the Yamaki *moromi*, it has been fermented in cedar barrels for two years so it has beerlike notes and is a thick, creamy, burnished, burnt umber that as kids we gleefully called "burumbager jones."

One reason for the confusion as to what *moromi* is, is that *moromi* in fact refers to any Japanese traditional mash due to be pressed,

whether soy sauce, sake, mirin, vinegar, or fish sauce. And it was really only through hands-on visits to these producers that this huge piece of information snapped clearly into place. The funny thing is that these days I find myself explaining the concept to city- and town-dwelling Japanese because *moromi* is not particularly part of the daily vernacular.

Nor is *shibori* or *kasu*. *Shibori* (pressing) is what happens to mashes (*moromi*) of any kind, and all *shibori* used to be performed in cedar *shibori fune* (pressing vessels) by filling *shibori bukuro* (pressing bags) with the sake, soy sauce, mirin, or rice vinegar mash (*moromi*). After a three-year ferment, fish sauce is allowed to drip out through a bore hole near the bottom of the barrel, using gravity, since pressing would cause cloudiness. Fish sauce solids float on the surface of the barrel so the barrel is only decanted until the fish sauce stops running clear. *Kasu* (lees) is what is left over after pressing. Although not used daily or even

widely, *sake kasu* (page 188) is a well-known specialized ingredient used in preserving and local-area soups. Now that I am pressing my own soy sauce, I have my own soy sauce lees (*shoyu kasu*), which resemble miso in texture and make a convenient instant pickling bed for vegetables. But even more brilliant are the lees remaining after pressing my Persimmmon Vinegar (page 177). The persimmon vinegar lees make an ingenious substitute for *ume* (pickled plum) in Smashed Cucumbers with Sour Plum (page 169) and Turnips Pickled with Sour Plum (page 171), or as is, to pickle daikon or turnips for about three days submerged in the bed of persimmon vinegar lees. While perhaps your head is spinning as much as mine was just a few years ago, suffice to say that as you start to create your own mashes (I especially encourage making persimmon vinegar), you will have your own lees with which to experiment. And with experimentation comes creative expression and testing your limits . . . and other invaluable lessons in life.

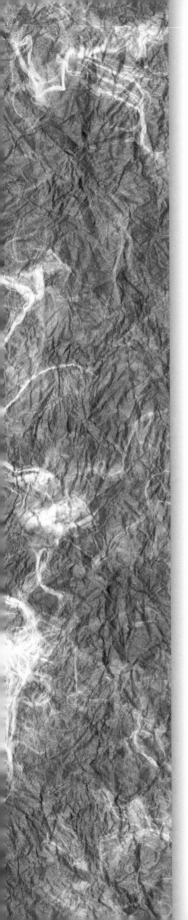

4

fish sauce

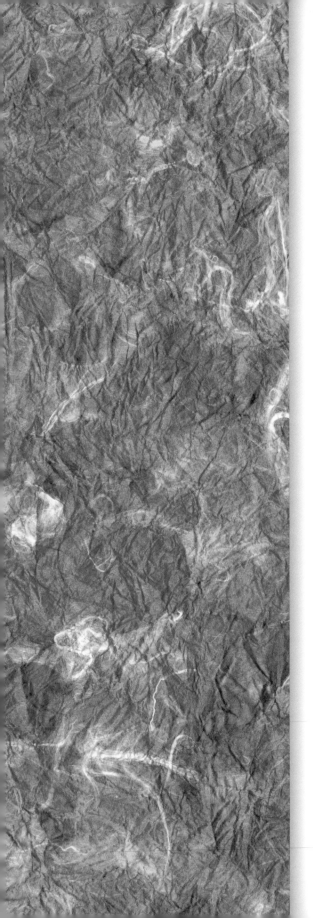

FISH SAUCE RECIPES

TOFU DOUSED IN FISH SAUCE	124
DAIKON IN FISH SAUCE	125
MYOGA PICKLED WITH FISH SAUCE	128
FISH SAUCE–SIMMERED EGGPLANT	133
FISH SAUCE–BROILED DAIKON	135
SANDFISH NABE	136
COUNTRY SOUP FLAVORED FOUR WAYS	138
FISH SAUCE FRIED RICE	140

Although soy sauce is the most common condiment in Japan today, fish sauce (in Japanese: *gyosho* or *uoshoyu*) has a long historical place in the local foods of coastal Japan. No big surprise, since as an island nation, Japan has plenty of fish and salt. Fish sauce is made from fish or sea creatures when they are in season and so plentiful that it is impossible to consume or sell the entire daily catch. There were three main areas that produced Japanese fish sauce: Akita, Ishikawa, and Shikoku. In the last couple of centuries, fish sauce was predominantly used in these local cuisines and was not a common flavoring in Japanese kitchens outside of those regions. With the increased familiarity of Southeast Asian cuisines starting in the 1990s, urban Japanese are now more ready to experiment with fish sauce in their own cooking. Currently what holds people back is lack of knowledge. "How can I use it?" is the most common question I hear. The easiest answer is to sprinkle in the delicate Japanese fish sauce as a hidden taste to most dishes, such as soups, blanched or sautéed vegetables, curry, or fried rice. (I add a few dashes to my Western stews and gratins as well.) When fish sauce is sufficiently nuanced, it can introduce a subtle salty overtone that hearkens back to the sea. You should never overpower a dish with it, and for the most part you should not even notice the flavor.

Tadaaki used to buy fish sauce by the case and he sprinkled it liberally on the dishes he cooked. I thought of it as foreign, or somehow hard to understand, so never used it in my own cooking. I became increasingly intrigued by Japanese fish sauce (initially Moroi Jozo's *shottsuru* from Akita prefecture), and I started seasoning sautéed vegetables with *shottsuru* instead of salt, miso, or soy sauce. The salty fish paired particularly well with eggplant, green beans, and snap peas. I began bringing Moroi Jozo's 10-year-old *shottsuru* to chef friends in California. (In a tasting between my best Italian *colatura* and the Moroi Jozo ten-year-old, the *shottsuru* won, hands down.) But I still did not have a feeling for the breadth of uses of fish sauce until a visit to a place where fish sauce is produced. An integral part of this book is the community of producers who make up "preserving Japan," and talking to them in situ was crucial for developing a deeper understanding of these fundamental preserved foods produced using age-old techniques. Through recording the producers' stories, I caught the idea of how they use the products, but more important I began to truly comprehend the philosophy of *kakushi aji* (hidden taste) that is the backbone of local food traditions. Dash drops of fish sauce in beef shabu-shabu to add a more rounded dimension, on simmered vegetables or mushroom-flavored rice instead of soy sauce, and on raw seasonal vegetables or rice balls before grilling. Splash liberally into curry rice, fried rice, tofu nabe, and vegetable-based soups. I encourage you to find the mildest fish sauce you can even if it is not Japanese; I recommend Nettuno Colatura di Alici di Cetara from Italy or Red Boat Fish Sauce from Vietnam. Do your own side by side taste test. Japanese fish sauce can possibly be discovered at specialty food stores in the U.S., but it is not yet widely available even in Japanese grocery stores or online. Be careful to avoid the ones that adds MSG (アミノ酸) with the salt, as it is not neccesary.

SHOTTSURU is made in the far northern perfecture of Akita in a remote coastal area. *Shottsuru* is the most widely known of all the Japanese fish sauces. The top maker, Moroi Jozo, markets to the mainstream population across the length of Japan and has been designated by Slow Food as an Ark of Flavor product. Although primarily sand fish (*hata hata*), *shottsuru* can also be fermented from small sardines or anchovy (*iwashi*).

ISHIRU/ISHIRI is a Ishikawa prefecture product, namely from the Noto Peninsula. While small sardines and anchovies (*iwashi*) and squid (*ika*) are arguably the most common commercially produced fish sauce in Ishikawa, I am partial to small-producer *ishiru/ishiri* made from mackerel or *megisu* (an anchovy-like fish of the silligo family that makes an exceptionally bright, very delicious fish sauce that you can drink by the spoonful). But any fish or shellfish can be salted and fermented into fish sauce. Ishikawa prefecture has probably the greatest variety of fish sauces in Japan and perhaps has the most fascinating food culture surrounding the use of *ishiru/ishiri*. Until quite recently, every fisherman's household made its own fish sauce. The majority of commercially produced fish sauce is still bottled in plastic bottles, so is less likely to be appreciated in areas outside of Ishikawa. Although I did find one brand of *ishiru* at my local supermarket, most Japanese are not familiar with either of the Noto terms for fish sauce: *ishiru* or *ishiri*. The local shops in Ishikawa prefecture are lined with a dizzying array of *ishiru/ishiri*. And small-batch, unlabeled fish sauces are available through older people hawking their wares at the morning markets such as the one in Wajima (page 130).

IKANAGO SHOYU was the other mainstay fish sauce along with *shottsuru* and *ishiru/ishiri* until the 1950s, when it went out of production. *Ikanago shoyu* was made in Shikoku (Japan's third-largest island), from sand lances (minuscule fish called *ikanago*). Thanks to a nationwide resurgence of local pride, *ikanago shoyu* has experienced a rebirth and is now, once again, being produced and marketed on a small scale. Like Moroi Jozo in Akita, the handful of *ikango shoyu* producers are looking to break out of local-area distribution, so are bottling their fish sauce in attractive bottles and shipping all over Japan.

Local governments in Japan are searching for products to develop using naturally available resources. To this end, several prefectures have begun producing and marketing their own fish sauces. Hokkaido's fish sauce is usually made from scallops or salmon but also from mackerel pike. Miyagi prefecture ferments small shellfish, sand lances, and saury; Kanagawa and Aichi use anchovies; Niigata ferments deep-sea shrimp; and Oita prefecture gathers the sweetfish when they are running. Kochi prefecture was fermenting skipjack tuna guts, but this product is no longer available commercially. All of these intrepid fish sauce makers sell directly from their own home pages, through local third-party Web sites, or via the giant conglomerate known as Amazon.co.jp. If you are an aficionado of fish sauce, I recommend a trip to Japan, for you will find no other country with such an array of well-made fermented fish products.

MAKING FISH SAUCE

I had been wanting to start a batch of fish sauce ever since seeing how (theoretically) easy it was on a visit to the Noto Peninsula. The local fish sauce producer had promised to send me a small barrel, but perhaps he forgot. In the meantime, I packed my fish mash into a crockery pot and stashed it outside with the other pickling projects. I was finally able to track down some hand-me-down pickling barrels and found a good possible alternative at the antique junk shop. It was a water bucket that leaked like a sieve at first. After soaking in water, the wood expanded and filled up the cracks, so it was good to go. The benefit to the water bucket is a spigot in the bottom for siphoning off the fish sauce when ready. Beware: This fish sauce takes at least one year to fully ferment and another half year or more to mellow out to a suitably elegant condiment. Also be sure to start with very fresh fish and the best-quality sea salt that makes sense for this kind of volume.

METHOD: Set a colander in the kitchen sink and fill it about three-quarters full with 13 pounds (6 kg) ungutted sandfish or other small to medium whole fish such as sardines, anchovies, or mackerel. Wash under cold running water while running your hands through the fish so they are all well rinsed. Shake off the fish by handfuls and drop into a large bowl. Continue rinsing the fish in batches until they are all sparklingly clean. (Do not remove the guts.) Process a couple of handfuls at a time by pulsing in a heavy-duty food processor. Adjust the amount of fish depending on the size and strength of your processor. The mixture should be a well-chopped creamy purple mass with visible small chunks. Scrape into a small wooden barrel (preferably with a spigot on the bottom for siphoning off the fish sauce once it is ready) or a crockery pot and stir in 2.2 pounds (1 kg) fine white sea salt (17% of the fish weight). Cover but make sure air can still enter. (I draped a muslin cloth across the top of the barrel and secured it with twine.) Since the barrel breathes, the fish sauce can be ready in 1½ years if you leave it out in the elements. Crockery pot fermentation will take at least two years. Inside fermenting and aging takes three long years, so be patient. In the first few months, stir every once in a while until the fish solids separate from the brine and start forming a grey coating on the surface. After that, let time take its course and taste the fishy liquid when you remember. The fish sauce is done when it has sufficiently mellowed and is a burnished Cognac color. Tap from the bottom.

Tofu made with organic Japanese soybeans is creamy with gentle notes of the heirloom beans from which the soy milk was made. Our friends at Yamaki Jozo (page 106) make such a tofu. And Yamaki's tofu needs nothing more than a pair of chopsticks (real tofu experts eschew soy sauce in tasting tofu, as it masks the natural flavor of the beans). On the opposite side, there is another philosophy of using tofu as a vehicle for absorbing interesting flavors, transforming it into a totally different textured food product such as for Tofu Marinated in Miso (page 65). Here the fish sauce just barely kisses the tofu before searing and makes an unforgettable dish.

tofu doused in fish sauce SERVES 4
TOFU NO ISHIRIZUKE

1 (10.5-oz/300-g) block Japanese-style "cotton" tofu

2 teaspoons Japanese fish sauce (page 119)

2 teaspoons organic canola oil

1 teaspoon best-quality dark sesame oil

7-spice powder (*shichimi togarashi*, page XXXI)

Remove the tofu from the package and set it on a chopping board propped up at one end, angled into the kitchen sink for draining. Place another chopping board on top of the tofu and leave to press out moisture for 1 hour. The board should not be so heavy that it smashes the tofu. Place the tofu on a small plate, spoon the fish sauce over the tofu, and rub it across the surface. Gently nudge the tofu off of the plate to make sure the bottom surface is filmed with fish sauce. Set a heavy frying pan over high heat and measure in the oils. Lift the tofu off of the plate with a long spatuala, taking care to leave any extra pooled-up liquid behind, and slide the fish sauce–filmed tofu into the hot pan. Sear on both sides for 1 minute. Cut into 8 pieces, sprinkle with *shichimi togarashi*, and serve for a bite before dinner or as a side dish to sake-steamed fish and Wasabi Leaves in Sake and Soy (page 98).

VARIATION: If Japanese fish sauce is not available, use another top-shelf fish sauce such as the Italian Nettuno Colatura di Alici or Red Boat from Vietnam.

I am a creature of habit. I favor the same restaurants, inns, or spots to visit in the world. Gone are the days when I traveled with my sons. Instead my travels center on teaching about Japanese local foods abroad or gathering new material for my writing. On a recent filming trip to the Noto Peninsula we stayed at the Sakamoto ryokan (page 126) and owner Shinichiro Sakamoto generously shared this local food preparation. Like many people, I am often in need of instant dishes, so this "morning pickle" is a slam dunk, since the fish sauce transforms the daikon into a succulent bite that tastes of the sea.

daikon in fish sauce SERVES 6
DAIKON NO ASAZUKE

1 small daikon, about 1 pound (450 g)

2 small dried red chile peppers, japones or árbol

¼ cup (60 cc) anchovy *ishiru* or other Japanese fish sauce (page 120)

¼ cup (60 cc) Katsuobushi Dashi (page 253), cooled

Whack the daikon in 2, through the center, to make 2 equal-sized pieces. Slice each of those pieces in half vertically. Cut the daikon halves into ¾-inch (2-cm) thick half-moons and toss into a gallon-sized freezer bag. Break the chiles into a few small pieces and drop them into the bag of daikon along with the fish sauce and dashi. Roll up the bag, squeezing out all of the air as you go, and refrigerate for 1 hour. Scoop these mildly flavored, yet spicy daikon pieces out with a slotted spoon and serve in a small bowl as a crisp afternoon snack or to accompany a simple supper of broiled fish and rice. Keeps well stored with the pickling liquid in the fridge.

VARIATIONS: Turnips substitute well for the daikon, but leave a small portion (¼ inch/6 mm) of the stem, since the green makes a pretty color presentation. Cut the turnips in half vertically, then crosswise into ¾-inch (2-cm) half-rounds. Baby turnips should be quartered instead of sliced. Eggplant cut as for Fish Sauce–Simmered Eggplant (page 133) is also excellent pickled in this way, though you should squeeze the slices before serving.

THE RYOKAN

Ryokan are upscale Japanese inns that include breakfast and/or dinner in the price of the stay. You pay per person, not per room, and the tariff usually ranges from about $120 to $280 a night. In actuality there is no cap on how expensive a ryokan can get, and while $500 per person is steep, it's not enough to gasp at. To Europeans, perhaps, our local ryokan in the hills above us might appear "primitive" for its lack of beds or showers in the room. Never mind that there is a private bath next door to the room that looks out over a lake at the bottom of a ravine and the plump futons are piled high with down comforters. A ryokan, by its very nature, is minimalistic in decor, though certainly not primitive. Also it is in the cool elegance of the sparsely furnished Japanese rooms where one derives an unfettered feeling of inner peace. Away from the clutter of home, your mind and spirit can become clear.

By outward appearances, Sakamoto ryokan on the Noto Peninsula could be 80 years old, but it is not. Sakamoto was designed by local architect Shinji Takagi and built in 1989 in the spot of Shinichiro Sakamoto's parents' *tojiba*— an inexpensive hot spring for local people to come take a rest. The entryway is veiled by a split hemp curtain (noren, page XIII), which lifts leisurely up at the whim of the afternoon breeze. Part the noren and you see the gleaming floors, a testament to daily rubbings. A perfectly formed cream-colored Japanese vase sits unadorned next to a haphazardly (yet deliberately) arranged branch of freshly harvested red chile peppers. And a lily floats on top of the stone reservoir in the corner of the room (I later learn that Takagi-san, the architect, sourced that massive piece of stone from the

deep mountains of the Noto Peninsula). Each time I enter, I am drawn to the ancient wood-burning stove that stands in the corner. I covet the stove. Badly.

All this is before you even enter the living space of the ryokan. The marvel of Sakamoto is how the architect has created that perfect balance of inside-outside, which is the hallmark of traditional Japanese construction. The long wooden sink looks out to the garden and has no wall or window separating the washing area from the outside trees. Attention to detail is what sets the best ryokan apart from the run of the mill (regardless of price): At Sakamoto one can soak in a red-lacquered bath fashioned by Kunikatsu Seto (page 134), the hand-washing bowls are hammered copper, and one sleeps between heavy indigo-colored cotton sheets. Original art pieces hang in the toilet areas. The feeling of unintentional is very intentional here, and exceptionally well conceived.

Some Japanese say that the mark of a good ryokan is when you cannot finish all of the food. I disagree. There are four measures to ascertain the quality of a ryokan. Most important is the deliciousness of the food, paramount is creativity in menus crafted from high-quality ingredients that adhere to the seasons. And originality in the kitchen should be mirrored on the table in the form of eclectic choices of ceramic, glass, and lacquerware. The ryokan should also demonstrate an innate aesthetic sense regarding the appointment of the rooms and bath area and the building that houses the whole. The last criteria by which to judge a ryokan is the least critical for me: the service.

Raising the level of service adds to the overall cost, no question. I'd rather pay for linen sheets and fantastic food than a private server attending to every wish (as at Honjin Hiranoya Kachoan in Hida Takayama). I am happy with a 10-year-old schoolboy bringing my food (as at Sakamoto in bygone years). Nonetheless I did thoroughly enjoy my stay at Kachoan and, except for the price ($80 more per night than Sakamoto), would go there again without hesitation. I discovered Kachoan in a *Gourmet* magazine article about sixteen years ago and stayed there with my youngest son, Matthew, twice when he was a baby and once when he was twelve. Kachoan is an elegant ryokan housed, ironically, in a high-rise. However the rooms are beyond pristine and the cuisine some of the best food in Japan. Our own private server greeted us each time we came in from ventures out on the town. She noted food likes and dislikes and was solicitous toward all of our desires. Matthew (always the lover of odd garb) was taken with the sage green down-filled silk vest worn over the dark blue–paned cotton *yukata*. I bought him the set for Christmas, which he wore once but never again. Perhaps I will start donning it on those cold nights when everyone else is in bed and the temperature of the house starts to drop, since my usual quilted housecoat still leaves me shivering.

Although I have visited Hida Takayama in Gifu prefecture countless times over the years, now the Noto Peninsula is where I yearn to go. And Sakamoto is where I found my perfect ryokan experience.

I had heard from veteran cookbook editor Kim Schuefftan about "the best fish sauce he had ever tasted," always qualified with "it's roughly bottled, with no label." That did not sound appealing. But I was wrong. While sipping coffee at Quai Gallery in Wajima (page 134), some *myoga* pickles appeared on the table. I pinched up a little clump with my chopsticks and popped them in my mouth. I had never tasted anything like them. I am extremely partial to *myoga*, so that does come into play here, but the subtle seasoning was haunting and beguilingly delicious. I kept reaching for more. The hidden taste here is that "rough" fish sauce that Kim had been talking about for years. Naturally, I bought four bottles at the morning market the next day . . . and wish I had bought more.

myoga pickled with fish sauce SERVES 6
MYOGA NO ISHIRIZUKE

⅔ pound (300 g) *myoga* buds

⅔ cup (150 cc) Katsuobushi Dashi (page 253)

⅓ cup (75 cc) mackerel ishiru (page 120) or other high-quality fish sauce

Slice off a sliver of the exposed stem bottoms to freshen the *myoga* buds, but leave the stems intact. Remove any discolored outside leaves and slice the buds in half vertically. Line up the *myoga* halves on a cutting board, cut side down, and slice thinly lengthwise. Scrape into a fine-mesh metal strainer as you go.

Bring a small teapot of hot water to a boil. Holding the metal strainer full of slivered *myoga* over the kitchen sink, pour the boiling water over the *myoga* for 10 seconds to slightly "cook" (*yudoshi*). Shake off the hot water and immediately run cold water into the strainer to cool the *myoga*. Feather your fingers through the slivers as the water is running to determine when they have sufficiently cooled. Turn off the tap and shake off the excess water.

Squeeze the cooled *myoga* threads by handfuls and drop into a gallon-sized resealable freezer bag. Pour in the dashi and fish sauce and stir with your fingers. Squeeze out the excess air, seal, and roll up. Store in the refrigerator overnight to infuse lightly. When ready to serve, dip a pair of chopsticks into the freezer bag to catch up a clump of *myoga* threads. Heap attractively in a small ceramic or glass bowl and serve as an accompaniment to drinks, tea, or a light summer dinner. These pickles stay perky for about a week, stored chilled in their soaking liquid.

VARIATION: You could successfully substitute threads of young ginger for the *myoga* slivers, but the pickle will be much hotter.

WAJIMA MORNING MARKET

Mention the Wajima Morning Market and inevitably you will hear two comments: "It used to be soooo cool; too bad it's only for tourists now." The Wajima Morning Market was originally the daily market where locals bought their fish and other necessities. The market was also famous for the plethora of wrinkled grandmas selling pickles. While farmers' and fishermen's wives still man the booths lining the morning market street, nowadays most of the pickles they sell are produced commercially. As the city-dwelling gawkers increased, the local shoppers decreased. Unfortunately this creates a situation where the stall vendors are discouraged by out-of-town visitors who sample the pickles but don't necessarily buy.

Despite the naysayers, we visited the market one early fall morning. Besides pickles there were plenty of vendors selling fish sauce (page 119) and other fish-related products such as fish nukazuke (page 224). Our favorite salt maker (page 9) had a table tended by his oldest daughter, set to take over from her father when he retires. As we wove our way through the foot traffic, we stopped occasionally when something interesting caught our eye. I was particularly taken with a

countrywoman selling a handful of greens she had obviously foraged. I spent a good twenty minutes chatting with her and wished I could buy more than a few bags of *myoga* buds. We still had one more night in Wajima, and I had to somehow make it back to my home in Saitama via plane and train, carrying all of my already alarming pile of packages. Nonetheless I commiserated with her on the state of the market and how difficult it is to eke out a living squatted on the side of the street. We swapped a few stories and I finally had to tear myself away as Seto-san (page 134) had arrived to escort us to the mackerel fish sauce lady.

The "stubborn grandma" tilted her head up to tell me about her sauce. She was amused that I wanted to try my hand at making it myself but happy that I bought four 500-ml bottles. She chops up whole mackerel when they are running and mixes in salt at 17% of the weight of the fish. It takes about one year for the fish to break down and for fermentation to evolve. She then only ages her fish sauce for another half a year or so before bottling it up and taking it to market. I worry about the day when she stops having the wherewithal to create her beautifully clear sauce, so am thinking to order a box of twelve. Maybe

by the time I finish the twelve, my own will be ready to "press" (technically the barrel is set at an angle and the fish sauce drips out by gravity through a bung hole toward the bottom of the barrel). Seto-san was also eager to introduce us to a fishmonger named Haruko whom everyone called "Otomi-san" (her grandma's name). Haruko-san took over her grandmother's stall, so the name stuck. She encouraged me to call her for fish and I will. It does seem a bit odd to order fish over the phone, but I am game to try. I liked her frank way of talking and her friendly cackle.

Another treasure I found in the Wajima market were hand-crafted cloth-covered zori (straw flip-flops). These zori caught my eye at the first vendor as we entered the market. I bought ten, though perhaps should have waited. As we strolled down the main street I came across a handbag and shoe shop with bins piled high with zori outside the shop. They had larger sizes than the first vendor and also quite a few that were woven with indigo-colored cloth. Just when I thought I could not carry another bulging package, I spied some *surikogi* (Japanese grinding pestles, page XVIII) carved from *sansho* tree branches laid out on a table in front of a smiling seventyish local woman sporting a sprigged cotton bonnet. I had been looking for more *sansho surikogi* for several years, so swooped down without hesitation. Her husband had gathered the *sansho* branches, sanded them down to a pleasing soft finish, and carved the fat rounded tip necessary for grinding seeds and sauces in the traditional Japanese ceramic grooved bowl (*suribachi*, page XVII). I also pawed through her pile of zori and selected another four to stuff in my bags. After all, I didn't know when I would be back.

Kunikatsu and Mikako Seto (page 134) served us a dead-simple dish of eggplant simmered in a whisper of broth. The heavenly broth was flavored with konbu, local mackerel fish sauce, and sake. Eggplant and fish sauce are a perfect match, since the bland eggplant always seems to want some punch. In the winter, Japanese leeks (negi) or thinly sliced daikon are used in place of the eggplant. You can also simmer chunks of peeled potatoes in the leftover simmering juices.

fish sauce–simmered eggplant SERVES 6
NASU NO KAIYAKI

6 Japanese eggplants, about
   1⅓ pounds (600 g)

1 (4-inch/10-cm) square of konbu

3 tablespoons Japanese fish sauce

2 tablespoons sake

Zest of 1 yuzu or ½ Meyer
   lemon, slivered

Slice the eggplants down the middle lengthwise and cut crosswise on the diagonal into 5/16-inch (7-mm) pieces. Discard the calyx and tip ends. Soak the eggplant pieces in a bowl of cold water to remove the bitterness while you prepare the simmering water and six small bowls.

Bring the konbu and 2 cups (500 cc) water to a simmer in a medium-sized pot over medium-high heat. Flavor the broth with the fish sauce and sake and simmer for 1 minute. Working in batches (a total of 3), throw in a large handful of eggplant and a pinch of slivered yuzu peel. As soon as the water comes back to a rollicking boil, skim out the eggplant and yuzu slivers into each of the prepared bowls and ladle in a tiny bit of the broth. The eggplant should be half raw and pleasantly springy. The broth should have a faint whiff of the sea. Give each person a pair of chopsticks and serve hot as a quick afternoon pick-me-up snack. Cook more as you go.

KUNIKATSU SETO LACQUER

I first ate off of some Kunikatsu Seto lacquerware when I visited Sakamoto (page 126), a life-changing ryokan in the town of Suzu on the Noto Peninsula. Holding the oversized soup bowl in my hand gave me a feeling of warmth and quiet. And there was a fabric-textured tray on which perched one small ceramic plate holding three delicately fried fava beans. I collect lacquerware and have handled quite a few bowls, plates, and trays in my travels through antique markets or in visits to high-quality lacquerware producers around Japan. But the lacquerware created by Kunikatsu Seto was like nothing I had ever seen. First, it had an extremely pleasing texture to the wood. And second, it followed an originality of style that made me want to meet the man behind the bowls.

Seto-san and his wife, Mikako, live in Wajima above a grey cement-walled gallery designed by architect Shinji Takagi. The front side of the gallery is a wall of glass facing the street, and when you climb the stairs to the living space, there is a vista out to the sea. Artists need light. We shook off our umbrellas and left them inside before stepping into the gallery. Seto-san was wearing natural-fibered, loose-fitting hemp pants with a sort of nubby tunic. Stylish.

When I had called to arrange our visit, I had dropped hints to Mikako Seto that we would welcome tasting some of their favorite simple bites (their cooking prowess having been well extolled by an old friend). Besides the excellent coffee, the Setos served us a bowl of delicate *myoga* threads that had been pickled in fish sauce (page 128). We whiled away the morning, perched on antique African chairs around a low plank table.

Next Seto-san brought out a small lacquer bowl for each of us. He emerged from the kitchenette carrying a steaming black stone pot of eggplant slices simmered in a clear soup flavored with mackerel fish sauce (page 120). Like in the *myoga* pickle, the fish sauce flavor was subtle, just barely there. Seto-san scooped some eggplant slices with a smidge of broth into each of our bowls and returned to the kitchenette. He made four more trips to cook eggplant and we never refused our dollop. The simple yet nuanced flavors of both dishes told me a geat deal about who Kunihiko and Mikako Seto were as people. The food attracted me for its understatement.

As we were winding down the visit, I wandered around the perimeter of the gallery space to take in the wares. Seto-san's lacquer is divided into two categories: art (not affordable for writers) and standard ware (reasonable, considering, though still dear). The art pieces showed a great breadth of style and strength. There was a deep originality to the works, yet they still maintained their functional integrity. I liked that dual element. I bought a lacquer soup bowl for Tadaaki's birthday present and vowed to return when I had increased means.

On the Noto Peninsula, this dish is made with winter daikon. If you use spring daikon, be sure to cut off (and discard) the light green portion of the daikon. That part of the root will be tough and fibrous because it pushed itself out of the ground and was exposed to sunlight. If you are able to grill these daikon slices over coals, you will be happy you did. That said, I pan-sautéed these at my sister's house using my brother-in-law Jeffrey Martin's Frantoio Grove olive oil and they were sensational. (Olive oil growers apparently don't stock any other oil.)

fish sauce–broiled daikon SERVES 4
DAIKON NO ISHIRI YAKI

1 small daikon, about
   1 pound (450 g)

¼ cup (60 cc) Katsuobushi
   Dashi (page 253)

¼ cup (60 cc) sake or hon
   mirin (page XXXI)

2 tablespoons *ishiru* (page 120)
   or other top-quality fish sauce

Flaky sea salt, for serving

Scrub the daikon with a stiff vegetable brush (*tawashi*) and dry well. Slice into ⅜-inch (1-cm) thick rounds and drop into a resealable gallon-sized freezer bag. Measure in the dashi, sake or mirin, and fish sauce. Tip the bag side to side to mix the liquids, then roll up, squeezing the air out as you go, and seal. Let the daikon slices absorb the marinade for 20 to 30 minutes while you prepare the coals or broiler. (If you use mirin and soak the daikon longer than 30 minutes they will caramelize more quickly, so be mindful of the soak time.) Grill over hot coals for 2 minutes on each side until the surfaces are slightly burned. Alternatively, sear quickly on each side over high heat in a heavy frying pan that has been filmed with a small amount of neutral oil. Serve with a sprinkling of flaky sea salt as a savory bite with drinks before dinner.

VARIATIONS: Brush summer vegetables such as thickly sliced eggplant, fat cherry tomatoes, small green peppers, and thick rounds of just-cooked potatoes with the sake and fish sauce, but omit the dashi. Grill as you would the daikon. Thick cuts of peeled lotus root substitute well for daikon.

Shottsuru Nabe is a dish that originates in Akita prefecture where sandfish (*hata hata*) are abundant. The fish sauce produced in Akita is called *shottsuru*, hence the name of the *nabe*. This is an easy dish to put together and makes a fun communal meal. Serve with a bowl of rice on the side. (N.B.: The Noto Peninsula has a similar dish called *ishiru nabe*, which uses their own local fish.)

You will need a portable tabletop gas burner to make this dish at the table.

sandfish nabe SERVES 4
SHOTTSURU NABE

1 (6-inch/15-cm) piece of konbu

12 shiitake or 18 *shimeji* or enoki mushrooms, discolored ends sliced off

1 large bunch of Japanese parsley (*seri*) or mizuna

2 thick negi (Japanese leeks) or thin leeks, bottom tendrils removed

¼ head of napa cabbage

2 (10.5-ounce/300-g) pieces of Japanese-style "cotton" tofu, cut into 1-inch (2.5-cm) cubes

6 sandfish (or other small delicate whitefish), gills and guts removed (if the fish have egg sacs, pop them into the *nabe* with the fish); substitute 6 filets of cod or snapper

1 tablespoon sake

2 tablespoons *shottsuru* (page 120) or any other top-shelf fish sauce

Cooked Japanese rice, for serving

Fill a flameproof casserole or clay pot (*donabe*, page xviii) with 2½ cups (600 cc) water. Drop in the konbu and bring to an almost boil over high heat. (Remove the konbu before the water boils and take the pot off of the heat.)

If using shiitake, remove the stems and reserve for another purpose such as making Konbu Dashi (page 266). If using *shimeji* or enoki, trim off the ends and separate into individual stems. Heap half of the mushrooms on one platter and the other half on another. Slice the discolored ends off of the *seri* stems or lop off the root ends of the mizuna. Cut the leaves crosswise into 2-inch (5-cm) pieces and mound on the platter with the mushrooms. Cut the negi or leeks into 2-inch (5-cm) lengths and heap on the platter as well. Remove the core from the napa cabbage and slice crosswise into 2-inch (5-cm) pieces. Mound on the platter. Divide the tofu cubes between two small plates. Arrange the fish or fish filets on a dinner plate and bring to the table with the platters of vegetables and the plates of tofu.

Set the *donabe* on the tabletop burner and bring to a gentle simmer over medium heat. While the water is heating, drop about half of the napa cabbage, negi, and mushrooms into the pot. Lower in half of the tofu pieces as well with a flat mesh skimmer. Once the liquid reaches a simmer, season with the sake and fish sauce. Taste for salt. Sprinkle in a bit more fish sauce if you think it needs it. Slide half of the fish into the *donabe* with half of the *seri* or mizuna. Simmer for about 5 minutes, until the fish is done, and divide all of the ingredients into 4 individual bowls. Serve with a half ladle of broth in a small bowl with a bowl of Japanese rice on the side. When ready for round two, repeat the steps starting with simmering the vegetables and tofu for about 3 minutes before sliding in the *seri* or mizuna and the fish (no need to add more sake or fish sauce). The leftover soup can be strained and refrigerated to be used as a base for simmering cooked rice as an impromptu Japanese-style risotto (*ojiya*).

We make *kenchinjiru* whenever we pound *mochi* (glutinous rice "cakes"). At our farmhouse, *mochi* pounding happens on several Japanese holidays and when we have a crowd of foreign visitors. On one such occasion, Tadaaki suddenly asked me to put sake lees in the *kenchinjiru*, something we had never done before. I was game because I happened to have some sake lees in the freezer from Imayotsukasa (page 308), my favorite sake producer, and had been hankering to try them. Typically, miso is the salt taste paired with sake lees, but Tadaaki wanted me to stick with soy sauce as we usually did. I disagreed but did not tell him. Instead I used all three: sake lees, miso, and soy sauce. The resulting soup that day was the best I had ever made. As it turned out, NHK television network came to film me that year for their Japanology program, so I ended up making *kenchinjiru* more times than I cared to. The bonus was the opportunity to experiment and I discovered that the soup was particularly tasty with the added hidden taste of fish sauce.

country soup
flavored four ways SERVES 8
KENCHINJIRU

2 large carrots, about ½ pound (225 g)

½ small daikon, about ½ pound (225 g)

1 thin burdock root (gobo, page 339), about ½ pound (225 g)

4 taro roots (*sato imo*, page 339), about ½ pound (225 g)

2 (10.5-ounce/300-g) blocks best-quality "cotton" tofu

4 pieces *usuage* (page XXIX, optional)

3 tablespoons organic canola oil

1-pound (500-g) block konnyaku, optional (see Note)

8 cups (2 liters) hot chicken stock or Konbu Dashi (page 266)

2 tablespoons sake lees (page 188)

2 tablespoons inaka miso (page 72)

½ cup (125 cc) best soy sauce

1 tablespoon best-quality fish sauce

7-spice powder (*shichimi togarashi*, page XXXI)

Cooked Japanese rice, for serving (page 172)

Pare off the tops and tips of the carrots, daikon, gobo, and scrub them with a rough brush (*tawashi*) but do not peel. You will be slicing all the vegetables into ⅛-inch (4-mm) thin pieces. The vegetables should be fairly uniform in thickness and size, as you will be cooking them together. Halve the carrot lengthwise and slice into half-moons. Scrape into a medium-sized bowl. Slice the daikon lengthwise into quarters and cut into thin triangles. Scrape into another medium-sized bowl, separate from the carrots. Slice the gobo diagonally into thin pieces. Drop in the bowl with the carrots. Peel and slice the taro roots (*sato imo*) into half-rounds like the carrots or rounded triangles like the daikon, depending on their size. Slide the taro in with the daikon. Cut the tofu in half horizontally through the middle to create two layers. Make 48 small cubes by slicing the two layers into 6 lengthwise pieces and 4 crosswise pieces. Pour boiling water over the *usuage*, if using. (This will remove residual oil. No need to perform this step if you are able to source *usuage* fried in quality oil.) Cut the *usuage* in half lengthwise, then crosswise into ¼-inch (6-mm) strips.

Film the oil in a large heavy soup pot over medium-high heat. When the oil is hot but not smoking, sauté the sliced carrots and gobo for 3 minutes. Scrape in the sliced daikon, taro, and konnyaku, if using. Sauté, stirring, for about 3 minutes longer. Pour in the hot broth and bring to a boil over high heat. Cook at a lively simmer until the vegetables are getting soft but not starting to fall apart, about 15 minutes or so.

Measure the sake lees into a medium-sized saucepan and ladle in a scoop of broth. Whisk over low heat to emulsify, then scrape the softened sake lees into the soup. Spoon the miso into the same saucepan and whisk in a small scoop of broth to form a thin paste. Add to the soup. Season with the soy sauce and fish sauce and slide in the tofu and *usuage*, if using. Simmer for a couple of minutes more until heated through. Sprinkle with *shichimi togarashi* if you like a little spice to your food. Serve with a bowl of white rice on the side.

NOTE: Fill a medium-sized pot three-quarters of the way up with water and toss in a small handful of salt. Bring the water to a boil over high heat. While the water is heating, slice the konnakyu into thin 1½ by ¼-inch (4 cm by 6-mm) strips. Boil the konnyaku pieces over medium-high heat for 15 minutes, drain, and reserve.

When the kids were small, Tadaaki often made fried rice for lunch. A busy farmer, he was always in a hurry, so the result sometimes felt a bit slapdash. Also I was put off by the style of serving: Pack it into a rice bowl and turn out onto a plate as a molded half sphere. I'm not a fan of molded or manipulated food, so it bothered me aesthetically. Once I started making my own fried rice at Sunny-Side Up! for my English immersion students' lunches, I developed a great fondness for the dish. Although I often take care to cook each vegetable separately, here I have not. And I always serve fried rice with a simple lettuce salad.

fish sauce fried rice SERVES 6
ISHIRU CHAHAN

4 cups (1000 cc) cooked Japanese rice (page 172)

About 4 tablespoons organic canola oil

⅓ pound (150 g) small bratwurst-style mild sausages, cut into ½-inch (12-mm) dice

2 usuage (deep-fried tofu pouches), cut into ½-inch (12-mm) dice (optional)

1½ tablespoons small dried Japanese shrimp (sakura ebi, page XXiX)

2 medium carrots (scant ½ pound/200 g), scrubbed and diced (¼-inch/6-mm)

½ teaspoon fine sea salt

2 medium to small onions (scant ½ pound/200 g), cut into ¼-inch (6-mm) dice

1 (1-inch/2.5-cm) piece of peeled ginger, finely chopped

3 small garlic cloves, finely chopped

1 small fresh green chile (japones or serrano), finely chopped

6 medium-sized eggs, at room temperature, beaten

4 tablespoons organic soy sauce

2 tablespoons top-quality anchovy fish sauce

Freshly shaved katsuobushi or hanakatsuo flakes (optional)

If you are using freshly cooked rice (rather than day old), it is wise to release some of the steam, otherwise the dish might become a bit heavy. Turn the cooked rice onto a flat wooden basin (handai, page XIX) or large wooden cutting board and cut into the rice with a rice paddle, spreading out the rice to aerate and cool.

Heat 2 teaspoons of the canola oil in a large, well-seasoned wok or frying pan over medium heat. When hot, drop in the chopped bratwurst until the meat juices dry up and the pan sizzles. Splash in a couple more teaspoons of oil and throw in the usuage, if using, to crisp up. Toss the dried shrimp into the pan, stir once or twice to distribute, and scrape the bratwurst mixture into a medium-sized bowl. Use a rubber scraper to remove any adhering meat, shrimp, or usuage from the pan.

Return the pan to the heat and dollop in 2 more teaspoons oil. Throw in the carrots and a pinch of salt. Toss for several minutes over medium heat until the carrots start to soften. Splash in a bit more oil and slide the onions into the carrots with a pinch of salt. Drop in the chopped ginger, garlic, and chile pepper and the rest of the salt. Stir with a flat wooden spoon and sauté a few minutes more until the onions are soft. Scrape into the medium-sized bowl with the bratwurst mixture.

Use a rubber scraper to remove any lingering vegetables from the sides of the pan and return the pan to the heat. Dollop in a little oil and roll it around the pan to coat the sides. Pour in the beaten eggs and cook quickly, constantly scraping the bottom of the pan to remove the cooked egg layer sticking to the bottom and to allow the raw egg mixture to slurp down underneath the cooked eggs to meet the hot surface of the pan bottom. Once the eggs are set but still slightly runny, scrape them into a clean medium-sized bowl. Wash the wok or frying pan.

Set the wok or frying pan over high heat and film the pan with the remaining oil (by now, a bit less than 1 tablespoon). Dump in the rice and sauté for several minutes, stirring constantly with a flat wooden spoon, turning the bottom layer up over the top layer to ensure even cooking and to dry out the rice. When all of the rice has been seared, stir in the soy sauce and the fish sauce. Lower the heat to medium (soy sauce tends to burn) and sauté for a few minutes more to disperse the liquids. Once the rice is evenly colored and no white remains, stir in the cooked vegetables. As soon as the vegetables are well incorporated into the rice, turn off the heat and add the cooked eggs, cutting them up with the flat edge of the spoon as you distribute them into the fried rice.

Scoop a few large spoonfuls onto a plate and strew some shaved katsuobushi, if using, on top. Serve with a mound of leafy green salad perked up with chopped chives or green onions, dressed with soy vinaigrette (page 113). Sprinkle the fried rice with a bit more fish sauce if you want more salt.

VARIATIONS: I am a big fan of green aromatics, so like to throw on some slivered shiso in the summer. While not particularly Japanese, we occasionally have cilantro in the field, and in that case, I chop it and use it liberally on everything. I've been known to strew with chopped green onions as well.

5

rice vinegar, sour plums,
and persimmons

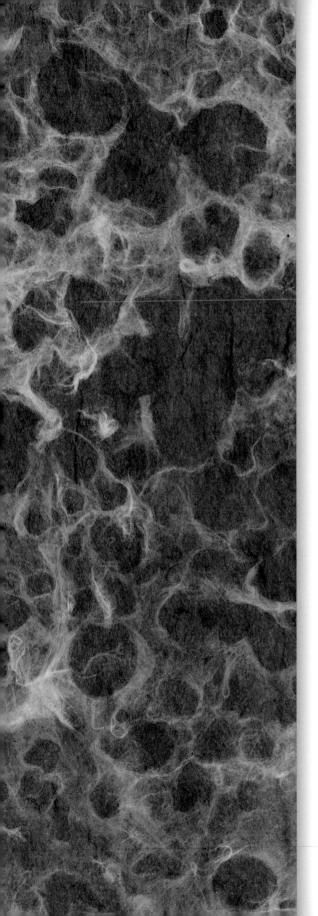

RICE VINEGAR RECIPES

THREE-WAY VINEGAR | 150

SOY VINEGAR | 150

SWEET VINEGAR | 151

DASHI VINEGAR | 151

PICKLED YOUNG SHALLOTS | 155

THINLY SLICED GINGER PICKLES | 156

SWEET VINEGARED TURNIPS AND PERSIMMONS | 157

CHOPPED VINEGARED FLYING FISH | 158

PORK BELLY SIMMERED WITH DAIKON AND LEEKS | 161

KABOCHA TEMPURA WITH THREE-WAY VINEGAR | 163

SOUR PLUM RECIPES

SALTED SOUR PLUMS	167
SMASHED CUCUMBERS WITH SOUR PLUM	169
TURNIPS PICKLED WITH SOUR PLUM	171
MINI RICE BALLS WITH SOUR PLUM	172
MYOGA PICKLED IN SOUR PLUM "VINEGAR"	175

PERSIMMON RECIPES

PERSIMMON VINEGAR	177
DAIKON PICKLED IN SMASHED PERSIMMONS	179
DRIED PERSIMMONS	180
MUSTARD WITH TOFU AND DRIED PERSIMMON	182

Approaching the organization of this book meant weighing different options. Organize by season? By pickling medium? Most of the year prior to actually writing this book was spent visiting producers around Japan, so it became clear that organization by pickling method made the most sense. Here, sour plums (*ume*) and persimmons are grouped with rice vinegar because they have crossover characteristics. For instance plum "vinegar," a misnomer, is actually the brine in which the *ume* soak before drying outside. Tossing some persimmons in a pot will yield a mind-blowingly delicious mild vinegar. In Japan, vinegar is used more for quick pickling or vegetable dishes called "vinegared things" (*sunomono*) than in pickling. Also vinegar makers recommend putting a dash in your miso soup to give it brightness. Here again is the "hidden taste" philosophy, the same as with fish sauce (page 119). A dash of vinegar in udon dough will relax the gluten and result in better-textured noodles. While you are at it, you might as well put a drop in the udon dipping soup to give it balance. And recently in Japan there is a boom of drinking vinegars, which has helped some of the premium vinegar companies grow their bottom line. It is perplexing to me that people buy inexpensive vinegar made from ethyl alcohol for cooking, yet spring for the top shelf for drinking. But then I would rather eat my vinegar than drink it. And our family's good health is thanks to our total diet, not a magic-fix drink.

RICE VINEGAR (KOMESU): Rice vinegar is fermented from alcohol (the quality of which ranges from ethyl alcohol to organic sake). The top-shelf vinegars made by large companies such as Mizkan (Mitsukan, Nakano brands) and Marukan, labeled as "all rice" or "organic," contain 120 grams of rice per liter (while Iio Jozo's red label Fujisu vinegar contains 200 grams per liter and their blue label Premium, a whopping 320 grams per liter). Fujisu is not yet available in the U.S., though the company does sell their sweet potato vinegar (Benimosu) at Dean & DeLuca in New York City and several of their vinegars at various venues in Paris, so there is hope.

I would avoid the cheapest vinegars made by Marukan and Mitsukan since they are quick brewed using ethyl alcohol and a naturally sweet koji drink (amazake, page 313), with only 40 grams of rice per liter. Stick with upper-echelon vinegars or, better yet, choose a "black" or brown rice vinegar made in the Kagoshima style. There are several Kagoshima black vinegars available online in the United States: Some are listed as "black brown rice vinegar" or simply "brown rice vinegar" (Eden Foods). Vinegars described as being fermented in stoneware pots from brown rice, koji, and water are all technically "black" vinegars (page 152). Do not, however, substitute Chinese black vinegar, because it is a completely different product and not suitable for Japanese cuisine. Red "vinegar" (page 165) is rare and not commercially available (except through wholesale sources). Not a rice vinegar, red vinegar (also known as *kasu su*) is pressed from three- to five-year aged sake lees thinned with water.

SOUR PLUMS (UME): Sour plums are a relative of the apricot family and are not edible raw. They should be either salted and dried or steeped with sugar and alcohol for a fruity cordial (page 317). *Ume* ripen in June, so look for them in the early summer. They are available in Japanese grocery stores at that time. Also if you live in an area where Japanese immigrants settled (such as California, Oregon, and Washington), there are certainly trees wanting to be picked. *Ume* go from being not ripe enough to falling off the tree in a matter of a day or two—be warned. If you are a fan of *umeboshi* (Salted Sour Plums, page 167), I recommend taking the time to make your own because it will be less onerous than you think and much appreciated over the course of the following years. *Umeboshi* improve with age, so usually we don't start eating ours until at least one year has elapsed. But if you cannot wait, there is no need to. If you buy *umeboshi* or *bainiku* (smashed *umeboshi* without the seeds), make sure there is no added MSG (アミノ酸) or artificial coloring, unless that does not bother you. *Umeboshi* sweetened with honey are also popular these days, so best read the label. Plum vinegar (*umesu*) is the nuanced fruity brine that forms from salting the *ume* when making *umeboshi*. Eden, Mitoku, and Ohsawa bottle organic *umesu* made in Japan. The flavor is good but somehow different from my homemade *umesu*—stronger and more fruity. Natural food companies and organic grocery stores are the most reliable sources for *ume* products.

PERSIMMONS (KAKI): There are two types of persimmons: astringent and sweet. Interestingly enough, we do not use the variety names Hachiya or Fuyu in Japan. Hachiya persimmons are astringent and typically elongated at the tip. (N.B.: Just to be confusing, there are rounded astringent varieties and elongated sweet varieties.) In Japan, the astringent varieties are used for various pickling projects such as Daikon Pickled in Smashed Persimmons (page 179) or drying for *Hoshigaki* (page 180). They can also be thrown in the pot with sweet persimmons to ferment into Persimmon Vinegar (page 177). Astringent persimmons are never eaten raw in Japan, though in the West they are used in desserts after they ripen to a gelatinous texture. Sweet persimmons, known as Fuyu in the U.S., are eaten raw while still firm. In Japan they are peeled and sliced like apples or apple pears to accompany green tea.

MAKING RICE VINEGAR

For the last two decades, I have been making my own red wine vinegar by pouring red wine over the "mother" sitting in my vinegar pot. If the pot stands undisturbed for a spell, a flat gelatinous membrane forms on top of the vinegar. I push this new mother down into the vinegar and add wine. I fished out a piece of the mother from one pot, popped it in a jar, and filled it with vinegar. I presented the mother to Akihiro Iio (page 159) when we visited his vinegar company and explained that this particular mother was started from the mother that formed on my pineapple vinegar fermented from organic Okinawan pineapple. Iio-san peered at the vinegar and deadpanned, "That kind of mother is formed from lactic acid, not acetic acid, so this is not really vinegar." I became a tad flustered and perhaps still do not quite understand the chemical differences between these various mothers. Why is the mother that forms on Kagoshima "black" vinegar or Iio Jozo brown rice vinegar acetic acid while the one that forms on pineapple vinegar or wine vinegar not? Or maybe it is. Iio-san tasted the vinegar, which he agreed was, in fact, vinegar, though lower in acidity than "official" vinegar. Phew.

This talk of mothers got me delving deep into trying to wrap my head around the science of vinegar making, since I had also been making persimmon vinegar. I have a much better handle on the process than before when I merely threw some skins and cores in a large glass jar of water with a handful of organic sugar and stuck it in the sun for three months (sometimes with success, sometimes not). Making rice vinegar was the logical next step.

Soyoung Scanlan, cheesemaker extraordinaire of Andante Dairy in California, was in Japan recently and came out to visit one day with her daughter, Jamie. We spent the day touring the area, tasting local food, and chatting about fermentation. Soyoung is also in the midst of making her own rice vinegar and understands the chemical properties of fermentation and alcohol conversion better than I. She shared her method. Soyoung makes *doburoku*, but feeds it 3 times with cooked rice until the alcohol reaches 10 to 12% (in a manner similar to the *sandan shikomi* method of sake making). She allows this high-alcohol mash to ferment into vinegar.

METHOD ONE: Toriki-san from Kakuida (page 152) shared with me the proportions for making "black" vinegar. My pot is still young, but hope springs eternal. Soak 1⅓ pounds (600 g) rice in water overnight. Fill a large pot or wok with water and bring to a boil over high heat. Line a bamboo steamer with a large piece of muslin cloth. Drain the rice, wrap in the muslin cloth, and place into the steamer. Cover and cook for 30 minutes. Dump the rice into a *handai* (page XIX) or the back of a large wooden cutting board. Cut and spread with a rice paddle to cool to body temperature. Pour 1⅓ pounds (600 g) of brown or white rice koji into the bottom of a large crock. Dump the cooled, cooked rice on top of the rice koji. Fill with 14½ quarts (13¾ liters) filtered water. Cover with a muslin cloth, tie around the circumference of the crock to secure, and set in the direct sun for 3 months. Top off with more filtered water and age for as long as you have the patience for.

METHOD TWO: Make *Doburoku* (page 311). Once the rice and koji mash fully converts into alcohol, add 1 cup (250 cc) cooked rice to the pot and allow the *doburoku* to convert that rice into alcohol. Repeat this step one more time before storing the pot in the hot sun. (The timing here is tricky. I started in April and put the pot out in May.) Stir every day. When the alcohol begins to convert into vinegar, it forms a thin membrane on the surface of the *doburoku*. Keep tasting the mash. It will take about 3 months for the fermentation process to convert the mash into vinegar. Add water to adjust the acidity and allow at least 3 months more to mellow. Press as you would Persimmon Vinegar (page 177).

METHOD THREE: If you have a red wine vinegar pot with some extra pieces of mother floating about, take a fistful-sized clump out and soak it in several changes of sake to dilute the red wine flavor that permeates the mother. Pop the sake-soaked vinegar mother into a ceramic pot with 1 cup (250 cc) each of sake and best-quality brown rice vinegar. Wait 2 weeks and add 2 cups (500 cc) more sake. After 2 weeks you can siphon off a cup or so of rice vinegar to use. Replace the vinegar you removed from the pot with the same amount of sake. Wait 2 weeks more before siphoning off any more from the pot.

three-way vinegar MAKES 2 CUPS (450 CC)
SANBAISU

Sanbaisu is the basis for making a pickle called *sanbaizuke*, though here it becomes the dipping sauce for tempura. This preparation was one of the many vinegar dishes we were served at Kakuida in Kagoshima. Kakuida produces a stunning Aged "Black" Vinegar (page 152), one more unforgettable Japanese product that I am actively advocating be exported abroad.

⅔ cup (150 cc) Katsuobushi
    Dashi (page 253)

⅔ cup (150 cc) organic soy sauce

⅔ cup (150 cc) brown rice vinegar

Mix the dashi, soy sauce, and brown rice vinegar together and pour into a well-labeled bottle or jar. Keeps for a couple of months, refrigerated. Good for making an instant pickle or on a vegetable salad with equal parts oil.

soy vinegar MAKES 1 CUP (250 CC)
NIHAISU

Soy vinegar is known as *nihaisu* (two-way vinegar). The classic method contains equal parts vinegar and soy sauce, though myriad variations exist today. This distinctive dipping sauce is good with sashimi or broiled fish. Endeavor to find the mildest brown rice vinegar you can, otherwise you might need to adjust the proportions and cut down on the vinegar.

½ cup (125 cc) mild brown
    rice vinegar

½ cup (125 cc) organic soy sauce

Measure the brown rice vinegar and soy sauce together into a jar. Shake. Keeps indefinitely at room temperature. Add equal parts oil and soy vinegar for an instant salad dressing.

sweet vinegar Makes 1 cup (250 cc)
AMASU

Vinegared vegetables are integral to Japanese cuisine and beloved by all. The proportions of sugar to vinegar vary widely, according to taste. Modern Japanese use much more sugar than a hundred years ago, but I like an old-fashioned taste and also have access to naturally sweet vegetables. Here, I opt for the minimum sugar you need to counteract the sourness of the vinegar. But I also use a mild brown rice vinegar, so you may feel this needs a bit more sugar than I have noted. Feel free to adjust.

1 cup (250 cc) brown rice vinegar

3 heaping tablespoons (50cc/50g) organic granulated sugar

Heat the vinegar and sugar together in a nonreactive saucepan over low heat to dissolve the sugar. Cool to room temperature before using to pickle salt-massaged sliced vegetables. Be sure to squeeze the excess water and salt from the vegetables before dropping in the *amasu*. Store sweet vinegar pickles in the fridge. They will keep for 1 week or more depending on the vegetable (weepy vegetables like cucumbers will deteriorate faster than whole roots, such as *Rakkyo*, page 8).

dashi vinegar Makes 1⅓ cups (300 cc)
WARISU

Adding dashi to vinegar softens it, which makes *warisu* a good match to drizzle on boiled refreshed vegetables such as in the variation for Fiddlehead Ferns Drizzled with Soy Dashi (page 265). Tadaaki advises using *warisu* when making smashed tofu dishes such as Mustard with Tofu and Dried Persimmon (page 182). It is also nice on mild salads, especially if you drop in a hint or two of fish sauce.

⅔ cup (150 cc) Katsuobushi Dashi (page 253)

⅔ cup (150 cc) brown rice vinegar

Measure the dashi and rice vinegar into a clean wine bottle or jar. Seal, mark it well, and store in the fridge. Keeps for about 2 months, refrigerated. Shake before using.

AGED "BLACK" VINEGAR

Friends had mentioned an intriguing black vinegar being made in Kagoshima, but it never sounded enticing. I could not rid myself of the image (and taste) of the slick, inky Chinese black vinegar in which we dip our *gyoza*, and could not imagine how it would be used in Japanese cuisine. But I was planning a photo and filming trip to Kagoshima to visit Sakai Kastuobushi (page 255), and we needed to fill out the schedule. So black vinegar it was. The Kakuida vinegar company in the Fukuyama area of Kirishima city in Kagoshima prefecture was the destination.

We pulled up in front of a nondescript modern building that did not prepare us for what lay beyond. The smiling general manager, Susumu Toriki, bowed ever so slightly as he extended his card. As I peered over Toriki-san's shoulder at the cavernous showroom behind him, it appeared they were doing a rollicking business. Toriki-san ushered us down a wide, sweeping hallway lined with historical photos of vinegar making.

We stepped out to a vista of rolling hillsides covered with stoneware pots almost as far as the horizon: 20,000 pots in all. As we stood blinking in the sun a gaunt septagenarian ambled over. I was taken by the orange garb sported by Akaike-san, the gentle brewer. We spent an hour strolling through the pots and tasting the vinegar; I could have spent two. Akaike-san was a patient teacher and immensely proud of his work. He had brought some small plastic tasting glasses and a bamboo scooper. He showed us the cloudy mother forming in one pot of newly fermenting mash and gave us tastes of an acrid 6-month-old clear vinegar. Strong. Weaving through the pots, Akaike-san stopped when it suited him

and unwrapped the paper tops or removed the ceramic tops. He pointed out the characteristics of each stage and explained the properties he was looking for in his vinegar. Each pot is unique, and "just like people, there are good boys and bad boys." However, Akaike-san was confident he could "fix" 50 percent of the "bad boys." (The lesson here is that if you try your hand at making rice vinegar, do not become discouraged if you are not successful. Just try again.)

Fukuyama-cho has a microclimate perfectly suited for making this style of vinegar. The method came from China about 200 years ago and has not changed a bit since. The Kagoshima black vinegar develops in large stoneware pots, which hold 50 to 60 liters. And the pots contribute their own microbes that help as a starter for future batches of vinegar. Although most of the pots are Japanese made (many have been in use for decades or more), newer pots are being sourced from Korea and Vietnam. The vinegars are started in the spring or fall when the sun is hot but not brutally so and the nights are cooled by ocean breezes.

Brown rice koji (page XXVIII) is placed in the bottom of the black stoneware pot, followed by cooked organic brown rice cooled to body temperature. The pot is filled with mountain spring water and a thin layer of koji is sprinkled on the surface of the water to protect the vinegar from putrefaction. The pot mouths are covered with paper, tied, and left in the direct sun to allow the contents to convert into vinegar. The pots are heated by the sun slowly over the course of the day, then cooled by the ocean breeze during the night.

After two or three months (depending on the weather), the koji that was scattered across the surface of the water has sunk, signaling that the mash has undergone saccharification and has fermented into acetic acid. In the next stage of fermentation, a cloudy, viscous "mother" forms on top of the vinegar surface and must be stirred in each time it forms (about every three days). After about six months to a year, the resulting liquid is a clear, fairly one-dimensional, fully fermented vinegar. At this point, the pots are topped off with water and left undisturbed to age. Traditionally the Kagoshima black vinegars aged from 1 to 1½ years before bottling. Now, thanks to the collaboration between Toriki-san and Akaike-san, a boom market has developed for longer-aged Kagoshima black vinegars and other companies are following suit.

Perhaps the term *black vinegar* is one way to differentiate between traditionally made alcohol-fermented brown rice vinegars and this kind of rice-fermented vinegars produced in Kagoshima. I have also read that the pots impart a slight "blackness" to the vinegar, although I did not detect that in my field tastings. Calling these vinegars "black" seems like a misnomer, but since, by all appearances,

they are not having any marketing issues, perhaps moot.

Akaike-san had been talking about and wanting to age the black vinegar longer than the typical 1 to 1½ years. In the meantime he retired. But Toriki-san, seeing the product potential in this aged vinegar, brought Akaike-san out of retirement in 2000. Marketing + know-how = a winning combination. The showroom shop had about thirty people milling around, tasting the various sauces, condiments, and vinegars at any given time. And there was a fairly consistent line five deep at the counter during the several hours we spent at Kakuida. The upstairs dining room, which sits over a hundred, was nearly full as well. Where did they all come from?

I was uninterested in the condiment concoctions being sold, though completely fascinated with the delicate, tan 3-year-old and whiskey-brown 5-year-old. The vinegars have a natural sweetness or caramelization not present in the (equally delicious) brown rice vinegars produced by Iio Jozo (page 159). I use the Kakuida black vinegars when I am looking for a soft round taste in the food, such as for Wild Arugula with Walnut Miso (page 75). They are worth seeking out.

The summer was wearing on, and my two plastic bags of salted young shallots (*rakkyo*) remained stashed in the fridge. It's easy to ignore what needs to be done, but it would be criminal to let those precious *rakkyo* grown by Suka-san's mother go to waste. Finally I rallied my energy and mixed up a batch of sweetened vinegar to extend their shelf life. And we were still eating them over the New Year holiday and well into the new year. They were that good. The trick here is to get good-tasting bulbs and not to oversweeten the vinegar.

pickled
young shallots MAKES ABOUT 2 POUNDS (1 KG)
RAKKYO NO SUZUKE

2 pounds (1 kg) Salted Young
   Shallots (page 8)

3 cups／750 cc Sweet Vinegar
   (*Amasu*, page 151)

Scoop out the salted *rakkyo* from its container using your hands and drop by handfuls into a large clean jar (or jars). Dilute the *amasu* with a scant 1/4 cup (50 cc) water when heating the vinegar to melt the sugar. Cool, then pour the diluted *amasu* over the *rakkyo* and refrigerate for 2 or 3 days before eating. These will keep for at least a year, though I wager you will not be able to keep them around that long! *Rakkyo* is a classic accompaniment to Japanese curry rice, but I like to serve these pickles with Thanksgiving dinner as a palate cleanser or with Miso-Cured Eggs (page 66) as part of an hors d'oeuvres plate.

Most commercial *gari* is full of additives, so I make a big batch in the summer from our field ginger. Late-season ginger will not show the characteristically lovely pink of new ginger. Nonetheless, the pickles are tasty as a palate cleanser or a quick bright bite before dinner—and of course to accompany sushi.

thinly sliced ginger pickles MAKES 1 QUART (1 LITER)
GARI

2 pounds (1 kg) fresh summer gingerroots

2 tablespoons sea salt

3 cups (750 cc) brown rice vinegar

2 cups (400 g) organic granulated sugar

Scrape off the ginger peel by running the edge of an upside-down spoon across the surface. Slice each root as thinly as possible with a razor-sharp knife or mandoline, trying to maintain the interesting natural shape of the ginger. Place the slices in a medium-sized bowl. When you have cut up about half of the ginger, toss in half of the salt and massage gently with your hands to distribute. Let sit for an hour or so and continue cutting the second half of the ginger (follow the same steps for the second half as you followed for the first; salting the first half while you cut the second helps avoid any discoloration of the roots).

After the first half of the ginger has rested in the salt for an hour, lift the slices out from any accumulated liquid and lay out flat on half of a clean kitchen towel (taking care not to break the shapes). Fold the other half of the towel on top of the ginger and press gently to wick out any lingering saltwater. Repeat this step with a second clean kitchen towel after you have finished cutting up and salting the second half of the ginger. Leave the second half of the ginger in the towel for 10 minutes, then drop all of the ginger slices into a medium-sized bowl.

Heat the vinegar and sugar in a small saucepan over medium-high heat, stirring occasionally, until the sugar has dissolved and the mixture has reached a slow boil. Remove from the heat and immediately pour over the squeezed salted ginger slices. Let the vinegared ginger cool naturally before pouring into a clean jar and storing in the refrigerator for several months or more.

Turnips have a natural bitterness that lends itself to pickling. The vegetal element of the turnip also pairs well with a slightly tannic fruit like the persimmon. The persimmons must be ripe but never soft or mushy. They should be the same consistency as the turnips. Use medium-sized turnips, so the turnips will yield similar-sized slices as the persimmons. These pickles keep for about a week or more in the fridge and are convenient to have around as a quick pick-me-up or as a low-cal, bright side dish to any simple meal.

sweet vinegared turnips and persimmons SERVES 6
KABU TO KAKI NO NAMASU

7 small turnips, about 1 pound (450 g)

2 tablespoons ½-inch (1-cm) thick chiffonade of tender turnip leaves

1 firm Fuyu persimmon

1 teaspoon sea salt

½ cup (125 cc) Sweet Vinegar (Amasu, page 151)

Slice off the tops and tails before paring away any discolorations on the surface of the turnips. Scrub them with a stiff vegetable brush (tawashi) and blot dry with a clean kitchen towel. Cut the turnips in half vertically and then crosswise into thin (⅛-inch/3-mm) half-rounds. Drop into a medium-sized bowl along with the chiffonaded leaves. Peel the persimmon, cut in half, and core. Turn the halves, cut side down, onto the cutting board and cut into ⅛-inch (3-mm) thin slices. Cut those slices in half crosswise. Drop the persimmon into the bowl with the turnips and massage the salt in gently. Let sit for 10 minutes to absorb the salt. Squeeze the turnip and persimmon slices by small handfuls and drop into a resealable gallon-sized freezer bag. Pour in the sweet vinegar and slosh around. Roll up the bag, squeezing out the air, and seal. Refrigerate for at least a couple of hours. Scoop some of the pickles out with a slotted spoon and serve in a small ceramic bowl with a little of the sweet vinegar to keep them attractively wet.

VARIATIONS: Omit the sliced persimmons and use slivered citrus peel, rinsed Salted Cherry Blossoms (page 23), Salt-Massaged Shiso Buds (page 20), Salted Red Shiso Leaves (page 19), or chiffonaded shiso leaves as the aromatic. Daikon can be used instead of turnips: Cut into quarters lengthwise before cutting into thin wedge-shaped slices. I also like to serve salted, squeezed spring onions and cucumbers with some slivered ginger in sweet vinegar. Refreshing.

Usually chopped silver fish preparations (*namero*) are seasoned with miso. Here Sakamoto-san (page 126) used a lovely brown rice vinegar, which makes sense, since silver fish varieties such as mackerel and sardines are often salted and given vinegar treatments before eating. The chopped chives complete this simple dish. Eat before dinner with a small glass of sake and you will think you are in Japan.

chopped vinegared flying fish SERVES 6
TOBIUO TATAKI

2 sashimi-grade, very fresh skinless flying fish filets (about 2 ounces/55 g each)

½ teaspoon fine sea salt

2 tablespoons brown rice vinegar

1 tablespoon squeezed grated daikon

2 tablespoons grated ginger

1 tablespoon best soy sauce, for dipping

Cut the long filets in half laterally and sprinkle both sides of the fish with the salt. Soak in the vinegar for 5 minutes, drain, and blot dry. Slice the flying fish filets into ¼-inch (6-mm) strips, then again into ¼-inch (6-mm) dice. Chop the diced fish with a razor-sharp knife until it amalgamates together into a roughly chopped mass. Fold in the squeezed daikon.

Squeeze the grated ginger into a small bowl. Measure out 1 tablespoon of the juice into another bowl and add the soy sauce. Give each person a small dish with a teaspoon of the ginger-soy. Portion out the chopped fish into individual bowls or saucers and serve as an appetizer before dinner. Sake is the pairing of choice here, though champagne would also hit the spot.

VARIATIONS: Substitute sardines, anchovies, or any other ultrafresh shiny fish that can be eaten raw.

IIO JOZO

Akihiro Iio, in his late thirties, is the fifth generation of a venerable vinegar house outside Kyoto: Iio Jozo. His family has been producing vinegar from locally grown rice for over 120 years; the vinegar has been 100 percent organic since the early sixties. Post-WWII Japan Agriculture pushed chemical fertilizers and insecticides on farmers as a means to lighten their load and increase yields. Iio-san's grandfather began to notice that there were no insects or little fishes in the flooded rice fields. Alarmed, he began knocking on the doors of the farmers that grew rice for his vinegar and convinced them, one by one, to convert to organic farming methods. This took two years and was very, very unusual at that time. The fact that Iio-san's grandfather was able to persuade not just one farmer but several is a testament to the man.

But that kind of mettle runs deep in this family. Iio-san's father developed a 20-year-long obsession to create a premium vinegar with unparalleled nuances. The basis for this obsession was his disappointment that some of his customers thought his Fujisu vinegar (already top shelf) had an unpleasant aroma compared to the large company vinegars. The reason for the aversion was the larger presence of rice in his vinegar (200 g per liter rather than 40 g per liter). He could not, in good conscience, decrease the amount of rice in his vinegar, so another solution had to be found. Iio-san (the son) attended graduate school to study the components that make up vinegar aromas and was thus able to eventually create that premium vinegar. It took five years. Iio-san came to understand that if the aroma of rice was bothering some customers, then he should increase the other components that make up the aroma profile. He also increased the amount of rice per liter from 200 g to 320 g. I have not tasted a more complex brown rice vinegar and use it when I want the vinegar to shine on its own, such as on raw fish or vegetables.

Iio Jozo is an anomaly in the climate of rice vinegar making and arguably the best. There are 400 vinegar makers in Japan. One-third of these companies make their vinegar in-house. The others buy their vinegar from large companies such as Mizkan or Marukan. A handful of the 130 or so companies that actually make their own vinegar brew sake in-house from which they ferment their vinegar. The rest buy inexpensive sake or combine ethyl alcohol with amazake (page 313) to produce their vinegar. Most of these cheaper vinegars are machine made. Iio Jozo vinegar is made by human labor at every step of the way, and these are the men that make it: Iio-san, the young scion of the family; Fujimoto-san, the brewmaster; Imai-san, the koji master; and Ito-san, the rice master. We spent two days at Iio Jozo watching (and partipating in) the koji-making process. The warmth and dedication of those four men was apparent in the kind and supportive communication between them.

They all wore a "uniform" of dark blue jeans and white T-shirts, with *tenugui* cloths (page XIII) tied around their heads. Their dapper style contributed to the air of brotherhood. It was clear that each young man valued the others and that the job of making sake was a deeply honorable one.

Iio Jozo is the only vinegar maker in Japan that has its own local farmers growing organic rice for them over a six-month period. Every other part of the process is effected on-site. The rice is milled, and the bran is returned to the rice fields as fertilizer. The top-quality sake is brewed in a hundred-year-old building over the course of forty days using equipment built fifty years ago. The sake naturally ferments into vinegar over 100 days and then rests for over 200 days outside in covered tanks. Other vinegar makers such as Marukan or Mitsukan spend only a week or two on their brewing process. After all, time is money.

Buta no kakuni is a family favorite that we always serve on New Year's Eve. It is also commonly found on izakaya menus since the soft fatty meat simmered in soy sauce goes well with drinks. For me, a little goes a long way, though I have started to change my mind. When on a consulting trip to Niigata recently, we were served a lighter version of *kakuni* while standing around a communal pot in a remote snow-impacted village. This version was lighter because the pieces were a quarter of the size we usually cut, therefore easier to eat in one bite and also easier to avoid any large pieces of fat better left for younger, more hearty eaters. While visiting the 120-year-old vinegar company outside Kyoto (page 159), I picked up a cookbook that the mother had published. My interest was piqued by her recipe for *kakuni* that included vinegar and negi (Japanese leeks). Here, I followed our family recipe but added their vinegar and also some daikon along with the negi. I thought it was the best rendition yet. Be aware that all *kakuni* benefits from long simmering or even starting the day before.

pork belly simmered with daikon and leeks SERVES 6
BUTA NO KAKUNI DAIKON TO NEGI SOE

1⅓ pounds (600 g) best-quality pork belly

½ pound (200 g) *okara* (page XXiX)

1 (1-inch/2.5-cm) knob of fresh ginger

2 cups (500 cc) sake

¾ cup (175 cc) best soy sauce

6 tablespoons hon mirin (page XXXI)

4 tablespoons brown rice vinegar (page XXVIII)

1 small daikon (about ¾ pound/375 g)

Dark green tops and light green stem portions of 2 thin negi (Japanese leeks) or very thin Western leeks

Japanese mustard (optional, see Note)

Cut the pork belly into 1-inch (2.5-cm) cubes. Drop the pork into a small, heavy saucepan and spoon the *okara* over the meat so that it falls into the cracks between the pieces. Fill the pan with cold water to cover by ½ inch (12 mm) and bring to a low simmer over high heat. Adjust the heat to the lowest setting, cover, and cook gently for 1 hour. Remove the pan from the heat and put outside if the weather is cold. Otherwise cool to room temperature before placing in the fridge to chill.

Once the excess fat has solidified in the *okara*, scrape off the *okara* from the pork pieces and set them in a mesh strainer. Rinse off any lingering *okara* from the meat and discard the *okara* mash in the saucepan. Clean the saucepan and dump the meat back in for the first simmer step. Scrape off the ginger peel with the edge of a spoon, slice thinly, and strew in with the pork. Measure the sake, soy sauce, mirin, and vinegar into a medium-sized bowl. Check for the flavor balance and adjust according to your own taste. Pour the flavoring liquids over the pork and bring to a low simmer over high heat. Adjust the temperature to maintain a low simmer and cook, uncovered, for 15 minutes.

Scrub the daikon but do not peel unless the root is not fresh and the skin is tough. Cut into 1-inch (2.5-cm) cubes. Peel off any withered outer layers of the leeks and slice into 1-inch (2.5-cm) lengths. If the leeks are 1-inch (2.5-cm) thick or more, slice in half lengthwise.

pork belly simmered
with daikon and leeks

After the initial 15-minute simmer, transfer the meat and simmering liquid to a slightly larger heavy saucepan to accommodate the addition of the daikon and leeks. Stir in the vegetables, bring almost to a boil over high heat, lower the heat to keep the mixture at a gentle simmer, and continue cooking, uncovered, for another 15 minutes.

Ladle the simmered pork and vegetables into a serving bowl along with the rich simmering juices. Serve individually at the table in small bowls. Dab with Japanese mustard, if using. Good on a cold winter's night.

NOTE: Muddle 1 teaspoon water into 2 tablespoons yellow mustard powder in a small bowl. Turn the bowl upside down on the counter for 30 minutes to let the flavor mellow.

Tempura is one of the trickiest Japanese foods to prepare, but this eggless batter (via Patricia Wells and Joël Robuchon) is light and almost foolproof. Tempura can be eaten with a classic dipping sauce, soy sauce, or even salt. The black vinegar maker (page 152) recommends *sanbaisu*, which I call Three-Way Vinegar. Kabocha tempura goes well with this complex vinegar, as do potatoes. If possible, serve as you cook, because tempura needs to be eaten hot and crispy. By nature of the cooking process, this dish lends itself to serving from the kitchen as people mill around with drinks. Just be careful of the hot oil.

kabocha tempura with three-way vinegar SERVES 6
KABOCHA NO TEMPURA SANBAISU-DE

½ medium-sized kabocha squash, unpeeled (about 1⅓ pounds/600 g)

Organic canola oil

1 cup (150 g) unbleached cake flour

1 cup (250 cc) chilled sparkling water

¼ teaspoon fine white sea salt

6 large ice cubes

Three-Way Vinegar (*Sanbaisu*, page 150), for dipping

Scoop the seeds and pulp out from the kabocha and slice into ¼-inch (6-mm) thick wedges (measured from the thick backside) with a sturdy-bladed kitchen knife. Cut those wedges in half crosswise.

Set a cookie sheet lined with a thick layer of newspapers covered with a layer of paper towels next to the stove. Warm 4 inches (10 cm) of oil in a medium-sized heavy, stainless steel saucepan over low heat. Whisk the flour with the sparkling water and salt in a medium-sized bowl. Take out two pairs of long cooking chopsticks or tongs. Use one pair to dip in the batter and one pair to remove the tempura from the oil. Increase the heat on the oil to about medium-high; the oil should not be smoking. Test the oil with a drop of batter before starting. It should sizzle and immediately form a small ball as it hits the oil but should not brown. Adjust the oil temperature as needed.

Drop the ice cubes in the batter and stir once or twice to chill the batter (depending on how long your tempura operation takes, you may want to remove the ice cubes occasionally to a small bowl, then put them back into the batter without the melted portion).

kabocha tempura with three-way vinegar

Working with 6 pieces of kabocha at a time (depending on the size of your pot), dip the kabocha in the batter, shake off the dripping batter, and drop into the hot oil. Turn gently as the batter takes on a light golden hue. When both sides are cooked, remove to the prepared cookie sheet. Arrange attractively on a salad plate lined with a piece of folded calligraphy paper (page XVI) to blot the oil and serve immediately with a few saucers of the *sanbaisu*. Eat with chopsticks.

VARIATION: Scrub 3 large potatoes and peel if the skins are tough. Slice the potatoes into ½-inch (12-mm) thick rounds before dipping in the batter and frying.

RED "VINEGAR"

Before touring the vinegar brewery at Iio Jozo (page 159) we were escorted into an elegant tatami-matted Japanese house where Iio Jozo receives visitors. As we waited, Akihiro Iio bustled about readying what, by all appearances, looked like a sushi rice tasting. He had set a small rice cooker by his side and a polished *handai* (page XIX) on the low table where we were sitting. He also had a box of obviously special Ariake nori (page XXX) from Fukuoka and a tray of assorted vinegars.

First he dumped the steaming rice into the *handai* and immediately began cutting into the rice pile and spreading it to cool. I was intrigued. The generally accepted method of making sushi rice involves fanning, cutting, and sprinkling the rice with sweetened vinegar all in synchronization (difficult with only two hands!). Iio-san explained his philosophy: It is crucial to sprinkle on the vinegar, then gently cut the rice with the rice paddle and never mash it. The reason not to fan right away is to allow the vinegar to penetrate the rice kernels more successfully. He also used less water than normal: 293 grams of water for 300 grams of rice. After several minutes of cutting in 3 tablespoons plus a little less than 1 tablespoon of mysterious Red Sushi Rice Vinegar (a 1:1 blend of Iio Jozo's blue label Premium vinegar and red vinegar), he set the paddle down and had me fan the rice. Then he cut the rice a bit more, fanned a bit more, and it was done. He caught up a clump of the rice and used his chopsticks to dab it across the surface of a square of the exquisite Ariake nori. He fashioned a rough roll and handed it to me. The nori crackled loudly as I took my first bite. The taste of the sea balanced well against the round vinegar profile of the rice. No need for sugar here and no need for fish. The "sushi" was perfect as is. I asked for another one. And another.

So what the heck was this red vinegar? Iio-san explained: Sake lees are packed into humongous vinegar tanks and aged for three to five years like miso (but without any weight on the surface). The creamy-colored sake kasu first turns tan before it begins to resemble miso. Finally, it develops into a dark reddish brown. In the Edo period, samurai were members of the upper class and so had access to sake, from which they made vinegar. But the plebeian class had to make due with the cast-off sake lees to make their vinegar. Historically, sushi was made by fermenting fish in rice (*izushi*, page 208) during the winter cold months. In the 1800s when the first *nigiri zushi* (nonfermented fish on vinegared rice) was developed, sushi rice was made with 100 percent red "vinegar" (pressed from aged sake lees), no sugar or salt. Nowadays true *Edo-mae zushi* (Tokyo sushi) is still made from half rice vinegar and half red vinegar.

Later, when Iio-san lifted the cover of the tank, I was assailed by the heady aroma of the *sake kasu* that had mellowed over the years. The aged lees are thinned with water, then pressed to exude the red vinegar in exactly the same method as we press soy sauce (page 99). I vowed to start making my own. Iio Jozo only sells its red vinegar to restaurants, but I did find one source online in Japan (one more have-to-have ingredient to put on your wish list!). In the meantime, I bought a few bottles of the Iio Jozo Red Sushi Rice Vinegar and used it to make sushi rice for my immersion preschoolers one day. It was phenomenal with charcoal-grilled *shiobiki* salmon (page 33) from Niigata prefecture. And the kids cried out, "More, more!"

I gained immeasurable self-confidence through making *umeboshi* myself. After my mother-in-law died, my husband tried to deal with the *ume* from our trees, but since he is busy, his method was to store the salted *ume* in alcohol (not my favorite). Recently I have heard more and more reports of *ume* trees all over California planted by the Japanese immigrants who came to the West Coast in the early 1900s. The *ume* should be ready to harvest in June, so look out for them. I harvest the *ume* with Tadaaki's youngest aunt, Katchan. The harvest time is tricky, however, and is one more test (Will I gauge it right this year? Will I have time to pick the *ume* on the exact day they have to be picked? Will I be the good farmwife?). Even if I check the *ume* each day as the time nears, somehow I always end up sifting through the weeds to gather any windfall fruit that has not discolored. It only takes about one day to develop brown spots on the skins in the damp early summer. Another twist is that we have trees in three different spots, and one of the trees is a completely different variety, so they all ripen at slightly different intervals. But the work is worth it because *umeboshi*, if stored well, never go bad. Also homemade *umeboshi* are much, much better than store bought. Photographer Miura-san still talks about my *umeboshi* as the best he has ever tasted, probably because the trees are heirloom varieties and I use good salt—still, I'll take the compliment.

salted sour plums MAKES 5 POUNDS (2.5 KG)
UMEBOSHI

10 pounds (5 kg) sour plums (*ume*)

13 ounces (400 g) fine white sea salt (8% of the weight of the *ume*)

Place the *ume* in a pail and run cold water over them to fill. Soak overnight in a cool spot. Dump the water the following day, transfer the *ume* to a large wooden, ceramic, or food-grade plastic tub, and measure the salt over the *ume*. Distribute the salt with your hand, making sure not to make cuts on the fruit with your fingernails. Place a clean muslin (or food-grade plastic) sheet across the surface of the salted *ume* and drape it down the sides of the tub. Lay a drop lid on top of the sheet and weight with rocks or similar heavy items equaling the weight of the *ume*. (Alternatively, you could line the tub with a thick food-grade plastic bag, squeezing out the air, and cinch it up before laying the drop lid.) Store these salt-weighted *ume* in a cool dark spot, but check after 2 or 3 days to make sure the brine has surfaced. If it has not, massage any residual bottom salt up to the top fruit. The *ume* should remain in the brine for several weeks until the weather turns sunny, but check periodically to make sure no mold is forming (if it has, pick the mold off carefully). After brining for at least 3 weeks (2 weeks for small *ume*), dry the *ume* for 3 days in the bright sunlight (they do not have to be consecutive days) on rattan mats (or the equivalent) stretched across a wooden frame for good air circulation. At night return the *ume* to the pickling pot. On the last day of drying, strain the brine left over in the bottom of the salting tub through a fine-mesh strainer and store in a clean jar or bottle. This is called plum "vinegar" (*umesu*, page 147). I refrigerate my *umesu*; Tadaaki does not. Pack the dried *ume* (*umeboshi*) in resealable gallon-sized freezer bags (fill the bags only half full). A syrupy liquid will pool

salted sour plums

at the bottom of the bags that aids in the long-term preservation of *umeboshi*. *Umeboshi* keep indefinitely at room temperature packed in airtight resealable bags.

VARIATIONS: Some people add Salted Red Shiso Leaves (page 19) to the salt-weighted *ume* while they are waiting for the sun to come out (typically, the red shiso is not yet ready to harvest at the time the *ume* ripen, hence the later addition). Dry the salted shiso leaves at the same time you dry the *ume*. While I have never tried it, it may be possible to make these with green apricots instead of sour plums.

My soba chef friend Kanchan served these to us one summer day several years ago and I never forgot them. I was back in his restaurant eating lunch the following summer and asked him how he had made these quick pickled cucumbers with *umeboshi*. He was hard pressed to remember, so re-created them on the spot. Like many dishes, the updated version had evolved and was even more delightful than the previous one.

smashed cucumbers with sour plum SERVES 6

TATAKI KYURI NO UMEBOSHI-AE

4 medium Japanese cucumbers, about 1 pound (450 g)

2 teaspoons sea salt

2 teaspoons finely chopped *umeboshi*

½ teaspoon organic soy sauce

¼ cup (60 cc) loosely packed shaved katsuobushi

Cut off the ends of the cucumbers and set them on a large cutting board. Give their surfaces some firm whacks with a Japanese pestle (*surikogi*, page XVIII) or rolling pin. Be sure to pull up slightly when the wood impacts the surface of the cucumbers so you don't smash them completely. Break the cucumbers into rough bite-sized chunks with your hands and scrape them into a medium-sized bowl along with the pooled-up juices on the board. Massage the salt into the cucumbers gently and leave to macerate for about 10 minutes.

Squeeze the cucumbers by handfuls and drop them into another clean, medium-sized bowl. Scissor the chopped *umeboshi* into the cucumbers with your fingers, then mix in the soy sauce. Sprinkle in the katsuobushi and toss until well distributed. Serve before dinner with drinks or as a side dish with any summer meal.

VARIATIONS: Stack 8 shiso leaves, roll into a cigar shape, and slice into fine tendrils; toss with the cucumbers instead of the katsuobushi. The cucumbers can be sliced into ¼-inch (6-mm) rounds instead of whacked and broken. Substitute Western cucumbers, but peel and seed them first.

I liked the smashed cucumbers so much that I cast about for other ways to showcase my home-cured sour plums (*umeboshi*). It was early fall, and I needed to thin the turnips in the field, so picked some of the small ones poking out of the ground. The turnips seemed to want more *umeboshi* and less katsuobushi, making this an elegant (and pretty) pickle. These are nicest soon after being made because they will weep a little when stored. Nonetheless they keep for several days in the fridge.

turnips pickled with sour plum SERVES 6
KABU NO UMEZUKE

2 small bunches baby turnips with tender greens attached (about 1¾ pounds/800 g)

1 teaspoon sea salt

1 tablespoon chopped sour plums (*umeboshi*, page 167)

1 large pinch freshly shaved katsuobushi or *hanakatsuo* flakes (page XXIX)

½ teaspoon soy sauce

Slice off the greens, leaving ½ inch (12 mm) of the stems. Save the greens for another dish such as boiled and refreshed greens or salted-massaged greens (page 24). Soak the turnips in a large bowl of cold water to help loosen the soil clinging to the area where the stem juts out of the root. Working with 1 turnip at a time, lop off the tail end and shave off any brown spots around the top with a sharp knife. Drop as you go into a metal strainer. When all the turnips are cleaned, give them one last rinse and set the strainer over a medium-sized bowl to catch the drips. Dump the turnips out onto a clean kitchen towel and pat them down. Wipe the medium-sized bowl dry and keep it by your workspace.

Cut the turnips into quarters or halves depending on their size (you want ¾-inch/2-cm pieces measured across the backs). Massage with the sea salt until some of the liquid is released. Squeeze by handfuls and drop into a clean, medium-sized bowl. Spoon in the chopped *umeboshi* and smooth it around the turnips with your clean hand. Sprinkle in the katsuobushi and soy sauce, toss to distribute, and serve mounded in a small ceramic bowl that complements the white turnips and pinky plums. Good as part of a Japanese pickle platter or with any Japanese meal. Also excellent accompanied by a cold glass of beer or Homemade Ginger Ale (page 321).

VARIATION: Instead of baby turnips you could use medium-sized ones. In this case, slice off the tops and tails, cut the turnips in half vertically, then crosswise into thin (⅛-inch/3-mm) half-rounds.

One summer I spent almost every day at SSU! to make up for being busy earlier in the year. Although we normally cook lunch for the children every day, they bring bentos during spring, summer, and winter break programs. Making my own lunch anyway, I thought it just as easy to make lunch for the handful of kids who had signed up for the optional day care weeks. Also testing recipes for my upcoming fall book tour, it was useful to have appreciative mouths to eat the food. I developed these mini rice balls to serve at bookstore signing events. The idea was to not overwhelm the audience with the unusually puckery *umeboshi*, but rather give them a hint of an essential flavor from Japan. My husband grew the rice, and one of the aunts made the *umeboshi*. I served them with cut-up local vegetables and a dab of homemade miso alongside and a glass of Cold Barley Tea (page 332).

mini rice balls
with sour plum MAKES 18/SERVES 4 TO 6
MINI UMEBOSHI-AE ONIGIRI

2 cups (500 cc) Japanese-
   style short-grain rice

2 tablespoons chopped sour
   plums (*umeboshi*, page 167)

Fine sea salt

5 sheets nori (page XXX)

Cook Japanese rice: Measure the rice into a rice cooker receptacle or a heavy, medium-sized saucepan. Fill the receptacle or pan to the very top with cold water and pour off any dust or debris. Scrub the rice in your fist to dislodge any extra bran. This is a bit of a mash-and-knead operation. Fill the receptacle (or pan) with cold water repeatedly, pouring off the water each time until the water runs clear. Drain one last time and pour 2 cups (500 cc) cold water into the rice, sloshing around the sides a little to dislodge any grains sticking to the sides of the pan. If possible, let sit for 30 minutes before cooking.

Cook in a rice cooker or a heavy, covered saucepan (cast iron or *donabe*, page XVIII) on the stove. Bring the rice to a boil in the covered pot over high heat (bubbly steam will escape around the edges of the pot lid). Turn the heat down immediately to the lowest setting and cook slowly until you hear little crackles when you lower your head close to the bottom of the pan, about 12 to 18 minutes. The heavy pan cooking method yields better rice than the rice cooker, but it is tricky to gauge when the rice is done and the rice will not stay warm very long.

Let the rice sit for 5 minutes, then fluff with chopsticks or a paddle to aerate. Store leftover cooked rice at room temperature for a day or two (no longer), since refrigeration will cause the rice to harden.

mini rice balls with sour plum

Make mini rice balls: Dump 6 cups (1500 cc/1 kg) of cooked rice into a large mixing bowl. Cut the chopped *umeboshi* into the rice with a rice paddle until well distributed (normally, 1 whole *umeboshi* is poked into the center of a large rice ball). Prepare 18 small sheets of plastic wrap about 6 x 6 inches (15 x 15 cm). Mini plastic wrap sold at Japanese grocery stores is most useful for making these rice balls. Hold a ¼-cup measuring cup in your nondominant hand and scoop up a heaping ¼ cup (75 cc/50 g) without packing down the rice. Dislodge the rice from the measuring cup with a table knife held in your dominant hand and drop the rice onto the center of each sheet of plastic wrap. Sprinkle each rice pile with a little sea salt. Fold up the plastic wrap by holding the long edge nearest you and laying it flush along the opposite long edge. After you have folded up the plastic on all of the rice balls, pick up each one and shake any errant rice grains back into the center mass to form a rough but coherent mass. Now fold the two sides into the center and the top edge of plastic wrap back over those folded edges. Shape the *onigiri* by cupping the rice ball in one hand and cupping your other hand on top to encircle. Squeeze together repeatedly to make a compact triangular ellipse, but do not manhandle or smash the rice so much it is completely impacted.

Cut the nori sheets into quarters and set the squares on a small plate. Let people wrap their own *onigiri*. At this point the rice balls can be stored at room temperature for 1 day but keep the nori in a resealable plastic bag. When ready to wrap, lay a rice ball on your nondominant hand and unwrap. Lay a sheet of nori on the rice ball while the plastic wrap is still draped across your hand. The nori square should be placed right below the tip of the rice ball and smoothed around the back side. Keep your fingers on the nori smoothed around the sides of the rice ball and let go of the plastic wrap. Fold up the bottom edge of nori around the back of the rice ball with your freed-up nondominant hand. Set the rice ball on a plate and eat immediately with a bowl of Cold Miso Soup with Cucumber and Myoga (page 83) or crudités dipped into miso.

VARIATIONS: Add 2 tablespoons shaved katusobushi flakes and 1½ tablespoons pan-warmed black sesame seeds to jazz up these simple rice balls. Katsuobushi alone or canned tuna flakes substitute well for the *umeboshi*, though in that case, mix 1 teaspoon sea salt into the rice along with the fish. You could also poke some filling into the center of the rice ball before wrapping with nori. I am partial to canned tuna smashed with pasteurized mayonnaise and a splash of rice vinegar or katsuobushi mixed with soy sauce (Okaka, page 262).

Myoga buds may be difficult to obtain, so you could substitute young ginger, though if you do, try and find the thinnest stalks. Ginger flavor gets hot very quickly as the root fattens. *Myoga* plants are in the ginger family, and the buds grow at the base of where the stem protrudes from the soil. We are lucky to have several plants in our garden, so this is a very quick and easy pickle for us to make. Plum vinegar is actually the salty brine that results from pickling sour plums at home. Commercial plum vinegar does not taste the same but can still be quite good. Be sure to buy a natural one, otherwise you risk preservatives or additives.

myoga pickled in sour plum "vinegar" SERVES 6
MYOGA NO UMEZUKE

⅔ pound (300 g) *myoga* buds

1 cup (250 cc) plum vinegar (*umesu*, page 147)

Pare off any discolored stem bottoms or outside layers of the *myoga* buds. Drop them into a resealable plastic freezer bag along with the plum vinegar. Let the buds marinate in the refrigerator for half a day before serving. The *myoga* will become more and more puckery as time wears on but will retain its crunch. Essentially these salty/sour pickles last forever. Serve with curry rice or Fish Sauce Fried Rice (page 140). Also good as a snack with Brewed Green Tea (page 325) or Homemade Ginger Ale (page 321).

VARIATION: Substitute thin young gingerroots with most of their stalks sliced off.

My Berkeley friend Sharon Jones came to visit for a month one fall, and she accompanied me on several of our filming and photographing jaunts around Japan. We also visited Brown's Field, an organic farm run by photojournalist Everett Kennedy Brown and vegan cookbook author–wife Deko Nakajima. Deko had a pot sitting on her shelf, and I peeked in to see a fragrant slurry. Persimmon vinegar, she breathed. (Deko is a calm, understated woman of great poise.) Captivated, I asked Deko to tell me how she made it. Deko advised me to stir the mash every day, though I did not. I stirred the mash every few days, then not at all. I also strained mine for a peachy-colored ambrosial liquid that will leave you wishing you had made more.

persimmon vinegar MAKES 2½ QUARTS (2½ LITERS)
KAKISU

8 pounds (4 kg) mixed persimmons: goopy windfall, baseball hard, sweet (Fuyu), and tannic (Hachiya)

Dump persimmons of any variety into a crockery pot. Cover with muslin cloth and tie around the perimeter to discourage fruit flies. Set the crock in a sunny spot and let nature take its course. In the first several weeks, it will be necessary to stir the mixture every 2 days to keep it from putrefying. By the end of the first week, you will have a pleasantly effervescent, fruity slush. Keep stirring and tasting over the next few weeks. As the winter sun softens, you will not need to stir the mash as often. Once you can taste that the persimmons are starting to throw off vinegary overtones, it is time to let the mash rest so that it can form a "mother" and mellow slowly over the course of the cool months leading up to spring. Keep tasting periodically, but do not disturb the gelatinous particles forming on the surface, as this is the mother.

Strain the vinegar when the taste has rounded out and has a clear fruit profile (about 3 months) but certainly before the weather turns warm. Set a fine-mesh strainer lined with a square of muslin cloth over a medium-sized bowl and scoop about 4 cups (1000 cc) of the mash into the strainer. Let the liquid drip out naturally. This will take several hours, so prepare to do this extracting operation over the course of a couple of days. Persevere, though; you will be happy you did. After dripping for a couple of hours, fold the muslin cloth over the top of the mash and set a small cast iron enameled pot on top to encourage the juices to press out. Add a few cans inside the pot for extra weight. Finally, remove the weights, twist the cloth ends to form a bundle, and squeeze with all

persimmon vinegar

your might. Store the squeezed mash in plastic containers in the fridge and use as a pickling bed for daikon (page 179) or instead of sour plum in Smashed Cucumbers with Sour Plum (page 169).

While it is possible that a full gelatinous disk (mother) will form on the surface of the persimmon mash, do not be alarmed if you only end up with small gelatinous patches here and there. It merely means you may have been a bit overzealous in your stirring. If your vinegar tastes like vinegar, it is vinegar. If the mash smells off or tastes of soap, it has gone bad. Toss it and try again the following year! Good paired with a bright oil such as organic canola on delicate spring vegetables or baby lettuce salads.

When I visited Akita prefecture for a Slow Food Japan meeting, I heard about these pickles but never ate them. But the daikon and persimmon pickle piqued my interest, so I tracked it down on the Internet. This is another one of those recipes that you can make only once a year when persimmons and daikon are in season. Also they take one month to cure. However, you can make a very intriguing substitute that only takes three days to cure from the mash left over after pressing out Persimmon Vinegar (page 177). That is, if you make persimmon vinegar first!

daikon pickled in
smashed persimmons MAKES 4 POUNDS (2 KG)
DAIKON NO KAKIZUKE

5 pounds (2.5 kg) small to medium-sized daikon

5 pounds (2.5 kg) firm tannic persimmons (Hachiya, page 344)

6½ ounces/200 g coarse sea salt (8% of the persimmon weight)

Scrub the daikon with a rough vegetable brush (*tawashi*, page XVII) and slice off the leaves. Put the tannic persimmons in a clean, heavy paper bag, such as is used for storing grain, or several double layers of grocery store bags. Bang the persimmons with a rolling pin to crush them roughly. Dump the crushed persimmons into a large bowl and massage in the salt. Smooth a ¾-inch (2-cm) layer of the smashed persimmons across the bottom of a wooden or plastic pickling barrel. Cut the daikon in halves or quarters to fit the pickling barrel and arrange on top of the persimmon mash. Smooth in a layer of persimmon mash, then more daikon. (You may have only enough for one layer of daikon.) The last layer should be persimmon. Place a drop lid on top of the persimmons and set a 10-pound (5-kg) weight on top before covering. Leave in a cool, well-ventilated spot for 1 month before eating. These pickles can be served as part of a pickle plate or on their own as a palate cleanser. These pickles are slightly salty with lovely persimmon overtones. They will keep immersed in their brine for several months or more, stored in a cool spot.

VARIATIONS: Hang a small daikon to dry for 2 days until slightly softened. Cut into manageable lengths and slice those lengths in half lengthwise. Bury in the pickling bed made from the mash left over from pressing Persimmon Vinegar (page 177). Let pickle for 3 days in the fridge. Remove from the pickling bed and slice into ¼-inch (6-mm) thick half-rounds. Be sure to leave some of the vinegary persimmon mash clinging to the daikon. Turnips are also tasty pickled the same way. Use whole baby (leave a little stem as well) or halved medium-sized turnips.

Except for a period when I ate peanuts and raisins in my lunch box, dried fruit was always something I cooked with rather than snacked on. However, dried persimmons (*hoshigaki*) always intrigued me. We first bought a rope of them in the city of Hida Takayama. In subsequent years, I bought the *hoshigaki* in small plastic packages when they started to appear in our local farm stands. The season is midwinter depending on the area. I liked the *hoshigaki* and used them often in vegetable dishes such as Mustard with Tofu and Dried Persimmon (page 182), but was never tempted to bite into one and eat the whole thing until given one made by a 75-year-old rice farmer in Niigata prefecture. It got me thinking that I should be making my own; I could not believe how dead easy they were to make. Or how blissfully satisfying they were to munch on when I was feeling peckish. Hanging under the eves ensures that the persimmons do not dry out too much. The flesh remains firmly gelatinous, and these *hoshigaki* are leagues beyond the ones dried in the direct sun by large-scale producers.

dried persimmons MAKES 30
HOSHIGAKI

30 hard, tannic persimmons (Hachiya, page 344)

Clip the persimmons from the branch, leaving the natural T-shape twig at the top of the fruit. Pare or peel off the skin, leaving the top crown. Spread the peels on flat round baskets and leave outside in the direct sun until completely dried. Use for pickling projects such as *Takuan* (page 217). Tie a loop in the top of a 30-inch length of thin hemp rope and poke the T-shape tops of 5 or 6 persimmons into the rope by opening up the strands. Alternate poking the T-top from each side of the rope (i.e., left side, right side, left side) at intervals of about 4 inches (10 cm). Hook each rope to a nail hammered underneath the eaves and dry until they are pleasantly orangy-brown but not black. This is a matter of taste, so if you like them more on the orange side, that is your prerogative. The drying process takes about 1 to 1½ months. The persimmons should be hung in a spot that gets sun and air but preferably not direct sunlight. If you buy persimmons already clipped without the T, cut a 2-foot (60-cm) piece of twine. Tie 2 persimmons together at each end of the twine by looping it around the calyx of each persimmon. Hang the persimmons from a pole in a semisunny spot in the garden or on your balcony.

When dried to your satisfaction, store the *hoshigaki* in a mesh basket and cover with a cotton or linen cloth. For long-term storage, freeze, though you probably do not need to. If stored properly (in cloth, at room temperature), *hoshigaki* keep well for at least 5 to 6 months or more. Just keep checking them since they are precious and you do not want them to go bad.

More and more places around the world are making tofu successfully. Living in Japan spoils me, but Meiji Tofu in Gardena, California is as good as the best Japanese tofu. I have also successfully used San Jose Tofu in the San Francisco Bay Area and Phoenix Bean in Chicago for cooking events in the States. The bitter mustard plays off well with the sweet-salty tofu, and the chopped dried persimmon adds the perfect last balanced note to this dish.

mustard with tofu and dried persimmon SERVES 6
KARASHINA NO SHIRA-AE

1 (10.5-oz/300-g) piece of Japanese-style "cotton" tofu

1 large bunch (about 1 pound/450 g) mustard greens (or rapini)

2 tablespoons sesame seeds

2 tablespoons brown rice or barley miso

2 tablespoons *Warisu* (page 151) or 1 tablespoon brown rice vinegar

2 dried persimmons or a small handful of dried unsulphured apricots

Place the tofu on a cutting board propped up on one end, angled into the kitchen sink for draining. Lay another chopping board or plate on top of the tofu to press out the excess water for 1 hour.

Fill a large pot with water and bring to a boil over high heat. Set a large bowl of ice water in the kitchen sink. Align the stem ends and grab the greens. Lower the thick stems into the boiling water. Count to 10, then drop the greens into the pot and cook an additional 1 to 3 minutes, depending on their thickness. Scoop out the greens with a strainer, shake off the excess water, and plunge the strainer into the ice water bath. Add cold water or more ice if the water does not feel icy cold. Once the greens are cooled, squeeze down their lengths and lay them across a cutting board. Slice the greens into 2-inch (5-cm) lengths. Squeeze the greens by handfuls one more time for good measure.

Heat a small, dry frying pan over medium-high heat until you feel the heat rise from the surface of the pan. Throw in the sesame seeds and roast them until they are fragrant and just starting to pop. The crucial point is the aroma, so shake the pan and pull it off the flame every few minutes to keep the seeds from burning. The roasting will be quick for this small amount of sesame seeds—maybe 3 minutes. Grind the sesame seeds in a *suribachi* (Japanese grinding bowl) or clean spice grinder until most of the seeds have broken down. Add the miso and *warisu* to the *suribachi* and blend to emulsify. If you are using the spice grinder, mash the ground sesame, miso, and *warisu* together in a medium-sized bowl. Squeeze handfuls of tofu to press out any lingering moisture and add to the grinding bowl (*suribachi*). Continue grinding to emulsify all the ingredients until creamy. Alternatively, process the squeezed tofu and mashed sesame-miso in a food processor or blender. Gently fold in the cooked and squeezed mustard greens and chopped dried persimmons. Scissor with your clean fingers to distribute the sticky dried fruit pieces. Serve in an attractive pottery bowl to accompany grilled meat or fish.

VARIATIONS: This dish would also be nice with arugula or peppery cresslike greens in place of the mustard. In that case just dunk the greens in and out of the water before refreshing immediately. I folded poached fava beans into *shira-ae* at a spring lunch I cooked in Paris and it was lovely. (In this case, skip the dried fruit and use slivered yuzu or Meyer lemon peel to add brightness.)

こうじ酒粕
ぬか

6

koji, sake lees, and rice bran

KOJI RECIPES

BITTER MELON KOJI PICKLES	191
SHIO KOJI	192
SHIO KOJI–PICKLED ONION	193
AVOCADO WITH SHIO KOJI DRESSING	197
SHIO KOJI–SAUTÉED SHIITAKE	198
SHIO KOJI–MARINATED SALMON	199
SHIO KOJI–GRILLED PORK	201
SHOYU KOJI	202
ZUCCHINI PICKLED IN SHOYU KOJI	203
TOMATO WEDGES DRIZZLED WITH SHOYU KOJI	204
SHOYU KOJI–MARINATED YELLOWTAIL	206

SAKE LEES RECIPES

SMALL MELONS IN SAKE LEES	209
SAKE LEES SOUP WITH SALMON	210
SAKE LEES–CURED CHICKEN	212
SAKE LEES ICE CREAM WITH FIGS	215

RICE BRAN RECIPES

HALF-DRIED DAIKON PICKLED IN RICE BRAN	217
RICE BRAN PICKLES	220

The three most important nonsalt or vinegar components for pickling are grouped in this chapter. They all are also the most unfamiliar and perhaps unconventional ingredients in the book. Now that we have discussed some of the more common methods, I want to give you some teaser explanations of more difficult or unusual methods. This second layer of preserving often uses these three very old and integral preserving mediums. Approach these ingredients with an open mind and start slowly. Take it step by step and as you gain confidence, branch out.

KOJI: Simply put, koji (*Aspergillus oryzae*) is a spore that in bygone days was harvested from the air around where fermentation was happening. The spores intermingled, so there was no one sake koji spore strain or no one miso spore strain. Eventually shops began specializing in selling rice koji for miso-making or pickling projects at home. About 1,000 such shops remain in Japan, of which one is Kojiya Honten, owned by Myoho Asari (aka The Kojiya Woman, page 194). When I arrived in Japan almost 30 years ago, rice koji was already being sold in supermarkets in machine-pressed cakes. Home fermenting projects using koji were not common, so koji was only used for the occasional pickling project and not on a daily basis. After the shio koji boom, thanks to the Kojiya Woman, artisanal rice koji is now much more readily available both in Japan and abroad (see Resources). Koji grows naturally in the right conditions (such as on the grains of young green rice during the rains), and Terada Honke in Chiba prefecture is one of the few sake producers harvesting wild koji from their organic rice stalks. The sake they craft is unusually funky, in a fruity, interesting way. (I love it.) However, Terada Honke is an anomaly. The vast majority (if not almost the complete majority) of miso, soy sauce, sake, shochu, and mirin makers buy koji spores (*koji kin*) from one of 7 koji spore laboratories in Japan. These laboratories developed in the Meiji period (1868–1912) as a means of harnessing the wild koji strains and developing the best strains to match the right fermentation process.

There are two main strains of koji spores. Shochu-making koji spores are a milk coffee–brown, while sake, miso, and amazake spores are a pale sage green. One hundred grams of koji spores can inoculate 100 kilos of rice, a ratio of 1:1000. Koji allows enzymes to develop to drive the fermentation process. (N.B.: There is also red koji [*Monascus purpureus*], which is mainly used in China, though occasionally for bread making in Japan.)

Confusion arises because both koji spores and rice koji are commonly called, simply, "koji." Rice koji is steamed rice that is inoculated with koji spores and left in a warm, moist, environmentally controlled room to propagate over the course of two to three days. The rice becomes covered in a furry white fuzz and is either used immediately to brew or ferment or spread out to dry for two days in a covered but well-ventilated spot.

Koji interacts directly with foods and thus imparts multidimensional flavor components, whereas MSG imparts a one-dimensional flavor punch that "seems" delicious (but ultimately merely masks what is missing in the food itself). Koji stimulates the inherent sweet, sour, bitter characteristics of foods and results in a more complex, well-balanced dish. And koji helps the body digest foods.

Writing this book, I got a view of the layers and layers of preservation techniques that exist in Japan. The world of Japanese fermentation has deep, deep roots, and much of this fermentation uses the ubiquitous koji.

SAKE LEES: In the past, all pressing of the mash of whatever was being pressed was done in a wooden boat-shaped apparatus. Hemp or heavy cotton bags were filled with the mash, then stacked on top of each other in the press. A board was placed across the bags, and a lever-weighting system pressed the liquid out slowly. The various lees resulting were used in pickling and preserving. Today a humongous hydrolic machine pumps the mash through a series of stainless steel vertical-meshed plates, where the lees are captured in huge sheets. Sake lees are sold in packaged sheets, whereas mirin lees (*kobore ume*) are crumbled (hence the Japanese name, which means "spilled plums" and refers to white *ume* flowers fallen on the ground). Mirin lees do not keep long and are not widely available but may be used as a natural sweetener; they are a softer alternative to sake lees for pickling.

RICE BRAN: Brown rice remains after removing the rice hulls. Polish off the bran and you have white rice + fresh rice bran. A Japanese farmer is the best source for this perishable item, but perhaps that is unrealistic. Bob's Red Mill Rice Bran is widely available in natural food shops and Whole Foods. Shiloh Farms in Pennsylvania and Rhapsody Farm in Cabot, Vermont, sell organic rice bran online. Also some conscientous smaller Japanese grocery stores abroad source higher-quality or organic rice bran. According to *Consumer Reports* and *New Scentist*, commercial rice bran products can contain inordinate amounts of arsenic, so, if possible, verify the growing conditions of the rice bran you buy.

MAKING KOJI

You need three things to grow koji: a room (or space) without outside pathogens, steamed and cooled grain, and koji spores (*koji kin*). A large table with shallow sides (similar to a tabletop sandbox) also helps. Koji is more and more on the minds of the members in our soy sauce–making community (page 93). The propagation of koji is what separates the men from the boys and is perhaps the most crucial step when making sake, shochu, miso, and soy sauce. When I visited the koji spore laboratory, the owner assured me that I could produce koji at my home, regardless of whether or not I had a environmentally controlled box or room. I have yet to put it to the test, but in my travels have assisted in three different koji-making operations. Iio Jozo (page 159) makes rice koji for brewing organic sake that will be turned into vinegar, so the process takes only two days. The rice koji produced by Kojiya Honten, run by the Kojiya Woman's family (page 194), destined for miso, amazake, shio koji, and shoyu koji, is allowed to grow furry over the course of three whole days. Iio Jozo and Kojiya are professionals and accordingly have dedicated rooms for cultivating their rice koji. Masashi Matsuda (page 78), my friend who grows organic soybeans for our miso- and soy sauce–making groups, makes do propagating his koji in washer-sized machines that control the temperature and humidity. A testament to Matsuda-san's commitment to DIY is the two $4000 machines he now owns (though one was a hand-me-down).

Matsuda-san had told me to arrive by 7 a.m. By the time I drove up, steam was billowing from the steamer boxes stacked five high on top of a vat of boiling water. Orange and blue

flames darted out and licked the edges of the blackened cauldron. Hiroshi Ninomiya, already gowned and hairnetted, was scooping the previous batches of koji (now air-dried for storage) into plastic bags to be used the following week to make miso. Hiroshi helps Matsuda-san whenever Matsuda-san needs a hand. He's that kind of guy. Always smiling, always projecting good humor, he's a fixture in our community. After the air-dried rice koji is weighed out and bagged, Hiroshi wipes the table down with alcohol in order to avoid cross-contamination between batches. The next two batches are due to be made into *doburoku* (page 311), though if anyone asks, amazake (page 313), since the Japanese tax man objects to citizens brewing alcohol.

Hiroshi gathers the four corners of the muslin cloth in which the rice has cooked and hefts the steaming bundle out of the box. Matsuda-san removes the empty box and grabs a second bundle. Two bundles at a time are inoculated,

so the bottom steamer boxes stay put. They each dump their bundle of rice on the table and attempt to remove all stubbornly adhering kernels, not an easy task considering their temperature. (The rice was steamed for one hour, until almost done.) We spread the rice across the table with large wooden paddles to cool to body temperature. After Hiroshi sprinkles the surface with powdery, pale green koji spores, we knead the rice with the edges of our palms to better distribute the spores around the kernels. Next, we cut square sections of rice with our paddles and flip the sections over like pancakes. Hiroshi floats a bit more koji spores on the back side, though this time not as much as the first. After another knead, we amass the rice into a mound in the center of a large cloth, gather it back up into a bundle, and nestle it into the koji culturing box. Matsuda-san sticks a thermometer in the center of the rice and clips the cloth together loosely. The temperature in the box is initially 86°F (30°C), but by evening it will have reached 100°F (38°C). Each of his two boxes can culture 15 kilos of rice at a time.

Since freshly cultured koji is time-sensitive (it takes three days to culture and you should use it within a week), it would be impossible for Matsuda-san to culture the 300 kilos of soybean-wheat koji that our soy sauce community needs, but he has been culturing his own. That day, we pressed the soy sauce that Matsuda-san had fermented in a cedar barrel using his own koji-cultured soybeans and wheat. I was struck by its heart, a pure reflection of Matsuda-san himself.

I tend to crave bitter flavors in the summer or early autumn when the days are hot and the nights are warm. Japanese bitter melon is glossier and softer-skinned than most of the bitter melons I have found in the States. Look for smaller varietals; perhaps even the mini Indian bitter melons might be a good choice.

bitter melon koji pickles SERVES 6
GOYA NO KOJIZUKE

½ cup (225 cc) shochu (page XXXii)

3 cups (720 cc/600 g) rice koji

2 medium-sized bitter melons, about ½ pound (225 g) each

Mix the shochu into the rice koji and let sit for 30 minutes to allow the rice koji to absorb the liquid.

Halve the bitter melons lengthwise and scoop out the seeds with a soup spoon. Cut the bitter melons in half crosswise and layer in a resealable freezer bag with the rice koji. Refrigerate for 4 hours or overnight. Scrape off lingering rice koji before serving, but do not wash. Cut into ⅓-inch (1-cm) slices and arrange nicely on a small plate. Good with drinks before dinner.

Shio koji is experiencing a significant boom in Japan and recently has moved its way abroad as well. I felt confident that shio koji and shoyu koji would become mainstream Japanese ingredients in the United States, so included some recipes in the photo shoot we did for a *Food & Wine* feature in the September 2014 issue. Making shio koji is ridiculously simple, and as it keeps for one year, there is little chance you will ever need to throw any out. This is magical stuff! The discovery and subsequent promotion of this ancient concoction is thanks to Myoho Asari, aka the Kojiya Woman (page 194).

shio koji MAKES 1¼ CUPS/300 CC

10.5 ounces (300 g) rice
  koji (page XXVII)

2 ounces (50 g) excellent sea salt

Measure the rice koji and sea salt into a medium-sized bowl. Pour in ¾ cup + 1 tablespoon (200 cc) water and cover loosely with a clean kitchen towel. Stir every day for 1 week to 10 days, depending on the ambient temperature of the room. Store in a jar in the fridge for 1 year. Drizzle on vegetables and eat after 30 minutes (or right away depending on the cut of vegetable); use with lemon and oil as a base for a salad dressing (page 197); marinate fish (page 199) for a few hours and duck or pork (page 201) for a day or so before grilling.

VARIATION: Emulsified Shio Koji: Whirl a batch of shio koji in a blender or miniprep and use to brush on vegetables before grilling or sautéing.

One morning I stopped by Yamaki Jozo (page 106) in the hills above us to pick up some supplies. Shopkeeper Sakurai-san called me over to sample some onion pickles she had made. I liked them so much that I quickly went home and whipped some up for the kids' lunch at SSU! Normally you wouldn't think to serve children raw onions, but I often do. It was early summer and the onions were sweet and juicy. Also the shio koji almost "cooks" the onions, so they are not quite raw. These do not keep longer than a day or so, since the onions tend to get droopy.

shio koji–pickled onion SERVES 6
TAMANEGI NO SHIOKOJI-ZUKE

4 small fresh onions, about
   ¾ pound (350 g)

3 tablespoons Shio Koji (page 192)

Cut the ends off of the onions and peel. Slice into ¼-inch (6-mm) thin rounds and place carefully in a resealable gallon-sized freezer bag. Fan the onions out a bit so the shio koji can reach all of the surfaces, but try to keep the onions in some semblance of order. Spoon the shio koji into the bag and spread it around the onion slices by dislodging them gently from each other before laying them back against each other. Roll up the bag tightly and leave for 30 minutes to macerate. Remove the onions from the bag and arrange on a pretty plate. Serve as a side dish with grilled meat or fish.

VARIATIONS: Sliced turnips or radishes, halved lengthwise, are also nice pickled in shio koji.

THE KOJIYA WOMAN

When I walked through the door of the Fuji TV set, her face lit up, and she approached me with arms outstretched for a warm hug. Japanese, while known to hug, normally don't do so on first meeting. Friends had told me about the Kojiya Woman, for she is a modern-day legend now in Japan. Myoho Asari was the woman who discovered shio koji in an Edo period food anthology and spread the word all over Japan through her blog.

Myoho favors Japanese outfits of old-fashioned patterned cloth. The pants billow out a bit but tie at the ankle, and the top is a belted jacket with a cream-colored shirt peeking out from underneath. Her glasses are attached with a chain cheater that drapes down her wide, smiling face. Does she ever frown? I doubt it. She has much to be happy about and even more to be proud of. Myoho is a sixty-something, outspoken, ebullient woman who is in love with her chosen métier. Our meeting was electrifying because we both had so much to say. The producer's response: "We need to get you together on film!"

Unfortunately Myoho-san was jetting off for a monthlong koji promotion tour in Germany and France, and I was leaving for the States soon after she got back. Not wanting to let any more time go by for an opportunity to collaborate, I changed my flight and managed to squeeze in a two-day trip to Kyushu. We left Haneda Airport at the crack of dawn; nonetheless time was tight if we wanted to participate in the koji-making cycle (page 189). To that end, Myoho and her husband, Shingan, made the hourlong trip to the Oita Airport to fetch us (and drove us back as well!). Still groggy from lack of sleep and the

drive, we unloaded our stuff and sat down for a warm glass of amazake (page 313) before a welcome caffeine jolt from a few cups of green tea (page 325). Over tea we talked koji.

During that 1½-day trip, we were able to participate in koji rice making from shoveling the burning hot rice out of the steamer to piling the koji-inoculated rice into mounds on stacking trays (about halfway through the process). Her koji master second son, Ryotoku, who will take over that part of the business, patiently allowed me to help him scoop the chestnut-smelling juvenile koji rice onto the trays. And her eldest son, Joei (who is handling a planned expansion abroad), demonstrated the most effective way to massage the koji into the rice (at each place the method was slightly different).

While we worked, Ryotoku told me the story of his decision to take over the company from his mother. In Japan, one son (or sometimes daughter), usually the eldest, is designated as the *atotori* (person to take over). In fact, Ryotoku is the second son, but at the time his older brother, Joei, was not interested. At university, Ryotoku formed several friendships with foreign students and through their eyes he began to better understand the treasures of Japan, of which koji was one. He changed his coursework to zymology (study of fermentation) and expressed to his parents the desire to become the 10th-generation koji maker for his family's company. Around that time, Myoho's father fell ill and in 2007 Myoho had to take over the reins of the koji shop. Sadly, most households no longer made their own miso and amazake, so the local market for koji had dwindled to almost nothing. As a result, the koji shop was not doing good business, and Myoho and her husband were considering shuttering the shop. The news that their son would come home after graduation to work side by side with his parents, eventually taking over, gave Myoho and Shingan renewed energy to push through and continue.

Myoho felt badly that her son would be taking over a dying business so, ever the researcher (she has shelves of scholarly tomes on her shelves in the shop), decided to explore new ways to use koji in daily life. At the time, she was already selling one original koji product in her shop: koji natto (soy sauce— and sake-flavored natto, cultured with koji). The story went like this: She had met someone from another area who knew of this dish but reported that the commercially produced version was not tasty since it was made from inferior koji. This woman traveled to Oita to teach Myoho how to re-create koji natto, and from that time the seed was planted in Myoho's brain. Why not explore ways to use koji outside of the mainstream? Myoho began perusing an Edo period anthology on Japanese foods and came across one small reference that gave her pause: "Put sardines in shio koji." Since Japanese cookbooks did not list amounts, the development was left to Myoho. Myoho also had the foresight to blog about her methods and recipes. The fire was ignited, and by 2011 she had published several recipe books and become a media darling.

Myoho-san's family is as warm as she is, though a bit more reserved. But they are all serious about food and cooking. The first day lunch consisted of at least fifteen different small dishes, and the community-cooked dinner probably had twenty.

ひとり勝ちでは
幸せはやって来ない
支え合い励まし合って
お互いの未来を
照らし輝かす
妙峰

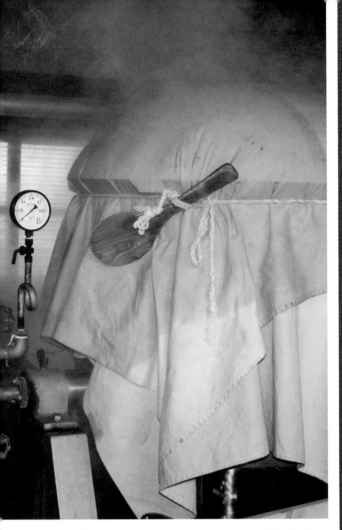

In between trips to the *koji muro* (the room where the rice koji propagates), the lot of us spent a few hours slicing fish, snipping seaweed, chopping vegetables, and simmering soup. The cooks rotated in, then left to attend other duties, though the constants were Myoho and me. Fuji TV had requested I create two original Western dishes using shio koji and shoyu koji, and I had brought the ingredients with me. In between preparing those dishes, I jotted notes and snapped photos. I was most taken with a version of hand-chopped jack mackerel (*aji*) that used shio koji rather than miso to season the fish and the squid cut into strips as for Raw Squid in Coral (page 287) where Myoho-san used shio koji in place of the squid coral. Also the ultrafresh seaweed that we swished in a pot of konbu-flavored water was a revelation. The dark greeny-brown seaweed is immediately shocked bright green when it hits the simmering water, and we dunked a corner of the seaweed in Soy Vinegar (page 150) before popping in our mouths. By the time all the dishes made it onto the three tables that had been pushed together, there was no more space. We squeezed chairs around, clicked glasses, and dove into the feast. Sometimes people are awkward around me because I am a foreigner, but this was not the case that night. The Asari family included us into their fold as if we were one of them. Had it just been that morning that we arrived?

Myoho Asari believes that it is important to pass on this fermented food culture to future generations and proclaims, "Through koji we will find good health and world peace." I agree.

Over coffee a few years ago, Max Bernstein (a college student pal) regaled me with his shio koji adventures. His favorite way to eat shio koji was smashed into an organic California avocado, seasoned with salt and lemon, then spread on Acme levain bread. I filed this away but was reminded of the method when served a similar rendition at one of the meals shared with Myoho Asari's family (page 194). I crave avocados but don't eat them much in Japan because they suffer from the long transit. A few days later, I stopped by the Thursday farmers' market in Berkeley, California, to pick up vegetables for my weekend of cooking. I was visiting my sister's mother-in-law in Healdsburg, and we had an ex–head chef, an ex–pastry chef, and an ex–pastry cook of Chez Panisse coming to dinner. Just a little intimidated, I put together a plate of Japanese small bites for each person and served them with flutes of champagne. Inspired by Myoho-san's salad, I created this dish, using my brother-in-law's freshly pressed Frantoio Grove olive oil. In the interest of maintaining a Japanese flavor profile, I substituted neutral canola oil here.

avocado with shio koji dressing SERVES 6
AVOCADO NO SHIOKOJI-AE

3 medium-large ripe avocados (about ⅔ pound/300 g each)

1 tablespoon Shio Koji (page 192)

2 teaspoons freshly squeezed lemon juice

2 tablespoons organic canola oil

1 tablespoon finely chopped chives

Cut the avocados in half, whack a large kitchen knife into the center of the seed, and pull it out. Scoop the avocado flesh from the skin, remove any discolored portions with a small, sharp knife, and cut the avocado into ½-inch (12-mm) dice. Toss the avocados gently with the shio koji, lemon juice, oil, and chives. Mound in a small bowl and serve as a salad with any meal or as part of a composed small bites plate before dinner with wine or sake.

VARIATIONS: Chopped cilantro is a natural partner to avocado, and, while not at all Japanese, works well in this treatment. Also good spooned onto toast, though again not quite Japanese.

I ate these at Myoho Asari's house (page 194) and, as she attested, the sautéed shiitake tasted like abalone (at much less the price). These take a while since they must be coaxed along at a low braise, but are worth it. Myoho used a fruity olive oil. Here I've substituted a pretty, organic canola.

shio koji–sautéed shiitake SERVES 4
SHIITAKE NO SHIOKOJI-YAKI

12 medium-large shiitake
(about ¼ pound/120 g)

4 teaspoons Emulsified
Shio Koji (page 192)

2 teaspoons organic canola oil

Remove the stems from the shiitake and dry them outside for using in Konbu Dashi (page 266). Brush the shiitake on all sides with the shio koji. Film a large skillet with the oil and heat over medium-high. Sear the shiitake for a minute or so on both sides, then turn the heat down to low and cook slowly for about 10 to 15 minutes. Keep turning and checking to avoid burning. The shiitake are done when they are sizzling and their juices are skittering around the pan. Serve immediately as a small bite before dinner or as a vegetable side dish to any Western or Japanese meal.

VARIATION: Substitute any kind of sturdy mushroom that can stand up to a slow sauté.

Although salmon has a distinctive flavor that one cannot characterize as mild, it is nonetheless a delicate fish. Marinating salmon with shio koji before grilling imparts an added dimension and mitigates the salmon's inherent richness.

shio koji–marinated salmon SERVES 6
SHAKE NO SHIOKOJI-ZUKE

4 (¾-inch/2-cm) thick salmon filets, skin on (about 3 ounces/80 g each)

¼ cup (60 cc) Shio Koji (page 192)

Marinate the salmon pieces with the shio koji in a heavy-duty resealable plastic bag. Seal carefully and store in the refrigerator for 2 hours. Remove the salmon from the bag and wipe off the shio koji with a few clean paper towels. Make sure you remove any lingering rice kernels.

These are best grilled over low coals for 5 minutes on each side. If you are not feeling the barbecue, broil on a grate set over a broiler pan placed in the second slot from the top of the oven. Cook for 5 minutes on one side, flip, and cook for 5 more minutes on the other side (the filets should not be red in the center). Serve with a bowl of Japanese rice (page 172) and a fresh vegetable side dish such as sweet vinegared spring onions and cucumbers (page 157).

VARIATIONS: Any mild fish such as red snapper, swordfish, or halibut lends itself to being marinated in shio koji.

Some Berkeley friends were in town a few years back to put on an event in Tokyo called OPENHarvest, and I helped them source ingredients. During this period, I often dropped by the Suka farm to discuss vegetables, and I noticed a small, reach-in freezer full of organic pork that my farmwife pal was selling for pocket money. I bought some samples and was blown away by the flavor of the fat (not usually my thing) and the succulence of the meat. Certainly more dear than the butcher shop pork, but certainly worth it. Around the same time, shio koji came across my horizon, so it was a natural to douse the meat with shio koji instead of salt (though both are equally delicious, the shio koji adds an element of *je ne sais quoi*).

shio koji–grilled pork SERVES 6
BUTA NO SHIOKOJI-ZUKE

3 (1½-inch/4-cm) thick, well-marbled boneless pork butt chops (about 2 pounds/900 g)

½ cup (125 cc) Shio Koji (page 192)

½ tablespoon organic canola oil

Slip the pork chops into a gallon-sized resealable plastic bag and measure in the shio koji. Stick your hand in the bag and massage the meat a little to distribute the shio koji between and around the chops. Seal carefully and store in the fridge for at least half a day or up to 3 days. About 15 minutes before serving, remove the chops from the bag and blot off all the shio koji, taking care to remove any residual rice kernel particles.

Heat a heavy, cast iron pan over low heat and film with the oil. If the oil starts to smoke, the pan is too hot. In this case, remove the pan from the heat and wait a minute or two before proceeding. Slap the chops into the pan and cook, covered, for 7 minutes on each side for medium-rare. Add 1 more minute for each degree of doneness. Water will bead up on the inside of the lid, so be sure to wipe the condensation a few times during the cooking process, otherwise the liquid will fall back onto the pan, causing the chops to steam rather than sear. Alternatively, cook for 3 minutes, covered, over low heat. Remove to a board to cool and finish by grilling over low coals for 5 minutes on each side. Let the chops rest for 5 minutes before cutting crosswise into ¼-inch (6-mm) strips. Serve with Tomato Wedges Drizzled with Shoyu Koji (page 204) or Smashed Cucumbers with Sour Plum (page 169).

VARIATION: Use duck breasts instead of the pork, but score the skin and grill over a medium-ember fire or under the broiler for 1 minute on the fat side. Flip and grill 4 minutes more on the meat side for rare or 5 minutes for medium-rare.

After developing shio koji, Myoho Asari (page 194) came up with the idea of shoyu koji. Use in place of soy sauce for marinating or drizzling.

shoyu koji MAKES 1¼ CUPS (300 CC)

10.5 ounces (300 g) rice koji (page XXVIII)

¾ cup + 1 tablespoon (200 cc) soy sauce

Combine the rice koji and soy sauce in a medium-sized bowl. Cover loosely with a clean kitchen towel. Stir every day for 1 week to 10 days, depending on the room temperature (warm room, 1 week; cool room, 10 days). Store in a jar in the fridge for 1 year. Drizzle on vegetables and eat after 10 minutes or right away, if tomatoes (page 204); marinate fish or steak for a few hours and chicken for a day or so before grilling.

This is one of those no-brainer but inspired uses of shoyu koji. Think anything that goes well with soy sauce will also go well with shoyu koji as a pickling agent, drizzle, or marinade. Onions are also nice pickled in the same way. If you do not have access to shoyu koji, substitute bottled or homemade ponzu (equal parts sour orange juice and soy sauce).

zucchini pickled in shoyu koji SERVES 6
ZUKKINI NO SHOYUKOJI-ZUKE

3 medium green zucchini
(about 1 pound/450 g)

4 tablespoons Shoyu Koji (page 202)

Slice the zucchini into ³⁄₁₆-inch (5-mm) thin rounds with a razor-sharp knife. Drop into a quart-sized resealable plastic bag and measure in the shoyu koji (or ponzu). Roll up the bag, squeezing out all of the air as you go. Let sit to soak up flavor for 10 minutes. Scoop the zucchini slices out of the bag with a slotted spoon and mound in the center of a wide soup bowl with a small amount of the soaking liquid. Serve immediately.

Although not a native Japanese fruit, tomatoes marry perfectly with soy sauce. Typically the tomatoes here in Japan are sold a bit less ripe than I have seen in the U.S. and Mediterranean countries. Don't reach for the reddest, juiciest tomato; it will be too sweet for this treatment.

tomato wedges drizzled with shoyu koji SERVES 4
TOMATO NO SHOYUKOJI-AE

4 medium-sized just ripe
  organic tomatoes

2 tablespoons Shoyu Koji (page 202)

Shiso leaves, cut into
  threads (optional)

Right before serving your meal, core the tomatoes and slice into 6 thick wedges. Arrange on a colorful ceramic plate and drizzle with the shoyu koji. Strew with the shiso threads, if using. Serve immediately as a salad-like dish for a cold summer supper or lunch.

VARIATIONS: Cut the tomatoes into thick slices rather than wedges, or substitute halved cherry tomatoes.

Soy sauce works well as a seasoning for meaty fish such as yellowtail. This shoyu koji souse transforms yellowtail into something very special, expecially when you grill the fish over coals, because the coals infuse a gentle, smoky flavor to the fish.

shoyu koji–marinated yellowtail SERVES 6

BURI NO SHOYUKOJI-ZUKE

4 (¾-inch/2-cm) thick yellowtail filets, skin on (about 3 ounces/80 g each)

¼ cup (60 cc) Shoyu Koji (page 202)

½ cup (125 cc) grated daikon, squeezed (optional)

Place the yellowtail filets in a resealable freezer bag and measure in the shoyu koji. Roll the bag up, squeezing out the air as you go, and seal. Store in the fridge for 2 hours. Remove the filets from the bag and blot off the shoyu koji with clean paper towels, removing all the rice kernels.

Grilling over low-ember coals for 5 minutes on each side is the easiest way to cook these. But you could also broil them on a grate set over a broiler pan placed in the second slot from the top of the oven. Cook for 5 minutes on each side (they should be cooked through to the center). Mound the squeezed grated daikon, if using, on the plate next to the fish. Serve with a bowl of Japanese rice (page 172) and boiled, dressed greens such as Mustard with Tofu and Dried Persimmon (page 182) or Fiddlehead Ferns Drizzled with Soy Dashi (page 265).

VARIATIONS: Any oily or strong-tasting fish, such as mackerel or cod, takes well to a shoyu koji marinade, as does steak.

NAREZUSHI

Every few years around the New Year, Tadaaki makes *kabura zushi*, a modern version of *narezushi*, the most ancient form of sushi that dates back to the Yayoi period (ca. 300 BC–AD 250). *Narezushi* is a method of packing salted fish and vegetables in rice mixed with rice koji to create an environment where lactic acid fermentation can naturally preserve the fish. Originally the vegetables and rice virtually melted away, so only the fermented fish was eaten. *Izushi*, an adaptation where all of the ingredients are eaten together, evolved in the Maromachi period (1337–1573) and is still prepared today by local grandmas and diehard fermenting aficionados. Quick sushi (raw or treated fish on vinegared rice) appeared in the Edo period (1603–1867), and a version of that remains as the sushi we know today (*nigiri zushi*). The sushi that Tadaaki prepares (*kabura zushi*) is a modern evolution of *izushi*, yet still falls under the *narezushi* umbrella.

It takes some of us a big leap of faith to play around with fermenting fish. But I had gained much self-confidence through vegetable-fermenting and fish-drying projects; it was time to jump. The first thing to be aware of is that *kabura zushi* takes two weeks to prepare, while *izushi* ferments for one month, so you need to think ahead. Also winter is typically the time to start your fermentation. You will need to leave the pickling container in a cool (50°F/10°C), dark spot. If no such spot is available, it is possible to try these projects in the fridge, though the result will not be quite as well balanced.

Tadaaki's *kabura zushi* is much simpler and quicker than *izushi* and one of my favorites on the table at New Year, when Tadaaki finds the time to make it. Each household seems to have its own variation on how to prepare either of these fish preserves. These are not fully tested recipes; but they are presented here for the intrepid to use as a rough guide. There are some caveats, however: Please be aware that if the water that exudes from any pickling barrel is cloudy or smells bad, the pickles have spoiled. Throw the batch out and start again.

TADAAKI'S KABURA ZUSHI: Scrub and slice 1¾ pounds (800 g) smallish turnips into ¾-inch (2-cm) thick rounds. Slice into the middle of the round but not all the way through to create a clamlike shape. Toss the slit turnips with 1 tablespoon/20 g salt (3% of the weight of the turnips) and layer in a large bowl. Add a drop lid and place a 1¾-pound (800-g) weight on top. Store in a cool dark spot for 1 week. After 4 or 5 days have elapsed, pack ¾ pound (350 g) of yellowtail filets with 2 tablespoons/35 g salt (10% of the weight of the fish) in a resealable freezer-style bag. Roll up, squeezing out all of the air, and refrigerate for 2 or 3 days. After the turnips and filets have salted the prescribed period, wash 1½ cups (350 g) of Japanese rice, wrap in a muslin cheesecloth, and steam for 30 minutes in a bamboo steamer. Fluff and cool the rice to body temperature. Crumble 4 ounces (100 g) of cake-style koji to separate the individual rice kernels, or sprinkle 1 cup (100 g) loose-style rice koji (page XXVIII) onto the rice. Mix in with a rice paddle. Drain the salted turnips in a sieve and blot the yellowtail filets with a clean kitchen towel. Slice the filets diagonally into ¼-inch (6-mm) pieces of sashimi. Sandwich a slice of yellowtail into the slit of each turnip slice. Press a ½-inch layer of the

rice mixture into the bottom of the (washed and dried) turnip pot. Arrange the turnip "sandwiches" on top of the rice in one layer. Cover with more rice, followed by turnips. The last layer should be rice. Cover the surface with plastic wrap or a muslin cloth and set a drop lid and a 3⅓-pound (1.5-kg) weight on top for 1 week in a cool, dark corner of your kitchen. Leave the weight in place, and reverse the pot onto a roasting pan to drain for 4 hours before cutting and serving.

IZUSHI: Salt 1 pound (500 g) salmon filets for 2 hours with 1 tablespoon sea salt. Refrigerate, stored in a resealable heavy plastic bag. Wash a scant 1 cup (200 g) of Japanese rice, wrap in a muslin cheesecloth, and steam for 30 minutes in a bamboo steamer. Fluff and cool the rice to body temperature. Mix 1¾ ounces (50 g) of crumbled cake-style koji (see Kabura Zushi method, page 207) or ½ cup (50 g) loose-style rice koji and 2 tablespoons sake into the rice with a rice paddle. Quarter a ⅔-pound (250-g) piece of daikon lengthwise and slice into ¼-inch (6-mm) triangular pieces. Scrub ⅓ pound (125 g) of carrots and cut into ¼-inch

(6-mm) half-rounds or rounds, depending on how fat they are. Slice ⅔ pound (250 g) of cabbage into rough 2 by 1½-inch (5 by 3-cm) pieces. Peel and cut 3 ounces ginger (100 g) into fine slivers. Toss all of the vegetables with 2 tablespoons coarse sea salt in a large mixing bowl, but do not massage. Remove the salmon from the refrigerated bag, pat dry, slice into thick 2- by 1½- by ½-inch (5-cm by 3-cm by 12-mm) sashimi-sized pieces. Line a deep, round container with a food-grade plastic bag and smooth a ½-inch (12-mm) layer of the koji and rice mixture across the entire bottom, reaching to the edges (make sure the plastic is completely flush on the bottom before you start). Arrange the salmon pieces side by side on top of the rice, without overlapping. Sprinkle a thick layer of vegetables over the salmon. Continue making layers until you have used up all of the ingredients. The last layer should be vegetables. Squeeze all of the air out of the bag, place a drop lid across the surface, and set a 3⅓-pound (1.5-kg) weight on top of the drop lid. Store in a cool, dark corner for about a month. As for many fermenting projects, the ideal temperature is 50°F (10°C). Once the vegetable water rises up (in about a week), you can remove half of the weight, so only 1⅔ pounds (750 g) remains. Taste the liquid. It should be vegetal but not unpleasant or too salty. It is commonly said that *izushi* takes 40 days, but it should be ready in about 35. Store in the refrigerator to maintain the vegetables' crunch. The taste will change over time—pleasantly sour is good, funky is not. Toss when that time comes if you have not managed to consume the whole batch already.

Tadaaki and Suka-san grow a small yellow melon called *makuwa-uri* that originated in Korea. Somehow I had been missing the chance to eat it when we have them in the summer, so began thinking of ways to put them more on the forefront of my menu planning. The first most obvious pairing was with prosciutto and chopped green chile peppers. Not particularly Japanese, nonetheless a lovely cold collation on a hot summer night. Since I have been delving into the world of sake, I have become a bit mad for sake lees and am always casting about for immediate ways to use it in my cooking or pickling (as opposed to making a Narazuke pickling bed, page 213). Here, I like the naturally sweet taste of the sake lees, so add nothing to it when pickling these melons.

small melons in sake lees SERVES 6
MAKUWA-URI NO SAKE KASUZUKE

3 small melons, about
  ¾ pound (350 g) each

2 pounds (1 kg) sake lees (page 188)

Whack the melons in half vertically and scoop out the seeds. Soften the sake lees with your hands by kneading them and fill the melon cavities with the lees. Store in a resealable plastic bag for a half day. Scrape off the sake lees and cut into ¼-inch (6-mm) wedges. Serve with beer on a hot summer night. Reuse the lees for other pickling projects or Sake Lees Soup with Salmon (page 210).

VARIATION: Chayote or bitter melon also do well smothered in sake lees for a spell.

Kasujiru is a country soup similar in base to a traditional *kenchinjiru* (page 138) made with Konbu Dashi (page 266), though you could just as well use Katsuobushi Dashi (page 253) or Niboshi Dashi (page 274). This is a very popular soup in Niigata, a seaside prefecture a few hours north of us famous for sake and salmon. If you are interested in cooking off any residual alcohol in the sake lees, add a bit more broth once it has emulsified and simmer it in the small pan over medium-high heat for 5 minutes, stirring constantly (be careful it does not burn). Heat up leftover *kasujiru* the following day for a hearty breakfast or light lunch.

sake lees soup with salmon SERVES 4 TO 6
SHAKE NO KASUJIRU

⅓ pound (150 g) belly-cut salmon filets

2½ teaspoons shio koji (page 192) or flaky sea salt

1 medium carrot, 2½ ounces (75 g)

1 small burdock root (gobo, page 339), 2½ ounces (75 g)

½ small daikon, scant ⅓ pound (150 g)

1 tablespoon organic canola oil

½ (9-ounce/255-g) block konnyaku (optional, see Note)

6 cups (1.5 liters) hot Katsuobushi Dashi (page 253)

8 tablespoons sake lees (page 188)

4 tablespoons inaka miso (page 72)

7-spice powder (*shichimi togarashi*, page XXXI)

2 tablespoons chopped scallions, for garnish

Whack the salmon into rough, bigger-than-bite-sized pieces (about 1 inch/2.5 cm square) and toss with the shio koji or salt. Reserve in the fridge.

Cut the tops and tips off the carrots, gobo, and daikon, but do not peel. Scrub the roots with a rough brush (*tawashi*). The vegetables will all be cut into ⅛-inch (4-mm) thin slices. Halve the carrot lengthwise, slice into half-moons, and drop into a medium-sized bowl. Slice the daikon lengthwise into quarters, cut into thin triangles, and drop into a different medium-sized bowl. Slice the gobo diagonally into thin pieces and add to the carrots.

Film the oil in a heavy soup pot over medium-high heat. When the oil is hot but not smoking, sauté the sliced carrots and gobo for 2 minutes. Throw in the sliced daikon and konnyaku, if using (see Note). Sauté, stirring, for about 2 minutes longer. Pour in the hot dashi and bring to a boil over high heat. When the soup comes to a boil, drop the salmon pieces into the pot and cook at a lively simmer until the vegetables are soft and the salmon is almost falling apart, about 10 minutes or so.

Measure the sake lees into a medium-sized saucepan and ladle in a scoop of broth. Whisk over low heat to emulsify, then scrape the softened sake lees into the soup. Spoon the miso into the same saucepan and whisk in a small scoop of broth to form a thin paste (no flame). Add to the soup and ladle into large soup bowls. Sprinkle with a bit of *shichimi togarashi* and chopped scallions. Serve with a bowl of Japanese rice (page 172) and some pickles on the side for a soupy supper on a cold night.

VARIATION: Use coarsely chopped, thinly sliced pork belly instead of salmon.

NOTE: Fill a medium-sized pot three-quarters of the way up with water and toss in 1 tablespoon salt. Bring the water to a boil over high heat. While the water is heating, slice the konnakyu into thin (1½ by ¼-inch/ 4 cm by 6-mm) strips. Boil the konnyaku pieces over medium-high heat for 15 minutes, drain, and reserve.

We had a freak snowstorm in the winter of 2014 (page 334), and Tadaaki's chicken coops were demolished by the weight of the snow. He lost one-third of the chickens. The remaining 2,000 chickens, now coopless, milled around in the mud. It was a nightmare. In the middle of all this, I was working crazily on this manuscript and getting ready to leave the country for a trip. Nonetheless, I got it into my head that we should put some chicken up in sake lees marinade. I rounded up some volunteers from the parents and grandparents of the SSU! preschoolers, and we had a chicken-cleaning party. We killed and cleaned ten chickens and I marinated all of the chicken pieces in shio koji. After a few days, I froze the thighs and smoothed the breasts with a sake lees–miso mixture. I served these at the graduation lunch, and even the kids loved them.

sake lees–cured chicken SERVES 6
TORINIKU NO KASUZUKE

4 boneless chicken breasts with skin (about 2⅔ pounds/1200 g)

½ cup (125 cc) Shio Koji (page 192) or 2 tablespoons coarse sea salt

¼ cup (60 cc) inaka miso

¼ cup (60 cc) sake lees (page 188)

1 tablespoon organic canola oil

Lay the chicken in a rectangular refrigerator container. Rub the shio koji or salt into the breasts, and flatten a piece of plastic wrap on top of the surface of the chicken. Cover with a lid and refrigerate for 2 days. Muddle the miso into the sake lees. Remove the chicken from the fridge and spread the sake lees–miso mixture on all surfaces of the chicken with your fingers. Re-cover with the plastic wrap and lid and refrigerate for 2 more days.

Preheat the oven to 400°F (205°C). Remove the chicken from the fridge and blot off the sake lees–miso mixture with thick paper towels. Line a cookie sheet with a piece of heavy-duty aluminum foil. Spread the oil around the foil with your fingers and place the wiped chicken breasts on the foil, skin side up. Cook in the center of the oven for 20 minutes, until the meat barely has give when poked with your finger. Alternatively, cook over a low-ember barbecue, turning occasionally. Shio koji and miso burn easily, so be vigilant. (Bone-in chicken breasts can be used as well but will need an extra 10 minutes of cooking time.) Let rest for 5 minutes before cutting. Serve with a Japanese salad such as Tomato, Onion, and Pepper Salad (page 113) and a small bowl of Japanese rice (page 172).

VARIATION: Thick pork chops also do well with this treatment.

NARAZUKE

Several years ago, a plastic container sat in a corner of our kitchen for most of the year. Tadaaki had explained that inside were *narazuke* cucumber pickles from Mochizuki-san, our octogenarian citrus grower friend. "Aren't they going to go bad?" was my response. Tadaaki assured me they never would, but I could not quite wrap my head around the idea. Toward the end of the year, the mash had darkened to brown-black. Tadaaki had maintained that they never go bad, so I bagged up some of the pickled cucumbers and brought them with me on a trip to California. Sylvan Mishima Brackett, of Peko Peko Japanese Catering, was hosting a sukiyaki party at his house in Oakland, and we brought out those blackened, shriveled cucumbers for everyone to sample. As we did not really quite understand what we were tasting, they were difficult to assess. Hmmm . . . they were interesting but perhaps too foreign for our untutored palates. (At the one-year-old funky stage is probably not the best way to first taste *narazuke*.)

Recently we received two more plastic boxes of *narazuke* from Mochizuki-san: One contained small Japanese melons (*uri*, page 340) and the other cucumbers. By that time, I was deep into writing this book, so knew that the cucumbers and *uri* had been salted before being sandwiched between layers of sake lees. I recognized the work involved to produce these treasures, so stored them in the fridge. I called Mochizuki-san to thank her and to confirm the pickles should not be left out. She equivocated, "In or out, either way is fine." I remembered the black cucumbers of a few years back, so erred on the conservative side, though wonder if I should have left them out.

Not ready to give an officially tested recipe, I still wanted to share the method to prepare *narazuke*, since there is not much information out there in English on these pickles. In my mind, *narazuke* belong to the second tier of traditional preserved vegetables and are a level up in commitment from *umeboshi*, *takuan*, and *hakusai* because more steps are required. Compared to fish

preserves, however, there is not much danger of spoilage, thus quite doable for even the less adventurous picklers out there. A farmwife grandma in Niigata prefecture passed the proportions for the sake lees pickling bed to me in a hand-scribbled note (though I took the liberty of decreasing the sugar from 20% to 12.5%). These pickles are started in the early summer, when the fields are prolific with cucumbers and *uri*. They take about 3 months to mature.

METHOD: Place 8 pounds (4 kg) of cucumbers in a wooden or plastic pickling barrel and rub with 1 pound salt (500 g). Salt is calculated at 12.5% of the cucumber weight. Lay a drop lid on top of the cucumbers, then two 8-pound (4-kg) weights on top of the drop lid. In a couple of days, the water will have risen above the drop lid. Remove one of the weights, leaving 8 pounds (4 kg). Press for a total of 1 week. Remove from the brine, rinse quickly, drain, pat dry very well, and air-dry overnight in a protected spot. Mix 1 pound (500 g) organic sugar into 8 pounds (4 kg) of sake lees. (Sugar is calculated at 12.5% to 20% of the cucumber weight, according to your taste.) The sake lees will be easier to work with if they are at room temperature. In the summer, sake lees become quite loose if you leave them in a warm corner of your kitchen. If the sake lees are not pliable, work a bit of sake into them to aid in spreading them into the container.

Smooth a ¾-inch (2-cm) layer of sweetened sake lees in the bottom of a wooden or plastic pickling barrel and line up a layer of cucumbers on top. The cucumbers should not be touching. Smooth another layer of sake lees across the cucumbers, making sure the cucumbers are covered by a thick ¾-inch (2-cm) layer and that all of the gaps have been filled with sake lees. There should be no air pockets. Lay the next layer of cucumber crosswise so that the layers alternate in orientation in a crisscross fashion. Continue layering the cucumbers and sake lees, with the last layer being sake lees. Be careful to seal up all the edges so no air can enter the bed. Cover with a nonairtight lid and leave in the coolest, most well-protected spot you have in the garden for 3 months. Some people stop here. Some people change the sake lees at 20-day intervals for a total of 3 changes. (The removed sake lees are saved and used as an impromptu pickling bed for quick pickles.)

These pickles keep almost forever, though will darken over time. Start sampling after about 3 months, and keep an eye on how they change at each 3-month interval. If you are happy with the pickles after 3 months, you could repack them in a rectangular plastic container and store them in the fridge. In this case, Mochizuki-san pats out the sake lees into thick sheets and sandwiches the pickles between the sheets without pressing down to totally surround the pickles with sake lees. When ready to eat, you only have to peel back the thick sheet of sake lees sheet and pluck out a cucumber or two. She also lays a clean towel across the top layer of sake lees to wick up moisture. Change the towel every once in a while. Despite my initial hesitation regarding these pickles, they are truly special and absolutely worth the commitment.

Sake lees lend a haunting alcohol note to creamy ice cream custard. Sometimes I serve sake lees ice cream with Sake Granita (page 316), though I like to use figs when they are in season, as the colors and flavors are complementary.

sake lees ice cream with figs MAKES ABOUT 1 QUART (1 LITER)

SAKE KASU AISU ICHIJIKU-ZOE

½ cup/120 cc sake lees (about 2.5 ounces/50 g)

¾ cup (180 cc) heavy cream

¾ cup (180 cc) milk

¾ cup (150 g) organic granulated sugar

3 egg yolks, at room temperature

6 ripe figs, quartered

Scrape the sake lees into a heavy-bottomed saucepan and whisk the cream in slowly to liquefy. Measure in the milk and sugar, and heat, stirring, over medium-high heat until the sugar has melted. Turn the heat down to low.

Whisk a soup ladle or so of warm milk mixture into the yolks to temper and scrape into the saucepan. Cook over low heat, stirring, until the custard has thickened slightly and coats the back of a wooden spoon. (N.B.: If you use an enameled cast iron pan, this will happen almost immediately, so have your strainer and container at the ready!) Strain into a plastic container, cool to room temperature, and chill overnight in the fridge. Freeze according to the directions for your ice cream maker. Keeps for several weeks in the freezer.

Scoop 2 small mounds of ice cream into a pretty dish and serve with a quartered fig on a saucer alongside.

Takuan can be one of the most intimidating vegetable preserves because there are so many things that can go wrong. Weather and timing both play a big part in making these pickles successfully. It is important to not dry the daikon too long, as they will become hard. Also if the pickling medium is too dry or the weather too warm, you might find some white furry mold appearing in the pickle mash. Just wipe it off and increase the weight on top of the pickles. Sprinkling a small amount of 3.5% saltwater over the surface of the *takuan* can help alleviate a too-dry batch. *Takuan* is said to have first appeared in the Edo period over 400 years ago and was consumed by Buddhist monks. *Takuan* also has a reputation of being one of those pungent Japanese foods that foreigners might have a hard time eating. This is difficult to understand, since these crunchy pickles are pleasantly earthy, with complex flavor notes, and quite addicting. My mother-in-law made fantastic *takuan*, and to this day I regret not learning from her while she was alive. Nonetheless, the first time Tadaaki tasted mine, he closed his eyes as he chewed, then looked up and pronounced them old-fashioned, "like my grandmother's pickles." Yes.

half-dried daikon pickled in rice bran MAKES 10

TAKUAN

10 freshly harvested smallish daikon, leaves intact, about 12 pounds/5.5 kg

About 7 ounces/200 g sea salt (6% weight of the dried daikon)

4 dried red chiles, torn (japones or árbol)

Peeled strips from 2 sour oranges or 3 yuzu (avoid the white bitter pith)

2 handfuls dried persimmon peels (optional)

About 17.5 ounces/495 g rice bran (15% weight of the dried daikon)

Tie one end of a thick 10-foot (3-meter) piece of heavy twine around the base of the leaves of one daikon and the other end around the base of the leaves of another. Tie all 10 daikon and hang over a pole to dry in the early winter sun (we start making *takuan* in our area in early December). Hang for about 5 days to 1 week in the sun, but cover at night with a tarp, blanket, or straw matting. (N.B.: If you use large daikon and you don't have much sun, they can take as long as 3 weeks to dry properly.) The daikon should become soft and pliable but should not dry or shrivel. Bring the daikon into the kitchen and slice the tops off right where the leaves jut out from the root (you want the leaves to stay together in 1 intact bunch, so don't cut too high). Save the leaf bunches for making the pickles.

Weigh the daikon and recalculate the salt and rice bran amounts. Sprinkle a layer of rice bran, aromatics, and salt (keep in mind how many layers you will be making and how much of each ingredient you have) in the bottom a wooden barrel or plastic pickling tub. Wind a layer of half-dried daikon around the circumference of the barrel, working your way into the center. Poke leaves into any spots where there is a gap. You do not want any air pockets to form, as they will encourage mold. You want a completely snug layer. This is crucial for the success of your *takuan* (and has been my downfall in the past). Sprinkle each layer with some of the salt, aromatics, and rice bran and continue layering the coiled daikon until all of the daikon has been placed in the barrel and you have used up

half-dried daikon pickled in rice bran

all of the pickling ingredients (the last layer should be aromatics, salt, and rice bran). Smash the remaining leaves on top of the rice bran, pushing it well into any cracks. Smooth a large muslin cloth across the surface and drape it down the sides of the barrel. Set a drop lid on top of the cloth and a 20-pound (10-kg) weight on top of the drop lid. Cover with a large muslin cloth and secure the cloth by tying a length of twine around the circumference of the pickling container.

Leave in a cool, shady spot in the garden for 1 month, but check after a week to see if the rice bran feels moist. If too dry, dissolve ¾ teaspoon sea salt in ½ cup (125 cc) water and sprinkle over the pickling bed. After 1 month, remove half of the weight, leaving 10 pounds (5 kg). The *takuan* will stay fine in the weighted pickle barrel, but should be refrigerated once the weather warms. Transfer the *takuan* with the pickling mash still clinging to the daikon to a resealable plastic bag or other refrigerator container. Scrape off any lingering pickling mash, wash, and slice into ¼-inch/6-mm pieces and serve with Green Tea (page 325), as a small bite with beer, or to accompany a bowl of rice and a hearty Japanese soup such as Country Miso and Vegetable Soup (page 80) or Country Soup Flavored Four Ways (page 138).

NUKADOKO

I packed my rice bran pickling bed (*nukadoko*) in plastic resealable bags (taped, double bagged), stored in a plastic food storage box placed inside a well-taped plastic bag for good measure, and took it on the road with me for my first book tour in the fall of 2012. During the course of the two months I was in the States, my rice bran pickling bed suffered through multiple airplane flights, overheated hotel rooms, and being handled by different people. By the time I got it home, the pickling bed was a bit sloggy and had lost about half of its volume. I set about reviving it, but sadly it took one busy November for me to neglect the bed and allow it to turn without my noticing. I gave up that year but started again the following summer, and that pickling bed remains happy and healthy, despite having already made its trip to the United States.

What I learned: *Nukadoko* does not like plastic or refrigeration—both brought on excess liquid. If liquid does accumulate, there are two methods to deal with removing the excess. Most orthodox: Smooth a clean muslin cloth on top of the surface of the *nukadoko* to sop up the excess liquid. In a pinch: Scrape the *nukadoko* into a fine-mesh strainer and let the excess drip out a bit.

Another thing I learned is not to bother scraping off the grey or white bloom that forms if you forget to mix the *nukadoko* for a day or two. Just remix it back into the *nukadoko* as part of the overall natural flora. But if the bloom is dark or discolored, scrape it off and discard. Keep in crockery, if possible, and at room temperature—not the fridge.

Pickling times will vary depending on the weather, the hardness of the vegetable, and the shape you have introduced (e.g., halved vegetables pickle faster than whole). Tadaaki likes a "morning pickle" type of taste, I like a more funky profile, so you are on your own about figuring out how you like your *nukazuke*.

If you are preparing pickles for an event, remember that once you take the vegetables out of the pickling bed, they can hold for a day or so in the fridge if placed in a plastic food storage box or bag. However, the vegetables will continue to pickle a bit, since you need to leave the residual rice bran clinging to the vegetables until just before serving. Caveat: Carrots will discolor after washing, so wait until the absolute last minute before washing, slicing, and serving.

And if possible, start your *nukadoko* in the summertime. It will "take" more easily.

It takes about a week in the hot, muggy Japanese summer to get the rice bran pickling bed to ferment enough in order to make properly sour rice bran pickles. On the fall 2012 book tour, this was a subject of great discussion among my various food friends and myself, since the book launch dinner was at Chez Panisse in Berkeley and the chef, Amy Dencler, was having a slight issue getting her pickling bed to mature quick enough. Blame it on the cool weather that August and September.

I thought storing the pickling bed in the car would be one way to raise up the ambient temperature—though this is a risky proposition, because the sun can suddenly beat down with a vengeance. My Boston friend, Sally Vargas, was in the middle of bread-baking experiments, so offered the bread-proofing oven as a possible storage spot for the pickling bed. My favorite (though untested) method was proposed by David Tanis one night over onion soup at his apartment in New York: Why not put the pickling bed in a cooler box and throw in some hand warmers to bring up the temperature gently? The summer pickles are looking for an environment of higher than 80°F (27°C), so be creative if you live in a cool climate.

rice bran pickles SERVES 6
NUKAZUKE

NUKADOKO

12 tablespoons
(about 6 ounces/165 g) salt

12 cups (1¾ pounds/800 g) rice bran

½ cup (125 cc/150 g) brown rice miso

2 (4 by 2-inch/10 by 5-cm)
pieces of konbu

3 dried red chiles

6 strips tangerine or sour
orange peel, such as *daidai*
or Seville (optional)

Mild vegetable cuttings or
pieces: carrot, zucchini,
squash, green beans, etc.

Bring 4 cups (1 liter) water to a boil with the salt; stir to dissolve. Leave the brine to cool while you parch the rice bran over a low flame in a large wok or frying pan until dry and powdery to the touch. (The bran should be warm but must not brown.) Remove from the heat and dump immediately in a large mixing bowl to stop the cooking and to cool a bit. Stir the saltwater into the cooled, parched rice bran to make a thick paste. Smash in the miso and mix well. Poke in the konbu, dried red peppers, and citrus peel and pat the mash down to create a smooth surface. Cover with a clean kitchen towel and leave on the counter within plain view.

The *nukadoko* needs about a week to ripen and ferment. As the healthy flora grows, you will be able to taste how the *nukadoko* progressively sours and develops a more complex flavor profile as each day passes.

Every day, starting with day 1, put a few cuttings or pieces of vegetable into the mixture and let sit overnight. The following day, pick out the vegetables and discard. Turn the mixture over with your hands to aerate and promote its health. Taste the mixture each day to understand how it is changing and how it is alive. If you forget to turn the mixture one day, it may have formed a fine white bloom. Just mix it back into the mash. If you forget for 2 days in a row, you risk souring the *nukadoko*, so be careful. Three or four days neglected, and it's most likely gone. If the *nukadoko* smells unpleasantly sour or develops a slimy texture, you might as well throw the whole thing out and start again.

rice bran pickles

Modern Japanese girls associate the smell of *nukadoko* with their grandmothers (or great-grandmothers). I prefer to use the word *aroma* over *smell* because I love the funky, wild fragrances that rise out of the pickling crock. Some people use rubber gloves to mix their pickling bed; I do not. Apparently there is something you can add to the pickling bed to eliminate odors—I don't quite get that. It seems like that would take away the heart of the process. Also no sense dwelling on the youth of your pickling bed—it will still make delicious pickles even if you do not have a pickling bed handed down from your ancestors. And what you add to the pickling bed is important, so look for high-quality (preferably fresh organic) rice bran. Adding a spoonful or two of koji to the *nukadoko* will increase the healthy flora of the mash and will result in a more forgiving *nukadoko* bed.

After a week, the *nukadoko* should be nicely seasoned and ready to use. Scrape the mash into a crock with a loose-fitting lid and store at room temperature, out of direct light. If tended, it will keep for years (if not generations).

Roll vegetables in a little sea salt before putting in the mash. If you want a quicker turnaround time, halve the vegetable before poking it into the pickling bed. Also make sure all of the vegetables and aromatics are completely covered by the mash and you have smoothed the surface evenly. Small porous vegetables such as turnips, radishes, mountain yams, cucumbers, okra, green beans, thin-skinned mild green peppers, Japanese eggplants, *myoga*, or thin greens such as mizuna will be done overnight or in half a day (depending on how you like them). Hard vegetables such as carrots, squash, or daikon can take up to a day or two—especially in the winter. Remove the vegetables from the mash, wash off the bran mash, dry well, and slice into ½-inch (12-mm) rounds or half-moon shapes. Leave radishes whole. Also you could introduce baby turnips already quartered or carrots cut into sticks.

Regardless if you make pickles every day or not, you must turn the mixture daily, or it will go off: once a day in the winter, but twice a day in the summer. Also the *nukadoko* should be saltier in the summer to hinder spoilage. As winter approaches, you can let the salt balance gradually soften. Taste the *nukadoko* whenever you think about it, and never forget that it is a living thing, so multiple variables come into play. It takes some trial and error, but don't be afraid to try and don't be afraid to fail.

VARIATION: If you have access to wheat bran of better quality than rice bran, you could substitute the wheat bran, though you will end up with a nuttier mash.

FISH NUKAZUKE

As the the time whiled by and we became chums, the *himono* fish-salting ladies in Wajima (page 35) vied with each other to teach me about their local culture of fish preservation. As they exchanged guffaws, my eyes fell on a Styrofoam box of what looked like dessicated fish packed in a dryish rice bran mixture. "Nukazuke," they revealed. I was confused since *nukazuke* in our house consists of vegetables pickled in a rice bran mash. They elucidated further: The fish is salted, then packed in unroasted rice bran to cure for several months. Aha! The *himono* ladies scooped a few different varieties of these pungent, preserved fish, tossed them in paper bags, and offered them as presents. We stashed the bags in the back of the car and could smell them the whole trip as they "perfumed" the air. I'm not sure what happened to the fish; perhaps Miura-san took them home.

On the trip to Iio Jozo, we visited a funky little izakaya whose master enjoyed using the more unusual cuts of meat and fish. Feeling a bit overwhelmed (and looking for a bite of something simple), I returned to the last pieces of raw fish on the sashimi plate. But I was also drawn to the *heshiko* mackerel, a dark, oily grilled fish redolent of sake lees. And I remembered that the *himono* ladies had advised us to stick the rice bran–fermented fish in a bed of sake lees to marinate in order to remove some of the salt of those very strong-flavored fish preserves. We had seen wooden barrels and plastic containers packed with these outwardly unappetizing long-fermented fish in the Wajima morning market (page 130) as well. Already having more *heshiko* than I wanted or needed, I was not tempted to buy more. I should have been more open-minded. The *heshiko* makerel we sampled at the izakaya that night was startlingly and deeply delicious and certainly worth trying to re-create.

A few months after I retuned from the Noto Peninsula, I was given a present of rice bran–pickled blowfish ovaries (*ranso no heshiko*) by a student's dad. I'm not a big fan of offal, but after arriving in Japan, never had a problem eating fish testicles (*shirako*) or squid guts. Still, fish ovaries were a bit of a stretch. First, they are golf ball–sized. Second, they have been fermented for about a year. Nonetheless, I girded my loins and broke out the *shichirin* (page 41). Washed down with some of that wild koji–fermented Terada Honke sake (page 352), the fish ovaries were surprisingly delightful.

METHOD: Pack whole mackerel (or anchovies) in plenty of sea salt and store in a cool place, no warmer than 50°F (10°C), for 2 weeks. Remove the fish from the brine and gut. Butterfly the body, but leave the head intact on one side (unlike the method for making air-dried fish, where you whack the whole fish in half, including the head, page 43). Wash the butterflied fish, scraping out all stubbornly adhering blood veins. Blot dry very well with clean towels, then let air-dry for 2 hours. Throw a ¾-inch (2-cm) layer of rice bran in the bottom of a wooden or plastic pickling barrel (do not roast the bran as you would for Rice Bran Pickles, page 220). Line the surface of the rice bran with one layer of salted (well-dried) filets. Sprinkle a ½-inch (12-mm) even coating of bran across the fish, then continue layering the bran and fish until finishing with a last layer of bran.

Many people throw in a few broken-up pieces of dried red Japanese chile with the bran. And some dash in some fish sauce, miso, soy sauce, or sake lees for a hidden taste. Place a drop lid on the surface of the rice bran and weight with stones equal to at least the weight of the fish and rice bran. Store in a cool, well-ventilated place for about 10 months. These pickles are traditionally made from autumn through winter after the rice harvest. A quick version can be made in the refrigerator by salting for 3 days, then packing in bran for 3 months. Scrape off the rice bran, but do not wash before curing in sake lees for 3 days to balance out the salt. Grill over low-ember coals for about 10 minutes on each side.

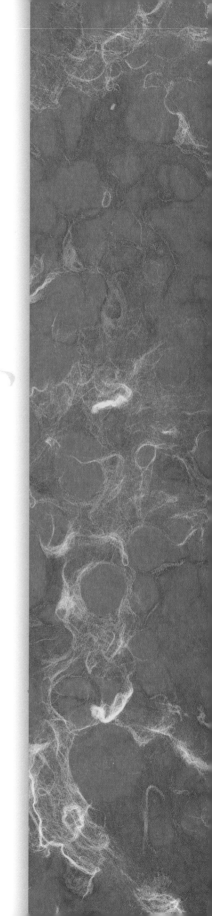

7

tofu, natto, and konnyaku

TOFU RECIPES

TOFU SIMMERED WITH VEGETABLES	234
HOMEMADE SOY MILK	235
SOFT TOFU	236

NATTO RECIPES

| HOT TABLE NATTO | 240 |

KONNYAKU RECIPES

| HOMEMADE KONNYAKU | 244 |

The organization of this book went through various phases, and the result is this focus on preserving mediums or similar ingredients. Because of the lack of good-quality tofu, natto, and konnyaku abroad, it was important to offer the wherewithal to make these yourself should you be feeling adventuresome. Do not feel daunted by occasional failure, but take comfort in the knowledge that just because the tofu doesn't set as well as you would like or the natto does not develop as expected, they will still be delicious if you start with good-tasting soybeans. And they will be yours.

TOFU: Soybeans, along with small fish, have historically been the main source of protein for Japan. Although an ancient form of cheese (*So*, page 28) was said to have been introduced to Emperor Kotoku in the mid-7th century, dairy consumption remained exclusive to the Imperial court and aristocracy. Dairy as a source of protein did not become prevalent until the late 1800s, after the Meiji Restoration.

Soybeans are simmered, seasoned, and eaten whole on their own but can also be thrown into curry rice or vegetable side dishes. Soybeans are also processed into soy milk for making tofu (the by-product of which is *okara*, page XXIX). And soybeans are fermented to create the most central flavorings in Japanese cuisine: miso and soy sauce. Tofu is (or should be) very perishable and, at its best, almost custard-like. The fresher the tofu, the more ethereal. Correspondingly, the better the beans and water, the better the flavor. In Japan, transcendent tofu is made from organic Japanese soybeans and pure spring water.

Soybean always refers to the dried bean. Edamame are young green soybeans that should be cropped when the pods are plump but before they yellow. I have noticed edamame being sold at farmers' markets in the United States; unfortunately, for the most part they appear to have been cropped too late. The window to crop edamame in the soybean growing cycle is extremely short. That said, the timing of the growing season varies with each soybean variety. Some varieties are sown late in the spring for a midsummer cropping, while others are sown in midsummer for a mid-fall cropping. If farmers are growing edamame, they could well be selling the soybeans after they dry in their pods on the plants. It is worth a conversation. Be warned, however, that the work involved to sort through and package the soybeans may not be worth it for them on a small scale. Having done it myself, I can attest to how time-consuming and painstaking the task can be. Machines make the sorting process much more practical.

While Tadaaki has grown soybeans in the past, his energy has flagged, so now we buy them from natural farmer friends. I stockpile them when the beans appear on the farm stand tables and keep them in a cool place. A refrigerator is preferable, however, because the beans can develop bugs. Thankfully, the pests and their debris are easily washed off. Organic, non-GMO soybeans are easily findable at any natural food store or online through Shiloh Farms in Pennsylvania, Rhapsody in Vermont, and Laura Soybeans in Iowa (see Resources).

Making your own soy milk (page 235) and consequently soft tofu (page 236) is the surest way to experience the closest you will ever get to Japanese tofu. Still, there are pocket areas around the U.S. where tofu is being made with varying degrees of success. Meiji Tofu in Southern California is the best I have tasted and the only one that compares favorably with the best Japanese tofu. San Jose Tofu in Northern California and Phoenix Bean in Chicago are fairly good as well. And Oakland, California's Hodo Soy soft tofu has a pleasant silky texture and mild flavor.

Whenever possible, it is better to place tofu in the bowl and pour the miso soup over it rather than putting the tofu in the soup itself. Tofu is usually weighted before marinating or mashing into a dressing. But no tofu preparation matches the pure pleasure derived from eating freshly made tofu, unadorned except for a drizzle of soy sauce or a sprinkling of sea salt, though good tofu seasoned with minimal toppings can also be satisfying. The classic trilogy for garnish is: freshly grated ginger, chopped scallions, and shaved katsuobushi. Freshly grated wasabi goes well with salt-sprinkled tofu.

NATTO: Natto is not for the uninitiated, but keep an open mind and you might grow fond of these funky, slimy, fermented beans. Natto is usually sold in small foam packs along with a teeny plastic package of hot mustard or wasabi and another of dashi-infused soy sauce. Be aware that the flavoring packages accompanying nonorganic natto can contain MSG (アミノ酸), fructose, or preservatives, so you may want to toss them. Dab in a smidge of Dijon mustard and a splash of soy sauce instead. Pop open the Styrofoam package and drop the natto into a small bowl. Whip the inert beans up with wooden chopsticks using a circular motion until the natto is suspended in a creamy mass of gossamer threads. Squeeze in the flavorings included (or your own soy sauce and mustard) and mix one more time before eating as is or spooned over a bowl of freshly cooked Japanese rice (page 172). Son Christopher adds a whole egg to his natto before scraping it over rice, though I would opt for only the yolk. Chopped scallions are the perfect garnish.

Since natto is a fermented product, it naturally has a long shelf life and should be good way beyond the expiration date, but use good judgment here. Natto is alive and will continue to ferment even in the fridge, so the taste will become more pungent over time. If any sourness develops, toss it in the bin. Almost without exception, the natto sold outside of Japan has been frozen, which is not necessarily a bad thing; however, it does indicate that the natto has been packaged in Japan and shipped abroad. There are several points where the natto can suffer in the packing and shipping process—usually due to heat fluctuations and storage issues. Mistreatment will cause natto to become a bit rank in the nose, even bordering on unpleasant. Megumi Natto in Northern California and Natto du Dragon in the Vars region of Provence seem to be the only producers actually fermenting and marketing their own organic natto. However, there are plenty of natto aficionados out there making their own at home, and Mitoku Traditional Natto Spores are available online through the Natural Import Company and Cultures for Health (see Resources).

KONNYAKU: Konnyaku (also known as konjac) is a corm that is processed into blocks or noodles. This food has been eaten in Japan for hundreds of years. On the farm, konnyaku was commonly grown and processed at home, though now the practice has waned considerably. For the most part, konnyaku is produced commercially, from roots that are sliced and gas-dried into chips, which are ground into a powder, which in turn is boiled and coagulated with calcium carbonate. Certainly more practical than starting from a fresh corm, though less appealing. We are lucky to have local grandmas still making fresh konnyaku in our area, though I suppose it won't be available for long, since the grandmothers are aging.

Konnyaku is a pure fiber, zero-calorie food, which takes well to frying or simmering but, when fresh, is also sensational chilled and sliced like sashimi (page 245). Konnyaku is available in Japanese grocery stores and online abroad (see Resources), though should be parboiled before using to remove the acrid taste of the liquid in which it is packed. Since freshly made konnyaku is so far not sold outside of Japan, the method for making your own is included here. When given my first konnyaku corm, I was daunted by what seemed like an impossibly laborious undertaking. Not so. Taken through the process step by step by Sakae Suka (page 242), I swelled with self-assurance: "I can do this!" I thought. And I could.

Konnyaku is planted in our local area in spring and harvested throughout November and December. When driving past the fields, they appear to be canopied by umbrella-like leaves. Approach more closely, and you can perceive the striking mottled brown stems jutting out like ramrods from the corm. Research online yielded several sources for konnakyu starts in the U.S. (see Resources), and I suspect the corms will start appearing in farmers' markets before too long.

MAKING TOFU

The first time I made tofu, it came out beautifully and tasted almost as good as our local organic tofu made by Yamaki Jozo (page 106). I was accordingly quite proud of my tofu-making prowess. When I took my tofu making on the road in the fall of 2012 for the first *Japanese Farm Food* book tour, I brought my tofu-making gear along with a mountain of other Japanese paraphernalia (grinding bowl, knives, vegetable scrubbing brushes, fish scaler, fish tweezers) and ingredients from home: 50 kilos of my husband's homegrown rice, 7 kilos of my homemade miso, and a 6-kilo rice bran pickling bed (page 219). I was committed.

Even in Japan, it is not self-evident that you will find conscientiously made tofu from Japanese soybeans. Most supermarkets carry brands produced by the larger companies, who use nonorganic U.S. soybeans. Machines take the place of human hands in some of the crucial steps when producing these low-priced blocks of tofu, but ultimately it is the quality of the beans and water that determines the subtly sublime flavor profile of top-shelf tofu. An integral part of my book events is always about introducing and sharing the great foodstuffs of Japan, which perhaps are not yet widely available abroad. While there was not even an inch more of space for soybeans, I managed to squeeze in two small cedar tofu forms in one of my eight pieces of luggage. I also ordered a couple more forms for my friend Amy Dencler, who would be the chef of the Chez Panisse book launch dinner.

Regrettably, the tofu I made in the States did not always turn out as perfectly as when I made it in Japan. What was different? Climate? Beans? *Nigari*? Certainly all of those factors come into play, though I'm not quite sure to what degree. Suffice to say, I had a moment of panic about the recipe in the book when I found that the U.S. wooden tofu forms, which looked exactly the same online as the Japanese, were actually almost twice as big. For some reasons the soy milk did not want to set, so I immediately doubled the amount of *nigari* and increased the setting time. (Thankfully, those changes got into the second printing.) I asked my assistant in Japan to send me some Japanese beans to assess the problem. No change. The U.S. beans had more pronounced overtones of soy than the milder Japanese varietal our friends grow, which produced slightly heavier, yet nonetheless creamy blocks of tofu. Skimming off the yuba skin (page XXIX) will tell you much about the innate quality of the soybeans. With the yuba comes any impurities or acridness, so the yuba skimming is a vital step. However, take off too much yuba (i.e., heat too slowly) and you don't end up with enough soy milk. Ultimately it is all about the pot, the stove, and the weather. And like so much of cooking: faith, personal balance, and self-confidence.

Every day, lunchtime sneaks up on me, and if I have not thought about what to make by about 11:30 a.m., I could be in trouble. Luckily, the vegetable stand down the street sells our local organic tofu and *usuage* (page XXIX)—both handy to have around for a quick Country Miso and Vegetable Soup (page 80). After visiting producers around Japan, I came away totally embracing the theory of hidden taste (*kakushi aji*) and now favor using small dashes of different ingredients to give balance or pop to food. And after a visit to the Noto Peninsula, I was very attracted to using Japanese fish sauce (in just about everything). This is a riff on the classic *yudofu* and is perhaps closer to a miso-less miso soup.

tofu simmered with vegetables SERVES 4
YASAI NO YUDOFU

1 medium carrot, about
   4½ ounces (125 g)

3 very thin negi or fat scallions,
   about 2½ ounces (70 g)

1½ cups/300 cc Katsuobushi
   Dashi (page 253)

1 (½-pound/250-g) block of
   konnyaku (see Note)

1 (10.5-ounce/300-g) piece of
   Japanese-style "cotton" tofu,
   cut into ½-inch (12-mm) cubes

Brown rice vinegar

Best-quality fish sauce

Soy sauce

1 finely chopped thin
   scallion, for garnish

Finely slivered peel from 2 small
   yuzu or 1 Meyer lemon, for garnish

Cooked Japanese rice, for serving

Scrub the carrot, but do not peel unless the skin looks distressed. Halve the carrot lengthwise, cut into ⅛-inch (4-mm) half-moons, and drop into a small bowl. Peel off any discolored outside layers from the negi or fat scallions, slice into ¾-inch (2-cm) lengths, and add to the bowl with the carrot.

Heat the katsuobushi dashi in a medium-sized saucepan until it comes to a gentle simmer. Slide the carrot, negi, and parboiled konnyaku into the simmering dashi and cook for 5 minutes over medium heat until the carrot and negi pieces are soft. Scoop the tofu off of the cutting board with a flat mesh skimmer and gently add it to the simmering soup. Heat through and serve immediately.

Ladle into deep soup bowls, drop in a speck each of organic brown rice vinegar and best-quality fish sauce, and drizzle in soy sauce to taste (about 2 teaspoons for each bowl). Sprinkle with the chopped scallions and slivered yuzu peel. Serve immediately with a bowl of rice for a light lunch.

NOTE: Fill a medium-sized pot three-quarters of the way up with water and toss in 1 tablespoon salt. Bring the water to a boil over high heat. While the water is heating, slice the konnakyu into thin (1½ by ¼-inch/ 4 cm by 6-mm) strips. Boil the konnyaku pieces over medium-high heat for 5 minutes, drain, and reserve.

Homemade soy milk only has a shelf life of about 3 days, so keep that in mind. You will also need patience to watch over the excruciatingly slow-heating pot. The bonus will be small milky treats in the form of the delicate yuba you skim off the surface of the soy milk. Sprinkle a little sea salt on before popping them in your mouth.

homemade soy milk MAKES 2½ QUARTS (2½ LITERS)
TEZUKURI TONYU

⅓ pound (150 g) small, flavorful dried soybeans

Soak the soybeans in 3 times their amount of fresh spring or well water (2½ cups/600 cc) for 9 hours in summer, 15 hours in spring, or 20 hours in winter. The soak time relates to ambient temperature.

Scoop one-third of the soybeans and soaking water into a blender, process on high for 2 minutes, and pour into a large mixing bowl. Repeat until all the beans have been processed. Bring 2¾ cups (650 cc) spring or well water to a boil over high heat in a medium-large, well-insulated pot. Add the foaming soybean mixture and bring almost to a boil, stirring constantly, to ensure the bottom does not scorch.

Remove from the heat source and let the foam subside for 15 minutes. Heat again slowly over low heat for 10 minutes.

While the soybean mixture is heating, set a fine-mesh strainer over a large mixing bowl. Line the strainer with a clean muslin cheesecloth (the reusable type). After 8 to 10 minutes have elapsed, pour the hot soybean mixture through the cheesecloth. Twist up the free ends to squeeze out the excess liquid, but let it cool for about 10 or 15 minutes before squeezing the bundle to get the last drops of liquid out of the solids. In the bowl you will have fresh soy milk ready to use for drinking or making Soft Tofu (page 236).

In the cheesecloth, you will have *okara* (soybean pulp). Use *okara* immediately or store in the fridge for up to 2 days. After that, freeze it. *Okara* is commonly stir-fried with vegetables (*unohana*), but it is also useful for preparing Pork Belly Simmered with Daikon and Leeks (page 161).

When restaurants abroad make soft tofu in-house, they get rave reviews from their loyal customers. For some reason, serving soft tofu raises the bar on a restaurant. Given how simple it is to produce, this always confounded me. That said, making or sourcing exceptional soy milk is not an effortless task. At a dinner I did with Peko Peko Japanese Catering, Yuko Sato (of Nama-Ya pottery) made beautiful soft tofu with Meiji soy milk, so I asked Yuko to share her method. As it turns out, there are many methods out there, all of which are equally straightforward. Method One will yield a looser style of tofu while Methods Two and Three will be slightly custard like.

There are several terms in Japanese for soft tofu. *Yosedofu* is the general term for tofu that is not formed into small blocks. *Kumidashi dofu* refers to the act of spooning the tofu out to serve, *oboro dofu* conjures up the shape of the rising moon, while *zaru dofu* refers to the bamboo strainer in which the tofu has been drained. But in the end they are all just about the same thing.

soft tofu SERVES 6
YOSEDOFU

2 teaspoons liquid *nigari*

3 cups (750 cc) Homemade Soy Milk (page 235) or best-quality unflavored, unsweetened soy milk of at least 10% concentration

METHOD ONE: Thin the *nigari* with 1 teaspoon water. Heat the soy milk in a double boiler over high heat until the soy milk reaches 167°F (80°C). Remove the pot holding the soy milk out from the double boiler, stick a flat wooden spoon in the milk, and immediately pour the *nigari* against the spoon. Slowly stir the soy milk, making 3 wide revolutions ONLY, and pull the wooden spoon straight up out of the coagulating soy milk. Cover with plastic wrap and let sit for 10 minutes before touching the container.

METHOD TWO: Fill the bottom half of a double boiler halfway with water and bring to a simmer over high heat. Pour soy milk and *nigari* into the top of the double boiler and set over the simmering water. Cover and steam on low heat for 10 to 15 minutes. Check for doneness with a thin wooden skewer or toothpick—it should come out clean when inserted. Gingerly (try not to jiggle) remove the top portion of the double boiler and let set for 10 minutes before serving.

METHOD THREE: Pour room temperature soy milk into a large pitcher and stir in the *nigari*. Divide between small ceramic bowls, cover with plastic wrap, and heat in the microwave for 3 minutes (the soy milk should almost, but not quite, bubble). Do not disturb for 10 minutes. Remove from the microwave and serve as described below.

Scoop tofu made by Methods One and Two into bowls and serve drizzled with a little soy sauce or sprinkled with sea salt. If you are looking for aromatics, garnish soy sauce—flavored tofu with chopped chives and a dab of grated ginger or salt-flavored with a smidge of freshly grated wasabi.

NATTO IN STRAW

A few years back, I began visiting the farm of my friends Junko and Toshiharu Suka ostensibly to pick up supplies, but the underlying reason was to chat for a spell with Suka-san's parents (page 242). Our relationship is uncomplicated, unlike mine with my parents-in-law and Suka-san with his parents. Suka-san thinks his mom talks too much, while I hang on her every word. I know her as Obaachan (grandma), so Obaachan (or Baachan) she is here. One day we were talking about the soy sauce–making community that I had joined and Obaachan began to regale me with stories of the days when they too

had made traditional foods as a community—namely, natto. She sketched out the method, which involved packing the steamed beans in rice straw. Apparently rice straw naturally contains *Bacillus subtilis* and is therefore ideal for growing natto. I went back to the Suka farm many times over the course of that winter and each time attempted to pin down Obaachan on the exact method of how to pack the steamed soybeans in straw. I should have Googled it!

Organic natto is not commonly stocked in Japanese supermarkets unless the market has a commitment to carry organic products. In our area, however, organic natto is sold at the local farm stands (thanks to Yamaki Jozo). Having organic natto readily available means there is not a big impetus to ferment one's own. Nonetheless, my pal Matsuda-san had been doing it for several years and he had piqued my interest. Matsuda-san tops fried brown rice and vegetables with natto and adds a squirt of his mayonnaise for a provocative combination. He also spoons a few natto beans on a margherita pizza, pulled hot from the brick oven, and strews it with a few fresh onion slivers and carrot fronds. Matsuda-san cultures his natto for 24 hours in the pizza oven two days after a pizza-making party once the oven has cooled to 113°-122°C (45°-50°C). The fire is extinguished, but the brick oven maintains the heat for long enough to ferment the natto. Since we do not have a brick oven but we do have rice straw, the straw method spoke to me.

Writing this book galvanized me to test several methods. Traditionally, fermentation was done without thermometers and thus seemed the natural method to pursue. My theory was that the hot, muggy Japanese summer would duplicate the temperature-controlled environment. This was not my first mistake.

After soaking the beans overnight, the iron cauldron had to be hauled out and a wood fire set. Being a town girl, I am not well versed in fire starting, so sought out Tadaaki's aunt, Katchan, for needed advice. As usual, Katchan took charge. We got the soybeans steaming over the pot of boiling water and Katchan fed the fire periodically while I assembled the other materials. The plan was to enfold some of the cooked beans in straw, inoculate some with a natto starter harvested from our local natto, and sprinkle a third portion with natto spores. Fashioning the straw boats for enclosing the natto was not as easy as for inexperienced fingers as Tadaaki made it look. Next time I will tie them with string rather than the temperamental rice straw.

Once all of the natto was safely encased in straw or smoothed into other containers, I stuck the soybeans in my car, thinking that since we were experiencing an unseasonably cool spell, the outside temperature was not high enough to culture the natto. The car would be the perfect environment. Unfortunately this reasoning did not take into consideration the sudden change in weather. Two days later, the sun had heated the car to an inferno. Oops! Prosaic (and hopeful), I stashed the natto in the outside fridge until the following day. The SSU! kids all thought the natto was tasty. Despite the lack of characteristic slimy threads, it still tasted like natto, though some of the beans were a bit dried out. The natto cultured in straw was noticably healthier, thus more flavorful.

A consultation with Matsuda-san yielded yet another intriguing method of culturing natto in straw that I am dying to try. Make a 1-foot (30-cm) deep hole in the garden. Line it with a good 4 inches (10 cm) of rice straw. Beat the rice straw against a hard surface to dislodge any debris, then fashion barquettes. Grasp a 2-inch (5-cm) thick bunch of rice straw, make sure the stem ends are flush, and tie a string or a few pieces of rice straw around the bunch at about 1½ inches (4 cm) from the stem end. Hold the tied end in one hand, pointing downward, and fan the rice straw out around your fist as if it were spilling out from a fountain. Secure the loose ends by tying them with a piece of string or a few pieces of rice straw about 10 inches (25 cm) down from the top. Create an opening for the soybeans by spreading out the straw toward the top portion into a boatlike shape. Trim off any loose straw ends about 4 inches (10 cm) from the bottom tie. Spoon a flat mesh skimmer full of steamed soybeans into the opened-up portion. Make a flat tie in one piece of rice straw and bury it in the middle of the beans as a starter. Fan the straw boat back into a cylinder to enclose the soybeans and tie string or rice straw around the circumference. Arrange the straw cones side by side in the straw-lined hole and pour a pot of boiling water over the cones. Cover with another 4 inches (10 cm) of rice straw, thick straw mats, or a plastic sheet, and shovel in a 4-inch (10-cm) layer of dirt. Leave for two or three days.

Since fresh natto is almost only available abroad online (for a price), it makes sense for natto lovers to attempt making their own. Providentially, Mitoku Traditional Natto Spores are sold through the Natural Import Company and Cultures for Health (see Resources). One small container of natto spores is enough to produce over 80 pounds of natto and the spores keep for 6 months in the fridge. The only caveat is to take care the natto spores do not infect other pickling projects because they are much, much stronger than koji. In Japan, people who work with koji never even eat natto lest some vestige of the threads transfer to the rice koji.

A *kotatsu*, consisting of a low, square table frame draped with a quilted cover and topped with a tabletop, was ubiquitous in Japanese households. If the table is set over a recessed hole in the floor, it is called a *horigotatsu* (page XIII). Post-WWII urbanization brought the electric *kotatsu* into popularity (an electric heating element was affixed underneath the tabletop frame). Today fewer and fewer households have *kotatsu* since rooms are warmed with heaters. Tatami-matted rooms are disappearing, and Western-style tables and chairs are favored. Nonetheless, making natto in the *kotatsu* was a popular fad and the idea is amusing, so it is included here. To better regulate heat circulation, however, a warm carpet under the *kotatsu* is advised.

hot table natto MAKES 8 (3-OUNCE/80-G) PORTIONS
KOTATSU NATTO

⅔ pound (300 g) soybeans

1 spoon of natto spores, measured with the teeny measuring spoon included with the spores (page 231)

Soak the soybeans for 9 hours in the summer or 12 hours in the winter in a large pot of cold filtered water. Drain the beans, return them to the pot, and refill the pot to about 5 inches (10 cm) above the beans. Bring to a boil over high heat, lower to a simmer, and cook for about 1 hour, uncovered, until the beans are soft. Since the beans were traditionally steamed over a wood-fired vat of boiling water, you want to simmer away most of the water to approximate the steaming method.

While the beans are cooking, dissolve the natto spores with 1 teaspoon of hot filtered water and preheat the oven or *kotatsu* (Japanese warming table) to 113°F (45°C). Cook the beans until they are soft enough to smash between your fingers but not mushy. Right before they are done, set twelve NEW (6-ounce/165-cc) plastic microwavable food containers on a baking pan deeper than the containers. Poke several holes in each of the lids and pour boiling water into each container and across a rubber scraper to sterilize. Dump the water right before the beans have finished cooking. It's OK if some of the water spills on the pan since the natto likes a humid environment.

Drain the cooked beans, return them to the pot, and immediately sprinkle with the dissolved natto spores. Toss with the sterilized rubber spatula to distribute well. Spoon the inoculated cooked soybeans into the plastic containers. The soybean layer should be only about ½-inch (12-mm) thick. Discard any beans that drop onto the counter. Cover the containers with their hole-poked lids and enclose the whole pan tightly with heavy-duty aluminum foil. Set the pan inside the *kotatsu* or oven and leave for 24 hours. Remove from the warm environment and discard the aluminum foil. Refrigerate overnight and start sampling the next day. The taste will mature over the course of the next few days, and since the changing nature is part of the enjoyment, have fun with it. Spoon the contents of one container into a small bowl and whip with chopsticks until the bowl is filled with gossamer threads. Season with a dash of soy sauce, a dab of Dijon mustard, and some chopped scallions, if you have any. Eat on top of a bowl of Japanese rice (page 172).

VARIATIONS: Rather than using natto spores, it is possible to inoculate the soybeans by folding a small package of natto into the hot steamed soybeans. An alternative way would be to mix 4 tablespoons warm water into a package of natto. Drain in a small sieve to harvest the soupy threads. Use 2 tablespoons of those threads in place of the natto spores mixed with hot water.

YOGURT MAKER METHOD: Set to 113°F (45°C) and ferment the inoculated beans in the yogurt maker (keep one dedicated container for this operation and sterilize before each use). Check after 24 hours. If the beans are not sufficiently funky, let them ferment for another day.

NATURAL FARMING PIONEERS

"Soil is a living thing" is almost a mantra for Sakae Suka, wife of Kazuo Suka, practicing natural farming (*shizen noho*) in Kamisato-machi, Saitama prefecture, for more than 60 years. Truly the father of natural farming in the Kanto (Greater Tokyo) area, Suka-san has quietly and gently mentored most of the organic farmers or producers in the region, including my husband, Tadaaki.

We live in the next town over, and in recent years I have been finding my way to the Suka Farm much more frequently than when I was raising three sons and struggling to get through the days jam-packed with homeschooling, running an immersion school, cooking, and helping in the field (when I could). These days I write. Writing is a (gloriously) solitary endeavor, though it can also be isolating.

I go to the Suka Farm not only to pick up vegetables that we are not growing ourselves or some organic pork that daughter-in-law Junka sells from her entry hall freezer but also to catch a few minutes with two people in my world who leave me feeling warm and valued. I always walk away from talking with Baachan and Jiichan (as we call the older couples in Japan) with some invaluable piece of knowledge about the growing process or increased understanding into the ways of country life, despite having lived it myself for over two decades.

During negi season, when I step into their barn, I am assailed by the warm sweetness of the Suka negi, stacked along the side of the vegetable packing operation. I want to drink that intoxicating aroma into my very pores

and I want to eat negi . . . immediately! I plop down on an overturned plastic milk crate next to Jiichan and Baachan and scribble furiously, hanging onto their every word, or sometimes just bask in their warm encouragement of my various endeavors. Baachan's dream is to "spread natural farming to all countries so the whole world will become healthy."

In August of 1948, Kazuo Suka's liver began to fail, and the doctors told him that no medicine would save him and he would certainly die. Still in his twenties with young children, dying was unacceptable. Searching for other options, he discovered that eating only natural foods could repair his failing body. It took one grueling month for his body to molt off the toxins of modern food, but by autumn, Suka-san had returned from the 50-kilo wraith he had become to his normal body weight of 70 kilos.

Sixty years ago, Kazuo and Sakae Suka were the only ones in our area cultivating food without pesticides, so they had no community. Today their son Toshiharu is the main farmer with the support of his wife, parents, and oldest son and daughter. And because Suka Jiichan (Kazuo) has inspired so many in our area with his clear and certain vision, we now have our own organic community. Not just satisfied with local or national recognition, Jiichan is particularly pround that his "oldest son [Toshiharu] goes out into the world to advocate for natural faming."

When asked why their vegetables were so powerfully flavorful, Jiichan cuts open a carrot to show the inside core. It is not the usual yellow but exactly the same color as the outside portion. "This carrot grew as it should. It is perfect." Baachan tilts her head to the side and with a confident smile tells me, "If you look at the shape, you can understand the soil." I often call her the "Tsuchi Obaachan" (Earth Grandma).

The Suka family negi is sweet, yet pleasantly hot. Baachan explains that "the long roots show the health of the negi." She laments that the ends, which are closest to the earth, must be lopped off and discarded, or that the tops closest to the sun are trimmed to fit the negi in a box. The part of the plant that "touches" the soil or sun contains the most natural energy. Baachan advises dropping the tops and ends into your stockpot for extra flavor. What impacts me the most about touching, cooking, or eating the Suka family vegetables is that I can taste the years and the heart that went into growing them. And that I have taken a piece of Suka Jiichan and Baachan home with me.

Creating relationships with producers or purveyors outside our immediate circle is a way to establish a connection to the world outside our own and to feel a part of a supportive community that was once the only way of life in Japan. It's a way to feel like we belong.

While I was writing and photographing *Japanese Farm Food*, we came upon some konnyaku farmers harvesting their crop. The grandma with her cotton garb and weathered visage caught my eye, so we stopped to grab some shots and chat. I had long been wanting to try my hand at making my own konnyaku from the corm itself, but was daunted by the idea of finding a wood-spiked grater to process the corm to a boilable mass. (Also it was the Christmas–New Year holidays, our busiest time of the year.) Two seasons later, I had a conversation with Suka Baachan about making konnyaku where she revealed that she makes it for her family whenever they felt like eating konnyaku. Not only that, she grows the corms herself and keeps them in her root storage house until needed. She walked me through the modern kitchen method of making homemade konnyaku. And she handed me one of her homegrown corms along with a baggy full of slaked lime made from calcined seashells for coagulating the konnyaku. I couldn't not make it. So I did. (N.B.: Most store-bought konnyaku is not sashimi quality.)

homemade konnyaku MAKES ABOUT 4½ POUNDS/2.25 KG
TEZUKURI KONNYAKU

½ konnyaku corm (about 1 pound/500 g)

Scant 1 ounce/25 g slaked lime (calcium hydroxide)

Scrub the halved konnyaku with a stiff vegetable brush like the Kamenoko *tawashi* made from hemp palm bristles (page xvii). Try to get as much of the outermost layer of the skin removed as you can. The corm will still be quite dark brown. Use your fingernails or a small sharp knife to dig out any indented spots. Don plastic gloves or stick each hand in a plastic bag before grating or cutting the konnyaku, as the flesh will make your skin itchy. To grate, cut the konnyaku into manageable pieces and grate using a circular motion on a coarse-toothed metal plate grater such as an *oroshigane* (page xviii). Or chop the konnyaku into ½-inch (1-cm) cubes and process in batches in a food processor until it is a well-grated mass.

Fill a wide kettle with 3 quarts (3 liters) of water and bring to a boil. Scrape in the grated konnyaku and cook for 3 minutes only, stirring constantly to ensure the konnyaku does not stick or burn. Smash any lumps with a potato masher. Adjust the heat so the water never comes back to a boil! Remove the kettle from the heat and leave it to cool naturally until the temperature drops to around 160°F (70°C). Whisk in the slaked lime powder (about 2 rounded soupspoons full) and continue whisking until well incorporated into the mixture and no lumps remain. Let sit for about 2 or 3 hours at room temperature.

Bring another large wide kettle of water to a boil. Scoop out rough, rounded ladlefuls of the cooled konnyaku gloop and drop into the boiling water. Boil for 30 to 45 minutes until the konnyaku blobs are firm. Depending on the size of your pot, you might need to cook the konnyaku in several batches. You should not crowd the pot while boiling.

Fill a large bowl with cold water in the sink. Plunge a metal mesh strainer into the simmering pot to scoop up the cooked konnyaku globs and immediately dump them into the bowl of cold water. Run more cold tap water to cool and to take off any residual acrid taste from the slaked lime. Store in a refrigerator container filled with cold water, but change the water each day to maintain freshness. Keeps for several weeks or more, but if the konnyaku or water smells off, toss.

Cut the fresh konnyaku into sashimi-like slices (1½ inches long by ¼ inch thick/4 cm by 6 mm). Arrange the pieces on a small plate like dominos falling against each other in a line. Dab the plate with wasabi or horseradish and serve with a couple of small saucers of soy sauce. Good with drinks or beer before dinner. Or with sake, of course.

Toss in any Japanese soups such as Country Miso and Vegetable Soup (page 80), Country Soup Flavored Four Ways (page 138), or Tofu Simmered with Vegetables (page 234). Also good sautéed in sesame oil and red chile, finished with a good glug of soy sauce and a generous handful of shaved katsuobushi (*kaminari konnyaku*).

かつお

にんぶ

8

katsuobushi, konbu,
and niboshi

KATSUOBUSHI RECIPES

KATSUOBUSHI DASHI	253
TOMATO AND EGGPLANT IN DASHI	254
KATSUOBUSHI AND TEA SOUP	261
KATSUOBUSHI WITH SOY SAUCE	262
KATSUOBUSHI MISO	263
TOSA ONIONS	264
FIDDLEHEAD FERNS DRIZZLED WITH SOY DASHI	265

KONBU RECIPES

KONBU DASHI	266
KELP-WICKED FLOUNDER	269
KONBU DASHI–SOUSED SANDFISH	270
SOY SAUCE–SIMMERED KONBU	273

NIBOSHI RECIPES

NIBOSHI DASHI	274
SOY SAUCE–SIMMERED NIBOSHI	275

When my husband and I were first married, he was the Japanese cook in our house. He shaved the katsuobushi by hand for making dashi or for sprinkling on boiled vegetables. As we had children, our life became busier and busier. The katsuobushi shaving box was relegated to the closet and replaced by bags of already shaved katsuobushi flakes. These flakes were large, fluffy pieces of pinky-tan katsuobushi (*hanakatsuo*), not the cheap minuscule shreds sold in small packs. I thought that *hanakatsuo* was shaved from the same whole fermented pieces of katsuobushi that my husband used to shave by hand. Not so. On a recent trip to Sakai Katsuobushi in Yamagawa, Kagoshima (page 255), my jaw dropped to learn that 90% of all packaged katsuobushi is shaved from pieces of smoked but not fermented skipjack tuna (*arabushi*). Sakai-san took us through the six-month-long process it takes to produce beautiful dusky pieces of hongare katsuobushi, fermented and dried on a rotation basis. In light of the UNESCO designation of Washoku as a World Heritage food, there is great irony in the fact that 60% of Japanese use powdered dashi. Beyond that, many hotels, restaurants, and company dining rooms use powder-filled paper sachets to make up their pots of dashi. Dashi, the backbone of Japanese cuisine, can easily be produced in 20 minutes—the time it takes to whip up a side dish or two to accompany a bowl of rice. Perhaps a reminder of this simple, homely food would be worth a second look.

Konbu (giant kelp) on its own forms the underpinning stock from which you build a *nabe* (one-pot dish), such as Sandfish Nabe (page 136). However, when substituting a vegetarian dashi for katsuobushi or niboshi dashi in soups such as Cold Miso Soup with Cucumber and Myoga (page 82) or Country Soup Flavored Four Ways (page 138), it makes sense to throw in some dried shiitake to add depth to the Konbu Dashi (page 266).

Second to katsuobushi-konbu dashi is niboshi dashi, which can be as simple as steeping the dried fish in water overnight or a combination soak-simmer for a quicker version. When I first came to Japan, this was the dashi that I made per the instructions of Mitsu-san, the grandmother of the tofu shop that became my home away from home. Niboshi are saltwater-simmered dried baby sardines, and the best ones are dried naturally under the sun. At Sakamoto (page 126) I tasted ago dashi for the first time and fell under the spell of its smoky overtones. *Ago* (baby flying fish) is either saltwater-simmered or charcoal-grilled before drying in the sun.

KATSUOBUSHI: Katsuobushi is smoked skipjack tuna (often called bonito). After smoking, arabushi katsuobushi is shaved into various grades. Single serving–sized packages resemble sawdust, so avoid these. Look for larger packages filled with airy pink shavings (*hanakatsuo*). Tadaaki often used thick, bronzed shavings (*araikezuri*) for making dashi in the past, but now has returned to shaving his own. Hongare katsuobushi undergoes a six-month fermentation process where it cycles between 20 to 30 days in a warm, humid environment to drying outside in the bright sun. Smoked skipjack tuna is inoculated with mold spores (*Aspergillus glaucus*), which, as they culture, break down the fats and suck up the moisture, leaving the katusobushi at only 15% residual moisture content. Whole katsuobushi (*hongare*) is listed in the Guinness World Records as the hardest food and resembles a bone, but it has a pleasantly chalky texture that compels you to stroke it.

Most Japanese have given up shaving their katsuobushi by hand, since it is much easier to just tear open a package. To shave, you need a *katsuobushi kezuriki,* the traditional wooden shaving box equipped with a heavy, well-honed planing blade. Shaving katsuobushi is harder than it looks. For one thing, the angle of the blade has to be adjusted precisely by tapping at the wooden box with a rubber mallet. Also the exact angle of how you scrape the katsuobushi across the planing blade is crucial for obtaining curled, almost sheetlike flakes rather than gritty crumbs. I am nowhere near as skilled as my husband, but am getting better with practice. It helps to warm the katsuobushi over a flame (or in the microwave) before shaving, but take care not to burn or overheat. Also be sure to rinse the powdery residue off of a whole katsuobushi before shaving.

Whole katsuobushi is available (like everything else) at Amazon as well as at Nihon Ichiban (see Resources) for a price. You will need a shaving box, but perhaps a planing blade could sub for the box. Whole kastsuobushi stays fresh for about a year at room temperature, whereas packaged *hanakatsuo* should be stored in the fridge once opened. *Hanakatsuo* or *araikezuri* tends to lose flavor as the weeks go by, and the color will fade as well. Use extra in your dashi if your shaved katsuobushi is over the hill. Or feed it to the cat and buy a new package.

Besides its use as a building block for dashi, sprinkling katsuobushi and soy sauce on boiled refreshed vegetables is one of the most classic Japanese dishes. Katsuobushi producers maintain that katsuobushi is wonderful sprinkled on anything—from curry rice to pizza to *tamago kake gohan* (raw egg on hot rice with soy sauce). I agree.

KONBU: Konbu is either farmed or gathered wild and is produced mainly in the northern island prefecture of Hokkaido. Kelp beds are like underwater forests and are therefore vital sources of oxygen for our planet. Kelp also is responsible for keeping the ocean clean, now more indispensable than ever. In 2007, the wild konbu harvests plummeted drastically, perhaps due to aftereffects of the 2005 Sanriku earthquake. Subsequently a method was devised to farm konbu that could be harvested in one year. (Wild kelp takes over two years to mature.) Konbu is harvested in June and July, and the wild harvest is strictly regulated. The strands are stretched out across the beach or hung to dry for about half a day. As the konbu dries, it is turned once or twice in order to dry evenly. However, it is not allowed to dry to the extent that it becomes brittle. The semidried konbu is rolled around a spindle, and workers pull out lengths to cut, fold, and stack for packing.

The most widely found types of konbu are ma konbu and Hidaka konbu, while Rishiri, Raus, and other konbus are only available at specialty shops or wholesale fish markets. Restaurants generally use ma konbu, a burnished-brown giant kelp whose fronds range from 12 to 15 inches (30 to 40 cm) wide and 6½ to 33 feet (2 to 10 meters) long. Ma konbu is valued for its clarity as well as its ability to become viscous when simmered or preserved. Hidaka konbu is softer than ma konbu, so lends itself to eating as is, once simmered or softened, in preparations such as Kelp-Wicked Flounder (page 269) or Soy Sauce–Simmered Konbu (page 273). Hidaka konbu also produces a fine dashi. Both ma konbu and Hidaka konbu are available on Amazon and Nihon Ichiban (see Resources), though the quality looks better on the latter. Some, but not all, Japanese grocery stores carry high-quality konbu. Check the Nihon Ichiban site for photos of what you should be looking for: simple, elegant packaging where you can see the konbu. Rishiri konbu, named after the island where it is harvested, is a sweeter, yet slightly saltier, style of konbu that produces a clear, deeply flavored dashi. Raus konbu is gathered in eastern Hokkaido and, when steeped, yields a yellowish soup with a pronounced fragrance. Neither Rishiri or Raus konbu seem to be easily available abroad.

Whenever possible, it makes the most sense to buy konbu from a fish market or specialty shop. Konbu is certainly not inexpensive, but there is a marked difference between the grades, so do a taste test if you can. But do not chew unsoftened konbu, no matter how addicting it is. You risk breaking your tooth (like I did). In the spirit of no waste, try to think of ways to reuse the konbu rather than throwing it away after making dashi or marinating fish. We like to cut the konbu into julienned slivers and serve a small pile alongside sashimi (page 269). I often do the same with the konbu I pull out from my Katsuobushi Dashi (page 253) and throw some in each soup bowl before serving miso soup (page 80). Buy the best-looking, most authentically packaged Japanese brands. Eden Foods sells wild, hand-harvested Hokkaido konbu and Gold Mine Natural Food Co. has "natural" Hokkaido konbu packaged by Ohsawa. On the U.S. domestic front, Maine Sea Vegetables sells sustainably harvested "Wild Atlantic Kombu" (see Resources).

NIBOSHI: Niboshi (also known as *iriko*) are dried baby sardines. The catch is brought in on ice to maintain freshness, cleaned immediately, and simmered in 3.5% saltwater to mimic the sea at 194°F to 205°F (90°C to 96°C). The quick cook hinders spoilage and solidifies the proteins. Because ultraviolet rays are too strong between April and September, drying during this period would result in bitter-tasting niboshi. The best niboshi are air-dried on cold, sunny days (preferably near the seaside, where the air currents are strong), and the season is from late autumn to early spring. For buying: If the bodies of the fish are bent, that is a good sign. If the stomachs of the fish are cracked or broken it could signal that the stomachs swelled during processing, which might yield a fishy-tasting broth (though some cooks pinch off the heads and stomachs before soaking or simmering for the same reason). Avoid reddish-brown niboshi; choose silvery-blue ones instead. Japanese grocery stores carry niboshi, though be very careful to check the quality. Nihon Ichiban's Katakuchi Iwashi, available either through their own Web site or Amazon, is about the best variety I have found in the U.S. (see Resources). Niboshi is well dessicated, so can keep for years if sealed in a package. Once it is open, oxidation will cause the dried fish to lose *oomph*, so try to keep them airtight.

I came across a cryptic notation in one of my Noto notebooks: "Tsuyu**... What katsuobushi?...Very smoky." Sakamoto (page 126) is legendary for its soba, and *tsuyu* is the dipping soup into which you dunk soba. This notation caused me to take a closer look into the local food culture of the Noto Peninsula. I discovered that on Noto, *ago* (baby flying fish) are slow-grilled over charcoal before drying at the seaside. *Ago* is also found in Nagasaki, where it is simmered in saltwater before sun drying, like niboshi. Clearly Sakamoto-san had used the slow-grilled. I ordered three packs right away and prepared udon for the kids at the school as soon as it came. The dipping soup was indeed smoky, though not as deeply flavored as Sakamoto-san's. Perhaps it's time for another trip to Noto.

Dashi is one of the most important building blocks in Japanese cooking, yet 60 percent of Japanese use powdered dashi. While perhaps it does not reach the heights of a Kyoto traditional restaurants, homemade dashi is dead easy to produce and more than sufficiently delicious. Katsuobushi dashi can be whipped up on the spur of the moment from two dry ingredients every Japanese should have in the kitchen cupboard (but maybe doesn't): konbu and katsuobushi.

katsuobushi dashi MAKES ABOUT 1⅔ CUPS/400 CC

1 (1½ by 2½-inch/4 by 6-cm) piece of konbu, about ¼ ounce/7 g

Handful of freshly shaved katsuobushi or *hanakatsuo* (page XXIX), about ⅔ cup/5 g

Place the konbu in a medium saucepan containing 2 cups (500 cc) cold water. Bring *almost* to a boil (you will see teeny bubbles form on the edges of the konbu) and remove the konbu. (If possible, try to reuse the softened konbu in a salad or soup.) Throw in the katsuobushi shavings and simmer gently for 8 minutes. Remove the pan from the heat, let stand for 8 minutes, then strain, but do not press the katsuobushi because it will make the dashi cloudy. Use within a day or so, if kept chilled in the fridge.

I like to slip away occasionally for solitary dinners at Soba Ro, our friend Kanchan's restaurant. One night during the rainy season the sashimi choices were slim. Instead, Kanchan served me a series of interesting vegetable dishes that I had never tasted. I was particularly taken by the chilled tomatoes that had been simmered in dashi and a broiled eggplant dish served cold with soy sauce–flavored dashi and topped with freshly shaved katsuobushi and grated ginger. A couple weeks later, Kanchan served us the tomatoes in individual bowls with a scattering of fresh corn kernels, a couple of edamame beans, a few stems of boiled *komatsuna* (page 341), and a spoonful of mozuku—all swimming in a light lashing of salt-flavored dashi. We slurped it down happily. I re-created this dish at the school as an homage to Kanchan when I was wanting a fresh taste to offset the teriyaki chicken I was serving that day for lunch. The dish was a hit with some young visitors from England and America who were staying with us.

tomato and eggplant in dashi SERVES 6
TOMATO TO NASU DASHI-NI

1 tablespoon fine sea salt

2½ cups (600 cc) warm Katsuobushi Dashi (page 253)

6 medium-small slightly underripe tomatoes (about ⅓ pound/150 g each)

4 medium Japanese eggplants (about 3½ ounces/100 g each)

2 small *myoga* buds

1 thin young gingerroot, finely slivered

1 tablespoon finely chopped scallion tops

Add the salt to the dashi and stir to dissolve. Scoop out a ladleful of salted dashi and chill in the fridge while you are cooking the tomatoes and eggplants. Bring the remaining dashi back to a simmer. Core the tomatoes and slide carefully into the simmering dashi. Cook for a minute or so until the peels start to show fissures. Cool, peel, quarter, and chill in the dashi.

Broil the eggplants on an open flame, turning with tongs, until all of the sides have blackened and the inside flesh is soft. Plunge in ice water to cool. Peel the eggplants, rinse off any lingering black specks, and blot dry carefully with a clean kitchen towel. Slice off the calyx and cut the eggplant crosswise into thirds (about 1½-inch/4-cm long long pieces). Add the eggplants to the chilling dashi and return to the refrigerator.

Slice the *myoga* buds in half vertically, turn the cut side down on the cutting board, and slice thinly. When the tomatoes and eggplants are fully chilled, spoon 4 tomato quarters and 2 pieces of eggplant into 6 small lacquered bowls. Ladle in a scoop of dashi from the tomato container, and sprinkle each bowl with a little bit each of the *myoga*, ginger, and scallion. Serve immediately as a first course to a summer supper or light lunch.

VARIATIONS: Can be also be made with boiled refreshed greens such as *komatsuna* or green beans instead of the eggplant or tomatoes. Large oval cherry tomatoes are pretty and make a nice one bite, but are a bit tedious to peel.

KATSUOBUSHI IN KAGOSHIMA

The local train bound for Yamakawa bucked and buckled down the coast, jouncing us until our teeth rattled. My pen skidded across the page. No chance of writing anything for the duration of that hour-long trip. Yamakawa was so dinky we had to walk across the train tracks to exit the station. But that also meant our destination was just across the street. The plan was to snag lunch at our inn before heading to Sakai Katsuobushi. As we pulled open the door to the inn, a waft of stale oil assailed us, which did not bode well for what lay ahead. Our misgivings were confirmed as we ordered off the chalkboard menu. Despite ordering local fish, supposedly in season, all of the fish had been frozen, even the sashimi—a conundrum given that the inn abutted the bay. Probably there was not enough business to warrant buying fresh, or perhaps they thought no one knew better.

Since the inn was the only game in town, we had intended to sleep and eat there that night. The previous night in Kagoshima, we had eaten at Cainoya, an innovative Tuscan restaurant run by Takayoshi Shiozawa, a chef dedicated to ferreting out the most pristine local ingredients, paired with organic produce from his kitchen garden. Finding a decent place to eat while on the road in Japan can prove problematic without reliable recommendations. Cainoya had been introduced to us by a close editor friend and, in fact, we had been treated to a lavish prix-fixe dinner there (a thank-you for helping out on an editing project). I stepped outside the inn and slipped into a recess away from the wind buffeting off of the bay to make the calls. First: Cainoya. Could he fit us in and could we have less courses, more casual food at the counter? Yes. Second: the hotel in Kagoshima. Could we rebook our rooms? Yes. In the meantime,

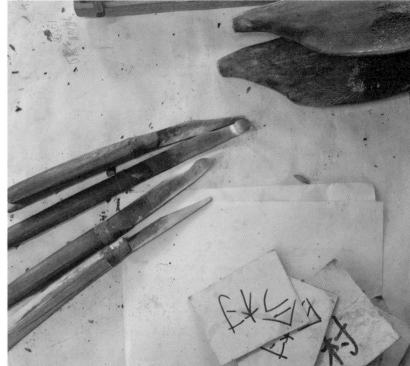

Fuji TV director Saori Abe had already talked to the innkeeper. Could we cancel? Yes . . . for a small fee, which we all willingly ponied up.

Although close, we grabbed a taxi for the 5-minute drive to Sakai Katsuobushi, located at the end of the dock area. The driver took us through a confusing rabbit warren of streets, and after asking directions several times, we finally alighted in front of the katsuobushi operation. The first thing Hiroaki Sakai asked me was, "Did you know that 90% of packaged shaved katsuobushi has merely been smoked but never fermented and sun-dried?" No, I did not. I just assumed it was the same, or at least close. My world turned around that day, and we are back to shaving our katsuobushi as we need it. No more preshaved bags.

Hiroaki Sakai is the 3rd-generation katsuobushi producer in his family which, along with most of the katsuobushi producers in this area, relocated from Kochi prefecture. Although Japanese have consumed dried skipjack tuna since prehistoric times, the technique to ferment using a combination of mold and sun drying only came about in the Edo period and originated in Tosa (present-day Kochi prefecture). While there are currently 26 companies producing katsuobushi around Yamakawa, of the 50 families that migrated to Kagoshima prefecture (coming for the busy port), only 8 remain due to the tough job it is to produce hongare katsuobushi (molded and sun-dried), the proliferation of cheaper production methods, and no son or daughter to carry on the family business. Despite this drastic drop in numbers of producers, yields have increased thanks to

a demand for *arabushi* (smoked, nonmolded, non-sun-dried katsuobushi) in instant and processed foods. Hiroaki left Yamakawa and spent ten years living and working in Tokyo after university. He eventually decided to return to his roots and feels better for it. If he had not come back, the company would have died.

The Sakai family produces katsuobushi from two kinds of skipjack tuna: those caught in Japanese waters during the season (spring to fall) and those caught all year long in far waters near the equator. I bought the Japanese-caught ones. In any case, all fish is frozen on ship and hoisted off the boats with helicopters to deliver to wholesale markets at the docks. Katsuobushi producers are located right next to these designated wholesale markets where the skipjack tuna comes in (Yaizu in Shizuoka prefecture and Makurazaki and Yamakawa in Kagoshima). Sakai Katsuobushi thaws the frozen fish in bubbling cold water overnight, circulating air through the water to aid in an even thaw.

Once thawed, the fish is cut down into four triangular-shaped filets, which are simmered for two to three hours in a shallow tank filled with baskets to hold the filets. The next step is deboning the filets. And the 1% of fish designated to be molded and dried for *hongare* will also be smoothed with mashed skipjack tuna meat to prettify the shape and to hide the bone striations. The rest get placed in the smoker as is. The smoker is a chimney-like, three-story-high room, which holds eight levels of trays. The filets remain in the smoker for twenty to thirty days and are rotated up as new trays are introduced. The trays are well marked for provenance before being slid into the smoking chamber and shut behind mottled copper doors etched with scratchings from the past.

The katsuobushi removed from the smoker looks like a piece of charcoal, and the black tar must be sanded off. The sanding room is equipped with four belt sanders behind each of which sits a surgical-masked worker who holds up a filet to the vibrating belt. My Berkeley friend Sharon comments on the windowless room that I had not noticed, a testament to my acceptance of Japanese life. The flinty black shavings are bitter, so have no use other than to be sold to farmers for fertilizer. At this point, the katsuobushi contains no more than 23% moisture content, and the smoked filets not designated for molding and drying will be shaved and packaged.

The katsuobushi pieces that were smeared with fish paste will undergo one more step before being fermented. Seventy-something Isamu Matsuue has spent over 60 years of his life working with katsuobushi, and he is the last artisan in Japan skilled at shaving the fish by hand. And Sakai Katsuobushi is the last katsuobushi company to perform this step. The special tools, shaped to follow the crevices of the katsuobushi, are no longer being fashioned, so this ancient art dies with Matsuue-san.

After each piece of katsuobushi passes through Matsuue-san's experienced hands, the katuobushi is set on trays and sprayed with *Aspergillus glaucus*, a mold spore akin to koji (*Aspergillus oryzae*). As with koji (page XXVIII), *Aspergillus glaucus* used to occur naturally in the fermentation process, though now is controlled by homogeneous, laboratory-made strains. The katsuobushi develops a dusting of greenish-blue mold that will eventually transform into dusky brown. It is held in the 84°F (29°C) mold room at 90% humidity for 20- to 30-day cycles before hauling out into the bright sunlight. The drying process takes six months and will yield hongare katusobushi with only 15% residual moisture, thanks to the mold sucking it out as it decomposes the fat. Using hongare katusobushi to make Katusobushi Dashi (page 253) will result in a clear, subtly nuanced broth.

After the tour, Sakai-san's family serves us tea. Sated from our bowl of *Chabushi* (page 261), we head back to the Yamakawa train station. As we careen around the curves, I recount our disappointing meal at the inn. Sakai-san laughs, agrees the food is egregious, and drops us off with these parting words, "Next time you should eat with us!"

After the Fuji TV episode of our visit aired, apparently the kasuobushi producers received a flood of orders. (Having seen a YouTube clip of the katsuobushi association members discussing the dismal state of the market and how to increase customer awareness, I was thrilled to hear this.) Sakai-san called my school one afternoon: "On behalf of all of the members of the katsuobushi association, thank you, thank you, thank you!" I reported that I would be ordering soon, as I was down to my last katsuobushi from the six I had bought during our visit. A couple of days later, a box arrived with five more. And this time it was my turn to call and say, "Thank you, thank you, thank you!"

After touring the Sakai Katsuobushi (page 255) operation, Hiroaki Sakai ushered us into a small room off of the main building, where they receive visitors. We perched on sofas in anticipation as Hiroaki's father swiped a piece of katsuobushi across their family's red lacquer katsuobushi shaving box (*kezuriki*). In the time it takes me to shave a couple of handfuls, the father had shaved a pile that filled the hopper of the shaving drawer. The father handed around the box and urged us to take a taste. Not wanting to be greedy, I pinched up a moderate amount but was admonished by Sakai-san to grab a fistful and jam the whole thing in my mouth to get the total feeling of the smoky katsuobushi shavings. Sakai-san's wife set a few black lacquer bowls on the table and the father heaped a handful of katsuobushi in each one. After adding a dollop of miso and a lashing of organic tea, she handed us each a bowl. "*Chabushi*," she smiled. "We eat it when there is no time to make miso soup."

katsuobushi and tea soup SERVES 4
CHABUSHI

4 handfuls freshly shaved katsuobushi or *hanakatsuo* (page XXIX)

4 scant tablespoons inaka miso (page 72)

1⅔ cups (400 cc) freshly brewed hot green tea (page 325)

1 tablespoon finely chopped scallion (optional)

Set 4 small lacquer or ceramic bowls on the counter. Heap a handful of katsuobushi (about ⅔ cup/5 g) into each bowl. Drop a tablespoon of miso into each bowl and pour the hot tea in a circular fashion over the katsuobushi (scant ½ cup/100 cc). Garnish with the chopped scallion, if using, and serve immediately as a 3 p.m. afternoon snack or warm breakfast.

Okaka is another name for katsuobushi and the common term for this popular *onigiri* filling. In our house, we often just mix some soy sauce into freshly shaved katsuobushi and poke that into our rice balls. Since that's a bit of a nonrecipe, I asked Hiroaki Sakai to divulge his family method. The return email: "We use the strained leftovers from making katsuobushi dashi." Of course. Waste not, want not. Store in a jar in the fridge and spoon on top of rice when the spirit moves you.

katsuobushi with soy sauce MAKES ½ CUP (125 CC)
OKAKA

Strained katsuobushi left over from making Katsuobushi Dashi (page 253)

2 teaspoons soy sauce

Dry the drained katsuobushi in a small frying pan over medium-low heat until the liquid has evaporated and the katsuobushi is dry and crumbly. Season with a splash of soy sauce and stir to incorporate. There should be no liquid pooling in the pan. Use as a filling for rice balls (page 172) or spooned on top of a bowl of hot Japanese rice (page 172). Also tasty with fried eggs instead of salt. Or as a tasty bite to accompany sake.

VARIATIONS: Cook the strained katsuobushi over medium-low heat in a small, dry pan until crispy. Dribble in ½ teaspoon sesame oil, 1 teaspoon soy sauce, 1 teaspoon mirin, and ½ teaspoon white sesame seeds. Continue stirring over medium-low heat until all of the liquid has evaporated. You will probably need to lift the pan off of the burner to avoid scorching the soy sauce and mirin.

When visiting a koji spore laboratory in Kagoshima, I poked around the shop to ferret out any local preparations that I might be able to re-create. Katsuobushi Miso caught my eye, so when Hiroaki Sakai from Sakai Katsuobushi (page 255) offered his family recipe, I gratefully accepted. This miso can be mixed into *onigiri* as in Mini Rice Balls with Sour Plum (page 172), poked in the center of a larger rice ball, or simply dolloped onto a bowl of steaming rice.

katsuobushi miso SERVES 6

2 tablespoons hon mirin (page XXXI)

⅓ cup (100 g) flavorful miso
(brown rice or barley)

2 tablespoons finely
chopped scallions

1⅓ cups (10 g) freshly
shaved katsuobushi or
hanakatsuo (page XXIX)

Muddle the hon mirin and sake into the miso and stir in a small frying pan over low heat, until warmed completely through but not bubbling. The point here is to cook off a bit of the alcohol. Remove from the heat and stir in the chopped scallions. Once incorporated, scrape into a medium-sized bowl and smash in the katsuobushi. Keeps, stored in the fridge, as long as the scallions stay perky—about 2 weeks.

VARIATION: Warm 1 tablespoon white sesame seeds in a small, dry frying pan over medium-high heat until you get a slight whiff of their aroma (they will not be as fragrant as golden sesame seeds). Toss the warmed seeds into the miso.

The trick to these simple and beguiling pickles is to make sure that they absorb the salt long enough, so they are no longer raw and unpleasantly hot. The Tosa region of southern Shikoku is famous for skipjack tuna, so preparations that bear that name refer to the use of katsuobushi. These are particularly good eaten alongside a strongly flavored, oily fish such as yellowtail. This recipe was adapted from one found in Eri Yamaguchi's long out-of-print book *The Well-Flavored Vegetable*.

tosa onions SERVES 6
TAMANEGI NO TOSA-ZUKE

2 medium yellow onions (⅔ pound/300 g), peeled and sliced into fine rings

1 teaspoon salt

1 tablespoon soy sauce

2 tablespoons sake

2 tablespoons freshly shaved katsuobushi or ¼ cup (60 cc) lightly packed *hanakatsuo* (page XXIX)

Drop the onion rings into a medium-sized bowl and separate them with your fingers. Sprinkle with the salt and toss with both of your hands to distribute the salt evenly. Leave the onions to soften for about 15 to 20 minutes. They should still retain their shape but be just starting to relax. Rinse lightly under cold water and pat dry on a clean, dry dish towel.

Measure the soy sauce and sake into a small bowl. Heat a medium-sized frying pan or wok over low heat and stir-fry (dry) the katsuobushi for a couple of seconds. Toss the onion, soy sauce–sake, and katsuobushi together in the medium-sized bowl and weight with 3 small plates. Leave for 30 minutes, then serve. The onions will start to droop (and exude water) as time elapses, so they are best eaten quickly. Serve with drinks before dinner or on the table as part of a full meal.

I read on Hank Shaw's highly regarded blog *Hunter, Angler, Gardener, Cook* that fiddlehead ferns could be considered carcinogenic. However, Hank further elucidates: The amount of fiddlehead ferns you would have to eat to affect your health would be tantamount to drinking a case of beer. I trust Hank, so had no qualms about including this recipe in the book. In any case, when fiddlehead ferns show up with the other mountain vegetables each spring, they are commonly eaten cooked, not raw (without alarm), all over Japan. While there are some cooks who use baking soda in the cooking water or who soak the ferns in saltwater overnight, we do not (and neither does Hank). Blanch the delicate fiddlehead ferns in salty water, then flavor ever so gently.

fiddlehead ferns drizzled with soy dashi SERVES 6
WARABI NO OHITASHI

2 small bunches of fiddlehead ferns, about 9 ounces (270 g)

2 tablespoons freshly shaved katsuobushi or 3 tablespoons *hanakatsuo* (page XXIX)

1 tablespoon soy sauce

4 tablespoons dashi

Bring a medium-sized pot of hot water to a boil and place a bowl of ice water in the kitchen sink. Cut and discard any discolored tips off of the fiddlehead ferns and throw the ferns into the boiling water. Depending on the variety, they will cook in 1 to 3 minutes. Scoop out the ferns with a strainer and plunge them immediately into the ice water. Stick your hand in the water to make sure it remains cool. Add some cold water if there is any residual warmth. Pull out the ferns, aligning the stem ends as you do. Roll in a clean kitchen towel to blot dry and cut into 1-inch (2.5-cm) lengths. Don't scatter the piles. Arrange in a shallow bowl as if they had been cut there. Strew the katsuobushi over the cut fiddlehead ferns. Mix the soy sauce and dashi in a small bowl and drizzle the soy dashi over the fiddlehead ferns. Serve with Konbu Dashi–Soused Sandfish (page 270) or Shio Koji–Grilled Pork (page 201) and a bowl of Japanese rice (page 172). The ferns hold up well as leftovers the following day.

VARIATION: I also like fiddlehead ferns dressed with Soy Vinegar (page 150), with or without the katusobushi garnish.

Most soupy dishes we cook in a stoneware casserole (*donabe*, page XVIII) on a burner in the middle of our table often just start with a piece of konbu in plain water. The broth is built up from the vegetables and fish or meat that get thrown and cooked together with tofu. But when putting together vegetarian-style miso or country soups, adding shiitake to the konbu gives the dashi enough depth to stand up to the miso or other hearty flavorings such as sake lees.

konbu dashi SERVES 6

2 (1½ by 2½-inch/4 by 6-cm) pieces of konbu, about ½ ounce/15 g

4 small dried shiitake (about ⅕ ounce/5 g)

Soak the konbu and shiitake in 2 cups (500 cc) cold water overnight or for at least 4 hours. If you are in a hurry, bring the konbu, shiitake, and water to a boil and let sit for 1 hour before proceeding. Simmer the soaked konbu and shiitake for 8 minutes. Cool to room temperature, remove the konbu, squeeze the shiitake, and take them out as well.

VARIATION: Throw in some of Baachan's Dried Eggplant (page 18) for a more complex taste.

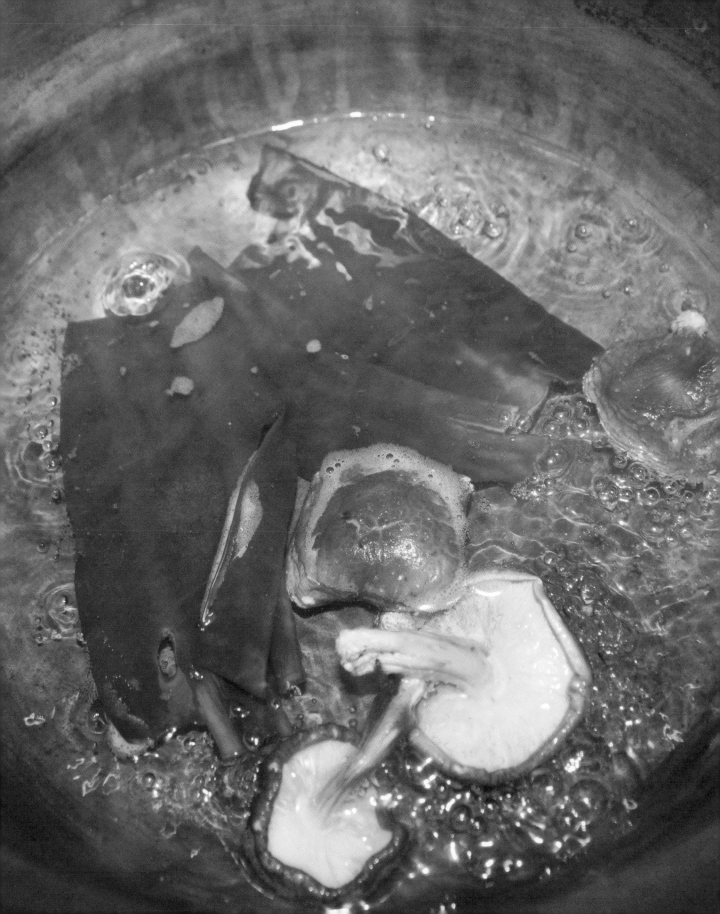

This is one of the easiest and most foolproof ways to prepare sashimi as a small bite before dinner, and I do it often, since kelp-wicked sashimi always seems gorgeous to the guests (even Japanese) because most people buy their sashimi already cut. If you are feeling particularly lazy, ask the fishmonger to remove the bones. The wicking-out process leaves pleasantly tight flesh that feels very nice against your tongue. The fish will stay for 2 days in the fridge, if kept well wrapped.

kelp-wicked flounder SERVES 4 TO 6
HIRAME NO KOBUJIME

1 ultrafresh *hirame* (flounder), skinned and fileted into 4 pieces (about ½ pound/225 g fish meat)

¾ teaspoon fine sea salt

4 tablespoons sake

2 to 4 pieces konbu (enough to cover the surface of the fish)

Flaky sea salt, for serving

Freshly grated wasabi (optional)

Remove the pinbones from the fish with flat-bladed tweezers and trim off any ragged edges. Sprinkle the salt evenly across the fronts and backs of the filets from a foot above. Pour the sake onto a dinner plate, lay the konbu in the sake, and set 2 dinner plates on top to speed the softening time. Separate the filets into 2 equal-sized sets for wicking. Cover the belly side of one filet with a layer of konbu (you can piece them together, if need be) and place the belly side of the partner filet on top of the konbu.

Tear off a connected piece of 2 spongy-style paper towels and lay the 2 konbu-sandwiched filets along the shorter edge, about 5 inches (12 cm) in. Fold that edge of the paper over the fish and gently roll up the fish to wrap. Repeat with the other 2 filets. Enclose in plastic wrap and refrigerate overnight (or at least 4 to 6 hours).

Remove the fish from the fridge, unwrap, and peel off the konbu from each filet. Cut the konbu into small squares or ⅛ by 1-inch (3 mm by 2.5-cm) strips. Slice the fish into ¼-inch (6-mm) thick pieces at a diagonal. Slide your knife under the sliced fish, and arrange on top of the konbu squares in 2 or 3 slightly askew lines on one large dinner plate or on two small ones. Or place directly on the plate and mound small piles of the slivered konbu in between the lines of fish. Serve sprinkled with flaky sea salt and a dab of freshly grated wasabi alongside, if using.

VARIATIONS: Any mild white fish filets such as red snapper, John Dory, or halibut are lovely treated with a kelp wick. Instead of the salt sprinkle, feel free to serve with a small saucer of excellent soy sauce.

While visiting Iio Jozo (page 159), Akihiro Iio took us around to the shops of his friend, Yoshikazu Taniguchi. Taniguchi-san is the fifth-generation owner of a traditional wholesale shop named Kanemasu. The storefront opens to the street with only a split curtain (noren) to separate the inside space from the outside. Taniguchi-san has kept the flavor of Meiji-era (1868–1912) Japan by leaving the old bins and shop chests in place and has added some new touches such as a sweeping indigo banner with the shop's logo standing next to the entryway. Across the road is his fish-drying operation. A few of his female high school classmates are in charge of cleaning, gutting, and sousing the daily catch. The day we stopped by, they had just put up a tub of *hata hata* (sandfish). The fish shimmered under the water, and I started to get very hungry. Luckily, Taniguchi-san also runs an eatery a short drive away. Taniguchi-san laid a few pieces of glowing charcoal in the *shichirin* (page 41) set in front of our places, and he started us off with local shiitake. It is important not to burn the vegetables or fish, yet you do not want it raw inside. Usually people salt the fish or soak it in saltwater for 30 minutes. This particular sousing method is Taniguchi-san's. And the dash of vinegar is at the behest of Iio-san, hence placement in the vinegar chapter.

konbu dashi–soused sandfish SERVES 6
DASHIZUKE NO HATAHATA HIMONO

6 small whole fish such as sardines, herring, or sandfish (about 2 ounces/60 g each)

1¼ cups (300 cc) Konbu Dashi (page 266), slightly chilled

1 tablespoon + scant 1 teaspoon fine white sea salt

2 teaspoons sake

1 drop of best rice vinegar

2 small yuzu or 1 Meyer lemon, for serving

Fine sea salt, for serving

Lay 1 fish on a cutting board, hold your flat hand across the surface length of the fish, and cut a slit from under the mouth bone to the end of the stomach area with a sharp knife held in your other hand. Scoop out the small amount of guts into a bowl, then wash under cold running water to remove the rest. Use your fingernails to scrape off any black blood tendrils. Repeat this process with the remaining fish.

Pour the konbu dashi into the container in which you will marinate the fish and stir in the salt to dissolve. Sprinkle in the sake and vinegar, slip in the fish, and let sit for 30 minutes. Cut six 1-foot (30-cm) lengths of kitchen twine. Tie a small loop in the top of each one by wrapping it around the handle of a wooden kitchen spoon. Remove the fish from the sousing liquid, poke the untied end of the string into the gill area, and thread the string through the open mouth. Tie. Hang the fish in a protected spot with good air currents. At Kanemasu they dry the fish for 2 hours buffeted by warm air emitting from a combo set up of a mild heating device and large fans to simulate drying the fish by the seaside. I hung the fish overnight under the rafters but felt they could use a bit more drying time. Since it was unusually cold (we were having a freak snowstorm) when I dried my fish, I left them out for 2 days (though brought them in at night). Normally storing the semidried fish in the fridge is recommended. The surface of the fish should be pleasantly taut and dry to the touch.

konbu dashi—soused sandfish

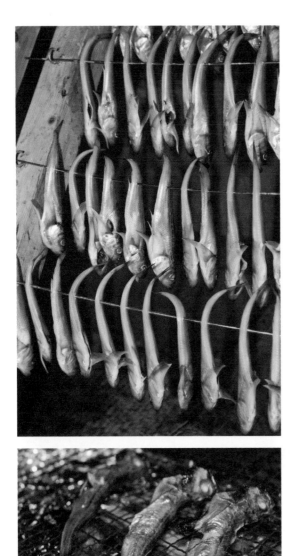

Cook over low coals on a *shichirin* (page 41) until the skin buckles a bit but is not burned. Or cook for 3 minutes on each side on a rack set over a foil-lined cookie sheet placed in the third rack from the top of the broiler.

Serve on individual plates with a piece of yuzu or Meyer lemon for squeezing and a small mound of white sea salt for dipping each bite before eating. Good as a casual appetizer or as part of a main meal.

VARIATIONS: Theoretically, any fish can be soused and dried using this same method. Taniguchi-san had whole squid as well as butterflied horse mackerel (*aji*), flounder (*karei*), butterfish (*ebodai*), and needle fish (*sayori*). Drying times depend on the weather and size of fish. Cooking times should be adjusted for thicker fish.

Make this after putting up some Konbu Dashi or Katsuobushi Dashi. This dish embodies the ultimate *motainai* (no-waste) philosophy of the Japanese traditional kitchen. The glossy konbu can border on viscous, but that quality gives this condiment its unique appeal. I like my konbu chewy, but if you prefer it softer, add more dashi and simmer it longer than 30 minutes.

soy sauce–simmered konbu SERVES 4
KOBU NO TSUKUDANI

Leftover konbu from Konbu
  Dashi (page 266) or 2 recipes of
  Katsuobushi Dashi (page 253)

1 to 1½ cups (250 to 350 cc)
  Katsuobushi Dashi or Konbu Dashi

2 teaspoons soy sauce

1 teaspoon hon mirin (page XXXI)

1 teaspoon sake

½ teaspoon organic sugar

1 tablespoon shaved katsuobushi

Snip the reconstituted konbu (about 1 ounce/30 g) into roughly 1-inch (2.5 cm) squares and drop into a small pot. Measure in ⅔ cup (150 cc) of the dashi and bring to a low simmer for 30 minutes. Check every 10 minutes to make sure the liquid has not evaporated. Add a scant ½ cup (100 cc) at a time to the pan, if needed. After simmering for 30 minutes, add the soy sauce, hon mirin, sake, and sugar, and cook while continually stirring until almost all of the liquid has been absorbed and the konbu is glazed. You will be able to smell the soy sauce caramelizing and the bubbles on the bottom of the pan will be large and glossy. Stir in the katsuobushi and serve as is with tea for an afternoon snack or dolloped on a bowl of Japanese rice (page 172). The sweet soy taste also complements the complexity of Country Soup Flavored Four Ways (page 138) and is nice served alongside.

VARIATION: Some people like to cut the konbu into thin strips instead of squares.

When I first came to Japan, I lived in Kumagaya, a city about 45 minutes away from where I live now (Kamikawa-machi). I befriended the owners of a small tofu shop down the street from my apartment and went there every day to buy a piece of tofu for my nightly dinner. Japanese tofu enthralled me, having previously only thought of tofu as an uninteresting substitute for meat. The affable shopkeepers were another draw. They gave me cooking tips, such as this method to make niboshi dashi. (N.B.: Some cooks pinch off the heads and tummies of the fish to clarify the flavor of the dashi.) Any dried fish can be used instead of niboshi, which are dried baby sardines. And if you can lay your hands on dried *eso* (a small whitefish) or dried *ago* (baby flying fish), you will not regret it, but be sure to break them in half before soaking. Also, the overnight soak method yields a bright, nuanced dashi and is well worth thinking ahead. Some cooks throw in a small piece of konbu when they soak the dried fish—a little goes a long way. I would not add more konbu than 50% of the weight of the niboshi.

niboshi dashi MAKES 1⅔ CUPS (400 CC)

5 niboshi, 1 or 2 *eso*, or 1 *ago*
(about ¼ ounce/7 g)

Soak the niboshi overnight (for 8 to 10 hours) in 2 cups (500 cc) cold water. Strain out the niboshi and use the dashi (soaking liquid) as is.

Niboshi dashi can replace katsuobushi dashi in miso soup or udon broth. Transform the soaked niboshi into Soy Sauce–Simmered Niboshi (page 275) if you are feeling energetic; otherwise stockpile them in the freezer to be simmered later.

A second dashi can be made from the soaked niboshi (and konbu, if using): Simmer in 1 cup (250 cc) water for 4 minutes. Let rest for 4 minutes before straining and using as a base for miso soup.

VARIATION: Soak the niboshi for 30 minutes in 2 cups (500 cc) cold water. (If you are in a hurry, skip the soak.) Bring to a simmer over medium-high heat and simmer over low heat for 8 minutes. Let sit for 8 minutes before straining out the niboshi.

During the first Japanese New Year spent at Tadaaki's house, I encountered many unfamiliar preparations in the traditional New Year food (*osechi ryori*). It was not until I began making *niboshi no tsukudani* myself from air-dried niboshi (rather than machine-dried) and Yamaki soy sauce that I could truly appreciate these sweet-simmered fishes. Start with the best dried fish you can find. It is possible to use frozen soaked niboshi that you have saved from making Niboshi Dashi (page 274), but you will lose some of the intrinsic structure of the fish and most likely the bones will separate from the meat. Also these are best if you use the smallest niboshi available.

soy sauce–simmered niboshi MAKES 2 OUNCES (60 G)
NIBOSHI NO TSUKUDANI

1 small handful of tiny niboshi, about 1 ounce (30 g)

2 teaspoons white sesame seeds

2 tablespoons soy sauce

2 teaspoons hon mirin (page XXXI)

1 teaspoon organic sugar

Soak the niboshi overnight (for 8 to 10 hours) in 1 cup (250 cc) cold water. Strain out the niboshi and reserve. The soaking water is concentrated strength Niboshi Dashi, ¼ cup (60 cc) of which will be used for making this recipe. Use the other ⅔ cup (150 cc) to make miso soup but dilute with some water to adjust the intensity. The dashi should taste of the sea but not be insistent. Warm the white sesame seeds in a small, dry frying pan over low heat until you get a hint of their aroma. Slide the seeds into a small bowl.

Dry the niboshi over medium-low heat in the small frying pan until they are crunchy. Turn occasionally with chopsticks, but be careful the niboshi do not fall apart. Sprinkle in the reserved niboshi dashi, soy sauce, mirin, and sugar. Increase the heat to medium-high to caramelize the sauce onto the fish. Tilt the pan so the sweetened sauce washes over the tops of the fishes as they caramelize. Cook until all of the liquid has been absorbed and the niboshi are glossy. Fold in the sesame seeds and use as a filling for rice balls (page 172), with beer or sake before dinner, or as a side dish at any hearty Japanese meal such as Sake Lees Soup with Salmon (page 210).

VARIATION: Toss in ½ tablespoon shaved katsuobushi along with the white sesame seeds.

とうがらし
キム
チ

9

chile peppers
and kimchee

CHILE PEPPER RECIPES

BITTER ORANGE RED KOSHO	281
CHILE PEPPER COD EGGS	282
RAW SQUID IN CORAL	287

KIMCHEE RECIPES

CUCUMBERS WITH CARROT THREADS	289
NAPA CABBAGE WITH SHREDDED DAIKON	290
CUBED DAIKON AND GARLIC CHIVES	292

Heat from chiles is not the first flavor that comes to mind when one thinks of Japanese cuisine. Salt, soy sauce, miso, sake, and mirin are the most classic seasonings . . . and of course sugar, though refined sugar is a fairly recent addition to the palate (post-WWII). In our area of landlocked Saitama prefecture, people did not have fish to ferment for giving that extra kick to their vegetable- and soybean-based diet. They relied on what was grown in the field: ginger, garlic, and red chile peppers. Those three aromatics appear in much of the food we eat in our locale.

I arrived in 1988, and Japan was in the midst of a spicy food boom: Korean barbecue was the hot ticket for nights out. Kimchee was a mainstream condiment at ramen shops or late-night drinking spots such as izakaya. On the other end of the spectrum lies Washoku, traditional Japanese cuisine, which at its best is characterized by subtle elegance whose roots lie in exclusive eateries (*ryotei*). Japanese food on a popular level has a wide range of flavors—pungent, sour, wild, funky, and yes, spicy. Red chile peppers have several centuries of history in the food cultures of the entire Japanese archipelago, including, if not especially, in preserving.

CHILE PEPPERS: While chiles have an over eight millennia–long history in Mexico, they were not introduced into Japan until the mid 16th century by Portuguese missionaries. The Japanese word for chile pepper (*togarashi*) roughly means "foreign mustard." Chile peppers are also called *yogosho*, "Western pepper," based on the Japanese term for black pepper (*kosho*). Confusingly, in Kyushu, green chiles are referred to as *kosho*, hence the name *yuzu kosho* (page XXXI). *Yuzu kosho* is a salty condiment of pulverized green yuzu peel and green chiles developed about fifty years ago in Kyushu. In the last several years, the use of *yuzu kosho* has exploded across Japan. While the most common use of *yuzu kosho* is in salt-flavored ramen, it can be dabbed on sashimi, tofu, tempura, pork cutlets, grilled meats, pasta, or whisked into salad dressings. Perhaps it's the new Sriracha.

The chile of choice in Japan not surprisingly is the japones chile, which is characterized by its clean heat. Because of its lack of complexity, the japones chile is well suited to the stronger flavors that profile robust Japanese cooking and preserving. In the summer, as the chiles turn from green to red, they are chopped up raw and appear on sashimi plates, in soups, and with noodles. And the leaves can be sautéed or simmered in sweet soy sauce like in *Kobu no Tsukudani* (page 273). In the late fall, the plants are yanked out of the earth and hung to dry. The dried chiles are used throughout the year in preserving, sautéing, and simmering. Japones chiles are available online through Purcell Mountain Farms and Spices, Inc. (see Resources). I have also seen them occasionally at stores that carry a wide range of chiles, such as Central Market in Texas. The closest substitute for the japones chile is the árbol chile, though it is perhaps 30% larger, so use less.

KIMCHEE: Although it appears that most food and cultural traditions (such as the kanji writing system and Buddhism) came from China, Japan has a very close (yet complicated) relationship with Korea and shares some DNA that dates back to the Stone Age. In fact, kimchee as we know it today exists thanks to a 16th-century gift of red chiles from Japan to Korea. The earlier version of kimchee involved vegetables pickled with salt and fish. After the advent of the chile pepper, Koreans began using red chile in these pickles and the term *kimchee* came into being.

While the 1980s brought a wave of immigration from Korea, the majority of Koreans who live in Japan today trace their ancestry to the immigrants who were forcibly or voluntarily patriated into Japan during the early 1900s, while Korea was under Imperial Japanese rule. During WWII, the numbers of Koreans in Japan increased drastically, as Koreans were recruited (or conscripted) by the Imperial army to aid in the war effort. Post-WWII, a large body of Koreans repatriated back to Korea, but there are still almost a million ethnic Koreans living in Japan (a quarter of whom are naturalized Japanese). Accordingly, there has been a significant influence on the food and popular culture of modern Japan.

Already in 1988, when I first landed in Japan, small yellow tubs of kimchee sat next to tubs of Fermented Napa Cabbage (page 11) at the local vegetable shops. Now you can buy kimchee in small jars at the convenience store. Kimchee shops run by Korean Japanese are dotted across Japan (we have one in the next town over) and kimchee is ubiquitous at *yakiniku* (Korean barbecue) restaurants. In Japan, cheaper kimchees have not gone through lactic fermentation and are artificially soured, while kimchee starter paste (*kimuchi no moto*) is sold for instant pickles. Kimchee is not difficult to prepare at home, especially in small amounts. Large batches are certainly more authentic but require a time commitment (and the ability to consume a mountain of kimchee). All of the kimchee recipes can be doubled or tripled (or quadrupled). Due to its overwhelming pungency, we store our kimchee in the drinks refrigerator. Many Koreans have a separate refrigerator whose temperature can be adjusted for fermenting and storing kimchee.

Green *yuzu kosho* is made from green chile peppers and green yuzu, whereas red *yuzu kosho* is made from yellow yuzu and red chile peppers (which makes sense seasonally in Kyushu, the southernmost island of Japan where *yuzu kosho* was developed). This bitter orange recipe is a departure from tradition, but the pungency of the skins are a good foil for the heat of the red chile. Use sparingly as a condiment for ramen or add a smidge to homemade mayonnaise for Japanese-style sandwiches like Ginger-Soy Pork Sandwiches (page 109).

bitter orange red kosho MAKES ABOUT 5 TABLESPOONS
DAIDAI KOSHO

4 *daidai* (page 343) or other bitter oranges such as Seville

4 medium-sized fresh red Japanese chiles

2 tablespoons fine sea salt

2 teaspoons *daidai* or other bitter orange juice

Pare off the outer zest of the *daidai* with a very sharp knife, taking care to avoid the white pith. Chop briefly, then scrape into a *suribachi* (Japanese grinding bowl) or miniprep food processor.

Slice off and discard the stems and calyxes of the chiles and chop the chiles coarsely. Drop the chopped chiles into the bowl or processor along with the zest. Mash in the salt or pulse in the processor until the zest and chiles have completely broken down and have formed a vibrant orangey-red paste. Dribble in the juice and scrape into a small jar and cover the surface with plastic wrap. Keeps for several months or more stored in the refrigerator.

VARIATIONS: Remove the seeds and veins before chopping the chiles if you prefer less heat. To make green *yuzu kosho*, substitute yuzu peel for the *daidai* and green chiles for the red.

When I first tasted *mentaiko* smeared on some rice, I loved the creamy red pepper components but disliked the MSG it contained. It's impossible to find *mentaiko* made without artificial ingredients in Japan, so I occasionally make my own. The process that I intended to put in this book involved a two-soak process that was a bit fussy but ultimately worth the effort (or so I thought). But by a great stroke of luck, my soba chef friend Kanji Nakatani set a dish of his home-cured *mentaiko* in front of me as I was having lunch one day at his restaurant in the final days of editing this book. The *mentaiko*, draped with slivers of konbu, was mounded on a bed of grated daikon. I savored every little section of spicy roe and wished for more. On the way home from lunch that day I stopped at the fish market to pick up some *tsukesodara* cod eggs and followed Kanchan's rough directions. Instinct kicked in and I nailed the proportions on the first try. The day they were fully cured, I raced out in the night to Kanchan's soba restaurant. He held up a piece to inspect, popped it in his mouth, and pronounced it "perfect."

chile pepper cod eggs MAKES ABOUT 1 POUND (500 G)
MENTAIKO

1 pound (500 g) small fresh
   cod roe sacs, about 3 to
   5 ounces (85 to 140 g) each

1 tablespoon/20 g sea salt, 4%
   of the cod roe weight

2 teaspoons/10 g organic sugar,
   2% of the cod roe weight

1 teaspoon/5 g *ichimi togarashi*
   and/or *gochutgaru* red chile
   pepper powder (page XXXI),
   1% of the cod roe weight

1 (1½ by 2-inch/4 by 5-cm) konbu,
   1% of the cod roe weight

Blot off any residual moisture from the surface of the cod roe with a clean cloth, but do not wash. Lay the roe in a shallow stainless steel container and sprinkle both sides of the roe with ⅓ of the salt (1 teaspoon). Press a piece of plastic wrap on top of the surface and refrigerate. Repeat the salting operation with another ⅓ of the salt (1 teaspoon) on the following day and then again on the day after that (2nd and 3rd days of the cure). Replace the piece of plastic wrap and return to the refrigerator each day. On the 4th day, sprinkle both sides with the sugar and refrigerate for 4 more days. After the cod roe has cured for 1 week, bring the konbu to a simmer in a small amount of water and snip into thin julienned strips with a pair of kitchen scissors. Sprinkle the cured cod roe evenly on both sides with the *ichimi togarashi* or *gochutgaru* (or a mixture of both), scatter with the konbu strips, and refrigerate for another day or two before using.

Cut into ½-inch (1-cm) pieces and, if possible, serve on a bed of grated, squeezed daikon. Perfect as an appetizer with drinks before dinner or with a bowl of rice for a quick lunch. Also sensational as an instant filling for rice balls (page 172) or simply with olive oil on pasta. Keeps for about a month, individually wrapped and refrigerated, or 2 to 3 months frozen.

MAKING SHIOKARA

Shiokara, or more precisely *ika no shiokara*, is often described as "fermented squid guts." No surprise that I mistakenly thought the white tendrils inside this delicacy were guts and not julienned slices of fresh squid. The raw squid pieces are cloaked in the creamy coral liquid squeezed from the inner sac of the squid and are seasoned with a bit of miso, salt, soy sauce, sake, red chile, and yuzu peel—heaven!

We had spent a better part of an hour winding our way through some narrow back streets in a god-knows-where neighborhood of Tokyo. My newfound pal Mike Veretto (a Harvard guy with mad Japanese skills) was intent on finding a Robata-yaki restaurant. We never did. He remained steadfast on me tasting *shiokara* and ordered it straightaway at the eatery we had eventually chosen. The server set the dish on the table, and Mike slid it my way. "Squid guts," he said. Salty, funky . . . downright stinky . . . unpleasant is putting it mildly. "When it's good, *shiokara* is very good," Mike assured me. Those words became a mantra for me in my life in Japan: The good is very good, the bad is very bad, and the mediocre is pretty common.

I was recently at a confab attended by long-term foreigners in Japan, Japanese trendsetters, and some members of METI (Ministry of Economy, Trade, and Industry). The theme of the meeting was to brainstorm about ways to introduce or promote Japan to countries overseas and to foreigners visiting Japan. One participant mentioned he had been thinking to bring a jar or two of *shiokara* as a way of introducing an unusual Japanese taste but then had reconsidered because it might not appeal to foreigners. The thought that immediately jumped into my head was: Who would want to eat *shiokara* from a jar? They don't even sell it at our fish market. When I asked one of the fishmongers, he was perplexed and pointed me to the semifresh plastic packs stacked in the fridge case. I sidled up to the case with my camera and snapped some shots of the label (squid, guts, sugar, salt, vinegar, honey, MSG, sorbitol, polysaccharide thickener, ethanol alcohol, annatto, paprika). Hmm.

Dodging the mob of people laying in provisions for New Year, I returned to the "real" fish area and selected three of the last squid of the year. My fishmonger scolded me for buying it at the expensive time. "You should have gotten it last week!" Hey, I did . . . but it was so good, I wanted to make *shiokara* again. Thrifty has never been my strong suit. I want it, I buy it. And anyway the increase in price was only ¥100 apiece (adding $3.44 to the total). I could handle that.

Here is the tricky thing about squid: Until you pull the gastric sacs out of the squid, you cannot tell what they will contain. If you are lucky, each sac will be plump, and the contents will be a dusky coral color; unlucky, and you could have flaccid sacs with brownish or even acrid black juices. The solution here is to buy extra just in case and air-dry the squid bodies (page 30) you don't use for *shiokara*. At least that is my solution. The other issue is that in Japan we use *surume ika* (Japanese common squid, Pacific flying squid) for *shiokara*. The only squid I had handled in the States recently was at Chez Panisse and I remembered that the guts oozed out a greyish color as we cleaned the squid. Pretty plump sacs of coral were nowhere to be found.

I asked my pal Sylvan Mishima Brackett, from Peko Peko Japanese Catering, to give me the lowdown on squid in the San Francisco Bay Area. Here is what he found: "I just talked to Tom Worthington at Monterey Fish, and he told me that most of the squid from Monterey Bay is caught in a seine, vacuumed up, and otherwise abused, causing the ink sac to rupture. He does occasionally get dip net squid, which would be in much better shape. However, I have also gotten a couple of really beautiful and LARGE squid from Humboldt from another fish vendor." Good to know.

There is no taste sensation that can quite match home-cured *ika no shiokara*, and I hope you can experience this gorgeously enticing dish yourself. It's dead easy to prepare, but perhaps just out of grasp without the Japanese fisherman who takes care to fish the squid gently and lays the bodies lovingly in Styrofoam boxes packed in ice, which are whisked to the nearest fish market—a different culture for a different way of eating. In Japan, raw fish starts with the fisherman, and without him, we would not be able to continue these food traditions that date back hundreds of years. Recently someone asked me if I take care to buy fish only from the Sea of Japan in order to avoid risk of radiation contamination from the Pacific side. I don't because I trust my fishmongers, and that is one compelling reason to buy from an honest professional with whom you have a relationship. For that kind of person does not have it in him to dupe his customers because he takes pride in his métier. He is a *shokunin*—a craftsman (page XXIV).

Rather than handing someone a pro forma jar of preservative- and MSG-laden *ika no shiokara,* I'd rather show them how to make the real thing. That is, if you can find dip net–caught squid.

Miura-san (my photographer) hails from Hokkaido, and as we work, often recounts his childhood spent foraging for food. As a Tokyo apartment dweller, he does not have close access to ultrafresh fish, so must rely on the supermarket. A haze of euphoria seems to settle on Miura-san when let loose to wander our local fish market. During one photo shoot, Miura-san taught me how to make *shiokara*, Hokkaido-style. We stopped by the fish market to grab provisions for our family's Christmas preparations and also picked up some squid to make *shiokara*. In the weeks following, remembering how good it was, I developed an insatiable craving for it. Running water makes the squid-cleaning process easier, but if you live in a water-poor state or country, making do with a basin of cold water may be more prudent.

raw squid in coral SERVES 6
IKA NO SHIOKARA

3 ultrafresh squid, with gastric sacs intact

1 teaspoon brown rice miso (page 72)

¼ teaspoon flaky sea salt

1 teaspoon soy sauce

½ teaspoon sake or shochu (page XXXii)

½ teaspoon finely slivered yuzu or Meyer lemon zest

1 small finely sliced dried red chile (japones or árbol)

Position a cutting board immediately to the left of the kitchen sink. Set the bag of squid directly behind the board and a wire-mesh strainer in the sink itself. Any squid refuse gets returned to the bag and later composted. Remove the squid from the bag and lay them on the board. Detach the tail portion of each squid by pulling it away from the main body. Drop the squid tails in the sink as you go. Gently dislodge the inner gastric sacs from the bodies by running your finger around the perimeter of the inside body walls. Grasp the tentacles around the eye area and pull the sac out in one piece. Place the sacs and tentacles on the board and add the bodies to the pile of tails in the sink. Move the board with the sacs and tentacles to a free counter space and bring out another board for your work space.

Score a vertical line down the outside skin of the squid with a sharp knife (don't cut the meat, just the skin). Ideally this line will be directly outside of where the plastic-like stick, called the *gladius*, is attached. Remove the skin by nudging it off laterally from the center in a rolling motion: Running water helps here. (The ease or difficulty of this step varies with the squid.) Pull the skin off of both sides of the tail, a welcomely easy operation. Rinse the tails and set to drain in the wire-mesh strainer. Lay the squid bodies on the clean board and slice them open vertically at the place where you scored the skin. Scrape off any remaining slimy tendrils inside, toss those into the squid refuse bag, and drop the cleaned squid bodies into the strainer with the tails.

raw squid in coral

Move over to the board with the tentacles and sacs. Cut off the tentacles below the eyes. Rinse them in the sink under running water and remove any hard portions of the suckers by running your fingernail down each leg. Drop the tentacles into the strainer with the bodies and tails. Dry the tails, bodies, and tentacles in a clean dish towel. Evaluate the amount of squid "guts" in the digestive gland sacs and make a decision about how much squid to keep for *shiokara* and how much to dry. I usually go with about 3 small sacs per 2 squid. Dry the extra squid body and tentacles that you will not cut and toss the extra tails into the refuse bag.

Cut the squid bodies in half vertically. Slice crosswise into julienne strips after excising the 2 hard lumps near the top. Slice the tail portion vertically into strips. Cut the legs off of the portion that joins them and cut into 3-inch/7.5-cm segments. Chop the remaining top portion by cutting through crosswise to free up each little leg nub. Slide the squid pieces into a medium-sized bowl.

Set a fine-mesh strainer or drum sieve (*uragoshi*) over the bowl with the squid and squeeze the creamy coral (gastric "juices") out of the sacs into the strainer. Press the coral through the sieve with the back of a small rubber scraper. Make sure you harvest the portion that remains stuck to the bottom of the sieve as well. Mash in the miso and mix until well incorporated before flavoring with the salt, soy sauce, sake or shochu, yuzu or Meyer lemon peel, and red chile. Toss with your fingers and taste for salt. Add a speck more, if needed. It should be flavorful and mild, not overly salty. Spoon into a jar and let "ferment" for 24 hours. Eat within 2 days.

VARIATIONS: Instead of the coral, toss the squid strips and legs in about 2 tablespoons shio koji and nothing else. Sakamoto-san (page 126) mixes squid strips with mashed-up avocado, seasoned with salt and a little yuzu or Meyer lemon juice. Unforgettable. (I used 1 small avocado, a few teaspoons of citrus juice, a sprinkling of salt, a small amount of chopped chives, and half of a fresh green chile, finely chopped.) N.B.: 3 small squid yields about a scant ½ pound/200 g of squid meat.

When our sons were small, we periodically made the 20-minute drive to a Korean barbecue (*yakiniku*) restaurant run by a Korean family. We always ordered the same thing: *shio karubi* (thinly sliced marbled meat with salt), *namul* (greens with an oil dressing), and an assortment of kimchee. As a rice lover, Tadaaki would also share a bowl or two of *bibimbap* with the boys. While Tadaaki dug into his towering bowl of rice, vegetables, meat, and raw egg, I reached for the kimchee, especially this cucumber one. Depending on the cook (especially mothers with small children), these can be more sweet than hot. For me, sugar masks the characteristic sourness, so doesn't make sense. Also, the *sakura ebi* here is strictly a Japanese addition. In Korea they might or might not use salted shrimp.

cucumbers with carrot threads MAKES 1½ POUNDS (675 G)

AOI KIMUCHI

1 pound (500 g) Japanese cucumbers (4 large or 7 medium)

2 tablespoons coarse sea salt

3 tablespoons Korean red chile powder (*gochutgaru*, page XXXI)

1 tablespoon anchovy fish sauce

2 tablespoons finely chopped dried shrimp (*sakura ebi*, page XXIX)

2 scallions, sliced into fine rounds

1 tablespoon finely chopped ginger

1 tablespoon finely chopped garlic

1 medium carrot (about ¼ pound/115 g), thinly julienned

6 garlic chives (*nira*, page 343), cut into 1-inch (2.5-cm) lengths

Slice the ends off the cucumbers and cut into thirds (approximately 2½-inch/6.5-cm pieces). Stand a piece of cucumber on the cutting board and make 2 cross-shaped, vertical cuts down about a quarter of the way from the bottom edge of the cucumber. Cut the other cucumber pieces in this fashion. Rub all of the cucumber surfaces with salt, taking care to reach the inside surfaces. Drop the salted cucumbers in a bowl as you go and let macerate for 30 minutes.

Mix 2 tablespoons boiling water into the red chile powder to form a paste. Let sit for 15 minutes before stirring in the fish sauce, dried shrimp, scallions, ginger, garlic, carrot, and garlic chives. Toss with your fingers to distribute (rubber gloves are optional).

Drain the cucumbers and rinse well with cold water. Blot all surfaces (including the inside cuts) dry with a clean kitchen towel. Rub the chile paste into the flower-like opening of the cucumbers and around the outside as well. Pack in a pot with a loose-fitting lid and leave for 24 hours at room temperature. Chill before serving, but eat within 1 week. Cucumbers weep, so this kimchee is best fairly soon after it is made. Good with grilled meats such as Soy Sauce–Soused Steak (page 111) or Shio Koji–Grilled Pork (page 201).

VARIATION: My Korean friend Soyoung Scanlan recommends substituting mushroom powder and/or konbu to replace the fish sauce and dried shrimp for a vegan/vegetarian version. In this case, you may want to omit the garlic and scallions but be liberal with the ginger.

One of my first girlfriends in Japan was Aino Ogawa, a Korean Japanese. Aino practiced the ancient art of ikebana (flower arranging) and the avant-garde Japanese dance, butoh. She was a study of duality. A soft-spoken, elegant young lady with a character of steel. Aino, although born in Japan, did not have Japanese citizenship. It took me many years to wrap my head around why she and her family retained their Korean citizenship. I first attributed the phenomena to what I naively perceived was the Japanese government's desire to maintain a homogeneous native Japanese population. Not so. Aino and her brethren choose to remain citizens of the culture to which they most identify: Korea. Becoming a Japanese citizen would mean giving up the Korean one (or, in my case, my American citizenship), and we are not prepared to forsake our national identity. Because of the very large population of Koreans in Japan, kimchee has become a mainstream food—especially this napa cabbage kimchee.

napa cabbage with shredded daikon MAKES ABOUT 3 POUNDS (1.3 KG)
HAKUSAI KIMUCHI

2 small heads napa cabbage, about 1⅓ pounds (600 g) each

1 cup (250 grams) sea salt

3 tablespoons Korean red chile powder (*gochutgaru*, page XXXI)

2 tablespoons anchovy fish sauce

1 tablespoon mashed garlic

1 tablespoon grated ginger

1 tablespoon finely chopped dried shrimp (*sakura ebi*, page XXIX)

¼ pound (115 g) scrubbed daikon, coarsely shredded on a box grater

2 scallions, cut diagonally into thin rounds

6 garlic chives (*nira*, page 343), cut into 1-inch (2.5-cm) lengths

Rinse any sandy bottoms, remove outside wilted leaves (but reserve), and halve the cabbages: Hold the cabbage upside down, make a 3-inch (7.5-cm) vertical cut through the bottom of the root end, and pull the 2 halves apart. Cut the halves in the same manner to quarter. Fill a large basin or bucket with 2 quarts (2 liters) cold water and swish the salt around in the water with your hand to dissolve. Immerse the cabbage quarters and reserved outer leaves in the salty water and place a flat circular weight on top to keep them submerged. Leave in the salty water for 6 hours, but rotate the cabbage pieces from bottom to top after 3 hours. (The leaves should be limp but retain some snap.) Remove the cabbage quarters and outside leaves from the basin or bucket, rinse to desalinate, and drain for 45 minutes.

In a medium-sized bowl, mix 2 tablespoons boiling water into the red chile powder to form a loose paste and let macerate for 15 minutes. Add the fish sauce and mash the garlic, ginger, and chopped *sakura ebi* into the red chile paste. Drop in the daikon, scallions, and garlic chives and toss with your fingers (gloves might be advised).

Squeeze each cabbage quarter and the outside leaves in a clean kitchen towel to blot dry. Working from the outside in, smear the red chile and vegetable paste around the cabbage, making sure to get in between each leaf and to push the paste into the base of the cabbage as well. Fold the outermost 2 leaves over the front of the cabbage to enclose the filling (one leaf should wrap around from the left side, the other from the right, as if they were two demurely folded hands). Pack, cut side up, in a ceramic, glass, or plastic pickling container. Continue until all the cabbage quarters have been rubbed with the paste and packed in the pickling tub. Lay the reserved leaves across the surface of the cabbage and pat the cabbages down with your hand to ensure that the pieces are well snuggled into the pot.

Let sit in a dark corner at room temperature (70°F/20°C is ideal) for 24 hours. Pull off a corner of a leaf to monitor the fermentation action and stick your nose down into the pot to get a good whiff to help determine where the kimchee is in its conversion process. In cooler weather, you may need several days to a week. Once the cabbage tastes pleasantly sour, it is ready to eat but will improve by refrigerating for a few days. Store in the refrigerator for several months, though it would be advised to double (or triple) bag since the smell can be overwhelming. Eat with eggs, on sandwiches, in soup or ramen, or just munch, as is, with a cold beer or Homemade Ginger Ale (page 321).

VARIATIONS: For a quick version: Chop the napa cabbages into 2-inch (5-cm) squares and massage the salt into the cabbage until it weeps a little. Weight and leave for 6 hours at room temperature. After 6 hours, rinse and drain for 45 minutes. Squeeze, blot dry, and mix in the red pepper slurry and all of the other aromatics and quick ferment as described in the main method. Darker greens such as bok choy can be successfully substituted for the napa cabbage.

This was the first kimchee I attempted. Pulling off three vintage Korean cookbooks from my cookbook shelf, I set about studying the hows and whys of kimchee. No one method spoke to me, so I developed a composite from what I had read and was extremely pleased with the results. And I was eager to use the celadon Korean pickling pot acquired years previously. The pot has a water reservoir around the top into which the lid is set, thus creating an airtight seal. You can find these ingenious pots on Heidi Swanson's exquisitely eclectic site: Quitokeeto (see resources). I served these to the guests after rice planting one year and was amazed at how well they had stood up in the fridge, as they were still perky after a month or two.

cubed daikon and
garlic chives SERVES 6
KKAKDUGI

1 medium-large daikon (about 2½ pounds/1.2 kg)

2 tablespoons coarse sea salt

2 tablespoons Korean red chile powder (*gochutgaru*, page XXXI)

2 tablespoons anchovy fish sauce

2 tablespoons finely chopped ginger

2 tablespoons finely chopped garlic

2 tablespoons finely chopped dried shrimp (*sakura ebi*, page XXIX)

4 garlic chives (*nira*, page 343), cut into 1-inch (2.5-cm) lengths

Scrub the daikon and trim off the leaves, leaving 3 inches (4 cm). Cut the top off the daikon and dispose of it in the compost bin. Slice the daikon into 3-inch (4-cm) cubes, and throw the cubes into a large mixing bowl. Slice the leaves into 1¾-inch (2-cm) pieces and slide them into the bowl with the daikon cubes. Massage the salt into the daikon and daikon leaves and leave to macerate for 2 hours.

Mix 1 tablespoon boiling water into the red chile powder to form a paste. Let sit for 15 minutes. Toss in the fish sauce, ginger, garlic, dried shrimp, and garlic chives. Crumble the ingredients between your fingers to incorporate all them into the paste (wear a rubber glove, if you like).

Drain the daikon and daikon leaves. Rinse with cold water and pat dry between two clean kitchen towels. Dump in the chile paste and toss well to distribute evenly. Pack in a pot and leave for 2 to 4 days (depending on the weather) at room temperature. Check each day to monitor the souring. The daikon cubes should be pleasantly sour and taste ever so slightly of fish, and the souse should have penetrated to the center of the cubes. Store well sealed in the fridge for several weeks or more. Good with beer or drinks before dinner or served with a rich meat dish such as Ginger-Soy Pork Sandwiches (page 109).

酒

焼

酎

10

sake, shochu, and tea

御

茶

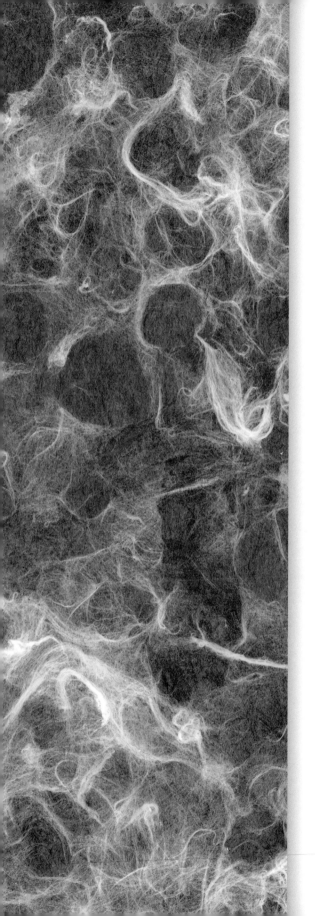

SAKE RECIPES

HOMEMADE SAKE	311
AMAZAKE	313
KUMQUATS SIMMERED IN SAKE	315
SAKE GRANITA	316

SHOCHU RECIPES

QUINCE-INFUSED CORDIAL	317
SOUR PLUM CORDIAL COCKTAIL	318
AKASHA COCKTAIL	320
HOMEMADE GINGER ALE	321

TEA RECIPES

BREWED GREEN TEA	325
JAPANESE "RED" TEA	326
COLD-INFUSED TEA	328
POWDERED GREEN TEA	331
COLD BARLEY TEA	332
BUCKWHEAT TEA	333

Thirty years ago we were all drinking hot sake with our sushi. (The heat masks the deficiencies in the sake.) One night Toshio Sakamoto of Sushi-ya in Palo Alto pulled down a bottle from the top shelf behind his sushi counter and poured me a cup. Like a good tequila, the flavor gap was broad. Toshi-san relinquished a few more cups of that eye-opening sake, but in subsequent visits the bottle had disappeared. Back to the hot flask. Toshi-san introduced me to an English school near Kumagaya, Japan, and that is where I first worked. Every day I walked down to the one-block-long shopping street and bought food for my nightly meal. Although the tofu shop family eventually became my closest friends, several other shopkeepers took me under their wing. I suppose the surfing shorts, flip-flop–wearing *gaigin* (foreigner) girl was an anomaly in their world. When I picked up a carton of Gekkeikan sake and pointed it toward the sake shopkeeper, he assured me it was fine. A fair assessment perhaps, though "adequate" might have been closer. It helped wash down my nightly dinner, but lacked subtlety. When Tadaaki came over with some other friends for a party at my apartment, he did not equivocate when I brought out the carton of Gekkeikan: "That sake is not good." Today we still buy cartons of sake for cooking . . . though not Gekkeikan.

Slow Food Japan put on a three-day event in Yokohama several years ago. One night they staged an outside drinking party where *kusaya* and shochu were served. *Kusaya*, a type of fermented fish, is famous for its pungent stinkiness. The funkiness of the nose is attributed to a several-week soak in a fish sauce–like brine that is reused with each subsequent batch, and the accompanying lacto-aciditic fermentation the fish undergoes. Before that night, I had never cared for shochu, and when offered a drink, usually chose sake. But that night we washed down the smoky, slow-grilled *kusaya* with shochu. Good shochu is a distilled spirit that can be harsh when young but mellows over time. We passed bottles down the table, sampling a splash of each. Some were silky smooth, evocative of sake, while others made my eyes water. The common thread among the bottles was that they all had character and held up well to malodorous fish. The shochu smoothed the insistent fermentation funk and rendered the *kusaya* a compelling bite. The conviviality of that party was palpable, and I am still friends with the two women I met there that night.

Upon arrival in Japan, determined to completely immerse myself in the culture, I echewed my daily cup of coffee and only ate with chopsticks. I enthusiastically drank green tea all afternoon at the English school where I worked to accompany my daily "lunch" of rice crackers or sweets left in the break room. But after the jet lag had worn off, an unexplained sleeplessness crept up on me. Erroneously thinking the green tea to be herbal, I began to suspect that it in fact contained caffeine. My queries were met with puzzlement. "Caffeine?" My Japanese coworkers and adult students had no concept of caffeine. Finally one of the students happened to be a chemist. The answer: Yes. Green tea has plenty of caffeine. But green tea also contains plenty of antioxidants, so, regardless of the caffeine, it is good for you.

SAKE: In Japan, the term "sake" refers to all alcoholic beverages, so what Westerners call sake is technically *nihon shu* (日本酒). Nonetheless, *nihon shu* is often referred to as "sake," or proceeded by the honorific *o* prefix in formal or polite conversations, as "*osake*." Sake is decidedly not rice wine (the legal definition of wine is alcohol fermented from grapes or the juice of other fruits and plants, not from grain). Sake is made from rice that is polished down in varying degrees. If you pick up a kernel of rice and look at it very closely, you can see a minute white core in the center of the kernel. This is the germ, and it is a concentration of starch where the vitamins and minerals are stored. Polishing off a portion of the starchy coating of the rice allows the koji (page XXVIII) to penetrate the kernel more quickly in order to begin converting the germ into sugars. First, the sake rice is soaked in water overnight, then it is steamed in a gigantic pressure steamer. The rice is cooled slightly and sprinkled with koji spores, which are kneaded in by hand. The koji-inoculated rice is raced to the *koji muro*, an enclosed, temperature-controlled, humid room where the koji spores are propagated over the course of two or three days at about 95°F (35°C). Well water or spring water is added to the koji rice, and it spends two more weeks in a small tank fermenting further (many breweries add yeast at this time). As the koji spores become active, the mash develops into a frothy, creamy slush, which is called the *shubo* (alcohol mother). This *shubo* will act like a starter in the sake-making process (similar to a levain sponge for bread making). The *shubo* is moved to a 793-gallon (3000-liter) stainless steel tank, where rice and water are added in three stages: a process called *san dan shikomi*. The mash ferments over the course of 14 days before being pumped into oversized canvas bags, which are placed on vertical plates in a hydraulic press. The pressed sake is heated to 140°F (60°C) to kill the yeasts and halt fermentation, then pumped back into the monstrous tanks to age for a few months or more. The sake lees are removed from the machine in huge sheets, cut into manageable portions, and folded into packages to be sold for pickling or cooking. Of course, in this age of mechanization, in large-scale sake breweries, these artisanal brewing practices go by the wayside and natural fermentation is accelerated by added yeasts and lactic acid.

Sake is produced in the cooler months starting from late autumn, after the rice harvest, and ending in late winter or early spring, depending on the region (large-scale breweries produce all year long in artificially controlled environments). Sake is produced in every prefecture in the archipelago, with the exception of Kagoshima. Nada, a district of Kobe in Hyogo prefecture, is one of the largest producers of sake, probably because of its excellent water and closeness to the port. Before visiting the barrel maker (who is conveniently located in Nada), we walked through the streets where the main sake breweries are located. Most of the buildings are traditional structures built decades ago yet were still well maintained. One of the breweries where we stopped informed us that of the 67 breweries that existed 40 years ago, only 29 are still operating. Across the street from the barrel

maker is a fascinating sake museum packed with traditional wooden sake-making equipment (including giant wooden barrels) that is worth a visit if you find yourself in Nada. Nada is also famous for *narazuke* pickles (page 213), thanks to the proximity of the breweries that provide a constant supply of sake lees. Niigata is arguably the most famous (and popular) sake-producing region, known for its exceptional rice and cold mountain streams. After all, sake is only as good as the rice and the water (and koji). Akita, also a snowy, mountainous prefecture on the sea of Japan, produces outstanding sake as well. Fukushima is another important sake-producing prefecture, known for its great rice and clean water, though the industry has been hit hard after the Fukushima Daichi Nuclear Reactor meltdown. Overall, sake consumption is way down, and thanks to a clever marketing strategy, a few years ago shochu consumption surpassed sake. It is safe to say that small-production sake breweries are in crisis.

Sake is typically sold in either 720-ml bottles (about the same size as a wine bottle) or 1.8-liter bottles, which are ungainly but more cost-effective. The 1.8-liter bottles (*isshobin*) are often decanted into small ceramic or glass flasks (*tokkuri*) but not always. The most common vessel used to drink sake is a small round ceramic or glass cup (*choko, guinomi*). Some traditional restaurants will present a selection of *choko* to allow the customer to choose which *choko* speaks to him or her. Less formal drinking spots may offer sake in a wooden box (*masu*) made of hinoki cypress or cedar (sometimes lacquered). Wooden *masu* of various sizes were once standard volume measures, but have all but disappeared, except for the miniature one used to drink sake. One rice measure equals 180 ml (called a *sho*: 升), and rice in traditional Japanese foods is still measured in *sho*, not cups. The *masu*

box is set on a plate and filled until it overflows—a custom to show generosity from the shopkeeper (though using the *masu* box is usually a sign that the sake being served is not of good quality). Wooden boxes tend to impart their intrinsic flavor onto the sake, so should not be used with more delicate, nuanced sake varieties. In our house, I often use short, straight-sided antique soba dipping cups because they are small enough to not be grossly oversized yet big enough to not require constant refills. Recently stemware has become popular for drinking sake, and Reidl has developed a special glass just for that purpose. We normally serve room-temperature (*jo-on*) or cold sake (*reishu*) at our house, though Tadaaki is partial to warm sake (*atsukan*) in the winter. He sets a flask inside a teapot of hot water and warms it gently over low heat. Each sake has its "best serving temperature," and certain good-quality sakes benefit from a slight warming to bring out their aromas and unpack their flavor notes. Cheap sake is served hot to mask its inferior flavor. Store sake in a cool, dark place. Once opened, sake should be consumed within a couple days to take advantage of its subtleties; however, it will not go bad if stored in the fridge for a month or so.

While there are certainly several other categories of sake that refer to aging conditions, concentrations of alcohol, or special factors, the following are the most common sake types you will encounter:

JUNMAI DAIGINJO (純米大吟醸): An elegant, usually higher-priced sake brewed from rice that has had 50% of the outside bran and starch polished off and to which no alcohol has been added.

DAIGINJO (大吟醸): Similar to *junmai daiginjo* in flavor profile and price point, also brewed from rice that has had 50% of the outside bran and starch polished off. However, alcohol has been added during the brewing process.

JUNMAI GINJO (純米吟醸): A full-bodied, flavorful sake brewed from rice that has had 40% of the outside bran and starch polished off and to which no alcohol has been added. Prices can range from reasonable to high.

GINJO (吟醸): Similar to *junmai ginjo* but with alcohol added while brewing. Brewed from rice that has had 40% of the outside bran and starch polished off.

JUNMAI (純米): A forward sake brewed from rice that has had 30% of the outside bran and starch polished off. No alcohol has been added. Usually reasonably priced.

HONJOZO (本醸造): Similar to *junmai* in that it is brewed from rice that has had 30% of the outside bran and starch polished off, with alcohol added in the brewing process. Similarly priced to *junmai*.

SHIBORITATE NAMA GENSHU (絞り立て生原酒): Freshly pressed (絞り立て), unpasteurized (生) sake to which water has not been added to lower the alcohol content. While most sake is typically 14 to 16% alcohol, *genshu* (原酒) is left at its original 18 to 20%. Highly perishable, nonetheless I have seen this coveted sake abroad and it can be reasonably priced.

NIGORIZAKE (濁り酒): A naturally sweet "sake" that is strained but not pressed, so it is cloudy. You must shake it before using, since the milky particles settle to the bottom of the bottle. (*Nigorizake* is not officially sake, since only clear liquids are designated as "sake" by law.)

DOBUROKU (どぶろく): Homemade "sake" (illegal to brew in Japan).

At about $30 a bottle for a decent bottle of *junmai ginjo* or *ginjo* and close to $50 (on up) for either of the *daiginjo*, purchasing sake is a financial commitment. Buy from a reputable shop such as True Sake in San Francisco, Sakaya and Astor Wines in New York City, or Workshop Issé and Sakebar in Paris. It is also recommended to learn something about the distributor who is selling the sake (check the back label): I can highly recommend Wine of Japan in New Jersey or perhaps World Sake Imports globally (see Resources). The biggest issue with sake is that it does not travel well, so many of the sakes I have tasted in the States have a certain funk factor that should not be there. There is a saying in Japan: "Sake should taste close to water." Sake that has been subjected to extreme temperature fluctuations will not fare well, so be cautious about its provenance. As for domestic U.S. sake, so far I have not liked any: Some are fair and one was downright spit-outable. However, there is a promising Canadian sake maker with a Japanese brewer off Vancouver on Granville Island auspiciously named Artisan SakeMaker. There are so many sakes out there, it is bewildering. Finally I settled on three sakes that fit different profiles: Imayotsukasa (Niigata) for its elegance, Takizawa Shuzo (Saitama) for its clarity and price, and Terada Honke (Chiba) for its wildness. I suggest you find *your* three and stop there.

SHOCHU (焼酎): Shochu is said to have originated in what is now Kagoshima prefecture on the southern island of Kyushu (the only prefecture that does not produce sake). The Japanese characters for shochu (焼酎) are translated as "burned liquor," (shochu is heat distilled, as opposed to sake, which is cold brewed). Although rough shochu has been produced in Japan since the mid 1500s, shochu as we know it today has come into being thanks to innovations in equipment and technique. Grade A shochu (*korui*, 甲類) is made using a continuous distillation method that began in the beginning of the Meiji era (1868–1912) after importing the machinery from the UK. This is sipping shochu. The majority of grade B shochu (*otsurui*, 乙類) is distilled from sweet potatoes multiple times rather than continuously. *Otsurui shochu* is what is used in canned cocktails and the white liquor (page XXXII) sold for making fruit cordials such as *Karinshu* (page 317). *Otsurui shochu* is much cheaper than *korui shochu*, but it has a slightly sickly smell that obviates drinking. Nonetheless, many people in Japan are happy to settle for the lower-grade shochu and often mix it into tea, juice, or low-alcohol beer.

Korui shochu (grade A) is made from inoculating cooked sweet potatoes, rice, wheat, buckwheat, Okinawan brown sugar (*kurozato*, page XXXIII), or even chestnuts with koji (page XXVIII) before adding water and yeast. This primary mash is fermented for five days, at which time more water is added, and the secondary mash ferments for an additional eight to ten days. The mash is distilled in a continuous cycle, filtered, then bottled or aged. *Otsurui shochu* (grade B) is made by distilling a molasses-like mash made from sweet potatoes (and sometimes cornstarch) into ethyl alcohol, then further distilling the alcohol multiple times to increase the purity (with inherent flavor loss).

I was never a big fan of shochu (mostly because I had never had a good one) until I attended a *kusaya* (fermented fish) and shochu party put on by Slow Food Japan one evening in Yokohama. The shochu that turned me into a convert, though, was the rice shochu (*komejochu*) I sampled in Kumamoto when doing a story on the revitalization of the Kumamoto oyster for All Nippon Airway's in-flight magazine, *Wingspan*. Miura-san and I discovered a local sushi bar where after a few beers we moved on to one of the excellent *komejochu* bottles displayed on the shelf. *Komejochu* is mild and reminiscent of sake (so a good starter shochu for the uninitiated). My next taste of excellent shochu came from a bottle of chestnut shochu that Darrel Corti of Corti Brothers gave me at a dinner in Sacramento. Darrel had received this rare shochu as a present and generously gave me the bottle to take back to Japan. The night my son Christopher came home from college, he immediately pounced on the bottle and we shared a glass each. It was hot on the tongue but mellow going down, truly special. But the shochu I fell in love with was the 10-year aged wheat shochu (*mugijochu*) that I had at Sakamoto (page 126) on the Noto Peninsula. I bought a gigantic 1.8-liter bottle and schlepped it home, only to kick it over accidentally on the kitchen tile floor (where it gushed out in a river). While I have never tasted it, a knowledgeable friend also recommends the fiery *awamori* (泡盛) distilled liquor native to Okinawa, made from long-grain *Indica* rice. Easily purchased on the Internet in Japan, *awamori* is probably difficult to come by abroad.

Once considered an older man's drink, shochu is now totally mainstream in Japan and favored by young women due to its supposed health benefits and tastelessness. The boom began in 2003 with creative marketing campaigns, which targeted young women. Cocktail bars have been the rage in Japan for several decades. Shochu splashed into the cocktail scene and was touted as a less caloric liquor for cocktails. The boom has quieted, though consumption is still steady and remains the same as (or more than) sake. Shochu is drunk straight, on the rocks, with cold water and ice, with warm water, or mixed into a cocktail. Shochu is available at Astor Wines or Sakaya in New York City, Nijiya Market in San Francisco, and Workshop Issé or Sakebar in Paris.

TEA: Tea is grown as far north as Niigata prefecture and as far south as Kagoshima prefecture, but the main growing regions are Shizuoka, Kagoshima, and Mie prefectures. The tea plants (called tea trees in Japanese) take four to seven years to mature from seedlings and are harvested three times a year, starting in the spring and ending in the fall. Although Japanese tea is typically grown in subtropical climates, some varieties are resistant to cold and some thrive in marine climates. As in harvesting grapes for wine, timing the tea harvest is essential because once the tender, bright green leaves develop, their caffeine, catechins, and amino acids increase, yet at one certain point will level off. As the leaves become more fibrous, the caffeine, catechins, and amino acids decrease, so quality is affected. (N.B.: Elevated cesium levels were detected in tea from Kanagawa, Chiba, Tochigi, Ibaragi and Shizuoka prefectures in the early summer following the Fukushima Daichi Nuclear Power Plant meltdown. In this same period, a large shipment of Shizuoka tea was refused by the French governement and destroyed. The current stance of the Japanese government is that there is no issue with cesium in Shizuoka tea.)

Tea is purported to have entered Japan in the early 800s from China and was used primarily as a restorative. The tea ceremony became a form of social play for aristocrats as well as a spiritual practice during the Heian period (795–1185), and tea remained a drink of the aristocracy for the following 500 years. Tremendous changes were effected to the overall infrastructure of Japan during the Edo period (1603 –1868), and this created watershed improvements in methods to preserve or process raw materials. The Edo period was also a time of great progress in arts and crafts. And it was in the Edo period that green leaf tea, in the form of *sencha* (page 306), became widely consumed.

The current method of processing green tea began in the Meiji era (which followed Edo). The tea leaves are steamed immediately after harvest before being placed in a hopper where they are kneaded and buffeted with warm air currents. According to Iijima-san of Fujimien (page 322), if dried in the open air, the inner leaves will not dry properly. *Kocha* (page 326) can be made from the same leaves as green tea. The leaves are wafted with cool, dry air for 24 hours to remove moisture from the leaves, though too much liquid loss will impede fermentation. After fermenting, the leaves are placed in a hopper, where they are tossed and kneaded in 86 to 95°F (30 to 35℃) air at 99% humidity for 1½ to 2 hours where they undergo oxidation.

As a coffee drinker, I had not given much thought to tea in Japan. I liked it when I drank it but chose coffee instead at home. But in my travels and in my writing I have developed a great curiosity for, and appreciation of, Japanese tea and the culture that surrounds it. When I was hospitalized for the births of each of my sons, a small plastic thermos pot full of *bancha* (番茶) stood on a table in the hall. This was everyday tea and not like the green tea my mother-in-law served. Whenever I walked into a tea shop, I was overwhelmed by the varieties, so as with sake, have eventually settled on three teas: Fujimien *kocha* and *sencha* (page 306), as well as an organic green tea from Kagoshima, simply labeled "Green Tea," produced by the Kozono family. Fujimien tea is available on a limited basis through The Brooklyn Kitchen in Brooklyn. In the San Francisco Bay Area: The Taste of Tea (online and bricks and mortar shop in Healdsburg, California) is an eclectic tea source that gives tea advice through a collective sage called "The Tea Docent"; Breakaway Matcha is one-stop source for all things matcha; and Leaves + Flowers in San Francisco is a mail-order source for loose organic green tea from the Kinezuka family as well as a wide range of other lovely teas. N.B.: The Kinezuka family has its own Web site, which represents 30 organic tea families in Shizuoka, Japan, and ships abroad (see Resources).

While there are many more types of tea in Japan, these are the most well known.

RYOKUCHA (緑茶): The umbrella term for green tea, which literally means "green tea." Known in Japan as *"ocha."*

SHINCHA (新茶): First-harvest green tea (either *gyokuro* or *sencha*).

GYOKURO (玉露): Translated as "Jade dew," *gyokuro* is a very high-grade tea that is grown in shade for 20 days before harvesting. The lack of sun results in a pale-colored, mild tea. Picked only the during the first and second flush harvests.

SENCHA (煎茶): *Sencha* technically means "simmered tea," perhaps referring to the previous habit of simmering rather than infusing green tea. The most common green tea in Japan, these are leaves that are gathered during the first and second harvest periods. When brewed, the tea is usually a deep green.

BANCHA (番茶): Literally "coarse tea," *bancha* is a common tea served all over Japan in restaurants and hospitals. *Bancha* is produced from the third or fourth harvests between summer and fall and has an almost off-brown tinge.

HOJICHA (保持茶): Charcoal-roasted green tea. Toasty and pleasant.

GENMAICHA (玄米茶): *Bancha* or *sencha* blended with roasted brown rice. Earthy.

KUKICHA (茎茶): Literally "twig tea," *kukicha* is made from the stems and twigs of the tea plant. Nutty.

KONACHA (粉茶): The bits and pieces left over from making *sencha* or *gyokuro*. *Konacha* ("powdered" tea) is inexpensive, so used by restaurants and offices.

MATCHA (抹茶): Stone-ground *sencha* or *gyokuro* powder, used in the tea ceremony. Matcha is at once bitter, yet creamy, and it is a taste I happen to adore. The bitterness lends itself to being used in Japanese and Western desserts. The kanji character for *ma* (抹) is the same as the one for ma konbu (page XXX) and means "the ultimate" or "quintessential."

KOCHA (紅茶): Although called "black" tea in English, the Japanese characters for *kocha* more appropriately mean "deep red tea." Iijima-san at Fujimien (page 322) ferments and dries his florally elegant *kocha* from green tea leaves, and his *kocha* has no harsh tannins. In Japan all fermented black teas are commonly referred to as "*kocha*."

MUGICHA (麦茶): Infusion made from roasted barley, usually sold in sachets (page 332). Although rare, organic whole roasted barley is obtainable in Japan (see Resources). Commonly served cold in the summer.

SOBACHA (そば茶): A warm infusion brewed from roasted and cracked buckwheat (page 333) sold loose in 1-kilo bags. Can be purchased at selective Japanese grocery stores or mail-order tea companies (see Resources).

KONBUCHA (昆布茶): Not to be confused with kombucha, a drink fermented from black tea. Konbucha is a delicate, tisane-like infusion made from pouring hot water over thinly sliced konbu (*ito konbu*) or powdered konbu, and seasoning with a drop of soy sauce or a pinch of salt. Also popular with a dab of chopped *umeboshi* (page 167), in this case dubbed *ume konbucha*.

Like so many traditional foods all over Japan, artisanal tea is at risk because the dynamics of society have changed. While tea consumption per capita has probably not declined over these last several years, the amount of people brewing tea at home in a small pot has plummeted. Thirty years ago, the designated office lady (O.L.) made small pots of tea for the workers in companies. Now there is a dispenser of tea brewed from the odds and ends left over from making higher-grade green teas (*konacha*). In rural areas the custom was (and still is for the ever-dwindling farmers, fisherman, and artisans) to take a tea break at 10 a.m. and 3 p.m. Bowls of tangerines, rice crackers (*senbei*), and some other Japanese sweets (*okashi*) were served alongside. The pot started out strong for that caffeine kick, then progressively (and welcomely) became paler and paler, until almost clear. It was the changing quality of each cup that gave one a feeling of anticipation (*tanoshimini*). This concept of *tanoshimini* is integral to many Japanese foods and drinks. The evolution of the thing you are tasting is exciting and something to look forward to. Understandably, making tea in a small pot for a large group is impractical (but wonderful in its impracticality). The pot invariably dribbles all over the table, and you have to pour little by little between the cups to create even-flavored brews. Also the leftover tea leaves are a pain to dispose of since they seem to not want to get out of the pot. The advent of canned and plastic bottled tea has skyrocketed to the point that many young people do not know how to make tea at home. I find that heartbreaking and worry for the fate of tea as the current generation silvers and eventually is no longer with us. Will artisanal tea production die as well?

THE SAKE MAKER

At twilight, Imayotsukasa sake brewery glows from the golden light emanating from the family crests affixed to newly resurfaced white-plastered earth walls. The main entry beckons warmly, though the garden entrance is more enticing, as its lights seep out through small peepholes cut in the thick, white garden wall. My initial visit to Imayotsukasa was as a consultant for a travel restaurant project. The heart of Imayotsukasa is made up of a series of traditional Japanese buildings, the oldest one of which dates back to the Edo period. The old had been preserved with care, and the modern had been integrated into the traditional in a coherent fashion.

On each subsequent visit, Heikichi Yamamoto, the gentle-mannered former owner (now serving as consultant), wore his *happi* coat, a heavy cotton unbelted indigo jacket stenciled with the name of the shop. Imayotsukasa was established in 1767 as a merchant trading company, but Yamamoto-san's great-grandfather began making sake over a hundred years ago. Yamamoto-san was the 9th-generation owner. What draws me to Imayotsukasa sake brewery in particular is Yamamoto-san's peaceful

stewardship and intuitive aesthetic sense. Before even tasting it, I knew the sake would be refined and "kind," like the man himself. (I also have a soft spot for Yamamoto-san because when the mayor balked at sitting next to a foreign woman, Yamamoto-san gallantly plunked himself down by my side.)

We don rubber clogs before entering the brewery itself to keep unwanted microorganisms from entering on our feet. The cavernous first chamber holds a monstrous metal cauldron set into the floor. In a previous incarnation, the cauldron was where they steamed the rice. Now sake is pumped into it for pasteurizing before being pumped into enamel-lined stainless steel aging tanks. As we pass through the ancient wooden doors into the holding-tank room, the temperature drops a welcome several degrees. The sake needs to stay cool, so Yamamoto-san quickly drags the heavy doors shut. We wander through the tanks and clank up the metal ladder to poke our heads in a row of fermenting tanks. "This work must never be done alone since falling in means certain death," he informs us as he demonstrates the stirring action.

On our way out, we stop at Yamamoto-san's
pride and joy: a 317-gallon (1200-liter) wooden
barrel ready to be filled soon with organic sake
mash made from rice grown by one of our Niigata
farmer friends, Hirofumi Miyao. Yamamoto-san's
vision had been to ferment and age the local
organic rice in a locally made barrel from Nara
cedar. Unfortunately this proved logistically
difficult since there are so few barrel makers
in Japan; in Niigata, none remain. Yamamoto-
san had the barrel made for him in Osaka, and
it was featured in a popular movie several
years ago. I remembered tasting that flavorful
barrel-fermented sake the previous winter and
how cleanly it lingered on my tongue. On a
subsequent trip Imayotsukasa's managing director
(CEO), Yosuke Tanaka, passed a few bottles
around as we stood next to a duck blind in the
middle of a duck preserve. That day Miyao-san
brought some of his wife's *takuan* (page 217) and a
condiment made from simmered semidried teeny
sardines (*chirimen jako*, page XXIX) and tiny red
shrimp (*sakura ebi*, page XXIX), which we pinched
up and dropped into our mouths (a welcome
snack on the rough).

Lights from underneath Plexiglas cubes in the
refurbished tasting room cast the space with
a feeling of modern luminosity as we step up
to the tasting bar. Usually accompanied by
a gaggle of others, it will be my first chance
to taste the Imayotsukasa lineup without
distraction. My friends, Sharon Jones from
Chez Panisse and Harry Rosenblum from The
Brooklyn Kitchen, have been my easygoing
companions on the trip, and we have fallen into
a comfortable rhythm. I am looking for sake
to serve at the upcoming *Food & Wine* shoot

scheduled at my house, and Harry has his eye out for possible sake exports to New York.

While sake consumption is falling at an alarming rate in Japan, thankfully it is on the rise abroad. Although wine is my beverage of choice, I certainly enjoy well-crafted sake, especially, but not exclusively, the clear-tasting, elegant ones. Finding and arranging delivery for excellent sake at restaurants that do not normally buy sake has proven challenging when doing food events in the States. So challenging that I temporarily gave up. Recognizing my responsibility vis-à-vis promoting traditionally produced foods, my resolve has strengthened, and I am finding ways to get good sake to food events staged abroad. And, whenever possible, extolling the virtues of sake has become one of my causes in Japan.

One watershed moment was while attending a Franco-Japanese dinner cooked at Imayotsukusa by Haruki Ikegami of Cachette Ikegami. No wine was served with the Japonified French food, and it was not missed. Sake bottles made their way around the tables. Each guest had three glass sake cups set in front of his/her place, and so could choose from one of the three sakes to pair with the dish coming next. Chef Ikegami had created French dishes using ingredients from local organic farms such as Miyao-san's. And each dish was complemented by or, more to the point, improved by the sake. This was a monumental revelation—and since Japanese are madly embracing Western food (especially French and Italian), a smart route to pursue for promoting sake over wine in Japan.

Tadaaki often makes *doburoku* when we have large Japanese-style gatherings. Although best made in the winter, it is still possible to make *doburoku* in the early summer or late fall if you have a cool spot where it can ferment. I was happy to leave the making of *doburoku* up to Tadaaki, since I had my hands full elsewhere, but in this fermentation journey I discovered a great interest in making it myself. One reason is the access to good-quality koji, made locally at Yamaki Jozo (page 106), rather than the supermarket cake style. Another reason is that there is an indescribable sense of empowerment in being able to convert rice into alcohol. You will need a small muslin cloth and a reusable muslin cheesecloth for making *doburoku*.

homemade sake MAKES 3 QUARTS (3 LITERS)
DOBUROKU

2 pounds/900 g uncooked Japanese rice

1⅓ pounds/600 g rice koji (page XXVIII)

Fill a large glass jar with boiling water, dump, and rinse to cool the jar (do not use soap). Measure 4½ cups (1080 cc) mineral water into the jar. (If you use tap water, you should boil it, then let it cool before proceeding.) Dunk a small piece of muslin cloth into the water, squeeze it into a ball, and set it aside in a clean bowl. Mix the rice into the water and drop in the balled-up cloth. Poke the cloth down with your finger and cover the jar loosely. Leave in a cool, dark spot for several days (depending on the weather, about 3 to 5 days). Stir the mixture once a day with a wooden spoon and press on the balled-up cloth at this time as well. This mixture will be the starter for your *doburoku* and is called the *kusare moto*. Smell the mixture every day when you stir it to gauge when it is done: The *kusare moto* should develop a sweet, fermented odor. Strain the rice and reserve the strained-out liquid (*kusare moto*). Hang the *kusare moto* cloth out to dry and store for subsequent batches, but do not wash, as you will remove the good "starter" bacteria.

homemade sake

Wet a reusable muslin cheesecloth or *tenugui* (page XIII) and enclose the strained rice in the cloth. Place in a steamer basket set over a large pot of boiling water. Cover and steam for 30 minutes, or until the rice is about 80% cooked (it should still have a slight bite to the kernels). If you are using cake-style koji (page XXVIII), crumble it to separate all of the rice kernels. When the rice has finished steaming, dump it onto a large wooden board, flat tub (*handai*, page XIX), or metal tray. Be sure to scrape all of the rice kernels off of the cloth. (Quickly fill a medium-sized bowl in the sink with water and dunk the cloth in the water to soak as you proceed.) Cut into the rice with a rice paddle to spread and cool. Once the rice is about body temperature, mix the koji into the rice with your hands and knead it in gently with the edge of your palms. Scoop the rice and koji mixture into a ceramic pot and measure the reserved straining liquid (*kusare moto*). It should be about 3 1/3 cups (800 cc). Stir the liquid into the rice and koji until well incorporated. The mixture should have enough liquid that it sloshes a bit, so you will probably have to add about 3 1/3 cups (800 cc) additional mineral water.

Rinse the soaking muslin cheesecloth to remove all of the rice kernels, wring out, and spread over the pot to cover. Tie a length of twine around the circumference of the pot to secure and stash in a cool, dark corner for about 7 to 10 days (or longer), depending on the weather. The optimal temperature is 50°F (10°C). The mixture will start fermenting after a few days and it will develop some spritz. Stir it once or twice a day and taste at that time. The enzymes in the koji and the wild yeasts of the *kusare moto* work together to convert the rice to sugar and ferment into alcohol. You will notice the mixture reach a pleasantly sweet peak before the sugars decrease day by day. The surface of the *doburoku* will have tiny bubbles from the carbon dioxide being released. As it reaches maturity, the surface will be thick and creamy like oatmeal, and many of the rice kernels will have almost melted. The day the *doburoku* is no longer sweet is also the day it tastes like alcohol and is ready to drink. Serve at room temperature and enjoy the changing flavor each day, or heat over the stove to halt fermentation and store in the fridge for a few weeks. If the mixture sours, then stick it outside and have a go at fermenting it into vinegar (page 148).

Whenever we visit Yamaki Jozo (page 106), invariably someone will scoop into a silver pot of amazake that they have standing by and hand out small cups filled with warm amazake in the winter or cold in the summer. Either way, the cups are welcome pick-me-ups. Amazake is healthy, as it is naturally sweet from the koji breaking down the rice, full of vitamins, and said to aid in digestion. Despite the name, there is no alcohol in this drink, making it well suited for children if homemade or organic. Be warned: According to the president of Yamaki, 99% of commercial amazake contains sugar and sake lees (so is not 100% naturally fermented, alcohol free, or sugar free). Amazake is also delicious as a frozen popsicle. Fill an ice cube tray with amazake and put a Popsicle stick in the center of each cube as soon as it is solid enough to support the stick.

You will need a rice cooker or a bulk yogurt maker for this method.

amazake MAKES 4 CUPS (1000 CC)

5¼ ounces (150 g) rice

7 ounces (200 g) rice koji (page XXVIII)

Rinse and drain the rice once to remove any dust, kneading the wet rice in your fist, and flush several times with cold water until the water runs clear. Drain off the last flush of water and measure scant ¾ cup (175 cc) water into the rice cooker receptacle. Cook the rice. When cooked, dump the rice into a large bowl and cut into it with a rice paddle to lift and cool. If you are using cake-style koji, crumble it until all of the rice kernels are completely separated. Once the rice cools to body temperature, mix the koji into the rice with the rice paddle. Return the rice koji–inoculated rice to the rice cooker receptacle and stir in 3⅓ cups (800 cc) hot tap water. Place the receptacle back in the rice cooker and switch onto the "Warm" setting but leave the top open. Cover with a clean kitchen towel, leave for 2 hours, stir, and let ferment for another 5 hours. Use as a sugar replacement in baking or dilute with equal parts water for drinking (the sweetness and depth of flavor varies with different rice varieties and koji, so you may want to add a little less water). Serve chilled or heated, depending on the season. Whirl in the blender if you prefer a smoother consistency. Stored in the fridge, it will keep for about a week.

VARIATION: Make in a bulk yogurt maker but leave the top shut and let ferment for 2 days at 150°F (65°C).

I had not eaten kumquats since I was a child, so did not pay much attention to the tree outside my parents-in-law's front door. But once I did, I became addicted and often plucked a couple off the tree when I was outside puttering around. I also began using kumquats in mizuna treatments (page 24) because they somehow matched in my mind. Here, I decided to poach the kumquats whole, but also used a hint of sake and shiso to give the kumquats an underlying complexity, which make these an admirable foil for Sake Lees Ice Cream (page 215).

kumquats simmered in sake MAKES ½ POUND (225 G)

KINKAN NO SAKE-NI

½ pound (225 g) kumquats

1 cup (250 cc) sake

½ cup (100 g) organic granulated sugar

10 large shiso leaves

Wipe the kumquats and poke about 6 small holes in each one with a toothpick. Pop the kumquats into a small saucepan and bring to a low boil with the sake over medium-high heat. Adjust the temperature, simmer for 5 minutes, and drain.

Measure the sugar into a small heavy saucepan and add 1 cup (250 cc) water. Bring to a boil over medium heat, stirring to help dissolve the sugar. Once the sugar has dissolved, toss the shiso leaves into the sugar syrup and simmer for 3 minutes. Remove the leaves with a pair of tongs and drop into a wire-mesh strainer set over a small bowl. Press on the leaves to extract any excess sugar syrup and scrape it back into the saucepan with the rest of the syrup. Drop the whole kumquats into the saucepan with the syrup and bring to a simmer over medium low heat. Cook gently for about 25 minutes. Scrape into a plastic container or jar and let cool to room temperature before storing in the fridge. Keeps for a couple of weeks.

When John Taboada did a dinner for my last book at his restaurant Luce in Portland, Oregon, he asked advice on the dessert. Sake lees ice cream and sake granita immediately leaped to mind, even though I had yet to make them myself. That trip I had brought several packs of organic sake lees given to us by our octogenarian fruit-growing friend, Mochizuki-san. At the Saltwater Oyster dinner in Inverness, California, Chef Anthony Starelli had made Sake Lees Ice Cream at my behest, and it had been the perfect balance of sweet and creamy, with a slightly alcoholic finish, so I was confident about recommending it again. The sake granita is delightful on its own as a palate cleanser but also makes a splendid partner for the ice cream.

sake granita MAKES ABOUT 3 CUPS/750 CC
SAKE NO GURANITA

¾ cup (150 g) organic
   granulated sugar

3 cups (750 cc) good-tasting sake

Heat the sugar and sake just to the boiling point in a medium-sized saucepan to evaporate some of the alcohol. Stir to dissolve the sugar. Pour the hot sweetened sake into a plastic container and cool. Cover and place the container in the freezer. Let sit, undisturbed, for 1 hour. Remove from the freezer and gently stir in the crystals that have formed around the perimeter with a fork. Repeat this operation every 30 minutes, breaking up any larger crystals as you go. The finished granita should be flaky.

Serve alone in a small tinted glass bowl or cup or, better yet, alongside Sake Lees Ice Cream with Figs (page 215). Keeps frozen for several weeks.

VARIATION: Any shochu-based fruit cordial such as Quince-Infused Cordial (recipe follows) would make a refreshing granita. Omit the sugar.

For years, I wondered if the fruit we call *karin* was indeed a quince. I did not come across quince too often when visiting the States, and Google then was not a household word. One night, while having dinner at Chez Panisse, I was given a tour of the kitchen. As I passed by the dessert station, I noticed a round, misshapen piece of fruit that looked quite like the *karin* that grew on our trees and that Tadaaki's mother made into quince cordial (*karinshu*). I asked the dessert chef if I could have a couple of the leaves off of the fruit (which was of course quince). She was taken aback: "Only the leaves?" but kindly denuded the quince on display and handed the leaves over to me. Still a Chez Panisse neophyte in those days, I did not realize that I had just destroyed the dessert display for the night (even in the Chez Panisse kitchen, things are displayed deliberately, not randomly deposited). Quince has an intoxicating fragrance and, when cooked or steeped, develops a gorgeous pink hue. But the fruit is a stubborn one: rock hard and prone to decay, so you have to put your elbow in and mind the brown spots when cutting up.

quince-infused
cordial MAKES ABOUT 2 QUARTS (2 LITERS)
KARINSHU

2 pounds (1 kg) quince

1 pound (500 g) organic
granulated sugar

2 quarts (1.8 to 2 liters) white
liquor (or plain vodka)

Wipe, quarter, and core the quince. Pare off any mottled sections or worm holes. Place the quince pieces in a large, clean jar or crock. Add the sugar and liquor and cap securely. Shake to distribute and help dissolve the sugar. (If the lid of your crock is not sealable, stir vigorously instead of shaking.)

Let the fruit and liquor macerate for at least 3 months in a cool, dark place. Shake (or stir) occasionally. Taste after 3 months, and if the liquor is sufficiently infused with quince, it is ready to serve. The flavor of this cordial deepens and mellows with age, and will keep practically indefinitely. Serve cold, over ice, as an aperitif.

VARIATIONS: This classic cordial in Japan is *umeshu*, made by steeping slightly yellow *ume* (sour plums) in white liquor and sugar following the same method here as for *Karinshu*. Quartered persimmons or whole apricots could be substituted for the *ume* or quince.

Sweet things often benefit from a touch of salt to draw out the deepest notes of the sugar. *Umeshu* is the quintessential Japanese summer evening aperitif and needs no embellishment. But when the nights are sultry and your thirst is not easily quenched, adding soda water makes the drink last longer. Salted red shiso leaves are often added to Salted Sour Plums (page 167), so make sense here to give this sour plum cocktail a complex kick.

sour plum cordial cocktail MAKES 1
UME SHU KAKUTE-RU

2 ounces (60 cc) sour plum cordial (*umeshu*, page 317)

5 ounces (150 cc) soda water

½ teaspoon Salted Red Shiso Leaves (page 19)

Fill a tall glass with ice, measure in the *umeshu,* and top with the soda water. Drop in the salted red shiso leaves and stir with a cocktail spoon. Serve immediately on a lazy Sunday afternoon to accompany a few dishes of pickles such as Myoga Pickled with Fish Sauce (page 128), Turnips Pickled with Sour Plum (page 171), or Pickled Young Shallots (page 155). Also goes well with tiny garlic cloves, young scallions, cucumber sticks, or green pepper wedges dipped in brown rice or inaka miso (page 72).

VARIATIONS: Use Salt-Massaged Shiso Buds (page 20) or a squeeze of citrus instead of red shiso.

Meeting Akasha Richmond was kismet. While attending the IACP culinary conference one year in San Francisco, we both spent the day as guests at *Sunset* magazine in Menlo Park, California. Pushing through the throng at the Host City Reception the next night, we spotted each other and stopped for a short chat. Akasha's friends were on the move, so she was swept up in their momentum. But as she was sucked into the fray, she shouted over her shoulder, "Let's do a dinner together at Akasha!" Akasha is the chef/owner of Akasha Restaurant in Culver City, California, and a big proponent of local and seasonal food. Her bartender put together a nectar-like cocktail, which I gratefully stuck in the corner and nursed throughout the entire 3 hours of food explanations and schmoozing. By the time I asked Akasha for the recipe, no one could remember. As an ex-bartender, I winged it here. Cachaça is a Brazillian rum-like distilled spirit also known as "pinga" that is particularly cocktail friendly. And is also readily available because of the Brazillian-Japanese population in our local area. Good on warm summer nights with a dish of kimchee such as Cucumbers with Carrot Threads (page 289) and some Miso-Cured Eggs (page 66).

akasha cocktail MAKES 1

AKASHA NO KAKUTE-RU

2 ounces (60 cc) cachaça

4 ounces (120 cc) freshly
    squeezed orange juice

½ tablespoon ginger syrup (page 321)

A wedge of lime

Fill a tall glass shaker cup three-quarters full with large ice cubes. Measure in the cachaça, orange juice, and ginger syrup. Place the metal top on the shaker cup and give it a smart rap with the flat edge of your palm. Make sure the glass and top nearest your tummy have formed a flush seal (otherwise you risk the top becoming dislodged). Hold the bottom of the shaker in one hand and the top in the other, raise over your shoulder, and shake briskly 5 times. Pour into a tall chilled glass. Squeeze a wedge of lime into the cocktail, drop it in, and serve immediately.

VARIATIONS: Use shochu (page XXX) or light rum instead of cachaça. For a lighter version, build the cocktail in a tall glass of ice, top with soda water, squeeze in the lime, stir, and serve.

Although not a fan of soft drinks, organic ginger ale can hit the spot after a few hours pulling weeds in the sweltering Japanese summer. Our local Italian restaurant, Fonte di Dio, serves ginger ale as well: a hot version and a mild. Since many of the dishes in this book are well suited for drinks before dinner, it made sense to offer a nonalcoholic choice. As a fan of ginger ale, I stopped by Fonte di Dio to ask Chef Hiroyuki Arai to share his method. He laughed and revealed that it was bottled: Wilkinson for the hot and Canada Dry for the mild. Although several friends had posted recipes on their blogs, David Lebovitz's method for ginger syrup caught my eye because it relied on the natural flavor of the ginger and contained no added spices. I make a big batch of ginger syrup once the local ginger harvest starts showing up at the farm stand down the street. David says the syrup keeps for a couple of weeks in the fridge, but in my experience, it's fine for several months or more.

homemade ginger ale MAKES 3 CUPS (750 CC) SYRUP
TEZUKURI JINJAEIRU

½ pound (225 g) ginger

2 cups (400 g) organic sugar

A pinch of salt

Soda water

Lime wedges

Scrub the ginger to dislodge any dirt in the crevices between the knob growths, but do not peel. Slice thinly with a sharp knife and chop the slices coarsely. Alternatively, slice with a 2-mm food processor blade before pulsing to chop roughly. Drop the ginger into a medium-sized saucepan with the sugar, salt, and 4 cups (1 liter) cold water. Bring to a boil and simmer slowly for 45 minutes. Cool, strain, and store the syrup in the refrigerator.

To make a glass of ginger ale: Fill a tall glass with ice, measure in 2½ tablespoons syrup, and top with ⅔ cup (150 cc) soda water. Squeeze in a healthy wedge of lime, and stir with a cocktail spoon. Serve immediately to accompany small bites before dinner.

MURAKAMI CHA

Goushi Iijima sits in front of the ash fireplace (*irori*, page XVI), back ramrod straight yet somehow deeply relaxed. With measured, fluid movements, he pours cold-infused green tea (page 328) into delicate clear glass cups set on lacquerware saucers. We balance the saucer in our hand and pick up the colored glass handles to take the first sip: grassy, tannic, yet sweetly well balanced. The cold green tea has been long steeped, and is a fresh bump of morning caffeine. As we greedily gulp our tea down, Iijima-san is readying the next round. This time: *kocha*. Known in the world as black tea, the Japanese word is more accurate regarding the actual color ("deep red tea"). The cold "black" tea is floral with almost no tannic aftertaste. The Murakami area of Niigata prefecture gets low sun exposure throughout the year, so the tea develops more sweetness than tannins, resulting in a noticeably mild tea with floral notes.

Iijima-san's family has been growing and selling tea for over 140 years, since the first year of the Meiji era, when current production methods were developed. The family grew tea plants and also ran a small tea shop: Fujimien. Iijima-san's uncle, the 4th-generation head of the family business, began phasing out the tea fields and drastically slashed the total area of family fields. Goushi Iijima, in his mid-thirties, is 6th generation. Although technically his father is still at the helm, under young Iijima-san's stewardship the fields have increased 6-fold (no mean feat considering it takes five to seven years for tea plants to mature). Recently Iijima-san discovered that his family used to produce fermented tea (*kocha*) during the Meiji period, and thus resolved to revive the practice at Fujimien. And he had the perspicacity to bring their Meiji-era label out from retirement to slap on their 21st-century tea canisters.

The first time I visited Fujimien, there was snow on the ground. The thirty-odd members of our group squeezed into the two raised tatami-matted rooms where Iijima-san receives guests. I was struck by his economy of movement as he first poured hot water into a black iron teapot and then into an array of small ceramic cups set before him. Each time he poured the water into another receptacle the water temperature decreased several degrees (-50°F/10°C). He scooped several heaping measures of loose black tea leaves into the (now warm) iron teapot and poured the water from the cups, now cooled to the precise temperature, over the tea. Half mesmerized by Iijima-san's conscious motions and half desperate for a cup, we waited patiently for the tea to steep. Every movement and every thought that Iijima-san shares shows us his deep respect for the process of growing and brewing tea. Finally, warm cup in hand, I took a small sip and aerated it through my mouth, as if tasting wine. Not a fan of black tea, I was seduced by the fragrant pale brown liquid that just barely kissed my senses. Beautiful.

The mountain town of Murakami in Niigata prefecture is the northernmost tea-producing area in Japan. Although blanketed in snow throughout the winter, Murakami perches above the Sea of Japan and has a microclimate well suited for tea (high rainfall, low snowfall, and short sun exposure). Murakami has been producing tea since the 1600s and was at one time a vital tea-growing region. Today Murakami cha is but a blip on the radar of Japanese tea. Tea cultivation all over Japan declined after WWI, thanks to the dire financial straights of the country. Urbanization and WWII eroded the total area of tea fields even further. Compared to the 1,600 acres in Murakami's heyday, the area's tea fields have dwindled down to a paltry 100 acres (of which 7.5 are cultivated by Iijima-san). Iijima-san laments the waning culture of brewing tea at home. The solution: He has begun teaching children the pleasures of brewing and drinking tea in the hope that the children will, in turn, teach their parents.

Green tea is said to be anticarcinogenic, good for lowering blood pressure, and helpful for delaying Alzheimer's disease. More to the point, green tea, with its mild yet bitter character, is truly satisfying. While drinking green tea has not been part of my daily routine, I drink it occasionally in the afternoon, and I look forward to drinking it when out on the road.

brewed green tea SERVES 4
RYOKUCHA

4 tablespoons (12 g) loose Japanese green tea (*ryokucha*, page 305)

Fill a large teapot with cold filtered water and bring to a boil. Fill a smallish teapot for brewing the tea with about 1¾ cups (400 cc) boiling water and leave the large teapot off of the heat. The 194°F (90°C) water should have dropped to 176°F (80°C). Now fill 4 small cups (the portion size per person is usually a scant ½ cup/100 cc) with the water from the smallish teapot. This will heat the cups and cool the water another 50°F (10°C). Measure the tea into the smallish teapot and pour the water in the cups over the leaves. Let steep for 20 seconds and pour out evenly in each cup. It is important to pour in short bursts, a little at a time, and to use up all of the water in the pot. For the second round, pour water directly from the large teapot (which now should have cooled to about 176°F/80°C). Set the lid back on the smallish teapot, but crack it a bit to let steam escape. Steep for 10 seconds and pour out again in the same fashion. Always pour all of the tea out of the pot before adding water. The tea will become weaker and weaker until it is almost clear. This changing quality is part of the appeal.

I am not a tea drinker, but that does not mean I don't like it. I am weak for caffeine and need my coffee in the morning. I had never tasted a fermented tea that was more delicately gentle in the aftertaste than the *kocha* grown and brewed by Goushi Iijima at Fujimien in Murakami (Niigata prefecture). It was truly special. Naturally, skillful brewing is a crucial element in getting this tea right.

japanese "red" tea SERVES 4
KOCHA

4 tablespoons (12 g) loose
  fermented Japanese "red"
  tea (*kocha*, page 306)

Fill a large teapot with cold filtered water and bring to a boil. Pour about 2¾ cups (650 cc) boiling water into a ceramic pitcher or glass measuring cup to cool the water to 176°F (80°C). Measure the tea into the small teapot and pour the 176°F (80°C) water from the ceramic pitcher over the leaves. Steep for 1 minute and pour out evenly into 4 small cups. Splash in a little at a time, going back over the cups several times until all of the tea has been poured out. When ready for more tea, refill the small teapot with water from the large teapot and replace the lid. Steep for 30 seconds and pour out again in the same fashion. Never add more hot water to the tea leaves if any tea remains in the pot. As the tea becomes weaker, you will be able to appreciate its complexities (which linger ever so slightly).

We visited Fujimien (page 322) one time in the late summer when the days were still a bit warm and humid. As soon as we had plopped down on our cushions, Iizuka-san served us some cold-infused tea. More a fan of cold beverages than hot, I welcomed the cup of cold-infused green tea and was pleased to hear that since no heat is used in the infusion process, the tea is lower in caffeine.

cold-infused tea MAKES 1 QUART (1 LITER)
HIYACHA

7 tablespoons (20 g) loose Japanese green or brown tea

Measure the tea into a glass container and pour 1 quart (1 liter) of filtered water over the leaves. (Hario makes handy glass serving pitchers that have a strainer in the spigot, so you can pour out without straining.) Refrigerate for 24 hours and strain before serving well chilled but without ice.

TEA CEREMONY CHARCOAL

On my first visit to Ohno Charcoal on the Noto Peninsula, I fell under the spell of Choichiro Ohno, as the pride and passion for his métier enveloped in me an equal swell of appreciation. Ohno-san had learned the art of making charcoal from his father, and after the untimely death of his parent took over the reins of the family company while still in his twenties. Artisanal charcoal makers cut trees from their own land, so must reforest by planting more trees. And they craft their own mound-shaped kilns for firing the charcoal. After logging the trees, hauling them in, and cutting the logs down to size, it takes ten days to load the kiln. The fire builds over the course of five days, followed by a low-ember five-day period in which the wood is transformed into charcoal. The charcoal cools in the kiln before unloading.

On my second visit three years later, a pervasive weariness surrounded Ohno-san's demeanor. This discouragement came from eking out a living on artisanal charcoal. Ohno-san is the only full-time charcoal maker in Noto; all the others have second sources of income. By now he had a small family and the weight of responsibility toward them was clearly heavy. Not wanting the cottage industry of charcoal to die, he perseveres. Japan used to have a strong culture of fire in daily life, and in some way Ohno-san would love to return to that way of life. A note of bitterness crept into his voice when he spoke of increased media exposure for his charcoal, which has led to a dramatic increase in Tokyo restaurants using the charcoal he sells loose in bags for cooking. He had come to realize that he was only breaking even on the loose charcoal he was selling. Short of doubling or tripling his prices, the only solution was to cut off all new customers until he could plant more trees and increase production. This will take six years. The subtle acrimony in his voice came from the dichotomy between the financially successful Tokyo restaurants cooking with his underpriced charcoal, which he literally was giving away, while he struggled to support his family. I empathized and tried to reach through to give him words of encouragement: None of us are getting rich at this kind of life, but it's not about the money; it's about the quality of that life, whether you are a farmer, a fisherman, an artisan, a writer, or even a cook.

Ohno-san was packing tea ceremony charcoal on the day of that second visit. A note of excitement, reminiscent of our last visit, crept into his voice as he deconstructed a box of charcoal destined for use in the tea ceremony. Each piece of charcoal had its own name and played a specific role in the formalized building of the fire to heat the water used in the tea ceremony. The box was expertly packed like a jigsaw puzzle to hold the precise number of each piece required for performing the ceremony. Some pieces were fat, some thin, some short, some long, some perfectly round, and some halved. Tea ceremony charcoal must be almost perfect in overall shape. The outside walls of the cross section of the wood should be seamless and the cross section's starlike slits should be small. Ohno-san carefully repacked each piece, each wedged into its exact space. "There is no limit to the price I can set on tea ceremony charcoal," he mused. Inherent in this ritualized ceremony whose roots lie in Zen Buddhism is the rarefied nature of every component used. A bowl or canister fashioned to be used in the tea ceremony will fetch many times the price of a bowl made to be used in the kitchen and can be hideously expensive. Although the practice of tea was originally limited to priests and aristocrats up through the Edo period, after the Meiji Restoration it became popularized and was incorporated into the genteel accomplishments expected of women. The tea ceremony still enjoys great popularity today, both in Japan and abroad, so thankfully for Ohno-san, the demand for tea ceremony charcoal is a constant.

In my first year in Japan, I drank more *matcha* than I have in the last twenty-five years. As an honored guest, I was invited to several tea ceremonies, all fascinating in their deliberate ritual. Eagerly anticipating the bowl of creamy tea, my limbs would go numb from having to sit formally on the floor cushions with both legs folded under me. But the pain was worth it. Tadaaki likes to whip up a few bowls of *matcha* whenever impromptu guests drop in because it is almost easier than making green tea leaf tea and seems so gorgeous. (An amateur potter, Tadaaki also makes ceremonial tea bowls.)

powdered green tea SERVES 4
MATCHA

16 heaping *matcha* spoons (*chashaku*) or 6 teaspoons powdered green tea (*matcha*, page 306)

Fill a teapot halfway with cold filtered water and bring to a boil. Pour 1 cup (240 cc) hot water into a glass measuring cup to cool. Divide the water among 4 deep, round bowls to heat the bowls a little and cool the water. Pour the water back into the measuring container. It should now be between 158-185°F (70-80°C). Measure 4 heaping *matcha* spoons (*chashaku*) or 1½ teaspoons of *matcha* into each bowl. Divide the water again among the bowls and whisk with a bamboo tea whisk (*chasen*) or a small metal whisk until frothy. Serve immediately for an afternoon pick-me-up with something intensely sweet.

A few years ago some designers rennovated an abandoned crane company down the street from the English school where I first worked in Konan-machi (now merged with Kumagaya city). This organic complex, auspiciously named Newland, has shops, restaurants, a gallery, an event space, a kitchen, gardens, and a dog run. I periodically teach workshops at Newland, and the little organic grocery store there is where I first discovered real barley tea. I had previously only seen unappealing sachets in the supermarkets, so bought a stockpile to bring home. I made *mugicha* often that summer and brought several packs along on my first book tour to serve at signing venues along with some farm snacks.

I was preparing for another book tour the following spring and was dismayed to find out that Newland no longer stocked the whole roasted barley. Panic! Luckily the roasted barley company is located in Ogawa-machi, a town about 45 minutes away. I looked around for the roaster, since my nephew Patrick Martin of Chromatic Coffee had shown me his when I consulted him on barley roasting techniques. Apparently the farmer grows the organic barley but sends the grain out to be roasted. So no machine. I bought ten packs, gave the woman my business card, and now order over the phone (see Resources).

cold barley tea MAKES 1 QUART (1 LITER)
MUGICHA

3 tablespoons roasted barley or 1 sachet roasted barley tea (page 307)

Bring 1 quart (1 liter) filtered water to a boil in a medium-sized pot. Throw in the roasted barley grains or sachet and simmer friskily for 3 minutes. Remove from the heat and let cool overnight to room temperature. (Do not attempt to speed this process up by sticking it in the freezer or fridge; the tea will not steep properly and consequently will be weak.) Strain and chill. Delightfully refreshing anytime but particularly well chilled in the summer. Do not serve over ice, as the melting cubes will dilute the tea.

Soba cha, ubiquitous at soba restaurants, warms your whole being and has a wonderful nutty profile from the roasted buckwheat. It is almost always served hot. *Soba cha* should be easier to find than the whole roasted barley. Look at Japanese grocery stores or Internet-based tea suppliers (see Resources).

buckwheat tea SERVES 4
SOBA CHA

1 tablespoon (10 g) roasted buckwheat (*soba cha*, page 307)

Pour 1 cup (250 cc) boiling water over the roasted buckwheat and let steep 2 minutes. Strain and serve immediately or save in a glass-lined thermos pot to keep warm.

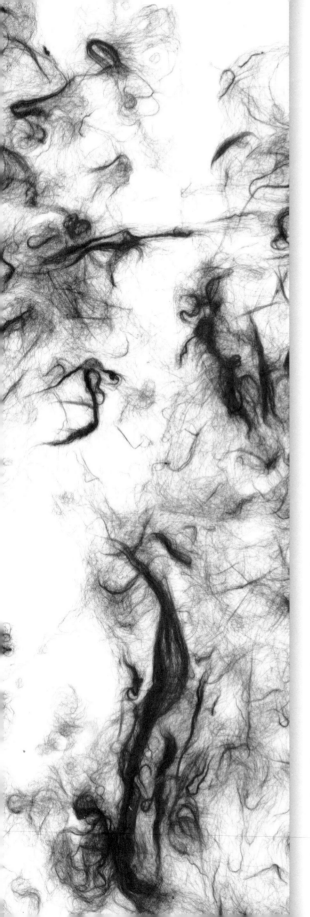

the snow of 2014

During the night of Friday, February 7, snow began to fall. On the return trip from Iio Jozo to learn about artisanal vinegar-making with my Fuji TV director, Saori Abe, we stopped in Kyoto for the night (and to have dinner at Kiln, the restaurant of a friend, Masayo Funakoshi). That night, as we slept, the snow continued to grow deeper. We settled our bill and dashed across the street to Kyoto Station, hoping to catch the bullet train back to Tokyo. No need for the haste—all the trains were behind schedule. We bought tickets and queued up for the next one, both of us anxious to get back home. The train was running slightly slower than usual but not abnormally so. Saori had been called in to capture footage of the snow in Tokyo, and I had duties at Sunny-Side Up! Remembering the previous February when 3 inches of snow had immobilized transportation in and around Tokyo, we were slightly on edge. We parted at Tokyo Station, and I made the transit to Saitama, thankfully only getting home an hour later than planned.

The snow fell steadily over the course of the day, as drifts built up on the fields and by the side of the road. By Sunday morning almost 11 inches of snow had been dumped in the Greater Kanto Tokyo area. A normal winter experiences light snow flurries once or twice a year, with the snow barely staying on the ground for a day or two. Eleven inches of snow was staggering. Sunday dawned sunny and white. Scheduled to make miso up at Matsuda-san's place (page 49), my ex-student Yoshie Takahashi stopped by to fetch me in her snow-tired car.

This particular year the members arriving from Tokyo were delayed by the unusually heavy snowfall, so we were a quiet, restful group. I welcomed the silence and the presence of just a few close local friends such as Adam Zgola and Yoshie. After depositing my miso-

making supplies, I climbed back up the driveway to chat with Adam. A Nova Scotia native, he seemed right at home wielding a snow shovel. We commiserated about being behind on each of our all-consuming projects: he building a traditional Japanese house for a friend, me finishing this manuscript. Adam paused and leaned his body on the shovel, a man at home in the outdoors. He had come to Japan in 2003 to teach at Sunny-Side Up! but eventually stayed to become a master at Japanese traditional carpentry (page XXIV). The first batch of beans was steamed, so we ambled down the driveway, heading for the makeshift kitchen to each start mashing and mixing our soybeans. As we packed up and were heading out, the Tokyo members were filtering in, having taken six hours to travel what normally takes two.

There were flurries throughout the week and warnings of another storm, but no one could have imagined the 2 feet of snow we eventually got. The snow started in earnest Friday afternoon. By the time I walked over to the school to hand the kids over to their mothers at 6:30 p.m., the branches on the Meyer lemon tree by the front door were straining under the heavy snow. After shaking the snow off the branches, they popped up, freed from the weight. Snow at first floats gently down, like soft feathers, tickling your hair and face. You tilt your head up to catch a few flakes on your tongue, and they make you smile. Not soon after, the flakes have become wet, stinging particles as they swirl around you, inducing tears over smiles. Also snow can be suffocating (having spent a winter in snow-locked Hanover, New Hampshire, I can attest to that). And snow can be devasting.

I started getting emails from the Sunny-Side Up! moms early Saturday morning, February 15: "Too much snow, no electricity, can't drive . . . not coming." I canceled the Saturday Program that day and, grateful for the solid block of time, hunkered down to write. Tadaaki climbed the stairs and poked his head in the room: "My chicken coops are totally destroyed by this heavy snow." His words were unfathomable. "Did you hear me?" Not able to think of an adequate response, I answered, "I'm sorry." Somehow that was not the reaction he was looking for. In the face of great loss, it is hard to fill the black void. What words could I offer to mitigate what could very well mean the end of his business? Certainly, I fell short that day.

The following few days were like the twilight zone. No one could move from their houses since, without snowplows, shoveling by hand was the only option to dig the cars out. Each day, I sent an email around to the moms: No school today.

And I wrote from morning to night. Four days after that unthinkable storm, we restarted school, though still could not get the cars out. We walked. Tromping through 4-foot-high snow mounds, I went to survey the damage at the coops. It was like a bomb had gone off. Unimaginable. I understood why Tadaaki had become deflated and listless in the aftermath of the storm.

However, Tadaaki gained energy from the outpouring of support from his friends. He had lost about one-third of the flock, while the remaining 2,000 chickens flapped about the wreckage and got underfoot. They laid their eggs in the mud, here, there, and everywhere. It was a horror. Tadaaki's brother, Noriaki, was a fixture during the weeks of grueling cleanup. Local friends dropped in whenever they could spare a few hours to haul broken lumber, bent iron poling, and meters of chicken wire from the caved-in coops. Many others came from far places to pitch in on the weekends. I cooked.

Experiencing great conflict for not helping out with the cleanup, I was already one and a half months past deadline on the manuscript, so in my own special hell. With no spare second to shovel the snow around my car, I continued to walk, cook, and write. And I worried about my editor in Japan, Kim Schuefftan, who lives in a remote mountain village about 40 minutes from here. Emails to him remained unreturned and phone calls unanswered— he was totally off the grid. Kim lives in a dilapidated farmhouse perched on a mountainside, so I feared the worst. Finally, after calling his town office, I learned that the residents of his village were still without electricity, but there were no casualties. Their power outage lasted 6 days, and the village was totally isolated during which time a helicopter came and dropped supplies.

The snow has melted, and the area where the chicken coops stood is now an expanse of leveled dirt with a temporary structure on the edge of the property. The remaining chickens are due to be sent away at the end of the summer, and Tadaaki still does no know if he will continue or not. The government intends to offer 90 percent relief to the farmers who have experienced damages, though no resolution is in sight. In the meantime, Tadaaki wavers, enticed by the notion of a life that does not require everyday work, yet pulled by that sense of responsibility toward Matsuda-san (page 78), his other egg customers, and birthright. For stewarding the land and house for the ancestors is his duty as the incumbent Hachisu.

ACKNOWLEDGMENTS

I am eternally grateful for the artisanal producers, farmers, and fishermen who opened up their lives to me and generously shared their time and expertise. They are the life and heart of this book.

Preserving the Japanese Way took on a life of its own over the course of a couple of years, sometimes leaving me breathlessly busy, unable to cook, clean, or even communicate with my family or school. I owe a deep debt to my husband, Tadaaki, for his patience, and to my sons, Christopher, Andrew, and Matthew, for pitching in both at home and at Sunny-Side Up! And to Alyssia Kenow, my head teacher, for stepping in for me in so many ways when I was detained elsewhere—I could not have written this book without her continual good humor and unquestioning support.

And of course, my team in Japan requires special mention. Veteran editor Kim Schuefftan, friend and mentor, with his expert advice on all things Japanese, who also gave two close editing reads on the manuscript, was a most crucial person in this process. It goes without saying how much I owe to photographer Kenji Miura for his gorgeous images and his tireless equanimity. Saori Abe, my Fuji TV director, has been my constant companion during these last years, and I continue to be amazed at her ability to fade into the background and capture footage, camera hoisted on her shoulder. And my dear colleague at Shogakukan publishing, Yasushi Ozaki, offered much valuable professional advice both day and night. Lastly I am also deeply grateful for being included in the Travel Restaurant and other Umari projects developed by visionary owner Hima Furuta and administered by the ever energetic Justin Potts.

Closer to home . . . without friends where would we be? Takashi Sekine and his family have been a fixture in our lives for over 20 years now, and I appreciate every time they show up several hours early to help me in the kitchen prepping for gatherings. Along with Sekine-san I gain strength and support from the whole Suka family as well as Masashi Matsuda (of Matsuda Mayonnaise fame), without whom I would be less grounded. And to all of the people at Yamaki Jozo, I am eternally grateful to be part of the community, and thank owner, Tomio Kitani, for his good-humored, gentle leadership of this outstanding company.

I should also get down on my hands and knees to thank my literary agent, Jenni Ferrari-Adler, for running interference for me when things got heated and my editor, Jean Lucas, for not losing her cool even when I did. I am grateful for each and every person at Andrews McMeel, including publisher Kirsty Melville for her intelligent leadership of this eclectic publishing house. Design under the guidance of Julie Barnes was flawless, while Diane Marsh showed a dead-on understanding of my vision for the book. Hats off to Robert and Cynthia Swanson for their inspired creativity in creating the index, and to my U.S. copy editor Libby Kessman and in-house production editor Maureen Sullivan for their minute attention to detail. And my continual thanks for publicist Andrea Shores, who answered every email right away and followed up on each request with professional confidence.

I also am greatly indebted to dear friends Cecily Dumas and Sarah Moulding with their darling daughters Izzy and Pinky and the little yappy dog, Beechie (who I pretended not to like), for letting me use their basement apartment as my pied à terre throughout various book tours over the last several years (sometimes for weeks on end).

And to my number one cheering section: old friend John Larkin, who wins the prize for attending the most book events all over the United States (Berkeley, Seattle, Woodstock, New York). Thanks for your infectious laugh and satirical jokes!

Last but not least, without Alice Waters and the community of Chez Panisse I would be a wayward soul. And specifically my sounding boards Sharon Jones and Sylvan Mishima Brackett: We all three share a passion for pristine foodstuffs and Japanese aesthetics, so each time one of them visits Japan we have unforgettable adventures together. I cannot wait for the next one.

To the Singleton family at large: Thank you for being patient with my fly-in, fly-out visits, which often prioritized book events over family.

And a special thanks to Katsue Nagano, aka "Katchan," Tadaaki's good-hearted aunt who helps me pick *ume*, cook rice over the fire, and is generally enthusiastic and encouraging in all of my activities. I don't always show my appreciation overtly, but I feel it keenly.

glossary of japanese produce

ROOTS, VEGETABLES, GREENS, MOUNTAIN VEGETABLES AND ALLIUMS, MUSHROOMS, AND AROMATICS

ROOTS

DAIKON: A large white radish, best in the winter. As the weather warms toward spring, the daikon push themselves out of the earth and the portion that is hit by sunlight turns pale green. Cut that part off before using. Try to buy daikon with the leaves attached. The skin of the root should be taut; peel if tough. Store in a cool place or in the fridge.

GOBO (BURDOCK): A long fibrous root that does well with soy sauce, miso, and sake lees treatments. Store in a cool, dark place. Scrub the surface vigorously with a vegetable brush before slicing diagonally. Do not peel.

KONNYAKU: A corm that is processed into gelatinous blocks and noodles, which are used in soups, simmered dishes, and stir-fries. Store in water in the refrigerator. Keeps well, but change the water daily if the konnyaku is homemade.

SATO IMO (TARO ROOT): A small round, pleasantly slimy potatolike root with dark brown barklike skin, which is usually peeled (or scrubbed, if freshly picked). Wonderful in soups and soy sauce–simmered dishes. Serve steamed or roasted whole (unpeeled) *sato imo* as an accompaniment to beer in the afternoon: Pop out of the skin while hot and eat dipped in salt. Keeps well stored in a cool, dark place.

SATSUMA IMO (SWEET POTATO): Similar to the North American sweet potato and yam. Used in simmered dishes, Japanese sweets, and tempura. Roasted in hot stones or the oven, it's a popular afternoon snack: Peel back the skin and eat as is, or scoop out the flesh and dab in some butter and salt. Store in a cool, dark place.

YAMA IMO (MOUNTAIN YAM): A cream-colored tuber speckled with small brown tufted eyes. The bright white flesh is grated into a wonderfully slimy mass and eaten raw with soy sauce or as an accompaniment to noodles. Also sometimes used as a binder when making soba noodles or tofu croquettes (*ganmodoki*). Store in sawdust or rice husks in a cool, dark place.

Sato Imo (Taro Root)

Goya/Nigauri (Bitter Melon)

Kyuri (Cucumber)

VEGETABLES

EDAMAME (YOUNG SOYBEANS): Sold on the branch or in small net bags in Japan. Best when freshly picked. The pods should be a deep sage green and not yellowed or discolored. Highly recommended to plant in the garden. Store in the fridge if not using right away.

GOYA/NIGAURI (BITTER MELON): A shiny, light lime green cucumber-shaped "melon" with blistered skin. Slice in half lengthwise and scoop out the white pith and seeds before pickling whole or slicing and sautéing.

KABOCHA (WINTER SQUASH): Most commonly a squat round shape with dark green skin. Heirloom varieties may have light green or peach-colored skin or be oval in shape. Store in a cool, dark place. Once cut, wrap in plastic and refrigerate.

KYURI (CUCUMBER): A slender, sometimes curled cucumber, usually about 7 inches (17.5 cm) long, with dark green shiny skin. Use without peeling or seeding. Store in the refrigerator.

NASU (EGGPLANT): Small purple elongated globes, about 4 inches (10 cm) long. Look for glossy specimens and avoid the dull ones. Store in a cool, dark place for a day or two, otherwise in the fridge.

NEGI (JAPANESE "LEEKS"): ½- to 2-inch (1.25- to 5-cm) thick Japanese green onions. Substitute fat scallions or spring onions. Store in a cool, dark place or the fridge.

RENKON (LOTUS ROOT): Tubular roots with a flowerlike cross section. Good peeled, sliced into thick rounds, and pickled in miso (page 59) or soaked in fish sauce and grilled (page 135). The surface of the roots should not be brown or mottled.

SHIRO URI (WHITE MELON): This cucumberlike melon has been consumed in Japan since prehistoric times. Most often it is pickled in sake lees (*narazuke*, page 213).

GREENS

HAKUSAI (NAPA CABBAGE): A ubiquitous vegetable in Japan (or perhaps all of Asia). Best salt fermented (page 11), in salads, or in soups (page 80). The cabbage heads are encircled with twine while still in the field to keep them straight and white and ideal for pickling, hence the name *hakusai* (literally "white vegetable").

KARASHINA (MUSTARD GREENS): A spicy, slightly prickly green, which is available much of the year, though perhaps best in the winter. *Karashina* does well salt fermented (page 14), sautéed, or in *nabe* (one-pot dishes, page 136).

KOMATSUNA (JAPANESE MUSTARD): A brassica, relative of bok choy, but with thinner stems and leaves. The most versatile green in Japan (or perhaps in the world!). Highly recommended for cultivation, as it can be grown year-round and is always welcome in a meal. Good salt fermented (page 14); in *nabe* (one-pot dishes, page 136); sautéed; or blanched, refreshed, squeezed, and dressed (page 182).

MIBUNA (BITTER GREENS): A native green similar to puntarella with long ⅓-inch (1-cm) wide leaves. Good salt fermented (page 14) or in *nabe* (one-pot dishes, page 136).

MIZUNA (BITTER SALAD GREENS): A peppery salad green with soft spiky leaves that are lovely as is, dressed with a citrus vinaigrette (equal parts mild citrus juice and oil), or salt massaged with kumquats (page 24).

NANOHANA (FLOWERING TOPS): When flowering brassica such as *komatsuna*, mustard, and turnip greens start to go to seed in the late winter and spring, they develop tender bud tops that are delicious salt pickled (page 14); boiled, refreshed, squeezed, and dressed with smashed tofu (*shira-ae*, page 182); or sautéed with thinly sliced pork belly, slivered ginger, and dried red pepper. Substitute tender rapini or any flowering tops sold at Asian farmers' markets.

SARADA KARASHINA (SALAD MUSTARD GREENS): Purple, zig-zaggy salad greens from the mustard family. Good for rustic salads with soy sauce vinaigrette (page 113) or as a vibrant bed to serve Miso-Cured Eggs (page 66). Shows up in the early summer and midautumn.

SHUNGIKU (CULINARY CHRYSANTHEMUM GREENS): Good salt massaged; in *nabe* (one-pot dishes, page 136); or boiled, refreshed, squeezed, and dressed with smashed tofu (*shira-ae*, page 182) or soy sauce–flavored dashi (page 265).

TAKANA (BITTER GREENS): A brassica relative of the mustard family that grows from ¾ foot to 2 feet (20 to 60 cm) high. Closely related to *komatsuna*. Commonly salt pickled (page 14). Pickled *takana* may be used to wrap rice balls (page 172).

Negi (Japanese "Leeks")

Koshi Abura (Mountain Vegetable)

Nobiru (Wild Onions)

MOUNTAIN VEGETABLES AND ALLIUMS

FUKI (GIANT BUTTERBUR): Celery-looking stalks that have a pleasantly bitter, astringent quality when stir fried or pickled. Fuki buds (*fuki no to*) are hauntingly beguiling as tempura or in miso (page 69). These buds are the harbingers of spring.

KOSHI ABURA (MOUNTAIN VEGETABLE): A feathery bud with the indescribably addicting bitterness that works so well as tempura. Midspring.

NOBIRU (WILD ONIONS): A multiplying onion with pinkish-white bottoms that sprouts up naturally in the spring on fields, near water faucets, by the rice fields, or just about anywhere. *Nobiru* is almost like wild garlic and is used in place of chives. Also sensational dipped in miso.

RAKKYO (JAPANESE SHALLOTS): A multiplying onion similar to slender shallots, though more pungent. Delightful salt pickled (page 8) or stored in sweet vinegar (page 155). Early summer.

SERI (JAPANESE CRESS): Spicy pink-stemmed curly cress that appears on the sides of rice fields in the early spring. Delicious as a salad or tempura.

WARABI (FIDDLEHEAD FERNS): Slender fiddlehead ferns that are simply blanched and dressed (page 265). Midspring.

MUSHROOMS

ENOKI: Mild white or orange-colored mushrooms that go well in miso soup or *nabe* (one-pot dishes, page 136). Slightly slippery. Store in the fridge.

SHIITAKE: Dark-capped meaty mushrooms grown on logs in the forest. The stems are thick, so cut them off the caps and dry them for stock (page 266). Look for dusky grey-brown caps with deep fissures; avoid wet or discolored shiitake. Wipe if necessary; do not wash. Store in a cool, dark place, cap sides down.

SHIMEJI: Spongy, grey-capped mushrooms that are good in *nabe* (one-pot dishes, page 136). Look for small caps and white stems. *Shimegi* stems can be eaten; the thick (often dusty) "stalk" that connects to the cultivation block should be discarded. Store in the fridge.

AROMATICS

HOJISO (SHISO BUDS): The flowerlike buds that form on the shiso plant as it goes to seed. Wonderful eaten with sashimi such as Kelp-Wicked Flounder (page 269), sprinkled into salads instead of shiso leaves, or merely pickled in salt (Salt-Massaged Shiso Buds, page 20). Late summer to early fall.

MITSUBA (TREFOIL): An aromatic herb with a light, astringent flavor. Substitute a peppery cress. Spring and early summer.

MYOGA: A relative of ginger that shoots pinkish-brown, candle flame–shaped buds up from the root area. If you find it, it should be fresh-looking and not tired. Spring to summer.

NIRA (GARLIC CHIVES): Used in *gyoza* filling and kimchee (page 280). Available most of the year.

SANSHO (PRICKLY ASH): Tiny tannic-flavored leaves that are good with miso or as a small garnish for tofu (page 65). Spring to summer. The dried seeds are also known as Japanese, Chinese, or Sichuan pepper.

SHISO (PERILLA): The most common Japanese herb, used throughout the summer in many dishes. Shiso is in the mint family and will reseed itself each year. Red shiso leaves (page 19) and green shiso buds (page 20) both do well preserved in salt.

WASABI (JAPANESE HORSERADISH): A small pale green nubby root that grows wild by mountain streams or is cultivated in running water (see Resources). Peel the skin before grating from the top of the root. Avoid the tubed variety if possible; better to use fresh Western horseradish instead.

CITRUS AND OTHER FRUITS

CITRUS

DAIDAI: The native bitter orange used to make ponzu (equal parts soy sauce and *daidai* juice). I substitute *daidai* peel for yellow yuzu in red kosho (page 281).

KOBOSU: A small green citrus with a distinctive flavor reminiscent of lime.

MIKAN: The ubiquitous citrus that all Japanese love. When in season we eat them by the bowlful after meals (technically a mandarin).

NATSUMIKAN: A large, pale orange–skinned, mildly sour citrus. Good eaten as is or in a citrus vinaigrette (equal parts citrus juice and oil).

OTACHIBANA: A native Japanese grapefruitlike citrus that yields a wonderfully aromatic zest, but not much juice due to the unusually thick pith.

SUDACHI: A small aromatic orange-colored sour citrus with bright-tasting juice and fragrant zest.

YUZU: A small citrus with a memorable rounded flavor profile. Starting in the late fall, we pluck green yuzu off the tree for their peels, then as the fruit matures, we begin paring off the yellow peels and squeezing the juice. Yuzu trees are being planted abroad, so the fruit will become more and more available.

Wasabi

Mikan

Shiitake

OTHER FRUIT

BIWA (LOQUAT): Good in place of kumquat with mizuna (page 24) or steeped in white liquor and sugar as a fruit cordial (page 317). Our loquats are ripe in the early summer, but the season is short, so sometimes I miss the window to harvest them.

ICHIJIKU (FIG): A nice addition to add balance to a pickle plate. Also the perfect foil to Sake Lees Ice Cream (page 215). Our fig tree seems to have a couple of growth cycles in a year: early summer and late fall.

KAKI (PERSIMMON): Kaki can be confusing: There are round ones and oval ones, astringent ones and sweet ones. In general, round *kaki* (called Fuyu in the U.S.) are sweet and eaten raw while still hard, much as you would a peeled and cut apple. Oval *kaki* (called Hachiya in the U.S.) are dried as *hoshigaki* (page 180). This is the variety Western countries use for desserts after it has ripened to the point of being almost gelatinous. *Kaki* ripen in our area in late October or early November.

KARIN (QUINCE): The quinces that grow on our trees are an Asian variety and are used for making a fruit cordial (page 317). My mother-in-law steeped an unsweetened version for her husband to swig as a restorative.

KINKAN (KUMQUAT): Our kumquats seem to perennially be in season, though at times are pithy. I did not pay much attention to them until a few years ago. Now I often grab a few when I'm passing by and pop them in my mouth on the way to my car.

MAKUWA URI (SMALL MELON): An oval, pale yellow–skinned melon about the size of a large avocado, with either green or orange flesh. Good for pickling with sake lees (page 209) or served with a squeeze of citrus juice and some chopped green chiles. Midsummer.

NASHI (APPLE PEAR): Harvested in our town throughout the summer starting in July and into September. Larger than an apple, these round juicy fruits should be chilled before serving. Peel and cut into eighths. Mildly pearlike and crisp, ubiquitous at tea break throughout the summer, and also intriging quick pickled in miso (page 60).

SUIKA (WATERMELON): A bowling ball–sized round watermelon that fits nicely in the fridge and is the perfect size for a small family. Mild, crisp, and sweet.

UME (SOUR "PLUM"): A member of the apricot family ready to harvest in June. *Ume* are soaked, packed in salt, then sun-dried for *umeboshi* pickles (page 167) or added to a generic white liquor with sugar to make *umeshu* (page 317).

FRUITS AND VEGETABLES BY PICKLING METHOD

	Dried	Salted	Miso	Soy Sauce	Fish Sauce	Vinegar	Sour Plum	Shio Koji	Shoyu Koji	Sake Kasu	Rice Bran	Kimchee
Asparagus		*	*	*	*	*		*	*	*	*	*
Bitter Melon		*	*	*	*	*		*	*	*		*
Bok Choy		*						*			*	*
Broccoli		*		*	*			*	*			*
Cabbage		*			*	*	*	*		*		*
Carrots		*	*	*		*		*	*	*	*	*
Cauliflower		*		*	*		*	*	*			*
Celery		*	*	*	*	*		*	*	*	*	*
Chayote		*	*	*	*	*	*	*	*	*	*	*
Corn	*	*						*				
Cucumbers		*	*	*	*	*	*	*	*	*	*	*
Daikon	*	*	*	*	*	*	*	*	*	*	*	*
Edamame								*				
Eggplant	*	*		*	*			*	*		*	*
Fava Beans								*				
Garlic		*	*	*				*	*			*
Gobo			*	*				*	*	*	*	
Green Beans		*	*	*	*			*	*	*	*	*
Green Peppers		*	*	*	*			*	*		*	*
Greens (Bitter)		*			*			*				*
Kabocha			*	*				*	*	*		
Lettuce				*	*	*		*	*			
Lotus Root			*	*	*	*	*	*	*	*	*	*
Melon		*	*		*	*	*	*		*		*

	Dried	Salted	Miso	Soy Sauce	Fish Sauce	Vinegar	Sour Plum	Shio Koji	Shoyu Koji	Sake Kasu	Rice Bran	Kimchee
Mizuna		*				*	*	*				*
Mushrooms	*	*		*				*	*			
Myoga		*	*	*	*	*	*	*	*		*	*
Negi				*	*	*	*	*	*			*
Okra		*	*	*	*			*	*	*	*	*
Onions		*	*	*	*	*	*	*	*	*		*
Peas								*				
Potatoes					*			*				
Radishes		*	*		*	*	*	*			*	*
Rakkyo		*	*	*	*	*	*	*	*		*	*
Snap Peas					*			*				
Snow Peas			*		*			*			*	*
Spinach					*			*				*
Taro Root								*				
Tomatoes				*	*	*		*	*			
Turnips		*	*		*		*	*		*	*	*
Zucchini	*	*	*	*	*		*	*	*	*	*	*

FISH AND SHELLFISH BY PICKLING METHOD

	Salt Seared	Half Dried	Long Dried	Miso Chopped	Vinegared	Kelp Wicked	Miso Broiled	Shio Koji	Shoyu Koji	Sake Lees	Sake Steamed	Hot Pot
FISH												
Albacore	*			*	*	*	*	*		*	*	*
Anchovies		*	*	*				*	*			
Bonito	*			*				*	*			
Cod			*		*	*		*	*	*	*	*
Flying Fish		*	*	*	*	*		*			*	

FISH AND SHELLFISH BY PICKLING METHOD CONTINUED

	Salt Seared	Half Dried	Long Dried	Miso Chopped	Vinegared	Kelp Wicked	Miso Broiled	Shio Koji	Shoyu Koji	Sake Lees	Sake Steamed	Hot Pot
Halibut	*				*	*		*			*	*
Herring		*	*					*		*		
Horse Mackerel		*		*	*		*	*	*			
Mackerel		*		*				*	*	*		
Monkfish							*	*	*	*	*	*
Salmon	*		*				*	*		*	*	*
Sandfish		*			*			*			*	*
Sardines		*	*				*	*			*	
Sea Bass					*	*	*	*	*	*	*	*
Snapper		*			*	*		*			*	*
Sole		*			*	*		*			*	
Sturgeon								*	*	*	*	
Swordfish	*						*	*	*	*	*	
Trout								*			*	
Tuna	*			*				*				
Yellowtail	*						*	*	*	*	*	
SHELLFISH												
Clams	*						*	*			*	*
Crab					*		*	*			*	*
Mussels	*							*			*	*
Octopus	*	*	*					*				
Oysters	*							*				*
Scallops	*	*		*	*		*	*	*		*	*
Shrimp	*				*			*		*		*
Squid	*	*	*	*			*	*	*			*

resources

Due to the rising popularity of Japanese foods outside of the sukiyaki-sushi paradigm, an increasing amount of goods and ingredients are becoming accessible. These items are mostly available via the Internet; however, small Japanese grocery stores and kitchen supply houses dot the landscape of the United States and the European Union. While impossible to name them all, here is a list of resources that I would personally recommend. Also Google any not-yet-available ingredients because the climate of artisanal Japanese foods will surely change each year. The movement is already well on its way. Alternatively, you could brave the labyrinth of Rakuten Global Market (page 253), a mind-bogglingly intricate site I discovered on the eve of finishing this book.

I blatantly favor the best-quality choices (within price range) of those important flavors you will need for Japanese preserving or cooking: salt, soy sauce, miso, fish sauce, rice vinegar, katsuobushi, konbu, hon mirin. Beyond that, I also believe that shopping at the farmers' market, fish market, or butcher shop will be cost-effective in the end because the food will stay fresher and will ultimately taste better.

UNITED STATES

MACROBIOTIC AND ORGANIC FOODS

GOLD MINE NATURAL FOOD CO. (WWW.GOLDMINENATURALFOODS. COM): The official distributor of Ohsawa® organic products, including Yamaki Jozo (page 106) soy sauce and miso, as well as top-quality tamari, brown rice vinegar, plum vinegar, pickled plums, plum paste, wakame, kelp, nori, agar, and *nigari*. A comprehensive source for most organic Japanese pantry items.

NATURAL IMPORT COMPANY (WWW. NATURALIMPORT.COM): A distributor for Mitoku macrobiotic and organic foods. An excellent resource for learning about ingredients (they have links to short, yet thorough explanations). Also carries many high-quality, hard-to-find Japanese ingredients such as amazake, koji, kuzu, and the ever-elusive gold sesame seeds. Many staple pantry items and Japanese cooking equipment are available as well.

EDEN FOODS (WWW.EDENFOODS.COM): One of the last single-owner organic food companies in the United States. Dedicated to repackaging high-quality artisanal Japanese ingredients for the Eden Foods brand. Readily available in the natural foods section of grocery stores as well as online or in specialty natural food shops.

OTHER ONLINE JAPANESE FOOD SOURCES

RAKUTEN GLOBAL MARKET (GLOBAL. RAKUTEN.COM/EN): Launched February 2014 by Japanese e-commerce giant Rakuten, the site is mammoth and a bit unwieldy to navigate. Nonetheless, this is THE source for almost every hard-to-find artisanal Japanese ingredient I use in my kitchen. To help unpack the wheres and whys of Global Rakuten Market, I have distilled the salient information needed to wrap your head around the complicated system (page 353).

AMAZON (WWW.AMAZON.COM): Almost everything is available through this mega-store. It boggles the mind. Caveat: The quality of Japanese ingredients is not uniformly high.

SALT

THE MEADOW (WWW.THEMEADOW. COM): A well-curated chocolate and salt shop located in Portland, Oregon, and New York City. Owner Mark Bitterman is a salt expert and the author of two books on salt. This is the source to turn to if you want to taste salts from all over the world, since The Meadow sells in small quantities as well as large. They also offer Trapani e Marsala coarse Italian sea salt in 2-pound (900-g) bags. Available online as well as in shop.

THE SPICE LAB (WWW.THESPICELAB.COM): An online source for "gourmet salts and spices," which carries Trapani sea salt and Cyprus flake salt for a reasonable price in bulk.

MISO AND RICE KOJI

SOUTH RIVER MISO COMPANY (WWW. SOUTHRIVERMISO.COM): One of the longest-running artisanal miso companies in the United States and arguably one of the best. Caveat: South River only ships between mid-September and mid-April (with a few exceptions in May). South River also sells brown rice koji and the impossible-to-find Miso Tamari (*almost* the real thing, which is the puddling on the top of the miso barrel and not anything like commercial tamari).

JORINJI (WWW.JORINJISOYBEAM.COM): A Portland, Oregon, company making a variety of absolutely delicious misos. Poised to expand their market base beyond Portland, this small company suffered huge setbacks in the spring and summer of 2013. At the time of this book printing, it was uncertain whether or not Jorinji would continue, but we should all hope owner Earnest Migaki will find a way.

COLD MOUNTAIN MISO (WWW. COLDMOUNTAIN.COM): Sold through Miyako Oriental Foods Inc. in Southern California. I have not tasted this organic miso, but from all appearances they seem to be doing a good job. Rice koji is also available through Cold Mountain Miso.

MISO MASTER (GREAT-EASTERN-SUN. COM): Miso Master is sold through Great Eastern Sun Trading Company in North Carolina. They carry a few other organic food brands such as Emerald Cove Sea Vegetables (mostly cultivated in China). Miso Master miso has great flavor but is a bit dense.

AEDAN FERMENTED FOODS (WWW. AEDANSF.COM): While I have not tasted any of the Aedan products, the Web site and packaging reflects an innate aesthetic sense, which bodes well for what lies within. Aedan sells several varieties of miso, fresh rice koji, shio koji, amazake, sagohachi pickling sauce, and *doburoku* at the Ferry Plaza Farmers' Market in San Francisco and through GoodEggs.com in the San Francisco Bay Area.

RHAPSODY NATURAL FOODS (WWW. RHAPSODYNATURALFOODS.COM): A small, conscientiously run organic family farm in Cabot, Vermont, producing traditional foods for a plant-based diet. Rhapsody Natural Foods makes their own miso (aged in oak barrels), tempeh, vegan egg rolls, rice milk, amazake, rice koji, and rice bran (all organic).

SOY SAUCE

BOURBON BARREL FOODS (BOURBONBARRELFOODS.COM): Along with several other bourbon barrel–aged products such as vanilla, salt, and Worcestershire sauce, Bourbon Barrel Foods makes a beautifully flavorful, Japanese-style soy sauce aged in bourbon barrels, Blue Grass Soy Sauce. The bottles carry a striking light blue label etched with a drawing of a soy plant. Expensive but worth it. Especially good on soy sauce vinaigrette salads (page 113).

GOLD MINE NATURAL FOOD CO. (WWW. GOLDMINENATURALFOODS.COM): Yamaki Jozo soy sauce, repackaged by Ohsawa® as Nama Shoyu, is available here in bulk at an extremely reasonable price.

SOYBEANS, TOFU, AND NATTO

PLEASANT HILL GRAIN (WWW. PLEASANTHILLGRAIN.COM): A comprehensive grain and kitchen equipment source that carries organic soybeans. Located in Nebraska; online or phone orders are accepted.

SHILOH FARMS (WWW.SHILOHFARMS. COM): A large-scale (mostly) organic farm enterprise in the Ozark Mountains of Arkansas specializing in grains, legumes, and nuts as well as organic bread, snacks, meat, and cheese. Shiloh Farms sells "adzuki" beans along with organic black and yellow soybeans.

LAURA SOYBEANS (WWW. LAURASOYBEANS.COM): A 100-year-old family farm operated by the Chambers family. The beans are non-GMO but not organic.

SOY MILK MAKER (WWW.SOYMILKMAKER. COM): Tofu-making supplies, including cypress tofu forms and soy milk makers, such as SoyaJoy.

MEGUMI NATTO (WWW.MEGUMINATTO. COM): High-quality organic natto made in Sebastopol, California. Available online.

CULTURES FOR HEALTH (WWW.CULTURES-FORHEALTH.COM): An excellent one-stop source for fermenting and tofu-making supplies, such as brown rice and barley koji, natto spores, *nigari*, Japanese tofu forms, fermenting crocks and weights, and yogurt makers for making Amazake (page 313).

RICE

MASSA ORGANICS (WWW. MASSAORGANICS.COM): Small-producer brown rice in California available online or at San Francisco Bay Area farmers' markets. Nutty brown rice grown by a fourth-generation ecologically dedicated rice farmer and his wife.

KODA FARMS (WWW.KODAFARMS.COM): A third-generation Japanese-American family growing rice in California's San Joaquin Valley. Koda Farms grows organically and conventionally. Their Heirloom Kohoku Rose would be the rice of choice to accompany Japanese meals. Use their Sho-Chiku-Bai "original, pure Japanese-style sweet rice" for making glutinous rice–based dishes.

LUNDBERG FAMILY FARMS (WWW. LUNDBERG.COM): Family owned, growing rice since 1937 in the Sacramento area using organic and "eco-farmed" methods. The rice they sell as "Organic California Sushi Rice" is the one closest to what we use in Japan. Available online and in selected grocery stores.

SAKE AND SAKE LEES

ARTISAN SAKE MAKER (ARTISANSAKEMAKER.COM): A Japanese sake brewer on Granville Island off of Vancouver, B.C., run by Masa Shiroki. Shiroki-san also sells his artisanal sake kasu. While I have not tasted his sake, I like his style.

WINE OF JAPAN IMPORT, INC. (WWW. WINEOFJAPAN.COM): Based in New Jersey, this family-run company is bringing in good-quality sake from Japan while keeping a close eye on the shipping process to protect the sake from being exposed to heat fluctuations. Look for their import label on the back of bottles, or check their Web site for sake recommendations. Also a respectable source for shochu.

WORLD SAKE IMPORTS (WWW. WORLDSAKE.COM): An extensive import company based in Hawaii with additional sales offices in New York, San Francisco, Miami, and London. Well regarded worldwide.

TEAS

LEAVES + FLOWERS (WWW. LEAVESANDFLOWERS.CO): A small well-curated, Web-based source for beautiful teas (including one from the Kinezuka family of Naturalitea), run in the San Francisco Bay Area by Anna Morton and Emily Erb.

NATURALITEA (NATURALITEA.COM): A Web site developed by tea farmer Toshiaki Kinezuka and Ian Chun from Matcha Latte Media to showcase 30 organic farming families' tea in Shizuoka, Japan. Daughter Ayumi studied at UC Berkeley and is now working with her father in the family business. A responsible and comprehensive site that ships abroad. Don't miss the video links on the About page.

THE TASTE OF TEA (WWW.THETASTEOFTEA. COM): A San Francisco Bay Area—based family tea business that is also opening a store in Healdsburg, California. They carry several organic Japanese teas and have a quirky Tea Docent who gives tea advice.

BREAKAWAY MATCHA (WWW. BREAKAWAYMATCHA.COM): A mail-order site that sells high-quality matcha and matcha supplies and is dedicated to teaching all about matcha. Run by cookbook author Eric Gower, a longtime resident of Japan who currently lives in San Francisco.

SEEDS, SPICES, PLANTS, AND KONNYAKU

KITAZAWA SEED CO. (WWW. KITAZAWASEED.COM): The oldest seed company in the U.S. specializing in Asian vegetables and THE source for all seeds Japanese. Order online or pick up packets at Japanese grocery stores.

PENZEYS SPICES (WWW.PENZEYS.COM): THE online source for best-quality spices. I stock my pantry only from Penzeys. Oriental mustard and more.

SPICES INC. (WWW.SPICESINC.COM): A spice and tea company carrying chile japones, the dried red chile we use daily, in bags ranging from 1 ounce to 5 pounds.

HEIRLOOM ONIONS (HEIRLOOMONIONS. COM): A project of Mulberry Woods Native Plant Nursery in Garden City, Alabama, dedicated to reviving endangered varieties of alliums. The only source I found for *Allium chinense* (*rakkyo*, page 8), well worth planting in your garden.

FROG EYES WASABI (WWW. FROGEYESWASABI.COM): Real wasabi roots grown on the Oregon coast. Available online. Pricey but well worth it for pristine fresh sashimi fish. Also sells wasabi leaves and stems, which are unforgettable pickled (page 98).

HALF MOON BAY WASABI COMPANY (HALF-MOON-BAY-WASABI.MYSHOPIFY. COM): Sells fresh wasabi by the quarter or half pound. Grown in Half Moon Bay, California, by part-time farmer-electricians.

BOBEROSA BARNWORKS (WWW. BOBEROSA.COM): An eclectic antique and craft shop in Capron, Illinois, that inexplicably also sells Voodoo Lily "bulbs" (konnyaku corms). The "bulbs" ship in the spring and fall, so mark your calendar.

KONJAC FOODS (WWW.KONJACFOODS. COM): All you ever wanted to know about konnyaku as well as a one-stop source for konnyaku products, namely *shirataki* noodles used in various Japanese simmered dishes such as sukiyaki and *nikujaga*. However, they do not appear to be making konnyaku blocks.

KITCHEN EQUIPMENT

HIDA TOOL & HARDWARE CO., INC. (WWW.HIDATOOL.COM): A compact but well-stocked traditional Japanese hardware shop at 1333 San Pablo Avenue in Berkeley, California. A smaller selection of the wares is available for purchase online through their Web site. Highly recommended for Japanese knives and sharpeners.

KORIN (WWW.KORIN.COM): A large Japanese kitchenware store located in Manhattan but also accessible online. A good source for Japanese barbecuing supplies, knives, and a wide range of Japanese kitchen supplies and tableware.

NATURAL IMPORT COMPANY (WWW. NATURALIMPORT.COM): In addition to carrying Mitoku macrobiotic and organic foods, also a good resource for Japanese kitchen equipment such as the "turtle brand" *tawashi* scrubbing brush, graters, *suribachi* and *surikogi*, *donabe*, iron pots, bamboo utensils, wooden tofu molds, and pickle presses.

TOIRO KITCHEN (WWW.TOIROKITCHEN. COM): Perhaps the only U.S. purveyor of *Igayaki donabe* (Iga ware refractory clay pots that can be used on a direct flame for cooking rice or *nabe*. I have (and recommend) the black *donabe* rice cooker they call "Kamado-san." It comes in different sizes and is not cheap. Although designed for cooking rice, it also pinch-hits as an excellent vessel for cooking *nabe* (one-pot dishes).

JAPAN BARGAIN (WWW.JAPANBARGAIN. COM): An exhaustive array of Japanese kitchen utensils, equipment, knives, paper, clothing, sushi and tea supplies, and tableware—including Japanese charcoal, calligraphy paper for blotting tempura (page 163), fish tweezers and fish scalers, tubs for aerating sushi rice (*handai*, page XIX), and plastic pickling presses.

PLEASANT HILL GRAIN (WWW. PLEASANTHILLGRAIN.COM): Zojirushi rice cookers and Japanese-style hot water dispensers, along with just about any other piece of equipment you might require for a serious kitchen, including food-grade plastic pickling buckets with lids.

PICKLING CONTAINERS

GARDENER'S SUPPLY COMPANY (WWW. GARDENERS.COM): A one-stop source for 1-, 3-, and 5-gallon stoneware pickling crocks, crock covers, and crock weights all made by Ohio Stoneware.

THE BROOKLYN KITCHEN (WWW. THEBROOKLYNKITCHEN.COM): A small but well-stocked kitchen and food shop housed, along with The Meat Hook, in the Williamsburg area of Brooklyn. Sells a limited amount of products online, including 1- and 2-gallon crockery pickling pots made by Ohio Stoneware.

LEXINGTON CONTAINER COMPANY (WWW.LEXINGTONCONTAINERCOMPANY. COM): An exhaustive source for food-grade plastic containers ranging from 1 ounce to 55 gallons.

QUITOKEETO (WWW.QUITOKEETO.COM): 101 Cookbook author Heidi Swanson's drop dead gorgeous collection of beautiful, yet highly functional hand-crafted items for the kitchen. I dare you to come away empty handed after checking out this site. THE source for fermentation crocks with a water seal built into the lid system (page 292).

TARUYA (TARUYA.COM): Run by 8th-generation barrel maker Yashima Nishikita (page 54) in Kobe, Japan. The Web site is only in Japanese, so best to call (+81-78-861-8717) or email (info@taruya.com). If he does not reply to your email, it might be wise to call, though pay heed to the time change and phone during the day in Japan.

AUSTRALIA/ NEW ZEALAND

CHEF'S ARMOURY (WWW. CHEFSARMOURY.COM): One of the top sources in the world for high-quality (mostly organic), hard-to-find Japanese ingredients. Also imports sake directly from the maker, which should eliminate any issues of sake becoming "fatigued" during shipping. Carries a wide range of knives and useful cooking equipment, including Oigen cast iron ware (page XIX), *shichirin* (page XVI), *tawashi* scrubbing brushes, and Japanese charcoal.

UNITED KINGDOM

CLEARSPRING (WWW.CLEARSPRING. CO.UK): The largest organic wholesaler in the EU, dedicated to selling and promoting organic and traditional foods. Run by a hands-on owner who lived in Japan for many

years and personally vets all of the products his company sells. Clearspring also distributes Mitoku.

SANCHI (WWW.SANCHI.CO.UK): Distributor for Muso Japan (one of the top organic food companies). Product information can be found on its Web site, though ordering should be done through Naturally Good Food.

NATURALLY GOOD FOOD (WWW. NATURALLYGOODFOOD.CO.UK): A mail-order natural foods clearing house that specializes in case and bulk discounts. Many Clearspring and Sanchi products are available here.

JAPAN CENTRE (WWW.JAPANCENTRE. COM): A mail-order source that also has a bricks-and-mortar shop in London. Most of the organic products available through Japan Centre are sourced through Clearspring, so perhaps it makes more sense to order directly from Clearspring. However, Japan Centre does carry Uchibori rice vinegar (one we use), organic misos, natto, and teas, as well as the hard-to-find fried tofu pouches, *abura age*.

THE WASABI COMPANY (WWW. THEWASABICOMPANY.CO.UK): An excellent source for organic spring water–grown wasabi rhizomes, wasabi plants, and wasabi accoutrements (such as graters and the useful bamboo brush for removing wasabi or ginger from a grater). Contact the company directly for EU distributors.

NAMAYASAI LLP (WWW.NAMAYASAI. CO.UK): Run by Robin Williams and Ikuko Suzuki, friends of ours who interned with the Suka family (page 242) and are growing a wide range of hard-to-find organic Japanese vegetables in East Essex, England.

FRANCE

WORKSHOP ISSÉ (WWW.FACEBOOK. COM/WORKSHOPISSE): A small shop in the 2nd arrondisement of Paris with a limited yet top-quality selection of vinegars, soy sauces, sake, and shochu. Also has a few seats and serves simple but (purportedly) delicious food.

KUROSHIO WASABI (WWW.KUROSHIO. FR): The French distributor for The Wasabi Company (UK). Kuroshio not only sells wasabi products, but also several very hard-to-find top-quality Japanese ingredients online, such as Fujisu's Premium Vinegar (page 159).

NATTO DU DRAGON (WWW.NATTO-DRAGON.COM): Artisanal natto made from organically grown French soybeans in the Var department of the Provence-Alpes-Côte d'Azur region of southestern France. Order online several days in advance (the natto is made on demand). Minimum order: 3 small packs.

SUPERSEC (SUPERSEC.COM): Artisanal dried mushrooms, pasta, and seaweed, including *aonori* and wakame (both wild).

GERMANY/AUSTRIA

UENO GOURMET (WWW.JAPAN-GOURMET.COM): An online sake-centric shop that also offers shochu and a few other artisanal Japanese products such as soy sauce, mirin, and *wasanbon* (Japanese native sugar). Click on the British flag icon if you need the English Web site. A link to the Japanese version is found at the bottom of the page: "日本語."

WORLD

MITOKU (WWW.MITOKU.COM): Contact for distributors. Also a good source for information on Japanese products and recipes.

MUSO (WWW.MUSO-INTL.COM): Check Mitoku's home Web site for a list of distributors worldwide.

JAPAN
JAPANESE FOOD SOURCES
AMAZON.CO.JP (WWW.AMAZON.CO.JP): As with its U.S. counterpart, an exhaustive source for Japanese ingredients, some artisanal, some not. Unfortunately they do not ship outside of Japan.

WINDY HILLTOP FARM (HOMEPAGE3. NIFTY.COM/TASHITA-FARM): An organic farm in the small town of Ogawa in Saitama prefecture that produces whole roasted barley tea. The name of the farm in Japanese is Kaze no Oka Farm (風の丘ファーム). It is possible this tea will become available on Rakuten Global Market in the future.

SAKE RECOMMENDATIONS

IMAYOTSUKASA (WWW.IMAYOTSUKASA. COM): A beautiful sake brewery (page 308) in the city of Niigata with a wide range of sakes ranging from completely affordable ($20) to fairly expensive ($45). Information only in Japanese.

TAKIZAWA SHUZO (HOMEPAGE3.NIFTY. COM/KIKUIZUMI): This sake brewery located in the city of Fukaya in Saitama prefecture uses organic rice and our local mountain spring water to brew their elegant, reasonably priced sakes. I buy the Daiginjo Nama and the Shinseienkyo. English Web site available.

TERADA HONKE (WWW.TERADAHONKE. CO.JP): An over 300-year-old organic brewery in Chiba prefecture that harvests wild koji from the rice stalks. Their most famous variety is Gonin Musume ("Five Daughters"), but I am also partial to Daigo no Shizuku, as it is unpasteurized. An invaluable one-page explanation of the brewery is offered in English and Italian.

PEOPLE DOING INTERESTING THINGS

BLUE & WHITE (BLUEANDWHITETOKYO. COM): A small, well-stocked indigo-oriented shop in Tokyo's Azabu-Juban district run by Amy Katoh (author of *Blue and White Japan*, *Japan Country Living*, *Japan: The Art of Living*, and others). Amy's books were inspirational in our house renovation.

ROPPONGI NOUEN (ROPPONGI-NOUEN. JP): An eclectic farm-to-table restaurant in the heart of Tokyo with close relationships to farmers and fishermen. Owned by the inimitable Hima Furuta, staffed by young people creating a freshened-up style of Japanese food. The Web site is in Japanese, but there is a small button on the first page to access an English menu.

NIPPON TRAVEL RESTAURANT (WWW. TRAVEL-RESTAURANT.JP): A food-related tour group run by Hima Furuta's Umari team developed to promote good food and interesting artisanal wares in local areas around Japan. Japanese Web site.

INTERNATIONAL TERAKOYA (INTERNATIONALTERAKOYA.COM): In their words, "Tokyo's locally supported, globally minded community schoolhouse." A project aimed at educating and building community between people of all ages and nationalities. The Web site is bilingual for the most part.

BROWN'S FIELD (WWW.BROWNSFIELD-JP. COM): An organic farm, macrobiotic café, and inn in the deep Chiba prefectural countryside. Although the Web site is predominantly Japanese, there is English on the About Us and Cottage pages.

KOJIYA HONTEN (WWW.KOJIYA.JP): Web site of Myoho Asari, "The Kojiya Woman" (page 194). A wealth of information about koji, all available in English.

JAPANESE WEB SITES AND BLOGS

INDIGO DAYS (WWW.INDIGODAYS.COM): My thoughts on life in Japan.

JUST HUNGRY (WWW.JUSTHUNGRY. COM): Maki Itoh, author of *Just Bento*, blogs from the south of France about all things Japanese, mainly food. The most comprehensive Japanese food blog around.

SAKE-WORLD (WWW.SAKE-WORLD.COM): John Gauntner's exhaustive Web site on sake. A longtime resident of Japan, John is the undisputed expert.

WITH A GLASS (WWW.WITHAGLASS.COM): An extremely well-written blog by a multinational young woman nicknamed "Sissi." While not exclusively about Japanese food, Sissi is a huge Japanophile and many of her posts have some sort of Japanese slant.

SHIZUOKA GOURMET (SHIZUOKAGOURMET.COM): An extensive collection of posts, mostly in relation to Japanese food, written regularly since 2007 by a Shizuoka-based expat.

HIROYUKI'S BLOG ON JAPANESE COOKING (HIRO-SHIO.BLOGSPOT.JP): An engaging bilingual blog written by a prolific Japanese man living in Japan who obviously loves to cook and enjoys sharing with the English-speaking world.

COOKING WITH KOJI (WWW. COOKINGWITHKOJI.WORDPRESS.COM): A blog jam-packed with many home-style recipes, written by a young Japanese woman living in Melbourne, Australia, who uses top-quality ingredients and makes her own soy sauce and miso.

COOKPAD.COM (ENGLISH SITE) (EN. COOKPAD.COM): The English version of Japan's largest recipe search engine communities. Recipes are submitted by readers, so beware of fluctuations in quality or authenticity. By all appearances, the recipes have been translated by a human being and not a computer, thus are understandable.

RAKUTEN GLOBAL MARKET

After the publisher had sent this book manuscript to the copy editor, I set to work on compiling the Resources section, and in the midst of that, stumbled upon Rakuten Global Market. Finally. A method for people living abroad to order almost every artisanal Japanese ingredient that I use in my kitchen! After spending all day looking into the nooks and crannies of Rakuten Global Market and delving deeply into how Rakuten functioned, I printed off almost 100 pages of great foods to recommend.

HERE IS WHAT I FOUND: Searching in English on the English Web site does not work. Searching in Japanese characters does because the same items listed in Rakuten Global Market are also listed in the Japanese site (rakuten.co.jp). I have explained this glitch to Rakuten Global Market, and hopefully it will be fixed by the time you try to use it. Another important point to understand is that because translation software was used, often the names of products are nonsensical. Without knowledge of Japanese, the site can prove frustrating, but it is worth persevering if you are interested in getting the best Japanese products.

Rakuten Global Market is an umbrella over a series of shops, all of which require checking out of and paying separately. Some shops do not ship overseas, but there are forwarding services that will. Otherwise it is cheapest to have the individual shops ship you directly, since the forwarder does not consolidate shipments, and you have to pay for their service. Most companies send via EMS (Japan Post's express

mail service), which is reliable but not cheap. The price gets progressively lower in the larger boxes. For instance, an 11-pound box will set you back $83, but a 50-pound box only $287. Shipping charges are not calculated until after you submit your order, so you will be contacted to approve shipping. However, if a large number of foreign customers consistently cancel orders, the shops will stop shipping overseas directly and require using a forwarder.

The best strategy is to find a few shops and stick with those for the bulk of your ordering. Navigation within the shop is a bit tedious but doable once you ferret out where the items you want are hiding. Be warned: The location of products is not always self-evident, and there are multiple dropdown menus. After about 12 solid hours, I had it licked, however. Some shops list their Japanese name in parentheses after their English name; some just use English. Since at this time it is impossible to search for these shops by name, advice on how to find them in Rakuten Global Market (GLOBAL.RAKUTEN.COM/EN) follows.

RECOMMENDED SHOPS

YUUKIYA0097(有機家): This shop ("organic house") has by far the largest percentage of ingredients that I use daily. Several sea salts, Yamaki soy sauce and miso (including their miso-making kit), fish sauce, a wide range of organic vinegars, including Iio Jozo Fuji brand, soybeans and soymilk (as well as other tofu and natto products, which probably cannot be shipped overseas), *niboshi* and other dried fish, every type of konbu mentioned in this book, nori, 7-spice powder, several different yuzu kosho, real wasabi paste, organic shio koji, various organic teas, dried shiitake, daikon threads, sesame seeds, organic roasted soybean flour and rice, organic rapeseed and sesame oils, and Matsuda Mayonnaise to boot. To search: Go to the main page of Global Rakuten Market and select Food & Drinks from the drop-down menu. From there, select Food. On the front page there will be a group of photos. Select Soy Sauce from the Seasoning section. You should be able to see a black-labeled bottle of soy sauce with purple writing (Yamaki), and it should be offered by this shop: yuukiya0097.

SHIZENKAN(PURE·HEART自然館): The main reason to purchase from Shizenkan is for their sesame seeds. They seem to be the only shop that carries nonroasted gold sesame seeds (*kingoma*, 金ごま) and whole dried Japanese red peppers. All of the following ingredients are available through Yuukiya, but if you wanted to fill up a box, here is what Shizenkan can offer: plum salt, most varieties of Iio Jozo Fuji vinegar (including their premium), Uchibori brown rice vinegar, organic white plum blossom vinegar, Japanese dried shrimp (*sakura ebi*, page XXIX), ma konbu, *mozuku* (page XXX), handmade 7-spice powder, shio koji, Japanese rapeseed oil, and Matsuda Mayonnaise. To search: Go to the main page of Global Rakuten Market and select Food & Drinks from the drop-down menu. From there, select Food. On the front page there will be a group of photos. Select Soy Sauce from the Seasoning section. One of the bottles offered on the first or second page will be by this shop: shizenkan.

MAGUU*S SHOP: Maguu is the only shop in Rakuten to stock red vinegar (page 165), well worth an order here for the chance to taste this ancient product. Maguu also carries some interesting salts: one from Christmas Island and another one infused with roasted seaweed ("burning" seaweed), as well as small bottles of an unusual sockeye salmon red pepper fish sauce, several yuzu kosho, and "economical" konbu. To search: From Food, select Seasoning, then in Vinegars, the Others section. Be patient: I found this vinegar on page 8; look for NAPIA (ナピア) and the name of this shop: magimaguu.

KENKO EXPRESS: I was stunned to find the oil I use on Rakuten and HIGHLY recommend trying to lay some in. You will not be disappointed. This oil is made by Yonezawa manufacturing and it is pristinely lovely. Kenko sells it in 3-pound (1400-gram) cans for $13.77. While Kenko also carries various dried fish and seaweeds, I would be inclined to just order oil for ease of packing. To search: From Food, select Seasoning, then in Oil, Rape Oil. I found the oil on page 2: It is in a light-colored can and has a green label with a cluster of yellow rape flowers; the shop's name is listed as: kenkoex.

TOKUSANHIN-CLUB: Tokusanhin is the only shop to carry the organic ginger ale I am addicted to. They also have a lovely persimmon vinegar and whole dried squid. To search: From Food, select Seasoning, then in Vinegar, Fruit Vinegars. I found the persimmon vinegar sold by Tokusanhin on page 3, but that could change. Several other shops stock this vinegar, so look for the name: tokusan-hin.

SATUMAYA (味は芸術 「薩摩屋本店」): This shop is the answer to your search for all marine-related foods such as katsuobushi, *niboshi*, *ago* (page XXIX), whole dried squid, konbu, and nori. You can also find a katsuobushi shaver here. To search: Go to the main page of Global Rakuten Market and select Food & Drinks from the drop-down menu. From there, select Food. On the front page there will be a group of photos. Select Dried Bonito from the Dried Food section. Some form of katsuobushi sold by Satumaya should appear on the first or second page; look for: satumaya.

ISEOTO (伊勢音): Another excellent source for marine-related foods, it carries everything Satumaya does except the *ago* (dried juvenile flying fish). Compare the prices and products and make your own decision. To search: From Food, select Dried Food, then in Dried Foods, Squids. A simple photo of 10 squid (cuttlefish) banded together should appear on the first or second page, sold by: iseto.

SUMISAKURA (炭・備長炭・オガ炭 サクラ産業): Here is THE source for Japanese charcoal and barbecue sets. Charcoal can be ordered in large or small lots; also they band the boxes together to keep shipping costs down. Sumisakura sells bamboo ware such as spoons, bowls, and bento boxes as well as bamboo charcoal for natural room deodorizing. Beyond that they feature a nice wooden katsuobushi shaving box and a wooden ridged daikon grater. Once you get to the shop, navigate by Selecting Kitchen, Dining & Bar from All Categories, and then Others. To search: From Food, select Seafood, then Others. A round *shichinrin* tabletop barbecue and some Tosa bincho charcoal were listed on page 1 under the name: sumisakura.

GETPLUS RAKUTEN MARKET STORE: Here is where you can find limited-time bargains on some staple items such as Yamaki soy sauce and miso, "Davy Jones/Sea Nymph" salt, and domestic rapeseed oil, Sokensha. To search: From Food, select Seasoning, then in Oil, Rape Oil. I found the "domestic rapeseed oil" being sold on Getplus Rakuten here on the second page, but since these are sale items, there is no guarantee you will find this elusive store as easily as I did. My best advice: Look for staple items and the shop name: getplus.

BIBLIOGRAPHY

Hisamatsu, Ikuko. *Quick & Easy Tsukemono*. Tokyo: Boutique-sha, Inc., 2005.

Homma, Gaku. *The Folk Art of Japanese Country Cooking*. Berkeley: North Atlantic Books, 1991.

Lee, Florence C. and Helen C. *Kimchi*. Elizabeth: Hollym Corporation, 1988.

Marks, Copeland, and Kim, Manjo. *The Korean Kitchen*. San Francisco: Chronicle Books, 1993.

Millon, Marc and Kim. *Flavours of Korea*. London: André Deutsch Limited, 1991.

Ogawa, Seiko. *Easy Japanese Pickling in Five Minutes to One Day*. Tokyo: Graph-Sha Ltd., 2003.

Shimizu, Kay. *Tsukemono*. Tokyo: Shufunotomo Co., Ltd, 1993.

Shurtleff, William, and Aoyagi, Akiko. *The Book of Miso*. New York: Ballantine Books, 1976.

Shurtleff, William, and Aoyagi, Akiko. *The Book of Tofu*. Berkeley: Ten Speed Press, 1975.

Tsuji, Shizuo. *Japanese Cooking: A Simple Art*. Tokyo: Kodansha International Ltd., 1980.

Wise, Victoria. *The Vegetarian Table*. San Francisco: Chronicle Books, 1998.

杵島直美。いつもの野菜でささっと漬けもの。東京：家の光協会、２００８。

杵島直美。つけもの漬けよっ。東京：主婦と生活社、２００５。

metric equivalents and conversions

APPROXIMATE METRIC EQUIVALENTS

VOLUME

¼ teaspoon	1 milliliter
½ teaspoon	2.5 milliliters
¾ teaspoon	4 milliliters
1 teaspoon	5 milliliters
1¼ teaspoons	6 milliliters
1½ teaspoons	7.5 milliliters
1¾ teaspoons	8.5 milliliters
2 teaspoons	10 milliliters
1 tablespoon (½ fluid ounce)	15 milliliters
2 tablespoons (1 fluid ounce)	30 milliliters
¼ cup	60 milliliters
⅓ cup	80 milliliters
½ cup (4 fluid ounces)	120 milliliters
⅔ cup	160 milliliters
¾ cup	180 milliliters
1 cup (8 fluid ounces)	240 milliliters
1¼ cups	300 milliliters
1½ cups (12 fluid ounces)	360 milliliters
1⅔ cups	400 milliliters
2 cups (1 pint)	460 milliliters
3 cups	700 milliliters
4 cups (1 quart)	0.95 liter
1 quart plus ¼ cup	1 liter
4 quarts (1 gallon)	3.8 liters

METRIC CONVERSION FORMULAS

TO CONVERT	MULTIPLY
Ounces to grams	Ounces by 28.35
Pounds to kilograms	Pounds by 0.454
Teaspoons to milliliters	Teaspoons by 4.93
Tablespoons to milliliters	Tablespoons by 14.79
Fluid ounces to milliliters	Fluid ounces by 29.57
Cups to milliliters	Cups by 236.59
Cups to liters	Cups by 0.236
Pints to liters	Pints by 0.473
Quarts to liters	Quarts by 0.946
Gallons to liters	Gallons by 3.785
Inches to centimeters	Inches by 2.54

OVEN TEMPERATURES

To convert Fahrenheit to Celsius, subtract 32 from Fahrenheit, multiply the result by 5, then divide by 9.

DESCRIPTION	FAHRENHEIT	CELSIUS	BRITISH GAS MARK
Very cool	200°	95°	0
Very cool	225°	110°	¼
Very cool	250°	120°	½
Cool	275°	135°	1
Cool	300°	150°	2
Warm	325°	165°	3
Moderate	350°	175°	4
Moderately hot	375°	190°	5
Fairly hot	400°	200°	6
Hot	425°	220°	7
Very hot	450°	230°	8
Very hot	475°	245°	9

Information compiled from a variety of sources, including *Recipes into Type* by Joan Whitman and Dolores Simon (Newton, MA: Biscuit Books, 1993); *The New Food Lover's Companion* by Sharon Tyler Herbst (Hauppauge, NY: Barron's, 2013); and *Rosemary Brown's Big Kitchen Instruction Book* (Kansas City, MO: Andrews McMeel, 1998).

index

A

Abe, Saori, 258, 334
abura age. See usuage
aburi, XXIX
Aedan Fermented Foods, 73, 349
aged "black" vinegar, 152–53
ago (juvenile flying fish), XXIX
Air-Dried Sardines, 38–**39**
air-dried squid (*surume ika*), XXIX
aka miso (red miso), 72
Akaike, Riki, **149**, 152–53
Akajiso no Shiomomi, **19**
Akasha Cocktail, 320
Akasha no Kakute-ru, 320
Akasha Restaurant, 320
albacore, pickling, 346
alliums, 339, 342
Amasu, 151
Amazake, XXXII, 313
Amazon, XVII, XVIII, XXIII, XXVIII, 4, 250, 251, 348
Amazon.co.jp, 351
anchovies, XXVII, 346
Andante Dairy, 148
anticipation (*tanoshimini*), 307
Anzen Hiroshi, XXIII
Aoi Kimuchi, 289
aonori seaweed, XXX
apple pear (*nashi*), 344
  Apple Pears in Miso, 60
Arai, Hiroyuki, 321
arai kezuri (thickly shaved katsuobushi), XXIX
arame seaweed, XXX
aromatics, 343
Artisan Sake Maker, 302
arugula, 75
Asari, Joei, 194
Asari, Myoho, 70, 187, 189, 192, **194**–197, 202, 352

Asari, Ryotoku, 194
asazuke (morning pickles), 36
asparagus, pickling, 345
Aspergillus glaucus, 250, 259
Aspergillus oryzae. See koji
Astor Wines, 303
atsukan (warm sake), 300
Australia resources, 351
Austria resources, 351
Avocado no Shiokoji-ae, 197
Avocado with Shio Koji Dressing, 197
awamori (Okinawan distilled alcohol), 303

B

Baachan (grandmother), 18, 238, 242, 243, 244
Baachan no Hoshinasu, 18
Baachan's Dried Eggplant, 18
Baby Turnips with Salt-Wilted Greens, 5–**7**
Bacillus natto, XXIX
bancha, 305, 306
banno bocho, XXII
barley miso (mugi miso), 72
barley tea (*mugicha*), XXXII, 307, 332
barracuda, **37**
The Barrel Maker, **54–56**
benriner (Japanese mandoline), XXIII
Bernstein, Max, 68, 197
bitter greens (*mibuna, takana*), 341, 345
bitter melon (*goya/nigauri*), **340**, 345
  Bitter Melon Koji Pickles, **191**
bitter orange (*daidai*), 343
  Bitter Orange Red Kosho, 281
bitter salad greens. *See* mizuna
Bitterman, Mark, XXVII

bittern (*nigari*), XXVIII, 10
biwa (loquat), 344
  "black" tea (*kocha*), XXXII, 305, 306, 322, 326–**27**
black vinegar (*kurosu*), XXVIII, 152–**53**
black walnuts (*onigurumi*), XXXII
Blue Grass Soy Sauce, XXVII, 91
Blue & White, XIX, 352
Boberosa Barnworks, 350
Bob's Red Mill Rice Bran, 188
bok choy, pickling, 345
bonito, pickling, 346
Bourbon Barrel Foods, 349
bowls, Japanese (*hachi*), XVIII
  grinding (*suribachi*), X, XVII–XVIII, 49
  kneading (*konebachi*), XVIII, **48**, 49–50
  pouring (*kataguchi*), XVIII
Brackett, Sylvan Mishima, 5, 23, 213, 285
brazier, charcoal warming (hibachi), XVI, 41
Breakaway Matcha, XXXII, 305, 350
Brewed Green Tea, **324**–325
bride (*oyome*), V
broccoli, 345
  Broccoli in Soy Sauce with Red Pepper, 92
The Brooklyn Kitchen, XVII, 305, 309, 350–51
Brown, Everett Kennedy, 177
brown rice (*genmai*), XXXIII
brown rice miso (genmai miso), 72
  Homemade Brown Rice Miso, 51
brown rice vinegar, XXVIII
Brown's Field, 177, 352
brushes, Japanese
  bamboo (*take burashi*), XVIII
  hemp palm–bristled (*tawashi*), XVII

buckwheat tea (*sobacha*), XXXII, 307
  Buckwheat Tea, 333
bunka bocho (everyday knife), XXII
burdock. *See* gobo
Buri no Shoyukoji-zuke, **206**
Burokkori no Shoyuzuke, 92
Buta no Kakuni Daikon to Negi soe, 161–**62**
Buta no Shiokoji-zuke, **200**–1
byobu (framed standing screens), XIII

C

cabbage, 345. *See also* napa cabbage
Cachette Ikegami, 310
Cainoya, 255
calligraphy paper, XVI
Campbell, Bill, VIII
Campbell, Christine, VIII
canola oil, XXXIII
carrots, 345
  Carrot Salad with Miso Vinaigrette, **83**
  Cucumbers with Carrot Threads, 289
cast iron kettles (*tetsubin*), XIX, XXII
cast iron ware, XIX
cauliflower, pickling, 345
celery, pickling, 345
Central Market, 280
cha dansu (tea cupboard), XIII
Chabushi, **260–61**
charcoal (*sumi*). *See also* Tea Ceremony Charcoal
  cast iron starter (*hiokoshi*), XVI
  grill (*shichirin*), VII, XVI, 42
  hearth, sunken (*irori*), XVI
  warming brazier (hibachi), XVI, 41
chayote, pickling, 345

Chef's Armoury, xix, 351
cherry blossoms, iv
    Salted Cherry Blossoms, **22–23**
chests and cupboards, Japanese
    (*tansu*), x
    clothes (*yofuku dansu*), xiii
    kitchen (*mizuya dansu*), xiii
    screened (*haicho*), xiii
    stair (*kaidan dansu*), xiii
    tea (*cha dansu*), xiii
Chez Panisse, 5, 70, 197, 220, 233,
    284, 309, 317
chicken, 212
chile peppers (*togarashi*), xxxi,
    279–80, **281**
    Bitter Orange Red Kosho, 281
    Chile Pepper Cod Eggs, 282–**83**
    Raw Squid in Coral, **286–88**
chiles, xxxi
Chin, Siew-Chinn (The Ramen
    Shop), 20
chirimin jako (larval-stage teeny
    fishes), xxix
choko (sake cup), 299, **300**
Chopped Vinegared Flying Fish,
    158
Chromatic Coffee, 332
CIA Worlds of Flavor Japan, 102
citrus, 343
clams, pickling, 347
Clearspring, xxviii, 73, 351
cloth
    bolt (*sarashi*), xiii
    carrying (*furoshiki*), xiii
    hand (*tenugui*), xiii, 160
cocktails
    Akasha Cocktail, 320
    Sour Plum Cordial Cocktail,
        318–**19**
cod, 346
    Chile Pepper Cod Eggs, 282–**83**
Cold Barley Tea, 332
Cold Miso Soup with Cucumber
    and Myoga, 82
Cold Mountain Miso, 51, 73, 349
Cold-Infused Tea, **328**
Cooking with Koji, 352
Cookpad.com, 352
cordials, 317–**19**
corms, 231
corn, pickling, 345
Corti, Darrel (Corti Brothers,
    Sacramento, CA), 303
country miso (inaka miso), 72
Country Miso and Vegetable Soup,
    80–**81**

Country Soup Flavored Four Ways,
    138–**39**
crab, pickling, 347
craftsman. *See Shokunin*
Cubed Daikon and Garlic Chives,
    276, 292–**93**
cucumbers (*kyuri*), **340**. *See also
    narazuke*
    Cold Miso Soup with Cucumber
        and Myoga, 82
    Cucumbers Soused in Soy, 101
    Cucumbers with Carrot Threads,
        289
    pickling, 345
    Smashed Cucumbers with Sour
        Plum, **169**
culinary chrysanthemum greens
    (*shungiku*), 341
Cultures for Health, xvii, xxviii, 51,
    231, 240, 349

D

daidai (bitter orange), 343
Daidai Kosho, 281
daiginjo sake, 301
daikon, 339, 345
    Cubed Daikon and Garlic
        Chives, **276**, 292–**93**
    Daikon in Fish Sauce, 125
    Daikon Pickled with Smashed
        Persimmons, 179
    Dried Daikon Threads, 16–**17**
    Fish Sauce–Broiled Daikon, 135
    Half-Dried Daikon Pickled in
        Rice Bran, **216–18**
    Napa Cabbage with Shredded
        Daikon, 290–**91**
    Pork Belly Simmered with
        Daikon and Leeks, 161–**62**
Daikon no Asazuke, 125
Daikon no Ishiri Yaki, 135
daily life and tradition
    chiles and mustard, xxxi
    cloth and paper, xiii–xvi
    dried fish, xxix
    fermented and distilled liquids,
        xxxi–xxxii
    fire vessels and tools, xvi
    house, xii–xiii
    knives, xxii–xxiii
    oils, xxxiii
    pantry, xxiii, xxvii
    pickling containers and
        accoutrements, xvii
    pickling mediums, xxviii
    rice, xxxiii

rice- and soup-related, xviii–xix
salt-related, xxvii–xxviii
seaweed, xxx
seeds and nuts, xxxii
soybeans, xxviii–xxix
sugars, xxxiii
tea-related, xix, xxii
teas and infusions, xxxii
vegetables, seeds, beans and
    dough, xvii–xviii
vinegars, xxviii
dashi, 265. *See also* konbu
    Dashi Vinegar, 151
    Katsuobushi Dashi, **253**
    Niboshi Dashi, 249, 274
    Tomato and Eggplant in Dashi,
        254
    vegetarian, 18
Dashizuke no Hatahata Himono,
    270–**72**
dasshi kako daizu (processed
    defatted soybeans), 89
Dean & Deluca, 146
deba bocho (fish knife), xxii
Dencler, Amy, 220, 233
doburoku (homemade sake), 149,
    301
Doburoku, 311-12
doma (earthen room), xii
donabe (ceramic casserole-style
    vessel), xviii–xix
doors, Japanese
    sliding (*shoji*), x, xi, xii
    thousand-slatted sliding
        (*senbongoshi*), xii
    wooden-framed, papered
        sliding (*fusuma*), xi, xii
dressing, shio koji, 197
dried, smoked skipjack tuna. *See*
    katsuobushi
Dried Daikon Threads, 16–**17**
dried fish, xxix. *See also* Wajima
    Air-Dried Fish
Dried Persimmons, 180–**81**
drop lid (*otoshi buta*), xvii

E

edamame (young soybeans), 340
Edamame Cropping Slow Food, 78
Eden Foods, xxiii, xxvii, xxviii, xxx,
    xxxiii, 73, 91, 146, 147, 348
Edo period, xxvii
eggplant (*nasu*), 340, 345
    Baachan's Dried Eggplant, 18
    Eggplant Pickled in Soy Mustard,
        103

Fish Sauce–Simmered Eggplant,
    132–33
    Salted Eggplant with Myoga and
        Shiso, 26–**27**
    Tomato and Eggplant in Dashi,
        254
eggs. *See also* cod; mullet eggs;
    salmon roe
    Miso-Cured Eggs, II, **66–68**

F

failure, fear of, ix
fava beans, pickling, 345
fermented and distilled liquids,
    xxxi–xxxii
Fermented Napa Cabbage, 11–**13**
fermented soybeans, xxix
fermented squid guts (*Ika no
    Shiokara*), 284–85, **286–88**
fermenting, viii
fiddlehead ferns (*warabi*), 342
    Fiddlehead Ferns Drizzled with
        Soy Dashi, 265
figs (*ichijiku*), 344
    Sake Lees Ice Cream with Figs,
        215
fiori di sale, xxvii
The Fire, xi
fire vessels and tools, xvi
fish, xxix, 346–47. *See also specific
    type*
    Shoyu Koji–Marinated
        Yellowtail, **206**
    Wajima Air-Dried Fish, **35–36**
fish nukazuke, 36, 224–**25**
fish sauce (*gyosho*), xxvii–xxviii,
    119–21. *See also ishiri; ishiru;
    shottsuru*
    Country Soup Flavored Four
        Ways, 138–**39**
    Daikon in Fish Sauce, 125
    Fish Sauce Fried Rice, 140–41
    Fish Sauce–Broiled Daikon, 135
    Fish Sauce–Simmered Eggplant,
        132–33
    Myoga Pickled with Fish Sauce,
        128–**29**
    making, **122–23**
    pickling fruits and vegetables,
        345–46
    Sandfish Nabe, 136–37
    Tofu Doused in Fish Sauce, 124
fleur de sel, xxvii, 3
flounder, **268–69**
flowering tops (*nanohana*), 341
flying fish, 346

Chopped Vinegared Flying Fish, **158**

juvenile (*ago*), XXIX

Fonte di Dio, 321

Food & Wine, 192, 309

food-grade plastic bag (*poly bukuro*), XVII

food-grade plastic tubs (*poly taru*), XVII

forgiveness, viii

France resources, 351

Frantoio Grove olive oil (Jeffrey Martin), 135

French Farmhouse Cookbook (Loomis), 3

fried rice

Fish Sauce Fried Rice, 140–41

Frog Eyes Wasabi, 350

fruits, 344, 345, 346. *See also* citrus; *specific fruit*

Fujisu vinegar, VI, 146, 159

Fuji TV, VI, VII–VIII, 70, 259

Fujimien (tea), **304–6**, 322–**323**, 326, 327

fuki (giant butterbur), 342, 351

Fukushima Daichi Nuclear Reactor meltdown, 299, 304

Funaba, Kazuo, 42

Funaba, Shinichi, **40**

Funaba, Yoneko, 41

Funaba Shichirin, **40–42**

Funahashi, Ayumi, XV, 71

Funakoshi, Masayo, **232**, **235**, 334

funayaku bocho, XXII

furikake, XXIX

furoshiki (carrying cloth), XIII

Furukawa, Kazuki, **40**

Furuta, Hima, 14, 352

fusuma (wooden-framed, papered sliding doors), XI, XII

Fuyu persimmons, 147

G

gampi, XIII

Gardener's Supply Company, XVII, 350

Gari, 156

garlic, **62**, 63–**64**, 319, 345

Garlic Embedded in Miso, **61**

New Garlic and Miso, **63–64**

garlic chives (*nira*), 343

Cubed Daikon and Garlic Chives, **276**, 292–**93**

Gekkeikan, 297

Gelb, David, XXIV

gender equality, VII

genmai (brown rice), XXXIII

genmai miso (brown rice miso), 72

genmaicha, 306

Germany resources, 351

Getplus Rakuten Market Store, 354

giant butterbur (*fuki*), 342

ginger

Ginger-Soy Pork Sandwiches, **108–10**

Shishito Peppers Sautéed with Miso and Ginger, **84–85**

Thinly Sliced Ginger Pickles, **156**

ginger ale, 321

ginjo sake, 301

glutinous rice (*mochigome*), XXXIII

gobo (burdock), 339, 345

gochutgaru (Korean ground red chile powder), XXXI

Gold Mine Natural Food Co., XXIII, XXVII, XXVIII, XXX, 72, 73, 348, 349

Goya no Kojizuke, 191

goya/nigauri. See bitter melon

grandmother. *See* Baachan

granita, 316

grater

wasabi (*wasabi oroshi*), XVIII

grating

plate for (*oroshigane*), XVIII

tool for (*oroshiki*), XVIII

green beans, 345

Green Beans Cloaked in Miso, **59**

green peppers, pickling, 345

green tea (*ryokucha*), XXXII, 298, 305

Brewed Green Tea, **324–25**

Powdered Green Tea, 331

greens, 341

Baby Turnips with Salt-Wilted Greens, 5–**7**

culinary chrysanthemum, 341

guinomi (sake cup), 299, **300**

gyokuro, 305

Gyokusendo, XXV–XXVI

gyosho. See fish sauce

H

hachi. See bowls, Japanese

Hachisu, Andrew (son), 111

Hachisu, Christopher (son), X, 8, 303

Hachisu, Matthew (son), 127

Hachisu, Mitsu (grandmother of tofu shop), 249

Hachisu, Nancy Singleton, IX, 81, **338**

about, IV

air-drying fish, 35

chopping mustard, 15

with daikon threads, 17

with dog, XXI

in kitchen, VII, 291, 293

making miso, 48, **72**

making miso squid, 77

making *myoga* pickles, 129

making soy sauce, 93, 95, 99

at market, 130

at sake brewery, 310

with shiso buds, 21

Hachisu, Noriaki (brother-in-law), 336

Hachisu, Tadaaki (husband), VII, XX, 140

doburoku, 311

as farming pioneer, 242

on garlic, 63, 64

kabura zushi recipe, 207–8

soybeans, growing and buying, 229

using *arai kezuri*, 250

Hachiya persimmons, 147

Hagiwara, Rise, XV

haicho (screened cupboard), XIII

hakusai. See napa cabbage

Hakusai Kimuchi, 290–**91**

Hakusai no Tsukemono, 11–**13**

Half Moon Bay Wasabi Company, 350

Half-Dried Barracuda, **37**

Half-Dried Daikon Pickled in Rice Bran, 216–**18**

halibut, pickling, 347

Hallowell, Charlie, 20, 114

hanakatsuo (pinky-tan katsuobushi shavings), XXIX

handai (wooden tub), XIX

Harigaya, Asako, 93

Harigaya, Takeshi, 93

Haruko, 131

hasami (iron scissors), XXIII

Hatcho miso, 73

Ha-Wasabi no Tsukemono, 98

hazakaiki (edge of season), 63

hearth, sunken charcoal (*irori*), XVI

Heirloom Onions, 8, 350

hemp palm–bristled brush (*tawashi*), XVII

herring, 347

Semidried Herring, **43**

hibachi (charcoal warming brazier), XVI, 41

Hida Takayama, 127

Hida Tool & Hardware Co., Inc., XXII, 350

hijiki seaweed, XXX

himono (semi-air-dried fish and seafood), 35–**39**

hiokoshi (cast iron charcoal starter), XVI

Hirame no Kobujime, 268–69

Hirokami, Yuko, 79

Hiroyuki's Blog on Japanese Cooking, 352

Hiyacha, 328

hiziki. See hijiki seaweed

hocho, See knives, Japanese

Hodo Soy soft tofu, 230

hojicha (roasted green tea), XXXII, 306

hojiso. See shiso buds

Hojiso no Shiomomi, 20–21

Homemade Brown Rice Miso, **51**

Homemade Ginger Ale, **321**

Homemade Konnyaku, 244–**45**

Homemade Sake, 311–12

Homemade Soy Milk, **235**

honjozo sake, 301

Horibata, Hiroshi, **56**

horigotatsu (warming table over a square hole in a floor), XIII

Horiuchi, Hayato, **107**

horse mackerel, pickling, 347

Hoshigaki, 180–**181**

Hosokawa *washi*, XVI

Hot Table Natto, 240–**41**

Hotei Wines, viii

hoya (sea squirt), 28

Hunter, Angler, Gardener, Cook blog, 265

I

IACP culinary conference, 320

ice cream, 215

ichijiku. See figs

ichimi togarashi (ground red chile powder), XXXI

Iijima, Goushi, 304–5, 306, 322–23, 326

Iio, Akihiro, 148, 159–**60**, 165, 270

Iio Jozo, VI, 32, 146, 148, 153, 159–**60**, 165, 189, 224, 270

Ika no Ichiyaboshi, 30

Ika no Misozuke, 76–77

Ika no Shiokara (fermented squid guts), 286–**88**

ikebana (flower arranging), 290

Ikegami, Haruki, 310

Ikezumi, Takako, 35

Ikura no Shoyuzuke, 104–5
Imai, Kaoruko, **71**, **107**
Imai, Rintaro, **107**
Imayotsukasa sake (Niigata), **300**, 302, **308–10**, 352
Imperial Cuisine (Kyutei Ryori), 28
inaka miso (country miso), 72
Inaka no Miso Shiru, 80–81
Indigo Days, 352
Ingenmame no Misozuke, 59
Intangible Cultural Heritage List, xvi, 107
International Terakoya, 352
iriko. See niboshi
iron kettles (*tetsubin*), xix
iron pots (*tetsunabe*), xix
iron scissors (*hasami*), xxiii
irori (sunken charcoal hearth), xvi
Iseoto, 354
ishiri, xxvii, **120**. *See also* fish sauce
ishiru, xxvii, 36, **120**. *See also* fish sauce
Ishiru Chahan, 140–41
isshobin (1.8-liter bottles), 299
itado. See fusuma
I-turn, ix
Iwafune, 33
Iwasaki, Yozo, 99. *See also* soy sauce
iwashi (anchovies or sardines), xxvii
Iwashi no Himono, 38–39
izushi, 208

J

Japan Bargain, xvi, 350
Japan Centre, 351
Japan Local Innovator's Committee, 14
Japan resources, 351–52
Japanese cress (*seri*), 342
Japanese eggplants. *See* eggplant
Japanese Farm Food, v, 20, 27, 55, 78, 93, 233, 244
Japanese "leeks" (negi), 340, **342**, 346
Japanese mandoline (benriner), xxiii
Japanese mustard (*komatsuna*), 341
Japanese paper (*washi*), xii, xiii, xv, xvi
Japanese "Red" Tea, 326–27
Japanese shallots. *See* rakkyo
Japanese sugar (*wasanbon*), xxxiii
Japanese websites and blogs, 352
Jiro Dreams of Sushi, xxiv
jizaikagi (giant hook), xvi
Jones, Sharon, 177, 259, 309–10

jo-on (room temperature), 300
Jorinji, 73, 349
junmai daiginjo sake, 300
junmai ginjo sake, 301
junmai sake, 301
Just Hungry, 352

K

kabocha (winter squash), 340, 345
  Kabocha in Miso with Red Pepper, **58**
  Kabocha Tempura with Three-Way Vinegar, 163–**64**
Kabocha no Misozuke, **58**
Kabocha no Tempura Sanbaisu-de, 163–**64**
Kabu no Shiozuke, 5–**7**
Kabu no Umezuke, 170–71
Kabu to Kaki no Namasu, 157
kabura zushi, 207–8
Kagoshima
  black vinegar, 152–53
  katsuobushi in, 255–59
kaidan dansu (stair chest), xiii
kaiseki, roots of, 28
kaki. See persimmons
Kakisu, 177–**78**
Kakuida, vi, 75, **148**–**150**, 152–**153**
kamado (brick or earthenware stove), xvi
Kamasu no Himono, **37**
kame (lidded ceramic pot), xvii, ix, **50**
Kanchan. *See* Nakatani, Kanji
Kaneko, Yoshinori, xiv
karashi (oriental mustard powder), xxxi
karashina (mustard greens), 341
Karashina no Shira-ae, 182–**83**
Karasumi, 29
karin. See quince
Karinshu, 317
kataguchi (pouring bowls), xviii
Katchan. *See* Nagano, Katsue
Katoh, Amy, 352
katsuobushi (skipjack tuna, fermented and sun-dried), vi, xxix, 249–50, **263**. *See also* Sakai Katsuobushi
  in Kagoshima, 255–59
  Katsuobushi and Tea Soup, 260–61
  Katsuobushi Dashi, **253**
  Katsuobushi Miso, 263
  Katsuobushi with Soy Sauce, 262

Tomato and Eggplant in Dashi, 254
  Tosa Onions, **264**
katsuobushi kezuriki (wooden shaving box), xxix, **253**, 263
Katz, Sandor, viii
kelp. *See* konbu
Kelp-Wicked Flounder, 268–**69**
Kenchinjiru, 138–**39**
Kenko Express, 354
Kenow, Alyssia, xv, **99**
Kikkawa (home of Murakamisake dried salmon), 31–**32**
Kikkoman, xxvii, 89, 91
Kiln restaurant, 334
kimchee, 280. *See also* chile peppers
  Cubed Daikon and Garlic Chives, **276**, 292–**93**
  Cucumbers with Carrot Threads, 289
  Napa Cabbage with Shredded Daikon, 290–**91**
  pickling fruits and vegetables, 345–46
kin goma (gold sesame seeds), xxxii
Kinezuka family, 305, 350
kinkan (kumquat), 344
Kinkan no Sake-ni, 314–**15**
Kiriboshi Daikon, 16–**17**
Kitani, Tomio, 82, 106–**7**
Kitazawa Seed Co., 350
kitchen. *See* doma
kitchen equipment, resources, 350
Kkakdugi, 292, **293**
knives, Japanese, xxii, xxiii
  everyday (*bunka bocho: banno bocho, funayaku bocho, santoku bocho*), xxii
  fish (*deba bocho, sakana bocho*), xxii
  sashimi (*sashimi bocho: takobiki, yanagiba*) xxii–xxiii
Knowlton, Andrew, 27
kobore ume (mirin lees), 188
kobosu, 343
Kobu no Tsukudani, 273
kocha ("black" tea), xxxii, 305, 306, 322, 326–**327**
Koda Farms, xxvii, 349
Kogure, Yusaku, xv
koji (*aspegillus oryzae*), xxiii, xxviii, 187–88
  Avocado with Shio Koji Dressing, 197
  Bitter Melon Koji Pickles, **191**

making, 189–**90**
  resources, 349
  Shio Koji, 182, 192
  Shio Koji–Grilled Pork, 200–1
  Shio Koji–Marinated Salmon, **199**
  Shio Koji–Pickled Onion, 193
  Shio Koji–Sautéed Shiitake, 198
  Shoyu Koji, 182, 192, 202
  Shoyu Koji–Marinated Yellowtail, 206
  Tomato Wedges Drizzled with Shoyu Koji, 204–5
  Zucchini Pickled in Shoyu Koji, 203
Kojiya Honten, 187, 189, 352
The Kojiya Woman. *See* Asari, Myoho
Komatsubara, Megumi, 93, 97
komatsuna (Japanese mustard), 341
Komatsuna no Tsukemono, ii, 14–**15**
kome. See rice
komesu. See rice vinegar
konacha, 306
konbu (kelp), xxx, 251–52
  Katsuobushi Dashi, **253**
  Kelp-Wicked Flounder, 268–**69**
  Konbu Dashi, 249, 266–**67**
  Konbu Dashi–Soused Sandfish, 270–**72**
  Sandfish Nabe, 136–37
  Soy Sauce–Simmered Konbu, 273
konbu tea (*konbucha*), xxxii, 307
konebachi (kneading bowl), xviii, **48**, 49–**50**
konjac. *See* konnyaku
Konjac Foods, 350
konnyaku, **211**, 231, 339
  Homemade Konnyaku, 244–**45**
  resources, 350
konro (tabletop cooking stove), xvi
Korean barbecue (*yakiniku*), 280
Korean ground red chile powder (*gochutgaru*), xxxi
Korin, xvi, xviii, xix, 350
korui shochu, 302
koshi abura (mountain vegetable), **342**
kosho (pepper), 279. *See also* yuzu kosho, daidai kosho
kotatsu (Japanese warming table), xiii
Kotatsu Natto, 240–41
kozo (paper mulberry), xiii
Kozono family, 305
Kubo Shotaro Washi, xvi

kukicha (stem tea), 306
kumquat (*kinkan*), 344
    Kumquats Simmered in Sake,
      314–15
    Salt-Distressed Mizuna with
      Kumquat, **24–25**
Kunikatsu Seto lacquerware, 126,
    127, **134**, **237**
kura (storage house), 64, 78–79
kuro goma (black sesame seeds),
    XXXII
Kuroshio Wasabi, 351
kurosu (black vinegar), XXVIII, 152–**53**
kurozato (Okinawan brown sugar),
    XXXIII
kusaya, 297
kyuri. *See* cucumbers
Kyuri no Shoyuzuke, 101
*Kyuri to Myoga no Hiyashi Miso
    Shiru*, 82
kyusu (teapots), XXII, **304**
Kyutei Ryori (Imperial Cuisine), 28

L

Larkin, John, **338**
Laura Soybeans, 230, 349
Leaves + Flowers, 305, 350
Lebovitz, David, 321
leeks. *See also* Japanese "leeks"
    Pork Belly Simmered with
      Daikon and Leeks, 161–**62**
lettuce, pickling, 345
Lexington Container Company,
    XVII, 351
Loomis, Susan Hermann, 3
loquat (*biwa*), 344
lotus root (*renkon*), 340, 345
Luce (Portland, OR), 316
Lundberg Family Farms, XXVII, 349

M

macrobiotic foods, 348, 352
magnesium chloride (*nigari*), XXVIII,
    10
Maguu*s Shop, 354
makuwa uri (small melon), 344
Makuwa-Uri no Sake Kasuzuke,
    209
Maldon salt, XXVII
mame miso (soybean miso), 73
Martin, Jeffrey, 135
Martin, Patrick, 332
Marukan, 146, 160
Massa Organics, XXXIII, 349
masu (wooden box), 300

matcha (powdered green tea), XXXII,
    306, 331
Matsuda, Masashi, 336, **338**
    making miso, 48, 49, 72
    making natto, 238
    mentor, motivator, friend,
      78–79, 81, 94, 189
Matsuda Mayonnaise, 78–79
Matsumura, Sho, xv
Matsunaga, Hitoshi, XXII
The Meadow, 4, 348
MegumiNATTO, XXIX, 231, 349
Meiji Tofu, XXVIII–XXIX, 182, 230
melons, **209**, 345. *See also* bitter
    melon: small melon
men, role of, vii–viii
Mentaiko, 282–**83**
METI. *See* Ministry of Economy,
    Trade, and Industry
mibuna (bitter greens), 341
mikan, 343, **344**
Mini Rice Balls with Sour Plum,
    172–74
Mini Umeboshi-ae Onigiri, **172–74**
Ministry of Economy, Trade, and
    Industry (METI), 284
mirin, XXXI
mirin lees (*kobore ume*), 188
miso, VI, XXVII, 47, **80**
    Apple Pears in Miso, 60
    Carrot Salad with Miso
      Vinaigrette, **83**
    choosing, storing, and using,
      71–73
    Cold Miso Soup with Cucumber
      and Myoga, 82
    Country Miso and Vegetable
      Soup, 80–81
    Garlic Embedded in Miso, **61**
    Green Beans Cloaked in Miso,
      59
    Homemade Brown Rice Miso,
      51–**53**
    Kabocha in Miso with Red
      Pepper, 58
    Katsuobushi Miso, 263
    making, **48–50**
    Miso-Cured Eggs, II, **66–68**
    Miso-Mustard Rapini, 74
    Miso Squid, **76–77**
    new garlic and, 62–64, **319**
    pickling fruits and vegetables,
      345–46
    resources, 349
    Shishito Peppers Sautéed with
      Miso and Ginger, 84–85

    Shiso Rolls, 57
    Tofu Marinated in Miso, 65
    Wild Arugula with Walnut
      Miso, 75
    Yuzu Miso, 69
Miso Master, 73, 349
Mitoku Company, Ltd., 73, 147, 351
Mitoku Traditional Natto Spores,
    231, 240
mitsuba (trefoil), 343
Mitsukan, 146
mitsumata, XIII
Miura, Kenji, X, 30, 41, 167, 287
Miyao, Hirofumi, 309
Mizkan, 146, 160
mizuna (bitter salad greens), 341,
    346
    Salt-Distressed Mizuna with
      Kumquat, **24–25**
Mizuna no Shiomomi, **24–25**
mizuya dansu (kitchen cupboard),
    XIII
mochigome (glutinous rice), XXXIII
Mochizuki, Kazuko (citrus grower
    friend), 213, 316
mold, VIII
momigami (crumpled Japanese
    paper), xv. *See also* washi
Monascus purpureus. *See* red koji
monkfish, pickling, 347
Monterey Fish, 285
Morita, Kazuhiko, 71, **107**, 114
moromi (soy sauce mash), 89, 95,
    96, 100, **114–15**
motainai (no-waste) philosophy,
    273
"mother"
    in making alcohol (*shubo*), 298
    in making vinegar, 148–49
mountain vegetable (*koshi abura*),
    342
mountain yam (*yama imo*), 339
    Mountain Yam in Spicy Soy, 102
mozuku seaweed, XXX
mugi miso (barley miso), 72
mugicha (barley tea), XXXII, 307, 332
Mukaiyachi, Akane, **99**
mulberry, paper (*kozo*), XIII
mullet eggs, 29
Murakami, Kazushi, IX, 94, 99–**100**
Murakami, Yuka, IX, 81, **93–94**, 99
Murakami Cha, 322–23, 326
Murakamisake salmon, **31–32**
mushiki (bamboo steamer), VII, XVIII
mushrooms, 346. *See also* shiitake
Muso, 351

mussels, pickling, 347
mustard, XXXI, 341
    Eggplant Pickled in Soy Mustard,
      103
    Miso-Mustard Rapini, 74
    Mustard with Tofu and Dried
      Persimmon, 182–**83**
    Salt-Fermented Mustard, II,
      14–15
mustard greens (*karashina*), 341
myoga, 343, 346
    Cold Miso Soup with Cucumber
      and Myoga, 82
    Myoga Pickled in Sour Plum
      "Vinegar," **175**
    Myoga Pickled with Fish Sauce,
      128–**29**
    Salted Eggplant with Myoga and
      Shiso, 26–27
Myoga no Ishirizuke, 128–**29**
Myoga no Umezuke, **175**

N

nabe (one-pot dish), XIX
Nada, 299
Nagano, Katsue, 11, **166–67**, 239, **338**
Nakamichi, Hajime, 9–**10**
Nakano, 146
Nakatani, Kanji, XXIV, 5, 29, 49, 169,
    170, 254, 282
Nama Shoyu, XXVII, 90. *See also*
    Ohsawa Nama Shoyu
Nama-Ya pottery, 236
Nambu Tekki, XIX. *See also* kyusu;
    tetsubin; tetsunabe
nanami togarashi. *See* shichimi
    togarashi
nanohana (flowering tops), 341
Nanohana no Karashimiso, 74
napa cabbage (*hakusai*), 341
    Fermented Napa Cabbage, 11–13
    Napa Cabbage with Shredded
      Daikon, 290–**91**
narazuke, 213–**14**
narezushi, 207–8
nashi (apple pear), 344
Nashi no Misozuke, 60
nasu. *See* eggplant
Nasu no Kaiyaki, **132–33**
Nasu no Karashi-zuke, 103
Nasu no Shiomomi, **26–27**
natsumikan, 343
natto, XXIX, **226**, 230–31
    Hot Table Natto, 240–41
    resources, 349
    in straw, 238–39

Natto du Dragon, xxix, 231, 351
Natural Farming Pioneers, **242–43**.
  See also Suka, Kazuo; Suka,
  Sakae
Natural Import Company, xxiii,
  xxviii, xxxii, xxxiii, 51, 231, 240,
  348, 350
Naturalitea, 350
Naturally Good Food, 351
negi. *See* Japanese "leeks"
Nettuno Colatura, xxiii, xxvii–xxviii
New Zealand resources, 351
Newland, 332
niboshi (juvenile sardines), xxix, 252
  Niboshi Dashi, 249, 274
  Soy Sauce–Simmered Niboshi,
  275
Niboshi no Tsukudani, 275
nigari (bittern; magnesium
  chloride), xxviii, 10
nigorizake sake, 301
Nihaisu, 150
Nihon Ichiban, 250, 251, 252
nihon shu. See sake
Nijiya Market, xxiii, 303
Ninjin Sarada Miso Vineguretto, **83**
Ninniku no Misozuke, **61**
Ninomiya, Hiroshi, **189–90**
Nippon Travel Restaurant, 352
nira. See garlic chives
Nishikita, Yashima, **54–56**, 351
Nishin no Himono, **43**
nobiru (wild onions), 342
noren (split curtain), xiii
nori (laver), xxx
no-waste (*mottainai*) philosophy, 273
nukadoko (rice bran pickling bed),
  219
Nukazuke, ii, **220–223**. *See also* fish
  nukazuke
nuts. *See* seeds and nuts; *specific
  type*

O

Obaachan (grandma). *See* Baachan
octopus, pickling, 347
Ogawa, Aino, 290
Ohno, Choichiro, 329–**30**
Ohno Charcoal, 329
Ohsawa, xxiii, 147, 348
Ohsawa Nama Shoyu, xxvii, 90–91,
  349
Oigen factory, xix, 57
Oikawa, Kuniko, 57
oils, xxxi, xxxiii, 135
Okaka, 262. *See also* katsuobushi

okara (soybean pulp), xxix
Okinawan brown sugar (*kurozato*),
  xxxiii
Okinawan distilled alcohol
  (*awamori*), 303
okra, pickling, 346
omoishi (pickling weights), xvii
one-pot dish (*nabe*), xix
onigurumi (black walnuts), xxxii
onions
  Heirloom Onions, 8, 350
  pickling, 346
  Shio Koji–Pickled Onion, **193**
  Tomato, Onion, and Pepper
  Salad, **112–13**
  Tosa Onions, **264**
  wild, **342**
online Japanese food sources, 348
Ono, Jiro, xxiv–xxv
OPENHarvest, 201
organic foods, 352
  granulated sugar, xxxiii
  resources, 348
  sugar, xxvii
oriental mustard powder (*karashi*),
  xxxi
oroshigane (plate for grating), xviii
oroshiki (tool for grating), xviii
otachibana, 343
otoshi buta (drop lid), xvii
otsurui shochu, 302
oyome (bride), v
oysters, 347
Ozaki, Yasushi, xxiv

P

pantry, xxiii, xxvii–xxxiii
paper, xiii. *See also* calligraphy
  paper; Preschoolers and
  Paper; *washi*
Park Hotel, 28
peas, pickling, 346
Peko Peko Japanese Catering, 5,
  213, 236, 285
Penzeys Spices, 350
people doing interesting things,
  352
peppers. *See also* chile peppers;
  red pepper
  Shishito Peppers Sautéed with
  Miso and Ginger, **84–85**
  Tomato, Onion, and Pepper
  Salad, **112–13**
persimmons (*kaki*), 147, **176**, 344
  Daikon Pickled with Smashed
  Persimmons, 179

Dried Persimmons, 180–**81**
  Mustard with Tofu and Dried
  Persimmon, 182–**83**
  Persimmon Vinegar, 177–**78**
  Sweet Vinegared Turnips and
  Persimmons, 157
pestle (*surikogi*), xviii, 49
Phoenix Bean, 230
Pickled Young Shallots, **154–55**
pickles (*tsukemono*), 109, 219.
  Bitter Melon Koji Pickles, **191**
  morning (*asazuke*), 36
  Rice Bran Pickles, ii, **220–23**
  Thinly Sliced Ginger Pickles, **156**
pickling, 345
  containers, xvii, 350–51
  fish and shellfish, 346–47
  fruits and vegetables, 345–46
  mediums, xxviii
  tools, xvii–xviii
  weights (*omoishi*), xvii
Pizzaiolo, 20, 114
plants, resources, 350
Pleasant Hill Grain, 349, 350
plums. *See* sour plums
poly bukuro (food-grade plastic
  bag), xvii
poly taru (food-grade plastic
  tubs), xvii
ponzu sauce, 203
pork
  Ginger-Soy Pork Sandwiches,
  108–10
  Pork Belly Simmered with
  Daikon and Leeks, 161–**62**
  Shio Koji–Grilled Pork, **200**–1
potatoes, 346. *See also* sweet
  potato
powdered green tea (matcha), xxxii,
  306, 331
Preschoolers and Paper, xiv–xv
preserving, salt, 3–4
pressing "boat" (*shibori fune*), xxxiii,
  97, 115
prickly ash (*sansho*), xviii, 343
Purcell Mountain Farms and
  Spices, Inc., 280

Q

quince (*karin*), 344
  Quince-Infused Cordial, 317
Quitokeeto, xvii, 292, 351

R

radishes, pickling, 346

rakkyo (Japanese shallots), 342,
  346. *See also* shallots
Rakkyo no Shiozuke, **8**
Rakkyo no Suzuke, **154**–55
Rakuten Global Market, 348, 353
rapini, 74
Raw Squid in Coral, **286–88**
rayu (hot chile oil), xxxi
Red Boat (fish sauce), xxiii, xxviii
red koji, 187–88
red miso (*aka miso*), 72
red pepper
  Broccoli in Soy Sauce with Red
  Pepper, 92
  Kabocha in Miso with Red
  Pepper, 58
red shiso leaves, **19**
"red" tea, 326
red vinegar, xxviii, 165
Reichl, Ruth, 102
reishu (cold sake), 300
renkon. See lotus root
Rhapsody Natural Foods, 188,
  230, 349
rice (*gohan; kome*), ii, xxvii, xxxiii. *See
  also* brown rice
  electric cooker (*suihanki*), xviii
  Fish Sauce Fried Rice, 140–41
  Mini Rice Balls with Sour Plum,
  172–74
  paddle for serving (*shamoji*), xix
  resources, 349
rice bran, xxiii, 188
  Half-Dried Daikon Pickled in
  Rice Bran, **216–18**
  pickling fruits and vegetables,
  345–46
  Rice Bran Pickles, ii, **220–23**
rice bran oil, xxxiii
rice bran pickling bed (*nukadoko*),
  219
rice koji, 188
rice paper. *See washi*
rice vinegar (*komesu*), vi, xxviii,
  146–47
  Chopped Vinegared Flying Fish,
  158
  Dashi Vinegar, 151
  Kabocha Tempura with Three-
  Way Vinegar, 163–**64**
  making, 148–**49**
  Pickled Young Shallots, **154–55**
  Pork Belly Simmered with
  Daikon and Leeks, 161–**62**
  Soy Vinegar, 150
  Sweet Vinegar, 151

Sweet Vinegared Turnips and
Persimmons, 157
Thinly Sliced Ginger Pickles, **156**
Three-Way Vinegar, 150
rice-related tools, XVIII–x
Richmond, Akasha, 320
risk taking, viii
Roppongi Nouen restaurant, 14,
352
Rosenblum, Harry, 309–**310**
Rukkola no Kurumi-ae, 75
The Ryokan, 126–**27**
ryokucha. See green tea

S

Saikyo miso, 72
Sakai, Hiroaki, IX, 249, 250, 258, 261,
262, 263
Sakai family, 258, 259, 262, 263
Sakai Katsuobushi, VI, IX, 152, 249,
255, **256–257**, 258, 259, 261,
263
Sakamoto (ryokan), 41, 125–**27**, 134,
249, 252, 303
Sakamoto, Shinichiro, 125–26, 158,
252, 288
Sakamoto, Toshio, 297
sakana bocho (fish knife), XXII
Sakaya, 303
sake, XXXI, 297–302
Amazake, 313
cold (*reishu*), 300
cup (*choko, guinomi*), 299, **300**
flask (*tokkuri*), 299
Homemade Sake, 311–12
Kumquats Simmered in Sake,
314–15
recommendations, 352
resources, 349–50
room temperature (*jo-on*), 300
Sake Granita, 316
warm (*atsukan*), 300
Wasabi Leaves in Sake and
Soy, 98
sake kasu. See sake lees
Sake Kasu Aisu Ichijiku-zoe, 215
sake lees (*sake kasu*), XXIII, XXVIII, 188
pickling fruits and vegetables,
345–46
resources, 349–50
Sake Lees Ice Cream with Figs,
215
Sake Lees Soup with Salmon,
210–11
Sake Lees–Cured Chicken, 212
Small Melons in Sake Lees, **209**

sake maker, 308–10
Sake no Guranita, 316
Sakebar, 301, 303
Sake-World, 352
sakura ebi (tiny shrimp), XXIX
Sakura no Shiozuke, **22–23**
Sakurai, Mitsue (Yamaki Jozo
shopkeeper), 193
salad. *See also* mizuna
Carrot Salad with Miso
Vinaigrette, **83**
Tomato, Onion, and Pepper
Salad, **112–13**
salad mustard greens (*sarada
karashina*), 341
sale marino di Trapani, 3
salmon
Kikkawa, **31–32**
pickling, 347
Sake Lees Soup with Salmon,
210–**11**
Salt-Dried Salmon, 33–34
Shio Koji–Marinated Salmon,
199
salmon roe, 104–**5**
The Salmon Whisperer, **31–32**
Salone del Gusto, 29
salt, XXIII, 3–4
Air-Dried Sardines, 38–**39**
Baachan's Dried Eggplant, 18
Baby Turnips with Salt-Wilted
Greens, **5–7**
Dried Daikon Threads, 16–**17**
Fermented Napa Cabbage, 11–**13**
Half-Dried Barracuda, 37
pantry items, XXVII–XXVIII
pickling fruits and vegetables,
345–46
resources, 348–49
Salt-Distressed Mizuna with
Kumquat, **24–25**
Salt-Dried Grey Mullet Eggs, 29
Salt-Dried Salmon, 33–34
Salted Cherry Blossoms, **22–23**
Salted Eggplant with Myoga and
Shiso, **26–27**
Salted Red Shiso Leaves, **19**
Salted Sour Plums, II, **166–68**
Salted Young Shallots, **8**
Salt-Fermented Mustard, II,
14–15
Salt-Massaged Shiso Buds,
20–21
Semidried Herring, **43**
Slightly Dried Squid, **30**
The Salt Raker, **9–10**

Saltwater Oyster, 316
San Jose Tofu, 230
Sanbaisu, 150
sanbaizuke, 150
Sanchi, 351
sandfish
Konbu Dashi–Soused Sandfish,
270–**72**
pickling, 347
Sandfish Nabe, 136–37
sandwiches, **108–10**
San-J Soy Sauce, 91
sansho (prickly ash), XVIII, 343
santoku bocho, XXII
sarada karashina (salad mustard
greens), 341
sarashi (cloth bolt), XIII
sardines, 347. *See also* niboshi
Air-Dried Sardines, 38–**39**
sardines or anchovies (*iwashi*), XXVII
sashimi bocho, XXII–XXIII
Sato, Yuko, 236
sato imo. See taro root
satsuma imo (sweet potato), 339
Satumaya, 354
scallops, pickling, 347
Scanlan, Jamie, 148
Scanlan, Soyoung, 148
Schuefftan, Kim, 101, 128, 336
sea bass, pickling, 347
sea salt (*shio*), XXVII
sea squirt (*hoya*), 28
seaweed, xxx
second chances, ix
seeds and nuts, XXXII, 350
Seeds of Change catalog, 63
seiro (stackable steamer), XVIII,
44, 48
Semidried Herring, **43**
senbongoshi (thousand-slatted
sliding doors), XII
sencha, 305, 306
seri (Japanese cress), 342
sesame oil
cold pressed, XXXIII
dark, XXXIII
sesame seeds
black (*kuro goma*), XXXII
gold (*kin goma*), XXXII
white (*shiro*), XXXII
Seto, Kunikatsu, 130, 131, 133, 134
Seto, Mikako, 133, 134
7-spice powder (*shichimi
togarashi*), XXIX, XXXI
Shake no Kasujiru, 210–11
Shake no Shiokoji-zuke, **199**

shallots
Pickled Young Shallots, **154–55**
Salted Young Shallots, **8**
shamoji (paddle for serving rice),
XIX
Shaw, Hank, 265
shellfish, pickling, 346–47
shibori bukkuro (pressing bags),
XXXIII, **99**
shibori fune (pressing "boat"), XXXIII,
97, **99**, 115
shiboritate nama genshu sake, 301
Shibuki, Yoshiyuki, xxv
shichimi togarashi (7-spice
powder), XXIX, XXXI
shichirin (charcoal grill), VII, XVI, 42.
See also Funaba Shichirin
shiitake, **344**
Shio Koji–Sautéed Shiitake, 198
Shiitake no Shiokoji-yaki, 198
Shiloh Farms, 188, 230, 349
Shimizu, Ryusei, **107**
Shimizu, Taiyo, **107**
shincha, 305
shio (sea salt), XXVII
Shio Koji, XXVIII, **182**, **192**
Avocado with Shio Koji
Dressing, 197
pickling fruits and vegetables,
345–46
Shio Koji Dressing, 197
Shio Koji–Grilled Pork, **200–1**
Shio Koji–Marinated Salmon,
199
Shio Koji–Pickled Onion, **193**
Shio Koji–Sautéed Shiitake, 198
shiobiki salmon, 32
Shiobiki Shake, **33–34**
shiokara, 284–85
Shiozawa, Takayoshi, 255
shiro goma (white sesame seeds),
XXXII
shiro miso (white miso), 72
shiro uri (white melon), 340
Shishito no Abura Miso, **84–85**
Shishito Peppers Sautéed with
Miso and Ginger, **84–85**
shiso (perilla), 343
Salted Eggplant with Myoga and
Shiso, **26–27**
Shiso Rolls, 57
shiso buds (*hojiso*), 343
Salt-Massaged Shiso Buds,
20–21
Shiso Maki, 57
Shisuian, 106

Shizenkan, 354

Shizuoka Gourmet, 352

Shizuoka tea, 304

sho measurement, 300

shochu, XXXII, 297, 302–3
Akasha Cocktail, 320
Homemade Ginger Ale, 321
Quince-Infused Cordial, 317
Sour Plum Cordial Cocktail, 318–**19**

Shoga Yaki Sando, **108**–10

shoji (sliding doors), X, XI, XII

Shokunin, XXIV–**XXVI**

Shotaro, Kubo, XVI

shottsuru, XXVII. *See also* fish sauce

Shottsuru Nabe, 136–37

shoyu. *See* soy sauce

Shoyu Koji, XXVIII, **182**, **202**. *See also* koji
pickling fruits and vegetables, 345–46
Shoyu Koji–Marinated Yellowtail, **206**
Tomato Wedges Drizzled with Shoyu Koji, 204–**5**
Zucchini Pickled in Shoyu Koji, 203

shrimp, 347. *See also* tiny shrimp

shubo (alcohol "mother"), 298

shungiku (culinary chrysanthemum greens), 341

Sicilian Trapani salt, 3

skipjack tuna, fermented and sundried. *See* katsuobushi

Slightly Dried Squid, 30

Slow Food Japan, 297

small melon (*makuwa uri*), 344
Small Melons in Sake Lees, 209

Smashed Cucumbers with Sour Plum, **169**

snap peas, pickling, 346

snapper, pickling, 347

Snow of 2014, **334**–36

snow peas, pickling, 346

Soba Cha (buckwheat tea), XXXII, 307, 333

Soft Tofu, 236–**37**

sole, pickling, 347

soup
Cold Miso Soup with Cucumber and Myoga, 82
Country Miso and Vegetable Soup, 80–**81**
Country Soup Flavored Four Ways, 138–**39**

Katsuobushi and Tea Soup, 260–61

Sake Lees Soup with Salmon, 210–11

sour plums (*ume*), VIII, 19, **142**, 147, 344
Mini Rice Balls with Sour Plum, 172–74
Myoga Pickled in Sour Plum "Vinegar," **175**
pickling fruits and vegetables, 345–46
Salted Sour Plums, II, **145**, 166–**68**
Smashed Cucumbers with Sour Plum, **169**
sour plum cordial, 317, 318
Sour Plum Cordial Cocktail, 318, **319**
Turnips Pickled with Sour Plum, 170–**71**

South River, XXVIII, 51

soy dashi, 265

soy milk, homemade, **235**

Soy Milk Maker, XVII, 349

soy milk skin (*yuba*), XXIX

soy sauce (*shoyu*), VI, XXVII
Broccoli in Soy Sauce with Red Pepper, 92
choosing Japanese-style, 90–91
Cucumbers Soused in Soy, 101
Eggplant Pickled in Soy Mustard, 103
Ginger-Soy Pork Sandwiches, **108**–10
Katsuobushi with Soy Sauce, 262
making, **93**–97
Mountain Yam in Spicy Soy, 102
pickling fruits and vegetables, 345–46
pressing, **99**–100
resources, 349
Soy Sauce–Cured Salmon Roe, 104–**5**
Soy Sauce–Simmered Konbu, 273
Soy Sauce–Simmered Niboshi, 275
Soy Sauce–Soused Steak, 111
Tomato, Onion, and Pepper Salad, 112–**13**
Wasabi Leaves in Sake and Soy, 98

soy sauce mash (*moromi*), 89, 95, 96, 100, **114**–15

Soy Vinegar, 150

soybeans, XXVIII–XXIX, **44**, 89, 229, 340, 349. *See also* miso

soybeans, processed defatted (*dasshi kako daizu*), 89

Spectrum Organic Canola Oil, XXIII

The Spice Lab, 349

spices, resources, 350

Spices Inc., 350

spinach, pickling, 346

squid
air-dried, XXIX
fermented guts, 284–85
Miso Squid, 76–77
pickling, 347
Raw Squid in Coral, **286**–88
Slightly Dried Squid, **30**

SSU!. *See* Sunny-Side Up! preschool

Starelli, Anthony, 316

steak, **111**

steamer
bamboo (*mushiki*), VII, XVIII
stackable (*seiro*), XVIII, **44**, 48

Steiki no Shoyu Marine, **111**

stove
brick or earthenware (*kamado*), XVI
tabletop cooking (*konro*), XVI

sturgeon, pickling, 347

sudachi, 343

sugar, XXVII, XXXIII

suihanki (electric rice cooker), XVIII

suika (watermelon), 344

Suka, Junko, **15**, 16, 97, 238

Suka, Kazuo, 106, **242**–43

Suka, Sakae, 231, **242**–43

Suka, Toshiharu, 24, 209, 238, 242, **338**

Suka Baachan. *See* Suka, Sakae

Suka Jiichan. *See* Suka, Kazuo

Sukiyabashi Jiro, XXIV

Sumisakura, 354

Sunny-Side Up! preschool, VI, XIV, XV, 335

sunomono ("vinegared things"), 3

Supersec, 351

suribachi (grinding bowl), X, XVII–XVIII, 49

surikogi (pestle), XVIII, 49

surume ika (air-dried squid), XXIX

sushi. *See* narezushi

sushi rice vinegar, XXVIII

Sushi-ya, 297

Swanson, Heidi, 292

sweet potato (*satsuma imo*), 339

Sweet Vinegar, 151

Sweet Vinegared Turnips and Persimmons, 157

swordfish, pickling, 347

T

table, Japanese warming
horigotatsu (over a square hole in floor), XIII
kotatsu, XIII

Taboada, John, 316

Takagi, Shinji, 126, 134

Takahashi, Takashi, **97**

Takahashi, Yoshie, 49, 50, 96–**97**, 99, 334

takana (mustard greens), 14, 341

take burashi (bamboo brush), XVIII

Takemura, Ryuki, **107**

Takizawa Shuzo sake (Saitama), 302, 352

takobiki sashimi knife, XXIII

Takuan, **216**–18

Tamago no Misozuke, II, **66**–68

Tamanegi no Shiokoji-zuke, **193**

Tamanegi no Tosa-zuke, **264**

Tanaka, Yosuke, 309

Taniguchi, Yoshikazu, 270

Tanis, David, IV, 70, 220

tanoshimini (anticipation), 307

tansu (Japanese chests and cupboards), X, XIII

taro root (*sato imo*), 339, **340**, 346

taru (wooden barrels), IX, XVII, **54**–56

Taruya, 351

The Taste of Tea, 305, 350

Tataki Kyuri no Umeboshi-ae, 169

tawashi (hemp palm–bristled brush), XVII

tea, XXXII, 304–7. *See also* Buckwheat Tea; green tea; *hojicha*
Brewed Green Tea, **304**, 324–25
Cold Barley Tea, 332
Cold-Infused Tea, **328**
Fujimien, 304–6, 322–**23**, 326, 327
Japanese "Red" Tea, 304, 326–**27**
Katsuobushi and Tea Soup, 260–61
kettles, iron (*testubin*), XIX, **304**, 323
pots (*kyusu*), XIX, **304**
Powdered Green Tea, 331
-related tools, XIX, XXII
resources, 350
roasted green (*hojicha*), XXXII, 306

Tea Ceremony Charcoal, **329–30**
The Tea Docent, 305
tempura, 163–**64**
tenugui (hand cloth), XIII, 160
Terada Honke sake (Chiba), 187, **286**, 302, 352
tetsubin (cast iron kettles), XIX, XXII, **304, 323**
tetsunabe (iron pots), XIX
Tezukuri Genmai Miso, 51–**53**
Tezukuri Jinjaeiru, 321
Tezukuri Konnyaku, 244–**45**
Tezukuri Tonyu, **235**
Thinly Sliced Ginger Pickles, **156**
Three-Way Vinegar, 150
    Kabocha Tempura with Three-Way Vinegar, 163–**64**
tiny shrimp (*sakura ebi*), XXIX
Tobiuo Tataki, **158**
tofu, XXVIII–XXIX, 229, 230
    form for making, XVII, **232**
    Homemade Soy Milk, **235**
    making, **232–33**
    Mustard with Tofu and Dried Persimmon, 182–**83**
    resources, 349
    Soft Tofu, 236–**37**
    Tofu Doused in Fish Sauce, 124
    Tofu Marinated in Miso, 65
    Tofu Simmered with Vegetables, 234
Tofu no Ishirizuke, 124
Tofu no Misozuke, 65
tofu tsukuruki (form for making tofu), XVII, **232**
togarashi. See chile peppers
Toiro Kitchen, XVIII, 350
toishi (whetstone), XXIII
tokkuri (sake flask), 299
Tokusanhin-Club, 354
Tokyo American Club, viii
Tokyo Fish Market, XXIII
Tomato, Tamanegi to Piman Sarada, 112–**13**
Tomato no Shoyukoji-ae, **204–5**
Tomato to Nasu Dashi-ni, 254
tomatoes
    pickling, 346
    Tomato, Onion, and Pepper Salad, 112–**13**
    Tomato and Eggplant in Dashi, 254
    Tomato Wedges Drizzled with Shoyu Koji, **204–5**
tools. *See* fire vessels and tools; rice-related tools

Toriki, Susumu, 148, 152, 153
Toriniku no Kasuzuke, 212
tororo konbu, XXX
Tosa Onions, **264**
Traditional Craft Industry, XIX
trout, pickling, 347
tsukemono. See pickles
tsukemonoki (small pickle press), XVII
tuna, pickling, 347
turnips
    Baby Turnips with Salt-Wilted Greens, 5–**7**
    pickling, 346
    Sweet Vinegared Turnips and Persimmons, 157
    Turnips Pickled with Sour Plum, **170–71**

U

Ubukawa, Jotaro, xv, **71**
Ueno Gourmet, XXVII, 351
ume. See sour plums
ume konbucha, XXXII
Ume Shu Kakute-ru, 318–**19**
umeboshi, XXXII, 147, **166–68**
umeshu (sour plum cordial), 317–18
umesu (sour plum "vinegar"), 23, 147, 167, 175
UNESCO, XVI, 107, 249
United Kingdom resources, 351
unohana, XXIX, 235
usuage (deep-fried tofu pouches), XXIX
usukuchi shoyu, 90

V

Vargas, Sally, 220
vegetables, XXIX, 340. *See also specific type*
    Country Miso and Vegetable Soup, 80–**81**
    pickling, 345–46
    Tofu Simmered with Vegetables, 234
vegetarian dashi, 18
Veretto, Mike, 284
vinaigrette, **83**
vinegar, VI, XXVIII. *See also* Iio Jozo; red vinegar; rice vinegar
    aged "black" vinegar, 152–**53**
    Dashi Vinegar, 151
    "mother," in making, 148–49
    Myoga Pickled in Sour Plum "Vinegar," **175**
    Persimmon Vinegar, 177–**78**

pickling fruits and vegetables, 345–46
    Soy Vinegar, 150
    Sweet Vinegar, 151
    Sweet Vinegared Turnips and Persimmons, 157
    Three-Way Vinegar, 150
"vinegared things" (*sunomono*), 3

W

Wajima Air-Dried Fish, **35–36**
Wajima Kaien salt, 4, 9
Wajima Morning Market, **130–31**
wakame seaweed, XXX
Wakayama, Junko, **79**
Wakayama, Sachi Matsuda, **79**
walnuts. *See also* black walnuts
    Wild Arugula with Walnut Miso, 75
warabi. See fiddlehead ferns
Warabi no Ohitashi, 265
Warisu, 151
wasabi (Japanese horseradish), 269, 343–**44**
    Wasabi Leaves in Sake and Soy, 98
The Wasabi Company, 351
wasabi oroshi (grater), XVIII
wasanbon (organic, Japanese sugar), XXXIII
washi (Japanese paper), XII, XIII, XV, XVI
washoku, 249
watermelon (*suika*), 344
Waters, Alice, **338**
whetstone (*toishi*), XXIII
white melon (*shiro uri*), 340
white miso (shiro miso), 72
white sesame seeds (*shiro goma*), XXXII
Whole Foods, 73, 188
Wild Arugula with Walnut Miso, 75
wild onions (*nobiru*), **342**
Windy Hilltop Farm, 351–52
Wine of Japan Import, Inc., 301, 349–50
winter squash. *See* kabocha
With a Glass blog, 4, 352
women, role of, vii–viii
wooden barrels (*taru*), IX, XVII, **54–56**
wooden box (*masu*), 300
wooden shaving box (*katsuobushi kezuriki*), XXIX, **253, 363**
wooden tub (*handai*), XIX
Workshop Issé, 303, 351

World resources, 351
World Sake Imports, 301, 350
Worthington, Tom, 285

Y

yakiniku (Korean barbecue), 280
yama imo. See mountain yam
Yamagishi, Hiroko, **42**
Yamaguchi, Eri, 101, 264
Yamaimo no Shoyuzuke, 102
Yamaki Jozo, VI, XXVII, 47, 51, **68**, 82, 90, **106–7**, 124, 238, 311, 313
Yamamoto, Heikichi, 308–**10**
Yamamoto, Masaki, **285**
Yamasa, XXVII, 89, 91
yams. *See* mountain yam
yanagiba sashimi knife, XXIII
Yanuma, Hiroshi, **122**
Yasai no Yudofu, 234
yellowtail, 347
    Shoyu Koji–Marinated Yellowtail, **206**
yofuku dansu (clothes chest), XIII
Yosedofu, 236–**37**
Yoshikawa, Akira, 31–32
yuba (soy milk skin), XXIX
Yuukiya0097, 354
yuzu, **69**, 343
yuzu kosho (fresh chile and yuzu peel paste), XXXI, 279
Yuzu Miso, **69**

Z

Zgola, Adam, XXV, 50, 334–**35**
Zojirushi, XVIII
zucchini
    pickling, 346
    Zucchini Pickled in Shoyu Koji, 203
Zukkini no Shoyukoji-zuke, 203

ALSO BY NANCY SINGLETON HACHISU
JAPANESE FARM FOOD

Andrews McMeel Publishing, LLC
an Andrews McMeel Universal company
1130 Walnut Street, Kansas City, Missouri 64106

www.andrewsmcmeel.com

15 16 17 18 19 TEN 10 9 8 7 6 5 4 3 2 1

ISBN: 978-1-4494-5088-5

Library of Congress Control Number: 2014931306

www.nancysingletonhachisu.com

EDITOR: Jean Z. Lucas

JAPANESE EDITORIAL CONTENT AND CONSULTING: Kim Schuefftan

DESIGN: Julie Barnes and Diane Marsh

PHOTOGRAPHY: Kenji Miura

ADDITIONAL PHOTOGRAPHY: Fredrika Stjärne for *Food & Wine* magazine: pages VII, XVI, XIX, XX, XXXI, 53, 69, 84, 103, 169, 175, 242, 300, 343; Kenji Wakasugi: pages II, 80, 137, 223, 366; Kenta Izumi: page XXV; Tetsuya Uragami: pages 145, 160; Masatoshi Uenaka: pages 268, 269; Asako Harigaya: page XXV; Saori Abe: pages 99, 162; Nancy Singleton Hachisu: pages XI, XV, 99, 126, 159, 160, 162, 178, 181, 190, 195, 196, 208, 267, 271, 272, 283, 294, 303, 308, 335, 336.

JAPANESE PAPER: Kubo Shotaro Washi, Ogawa-machi, Saitama Prefecture

ART DIRECTOR: Julie Barnes

PRODUCTION MANAGER: Carol Coe

PRODUCTION EDITOR: Maureen Sullivan

DEMAND PLANNER: Sue Eikos

ATTENTION: SCHOOLS AND BUSINESSES
Andrews McMeel books are available at quantity discounts with bulk purchase for educational, business, or sales promotional use. For information, please email the Andrews McMeel Publishing Special Sales Department: specialsales@amuniversal.com